STARTER

Context

Lehrkräftefassung

Legende zur Lehrkräftefassung

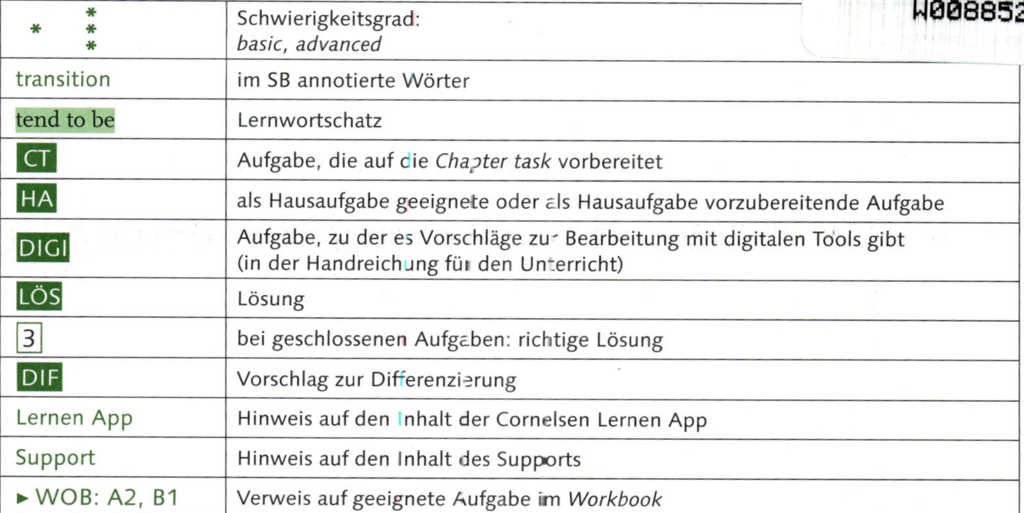

* ***	Schwierigkeitsgrad: *basic, advanced*
transition	im SB annotierte Wörter
tend to be	Lernwortschatz
CT	Aufgabe, die auf die *Chapter task* vorbereitet
HA	als Hausaufgabe geeignete oder als Hausaufgabe vorzubereitende Aufgabe
DIGI	Aufgabe, zu der es Vorschläge zur Bearbeitung mit digitalen Tools gibt (in der Handreichung für den Unterricht)
LÖS	Lösung
3	bei geschlossenen Aufgaben: richtige Lösung
DIF	Vorschlag zur Differenzierung
Lernen App	Hinweis auf den Inhalt der Cornelsen Lernen App
Support	Hinweis auf den Inhalt des Supports
▸ WOB: A2, B1	Verweis auf geeignete Aufgabe im *Workbook*

Abkürzungen in der Lehrkräftefassung

SuS/L	Schülerinnen und Schüler/Lehrkräfte
EA/PA/GA	Einzel-/Partner-/Gruppenarbeit
UG	Unterrichtsgespräch
AE/BE	American English/British English

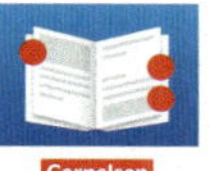

Dein Buch findest du auch in der **Cornelsen Lernen App**.

Siehst du eines dieser Symbole im Lehrwerk, findest du in der App

- alle **Audios**
- alle **Videos**
- **Ideen, Informationen** und **Lösungen zu gewählten Aufgaben**

Cornelsen

Context • Starter

Lehrkräftefassung

Im Aufrag des Verlages herausgegeben von
Dr. Annette Leithner-Brauns, Dresden

Erarbeitet von
Ramin Azadian, Berlin; Irene Bartscherer, Bonn; Dr. Sabine Buchholz, Hürth; Dr. Wiebke Bettina Dietrich, Göttingen; Björn Jörgeling, Berlin; Claudia Krapp, Geestland; Sylvia Loh, Esslingen; Dr. Paul Maloney, Hildesheim; Britta Rössner, Leipzig; Dr. Andreas Sedlatschek, Esslingen; Sabine Struß, Verden

Beratende Mitwirkung
Dr. Christine Ayorinde, Braga; Ramin Azadian, Berlin

In Zusammenarbeit mit der Englischredaktion
Dr. Christine Hehle, Freya Wurm (koordinierende Redakteurin), Michelle Fridman, Annegret Hauser-Teubner (Projektleitung), Solveig Heinrich, Dr. Marion Kiffe, Marie Kindler, Mai Weber *unter Mitwirkung von* Irja Fröhling, Katrin Gütermann, Neil Porter

Layoutkonzept
Klein & Halm, Berlin

Layout der Lehrkräftefassung
Yvonne Thron, designcollective, Berlin

Technische Umsetzung der Lehrkräftefassung
Zweiband Media, Berlin

Umschlaggestaltung
Rosendahl, Berlin

Weitere Bestandteile des Lehrwerks

- Schulbuch als E-Book
- Lehrkräftefassung des Schulbuchs (*print* und als E-Book)
- *Workbook* (*print*)
- Handreichungen (*print* und im Unterrichtsmanager Plus)
- Unterrichtsmanager Plus
- Cornelsen Lernen App

www.cornelsen.de

Die Webseiten Dritter, deren Internetadressen in diesem Lehrwerk angegeben sind, wurden vor Drucklegung sorgfältig geprüft. Der Verlag übernimmt keine Gewähr für die Aktualität und den Inhalt dieser Seiten oder solcher, die mit ihnen verlinkt sind.

Alle Drucke dieser Auflage sind inhaltlich unverändert und können im Unterricht nebeneinander verwendet werden.

Die **Cornelsen Lernen App** ist eine fakultative Ergänzung zu *Starter Allgemein*, die die inhaltliche Arbeit begleitet und unterstützt. Als solche unterliegt sie nicht der Genehmigungspflicht.

1. Auflage, 2. Druck 2024

Druck: Athesiadruck GmbH

ISBN: 978-3-06-034970-8

PEFC-zertifiziert
Dieses Produkt stammt aus nachhaltig bewirtschafteten Wäldern und kontrollierten Quellen
www.pefc.de

Contents

Contents

Abbreviations and labels used in *Context Starter*

AE/BE American English / British English
ca. *(Latin)* circa = about, approximately
cf. confer (compare), see
derog derogatory *(abfällig, geringschätzig)*
e.g. *(Latin)* exempli gratia = for example
esp. especially
et al. *(Latin)* et alii = and other people/things
etc. *(Latin)* et cetera = and so on
f./ff. and the following page(s)/line(s)
fml formal English
i.e. *(Latin)* id est = that is, in other words
infml informal English
jdm./jdn. *jemandem/jemanden*
l./ll. line/lines
n noun
pt(s) point(s)
p./pp. page/pages
pl plural
sb./sth. somebody/something
sg singular
sl slang
usu. usually
v verb
vs. *(Latin)* versus *(gegen, im Gegensatz zu)*

[map icon] marks tasks that refer you back to the chapter's guiding question
Challenge marks a more difficult task
► Support refers you to the Support and Partner B pages (p. 182) where you can find more help to do the assignment
You choose lets you decide which of the two given assignments you'd like to do
Intercultural communication marks a task that focuses on intercultural communication
*metaphor indicates that a word or expression (here: *metaphor*) is explained in the Glossary (p. 272ff.)
► SF 9 directs you to the Skills File (here: Skill 9)
[audio icon] indicates that the sound file can be found in the Cornelsen Lernen App, eBook and Unterrichtsmanager Plus
[video icon] indicates that the video can be found in the Cornelsen Lernen App, eBook and Unterrichtsmanager Plus
► More info indicates that additional information can be found in the Cornelsen Lernen App
► More language indicates that tips or further information regarding language can be found in the Cornelsen Lernen App
► Check indicates that solutions to tasks can be found in the Cornelsen Lernen App
► Getting started indicates that tips or ideas to get started on tasks can be found in the Cornelsen Lernen App
► WOB indicates relevant sections in the Workbook

Chapter 1

Youth and Adolescence – the Growing-up Years

*51 Things to do while you're young

Richard Horne, Helen Szirtes

1 Send a message in a bottle
2 Run up an escalator the wrong way
3 Make an origami crane
4 Learn to play an instrument
5 Have an embarrassing moment and get over it
6 Paint a picture good enough to hang on the wall
7 Learn to whistle (and make other noises)
8 Make a swear box
9 Act in a play
10 Win something
11 Make a T-shirt
12 Stay up all night
13 Sleep all day
14 Grow something from a seed
15 Start a collection
16 Help save the planet
17 Climb to the top of a mountain
18 Host a party
19 Learn to bake a cake
20 Hide a treasure and leave a map for friends to find
21 Learn how to ask someone out (and how to dump them)
22 Start your own blog
23 Write lyrics for a song
24 Take care of an animal
25 April fool someone
26 Teach your grandparents something new
27 Invent a new game
28 Pretend to be ill convincingly
29 Save your pocket money for a month and spend it all at once
30 Succeed at something you're bad at
31 Invent a new trend
32 Start a band
33 Camp out in the back garden
34 Learn to live without something you love for a week

Annotations
25 **April fool** play a trick on sb. on April Fool's Day
47 **dye** change the colour of sth. using a special liquid

DIGI Top 3-Listen als digitales Poster erstellen und illustrieren

DIGI digitale Mindmap nutzen

DIGI Vorschläge digital sammeln

1 **a** * List five fun things you want to do before you turn twenty.
b * Read the list above. Note down the things you have already done.
c * Add five things you would like to do from the text to your list from **1 a**.

HA **2** * What kind of wishes and dreams could the people in the picture above have for their future?

CT **3** **a** * **Think** Collect five wishes or dreams and five challenges you think modern teenagers have to face.
CT **b** * **Pair** Compare your list from **a** with a partner. Together, decide which five dreams or wishes and which five challenges make it into a new list.
CT **c** * **Share** Discuss your lists in class. Decide on the three top wishes and dreams and the top three challenges.

4 **a** Take a look at the Chapter map on the right. How would you answer the guiding question at this point?
b * In a group, explain how the words and ideas in the Chapter map relate to the topic 'youth and adolescence' and give examples.

35 Cook a meal
36 List the things your parents say they'll tell you when you're older
37 Learn to juggle
38 Have a snowball fight and fun in the snow
39 Build the ultimate sandcastle and have fun in the sun
40 Take part in a TV show
41 Make a scene in a public place
42 Spend Christmas in another country
43 Do something nice without being asked
44 See your music idol perform live
45 Learn to say useful phrases in other languages
46 Learn to skim stones
47 Dye your hair
48 Sing in front of an audience
49 Blame someone else
50 Get from A to B using a map
51 Be vegetarian for a week

From: 101 Things to Do Before You're Old and Boring, *2005*

Annotation
46 **skim stones** throw stones so that they hop along the surface of water

351 Wörter

Chapter map

Lernen App: Useful vocabulary for the chapter
▶ More language

Lernen App: Teenagers – standing at the crossroads (00:03:52)

Teenagers – standing at a crossroads

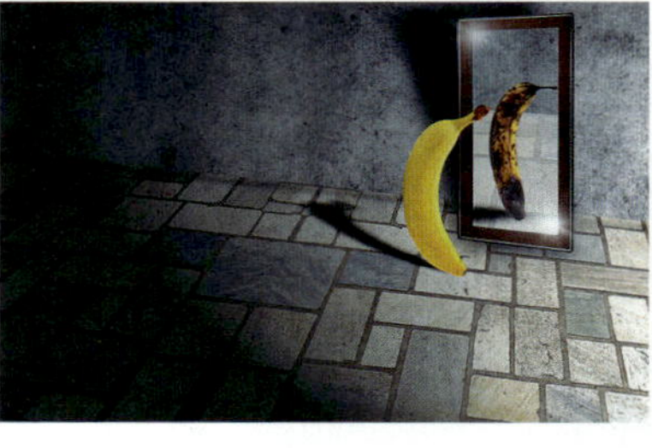

Teenagers throughout the years

Teenagers have been perceived differently throughout time: from rebellious to docile, from curious to calm, from problematic to socially engaged, all these characteristics were and still are used to describe teenagers. But how accurate are these attributes? It is undoubtedly true that each teenage generation has to face its own challenges and pitfalls. There are many different expectations adolescents have to meet: Parents urge them to succeed in school, friends and peers want them to be fun and trustworthy, and then there is school and exams, which can put a lot of pressure on everyone. All of this comes on top of finding one's own place in society. As if this isn't enough, there are also issues with the ever-changing state of technology and the pervasiveness of social media that one has to deal with every day.

Einstiegsmöglichkeit: Brainstorming ausgehend von den Bildimpulsen

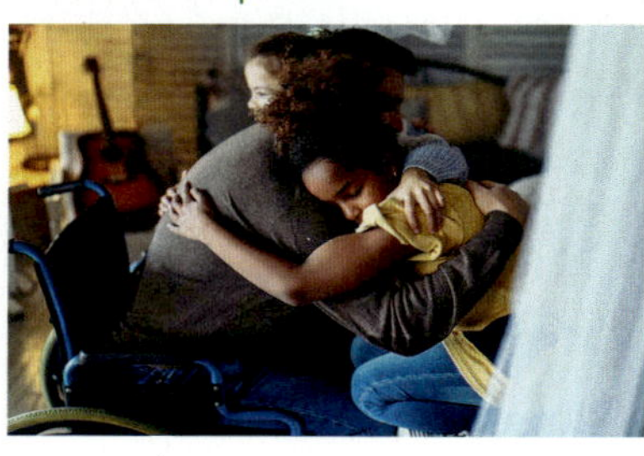

Modern families

Families have become smaller in recent years. Therefore, parents are likely to have more time to spend with their children. Some researchers assume that the parent-child relationship has become closer and teenagers confide in their parents more often than before. On their side, parents also expect more from their children. They want them to do well at school, so they can have a successful career in later life – this might in turn put even more stress on teens. At first glance, the youth of today seem to be less rebellious and less defiant than former generations. But if you look closer you can find many young people actively participating, e.g. in protests against global warming, marches for equality etc.

Peer pressure

Peer pressure or rather peer influence has always been an issue for young people and is especially important while forming one's own identity. Peers and their opinions and attitudes appear more important to young people than parents' or teachers' opinions. Young people can go along with the crowd because they don't want to debate the issue openly, even though they inwardly disagree. This is something that can also happen to adults. Nevertheless, teenage years are formative years as young people acquire and develop new skills such as impulse control, the ability to think ahead and resistance to pressure from others. Everyone deals differently with pressure and stress and although substance abuse, e.g. alcohol and drugs, has seemingly declined, social media often serves as an outlet for stress, while simultaneously being a source of new stress.

Dreams and wishes

If the world were perfect, everyone would have the same chances to improve their situation in life. Unfortunately, the reality is that someone's success is often based on preset factors. In countries such as Germany access to a good education very much depends on the social background of a person. Climbing the social ladder thus becomes yet another challenge young people must face to achieve their goals and dreams for the future.

479 Wörter

1 Main ideas

HA a Explain the main idea of the text in two or three sentences. DIF *true/false statements* vorgeben
HA CT b Read the text again and create a *spidergram about challenges that teenagers face today using the information in the text. DIGI/DIF *spidergram* digital und in PA erstellen

2 Reflect

a Assessing the text, which paragraph was most difficult for you? Give reasons. Refer to content, vocabulary or sentence construction.
HA b Find ...
1 three words or phrases that were new to you and explain them.
2 two interesting sentence constructions or grammar aspects.
3 one sentence that you would like to keep in mind and use as a model for one of your next assignments.

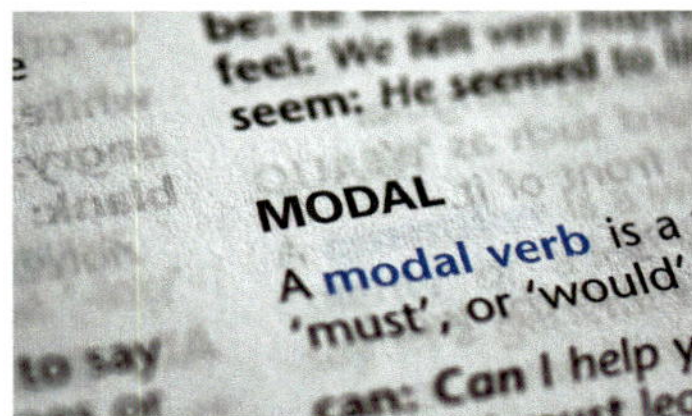

Lernen App: Video on modal verbs
▸ Getting started (task 3 a)

3 Modal verbs KV 1: Modal verbs

HA a* The modal verbs *can*, *have to* and *would* are used in the text on p. 12. Scan the text and find the modal verbs.
HA b* Note down the function of each modal verb in each sentence.
HA c For each modal verb, write a new sentence on challenges adolescents face and explain the function of the modal verb in the sentence.

Lernen App: Answer key for tasks 3a and 3b ▸ Check (task 3a/b)

HA 4 * Chunk it!

Match the adjectives with the nouns below to form common *collocations.
Adjectives: social • formative • acquired • academic • recent • teenage
Nouns: success • skills • ladder • years

Lernen App: Video about chunks ▸ Getting started
▸ Check
Lernen App: Answer key for task 4
▸ WOB: A1

HA 5 Working with cartoons

Describe the cartoon. To what extent does it mirror the content of the text on p. 12?

▸ SF 25: Analysing cartoons, p. 231
▸ Getting started
▸ WOB: A1 Reading for analysis, pp. 4–7
Lernen App: Things to consider when describing a cartoon

"You can chase your accounting dream later, son. Your mother and I just want you to finish film school."

CartoonStock.com

Growing up too fast? Richard Fisher

The article below deals with the characteristics attributed to teenagers throughout the years and examines the reasons for behavioural changes.

Titel in drei Ecken des Klassenzimmers aufhängen → SuS gehen zu ihrem gewählten Titel

* • Imagine you had to find a new title for this article on characteristics of teenagers throughout the time, which of the three alternatives 1–3 below would you choose? Talk to your partner and explain the reasons for your choice.
  1 The wild bunch – teenagers are getting more reckless every decade
  2 Teenagers are less rebellious and more dedicated nowadays
  3 Same old story – teenagers are as wild and rebellious as former generations

Annotations
3 **measure** (here) criterion; standard
21 **delay sth.** *etw. verzögern*

Teenagers dancing at a party

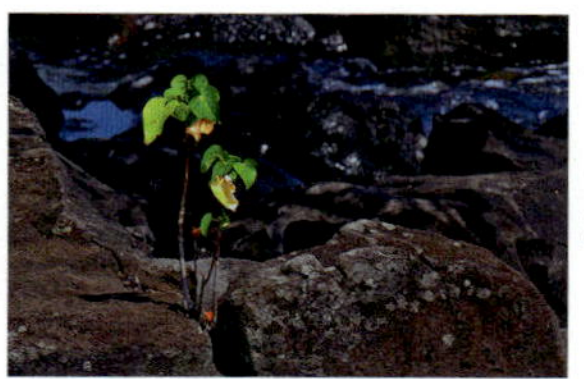

Fehlerquelle: Aussprache von *hypothesis* [haɪˈpɒθəsɪs] (Z. 16)

Over the past decade or two, there have been some intriguing changes in the attributes of the teenager. The psychologist Jean Twenge of San Diego State University notes that teens are growing up more slowly by many measures, compared with their 20th-century counterparts. A typical 17–18-year-old in the US, for example, is now less likely to have tried alcohol, have had sex, or acquired their driver's licence, compared with similarly-aged teens only 20 years ago. A 13–14-year-old is less likely to have a job or to have gone on dates. Meanwhile other measures of early adulthood, such as teenage pregnancy, have reached historic lows in the US and Europe.

Twenge points to a number of reasons why growing up is slowing down. There's little doubt that technology and the internet has played a major role, meaning more interaction with peers happens online and in the home, where sex, experimentation and trouble are perhaps less likely. For this reason, she calls this latest crop of young people the 'iGen' generation [...]. But she also points out that some of these trends were already beginning before the online culture of the 21st century, and so the internet can't be totally blamed.

Her hypothesis is that teens behave differently depending on how hostile and unforgiving their local environment feels to them, an idea that social scientists called 'life history theory'. In tougher times in history, teens were forced to take a 'fast life strategy', growing up faster, reproducing earlier and focusing on basic needs. Now life in the West is generally more forgiving, and families are wealthier – at least on average – so it's possible for teens to take a 'slow life strategy', delaying the transition to more adult behaviours. [...]

There may also be a greater emphasis on safety among this latest teenage generation, Twenge suggests, both physically and emotionally, which encourages young people and their parents or guardians to keep them insulated from the harshness of the adult world for longer.

So, what will this mean for our ideas about teenagers if these trends continue? It might suggest that the 20th-century notion of a teenage rebel-without-a-cause is becoming outdated. Whereas many teenagers in the 1950s and 1960s were driving their own cars, getting into trouble, and experimenting with drink and drugs, their similarly-aged counterparts today are often far more clean-living and safety-conscious. If there is reckless behaviour and an urge for independence, it's coming later.

A slower path to adulthood is not the only way that cultural perceptions of youth may need updating. In recent years, science has also shown that adolescence doesn't finish at the end of the teenage years. By 20 years old, a young person is usually considered an adult: their body size is fully grown, they can vote, get married, and many have already entered the workplace. But the evidence suggests that, by many important measures, adolescence continues until around the age of 24 to 25.

Annotation
48 coddle *(disapproving)* take care of sb. excessively

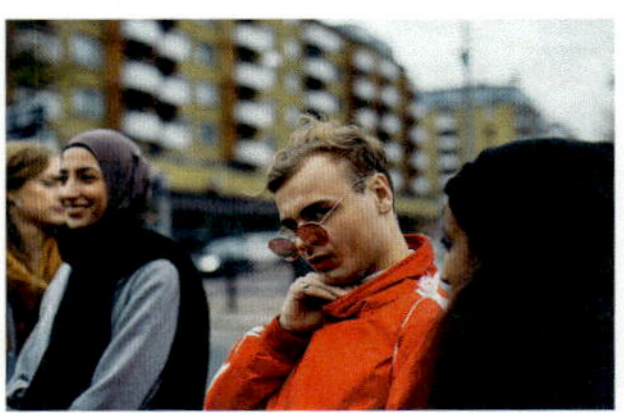

At the end of the teens, puberty may have finished but the development and maturation of the brain is far from complete. […] Some researchers now also see these years as an important developmental social stage too, where young people are still learning about intimacy, friendship, family, self-expression, and political and social awareness, and so deserve more support and protection than they currently receive from society.

Could there therefore be a case that these older adolescents should become more clearly recognised as a distinct demographic group? Should we allow them to delay their entry into the fully adult world of life and work? It might seem like coddling to some, but then again, our ancestors might have said the same about how we treat teenagers.

Fehlerquelle: Aussprache von *ancestor* [ˈænsestə(r)] (Z. 49)

Signs of this cultural change may be happening already. The 'boomerang' phenomenon describes recent rises in the number of young adults returning to the nest to live with their parents after higher education, or because they can't afford their own property or rent. (Some never move out in the first place.) In the UK, around 3.5 million single young adults now live with their parents, which is a third more than a decade ago […]. Wealth imbalances between older generations and today's young people have only strengthened this trend. […]

'One difference we should consider is the assumption that in our 20s we are meant to go immediately from schooling to a career. In the 100-year life we should consider taking a period of our 20s and dedicating it to a new stage, exploration,' write Gratton and Scott. 'Your decisions early in life impact the entirety of the rest of it… so it is rather absurd that we expect people in their late teens and early 20s to make decisions like what direction they want their lives to take. Instead they should have a period of exploring the world and trying different paths.' 821 Wörter

From: 'Why teenagers aren't what they used to be', BBC.com, *2 February 2022*

Comprehension

1 You need a number of small paper slips or file cards for this activity.

a Work on your own. Read the text. Identify keywords and phrases.

b Write the most important keywords on one side of the cards. Write one keyword per card only. Add explanations of these keywords on the back of the card.

c Arrange the file cards in a logical order, e.g. alphabetically, chronologically, like a mind map, etc. The structure should enable you to summarize your text by only looking at the keywords on the file cards.

d Find a partner. Each one of you summarizes the text. If you get stuck, take a look at the back of the respective file card for your backup information.

▸ WOB: A1

DIF *key words* vorgeben

DIF zunächst mehrfach üben; Anzahl der Karten variieren

DIGI digitale Mindmap erstellen

Analysis

HA **2** Analyse how adolescents are presented in the text. DIF Lösung in PA

HA **3** *** Examine the line of argument the author develops. Underline your results with examples.

▸ WOB: A1

DIF Hauptargument gemeinsam besprechen → dann untersuchen, wie der Text darauf hinarbeitet

Lernen App: Video on modal verbs
▶ More language

Language awareness

HA **4** **a** * The text includes modal verbs. Identify at least two of them and reflect which function they have.

HA **b** * Write two example sentences about modern teenagers using the modals verbs from **a**.

▶ Getting started
▶ SF 22: Analysing diagrams, p. 227
Lernen App: Video on analysing diagrams

Beyond the text

HA **5** **a** *** Describe the line graph below. DIF *true/false questions* zum Diagramm stellen

▶ WOB: A1

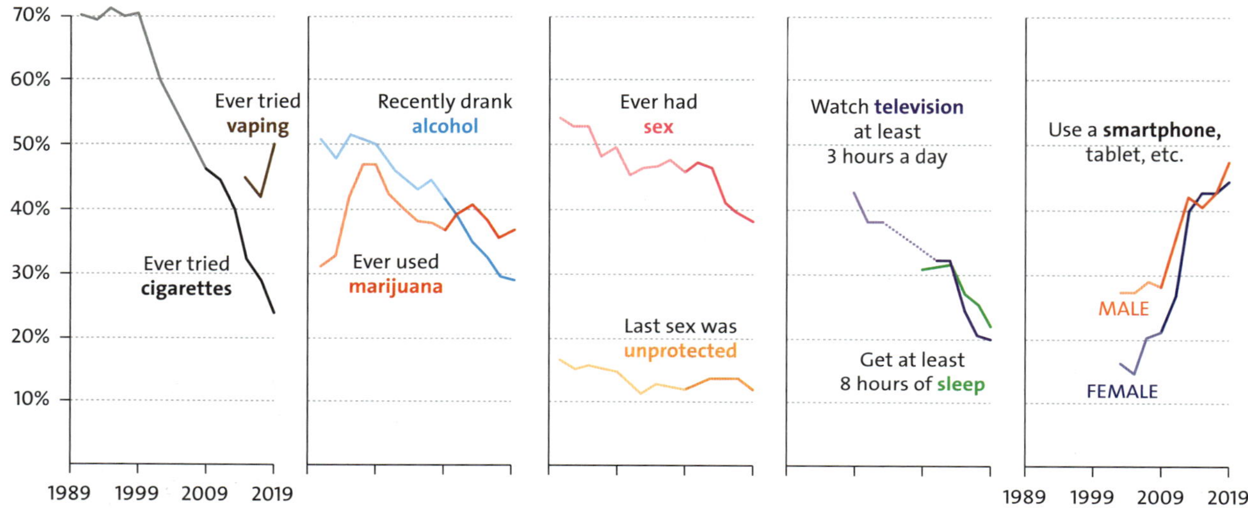

Source: Centers for Disease Control and Prevention High School Youth Risk Behavior Survey

Annotation
vape *E-Zigaretten rauchen*

Language help

The graph/table/chart deals with ... • It was taken from ... • It shows / compares the ... with respect to ... • The percentage decreases/ increases slowly/ moderately/quickly/steeply ... / is as big as ... / is twice as big as ... / ... is bigger than ... • The vast majority of ... • A clear trend becomes obvious ... • The percentage reaches a peak / a low point in ...

HA **b** Compare the line graph with the information given in the article. Support your findings with examples. ▶ WOB: A1

Lernen App: A picture stimulus: Topics of conflict
▶ Getting started (task 6 b)
▶ SF 28: Argumentative writing, p. 236
▶ SF 43: Giving a presentation, p. 259
▶ WOB: A2 Writing, pp. 8–11
▶ WOB: A4 Speaking – presentation, pp. 16–17

6 You choose Do either task **a** or **b**.

HA **a** *** Writing 'Modern teenagers are less likely to seek conflict.' Comment on this statement. Include the findings from the text and statistics above as well as your own arguments. ▶ WOB: A2

DIF *comments* als Blogartikel gestalten

b * Speaking What topics could be a cause of conflict for modern teenagers? Brainstorm some, research more and present them to your class. HA ▶ WOB: A4

DIGI/DIF Präsentation digital unterstützen und in PA halten

Reactivate

Giving a well-structured and convincing presentation is one of the skills you will need throughout the rest of your life, not just at school.

1 Revising the golden rules of giving a presentation

a ✱ With a partner, think about presentations you gave or witnessed. Note down the aspects that made these presentations successful or not.

b ✱ Copy the *method card below and add aspects from a that contribute to a good presentation (dos) and those that prevent it (don'ts). DIGI *method card* digital erstellen

Method card – giving a presentation	
Dos:	Don'ts:
...	...

c ✱ Discuss your findings in class. Add aspects to your method card that aren't already included.

► WOB: A4

Lernen App: Video on giving a presentation

► SF 42: Essentials: speaking, p. 258

► Getting started

Step ahead

2 Useful phrases for giving a presentation

HA **a** ✱ There are some useful phrases that can help you to give a good and structured presentation. Match the phrases listed in the box below to the three phases of a presentation:

1 introduction
2 starting a new section
3 conclusion

Now, let's turn to ... • So, as I've pointed out ... • Today, I'm going to talk about ... • I'd now like to talk about ... / to discuss ...• Are there any questions? • First, I'll give you a general idea of ... Then I'll go on to ... After that I'll tell you ... Finally, I'll ... • The next issue I'd like to focus on ... • That was my presentation on ... • The topic of my presentation is ...

HA **b** Add one more phrase that could be helpful to each part.

► Check

Lernen App: Answer key for task 2a

LÖS **2b**
1 Hello everybody. My talk is going to be on ...
2 The second topic/area I'd like to present to you is ...
3 Thank you for listening. I hope you enjoyed my presentation.

3 Preparing the content of your presentation

*The phrases in task **2** can help you to structure your presentation. But to be able to give a convincing presentation, you have to research your topic and decide what is important enough to be included.*

HA **a** ✱ Choose one of the topics below for your presentation

1 Peer pressure among teenagers
2 Teenage problems
3 Teenage dreams

► WOB: A4

Lernen App: Answer key for task 3b
► Check

HA CT **b** * Match the ideas below with the topics from **a**. Some might be relevant to more than one topic.

1 good grades
2 different financial means
3 finding your place
4 loyal friends
5 experimenting with substances
6 bullying
7 finding love
8 not fitting in
9 not being able to keep up
10 disappointing others

c * HA Research can help you to find more relevant information for your presentation. Research or brainstorm more ideas for your chosen topic and add them to the list from **b**.

d * Now decide which pieces of information are important enough to be included in your presentation. Cross out the ones you think you should leave out. HA

DIGI Ideensammlung auf digitaler Pinnwand/ Mindmap

► WOB: A4

4 Preparing your presentation

An outline can help you to structure your presentation once you have collected all relevant information. Apart from an outline, a convincing introduction and ending can help to give a successful presentation.

Info

A good **introduction** can help you to engage your audience right away. That's why your introduction should not only include the topic of your presentation and give an overview. With an interesting example, a funny story or an astonishing fact you can catch the audience's attention.

a * Discuss the two introductions below. What do you like/dislike about them?

1 Hey everybody, today's topic is 'Teenage dreams' and I'm going to tell you everything you have to know. So, I hope you're ready for the ride.

2 Today I'm going to talk about 'Teenage dreams'. First, I'll tell you something about teenage dreams throughout time, then I'll give you some concrete examples of modern teenage dreams before moving on to the reality of those dreams.

KV 2: Engaging introductions to presentations

HA **b** Choose the introduction from **a** you liked best and improve it. Use the phrases from **2 a** if possible.

c Exchange introductions with a partner. Give feedback on each other's introduction and improve it if necessary.

► WOB: A4

5 Guiding through your presentation

* **a** There are several tools you could use to accompany your presentation. Brainstorm pros and cons for each medium.

1 poster
2 handout
3 digital presentation tool

DIGI die Visualisierungsformen gruppenweise behandeln

* **b** Choose one of the tools mentioned in task **a** and prepare it accordingly for your presentation.

* 6 Focus on body language

An aspect that hasn't been covered yet is the use of body language, which is also very important when giving a presentation. It shows your attitude towards the topic and your audience.

Act out one of the following attitudes without speaking. The audience should guess which attitude you chose.

1 You are happy about your topic and your audience.
2 You are afraid of standing in front of a big audience.
3 You have prepared your presentation so well that you are very self-confident.
4 You are not interested in what you have to present.

Practise ▸ WOB: A4

7 Giving a presentation

a Find others who have chosen the same topic as you did in task **3 a**. Form a group.

b Take turns to deliver each of your presentations to your group. Use everything you have learned so far. Gruppen wählen die jeweils beste Präsentation, die im Plenum nochmals gehalten und kommentiert wird

Info

Follow the **golden rule of presenting**:
- Tell them what you are going to tell them.
- Tell them.
- Tell them what you have told them.

Take another look

8 Peer assessment

* a In your group, evaluate each person's presentation. Use the *method card you created in **1 b** to give feedback. Add more *dos* and *don'ts* if possible.

b Think about the *don'ts* that found their way into your presentations. How could you prevent them from happening again? If you haven't done so already, add a counterstrategy for every *don't* to your method card.

Method card – giving a presentation	
Dos:	Don'ts:
...	...
Strategies to avoid the don'ts:	
...	

Hinweis zum Feedback: zwei positive Punkte hervorheben, bevor ein Verbesserungsvorschlag gemacht wird

▸ WOB: A4 Speaking – presentation, pp. 16–17

▶ More info
Lernen App: Jennifer Clement

Living in a car Jennifer Clement

* • *Gun love* is the title of the novel the excerpt below was taken from. Speculate about this title. What do you think the story might be about? When and where would you set a story with such a title?

Gun Love *is told from Pearl's perspective. She is a teenager and lives with her mom.*

Annotations
- **2 tow truck** *Abschleppwagen*
- **21 foster home** *Kinderpflegeheim*
- **31 dilapidated** [dɪˈlæpɪdeɪtɪd] old and in bad condition
- **35 Everglades** national park in Florida
- **36 canopy** *Baldachin*
- **37 convertible** *(n)* car with a removable roof
- **37 Animal Kingdom/ Magic Kingdom** theme parks at Walt Disney World in Orlando, Florida

Me? I was raised in a car and, when you live in a car, you're not worried about storms and lightning, you're afraid of a tow truck.

My mother and I moved into the Mercury when she was seventeen and I was a newborn. So our car, at the edge of a trailer park in the middle of Florida, was the only home I ever knew. We lived a dot-to-dot life, never thinking too much about the future.

The old car had been bought for my mother on her sixteenth birthday.

The 1994 Mercury Topaz automatic had once been red but was now covered in several coats of white from my mother painting the car every few years as if it were a house. The red paint still appeared under scratches and scrapes. Out the front window was a view of the trailer park and a large sign that read: WELCOME TO INDIAN WATERS TRAILER PARK.

Mercury Topaz

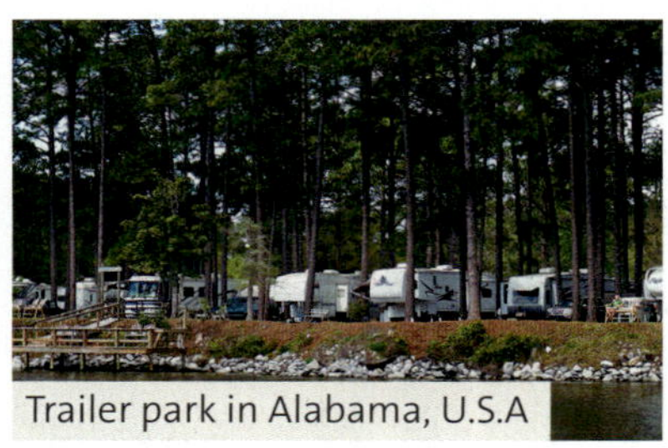
Trailer park in Alabama, U.S.A

Our car was turned off under a sign that said VISITORS' PARKING. My mother thought we'd only be there for a month or two, but we stopped there for fourteen years.

Once in a while when people asked my mother what it was like to live in a car, she answered, You're always looking for a shower.

The only thing we ever really worried about was CPS, Child Protective Services, coming around. My mother was afraid that someone at my school or her job might think they should call the abuse hotline on her and take me off to a foster home. [...] We can't go around making too many friends, my mother said. There's always some person who wants to be a saint and sit on a chair in heaven. A friend can become Your Honor in an instant.

Since when is living in a car something you can call abuse? She asked without expecting me to answer.

Annotation
23 Your Honor title for addressing a judge

The park was located in Putnam County. The land had been cleared to hold at least fifteen trailers, but there were only four trailers that were occupied. My friend April May lived in one with her parents, Rose and Sergeant Bob. Pastor Rex inhabited one all by himself while Mrs Roberta Young and her adult daughter Noelle occupied one right next to the dilapidated recreation area. A Mexican couple, Corazón and Ray, lived in a trailer toward the back of the park, far from the entrance and our car.

We were not in the south of Florida near the warm beaches and the Gulf of Mexico. We were not near the orange groves or close to St Augustine, the oldest city in America. We were not near the Everglades, where clouds of mosquitos and a thick canopy of vines protected delicate orchids. Miami, with its sounds of Cuban music and streets filled with convertibles, was a long drive. Animal Kingdom and the Magic Kingdom were miles away. We were nowhere.

Two highways and a creek, which we all called a river but was only a stream off the St John's, surrounded the trailer park. The town dump was at the back through some trees. We breathed in the garbage. We breathed in gas of rot and rust, corroded batteries, decomposing food, deadly hospital waste, odors of medicines and clouds of cleaning materials. […]

One time we even found a bullet hole in our car. It had pierced the hood and must have lodged somewhere in the motor because we couldn't find the bullet or exit hole.

When did this happen? My mother said on the day we discovered the clean hole in the steel with a dark ring of residue around it.

We never felt it.

People are hunting cars these days, she said. That's a joke. It must have been a stray.

But we both knew this was not unusual. In our part of Florida things were always gifted a bullet just for the sake of it. […]

On rainy mornings, with the car windows blurred with water, I never daydreamed about a house. That dream was too big. My dreams were about furniture. I imagined having a chair and a desk.

At night I placed a pillow over the hand brake so that the two front seats became one bed. In the dark space of the brake and accelerator pedals, I kept a pair of tennis shoes and sandals.

My books and comic books were laid out in short piles in a row along the dashboard and were warped from the sun shining down on them day after day.

We kept our groceries in the trunk and ate foods that didn't need refrigeration.

Our clothing was folded into plastic supermarket bags. In the glove compartment we kept our toothbrushes, toothpaste, and soap. In this space my mother also kept the can of Raid Flying Insect Killer. Every night before we went to sleep, we closed the windows and doors and sprayed the inside of the car with insecticide. Every morning as we stretched and yawned, the taste of Raid filled our mouths and mixed with the breakfast taste of cheerios and powdered milk mixed with water.

857 Wörter

From: Gun Love, *2019*

Annotations

51 **stray** *(n)* (here) bullet that missed its target

61 **warped** bent or damaged by heat or water

Fehlerquelle: Aussprache von *residue* [ˈrezɪdjuː] (Z. 48)

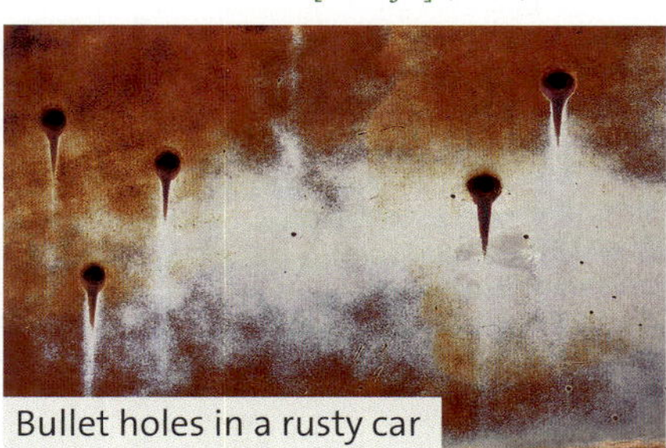

Bullet holes in a rusty car

Fehlerquelle: Aussprache von *insecticide* [ɪnˈsektɪsaɪd] (Z. 67)

Comprehension

HA **1** Outline Pearl's living conditions in not more than four sentences.

► WOB: A9

► SF 34: Writing a summary or an outline, p. 244

Erzählperspektiven wiederholen

Analysis

2 Identify the *narrative perspective used in the text and examine the effect(s) it has on the reader.

Lernen App: Video on narrative perspective

► Getting started

► SF 19: Reading and understandig narrative texts, p. 223

Language awareness

3 a HA Pearl juxtaposes the image people have of Florida with the part of that state she lives in. Make a list of adjectives and nouns from the text, which show the difference between these two worlds clearly.

HA **b** Read ll. 33–38 again and assess the effects the adjectives have on the reader.

LÖS **3b**
create a warm atmosphere/a holiday vibe of a beautiful and sunny place where life is easy → sharp contrast with the description of the actual trailer park Pearl lives in

Beyond the text

▸ WOB: A5

▸ SF 46: Having a discussion, p. 264

▸ SF 38: Creative writing, p. 249

4 You choose Work on task **a** or **b**.

DIGI Aufgabe mit *prompts* an KI delegieren → Ergebnisse bewerten

* **a** Speaking Discuss the challenges Pearl faces as a teenager living in a car with her mother. Together decide which three aspects are the most challenging.

b Writing Write a continuation of the story which follows up on at least one of the elements introduced in the excerpt, e.g. the CPS, living in a car, lack of future perspectives, living next to a dump, etc. HA

▸ SF 13: Doing research, p. 214

▸ SF 12: Communicating across cultures, p. 213

▸ SF 50: Paraphrasing, p. 270

HA *** **5** Writing Intercultural communication After having read the excerpt above you are quite shocked and want to know from your friend in the U.S. whether a situation like Pearl's is realistic. Out of interest, you have researched the support young people from low-income families can get in Germany and tell your friend about it in your email. im Anschluss an Aufgabe 5: Diskussion über kulturelle Unterschiede zwischen USA und Deutschland

Text 3

Info

Almost all societies function according to certain social hierarchies. The decision to which social class someone belongs is determined by different factors, amongst them income and education. The term ***social mobility*** describes the process of someone moving to a different position in a societal structure. For example, a former CEO could lose a lot of money and move downward in the societal structure, while a hard-working person could get a better job and move upward.

Annotations
council estate *Siedlung mit Sozialwohnungen*
bursary grant; scholarship

*** Social mobility – real opportunity or only a dream?

- Brainstorm people, services or supports that help individuals to improve their situation in life. Brainstorming in PA, GA oder im Plenum
- Rate them according to their effectiveness. Present your findings.

The following video by The Economist *focuses on the topic of social mobility in our time and questions whether young people can improve their position in society or whether they are destined to follow their parents' lead.*

Partner B: Go to p. 182 and do task **1 a**.
Partner A: Watch the video about social mobility and do task **1 a** on this page.

DIF Die Partner-A-Aufgabe bietet sich für leistungsstärkere SuS an.

Comprehension

1 a Viewing While watching the video for the first time, make notes on the following topics. Don't write complete sentences. ▸ WOB: A8

1 two pieces of information about the chances of 'climbing the social ladder' in modern times
2 two facts about social mobility in Britain, the U.S., Canada and Denmark
3 three pieces of information about Newham College
4 three differences between Newham College and other schools

HA **b** * ***Quick write**: What part of the video did you find most interesting? It can be an example that affected you, numbers that surprised you or something else.

Lernen App: Video on social mobility

Analysis

(08:47 min.)

2 Viewing Watch the video again. Analyse which cinematic devices are used to convey the information. Aufgrund der Komplexität des Videos reicht eine allgemeine Antwort aus.

▸ WOB: A8

DIGI mit KI zum Thema recherchieren

Beyond the text

HA **3** **a** Make a list of films, books and songs that describe the situation of teenagers who are limited in their options due to their backgrounds.

b Speaking Choose one example from the list and present it to your class. Explain why it is a good choice when talking about social mobility.

4 Reconsider the guiding question. How would you answer it at this point?

DIGI/DIF Präsentation digital unterstützen und in PA halten

▸ Getting started (task 2)
▸ SF 41: Analysing films, series and videos, p. 253
▸ Support (task 3 a), p. 182
▸ SF 43: Giving a presentation, p. 259
Lernen App: Video on viewing skills

Text 4

Lernen App: Nancy Jo Sales

▸ More info

* Living through social media

Nancy Jo Sales

* • Which social media sites do you know and what function do they have for you?

The following excerpt is taken from the book American Girls – Social Media and the Secret Lives of Teenagers *by Nancy Jo Sales. The author talked to girls between the ages of 13 and 19 and analysed their use of social-media platforms.*

DIGI digitale Umfrage zur Beliebtheit einzelner *social media sites* in der Klasse → Visualisierung in digitalen *graphs/charts*

Los Angeles, California

'Social media is destroying our lives,' said the girl at the Grove. 'So why don't you go off it?' I asked.

'Because then we would have no life,' said her friend.

The girls had been celebrating a birthday at the busy L.A. mall and now were on their way home. They carried bags of leftovers from the Cheesecake Factory. There were four of them: Melissa, Zoe, Padma, and Greta. They stopped to sit down and talk awhile at an outdoor table near the Gap. It was a steamy Saturday night and the mall was thronged. A salsa band was playing on a nearby stage; parents watched as little girls twirled around in princess dresses.

The girls were sixteen, with long straight hair, two blond and two brunette. They wore sleeveless summer dresses, flats and sandals. Melissa, Zoe, and Greta were white and Padma was Asian Indian. They all went to the same magnet high school in L.A. Zoe's parents were teachers; Melissa's father was a lawyer and her mother was a stay-at-home mom; Padma's parents were doctors; and Greta's father was in real estate. All the other girls' parents were married.

Greta, they said, was Instafamous, having thousands of followers on Instagram. She showed me a gallery of her Instagram pics; some were of Greta smiling, holding her dog, and some were of her in tank tops and crop tops, doing the duckface. In some of these pictures, Greta stared into the camera with the kind of intense

Annotations
6 **the Cheesecake Factory** popular U.S. American restaurant chain
8 **the Gap** clothing store
9 **thronged** full of people
13 **magnet high school** public school with specialized courses
16 **real estate** (here) *Immobilienbranche*

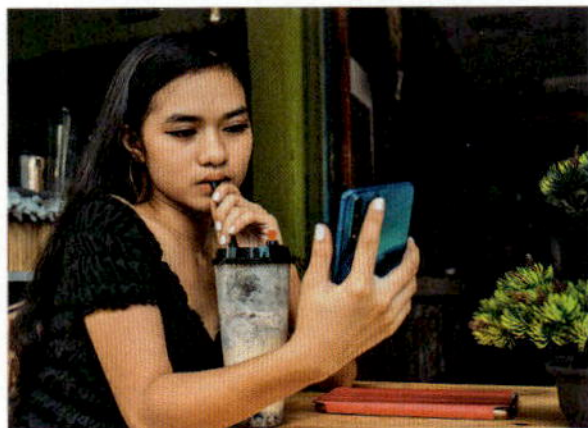

Annotations
28 strained uneasy; tense
31 Path former social media service (2010–2018)

expression seen on the faces of models and Hollywood stars. Some of her followers, Greta said, were people she knew, and some were 'random dudes in Italy and Arabia'.

'Almost every person I meet comes up to me because I have close to five thousand followers on Instagram,' Greta said breezily. 'It's almost like a title people associate me with'– meaning 'Instafamous.'

She relayed all this as if she thought it were ridiculous. The other girls listened with slightly strained expressions. I asked them what social media accounts they were on.

'I have Facebook, a YouTube, Twitter, Instagram, Snapchat,' Melissa said, 'Vine ...'

'Path, Skype,' Zoe added.

'Tumblr,' said Padma.

'I have a Twitter, but I don't use it except for stalking other people,' Greta said.

The other girls smiled knowingly.

'I think everyone does it,' said Greta. 'Everyone looks through other people's profiles, but especially being teenage girls, we look at the profiles of the males we find attractive and we stalk the females the males find attractive. Like Hunter Hayes,' she added, referring to a twentysomething country singer with boyish good looks. 'He's beautiful and going to be my husband someday. I mean it.' She laughed. 'I just, like, go on his Twitter and look at what he's saying and pretend he's saying it to me.'

'Stalking isn't really stalking,' Melissa explained. 'It's just a way to get to know them without them knowing that you're doing it. It's not like you're following them around and finding out where they live and looking in their windows.'

'It's a way to get to know them without the awkward, like, Oh, what do you like to do? You already know,' Padma said.

'You can know their likes and dislikes,' said Greta. 'Oh, they like this band. So you can, like, casually wear that band's T-shirt and have them, like, fall in love with you or something. Or you can be like, Oh, they listen to that music? Ew. Go away.'

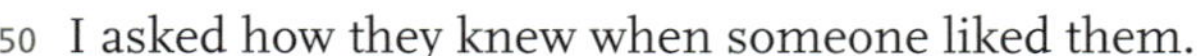

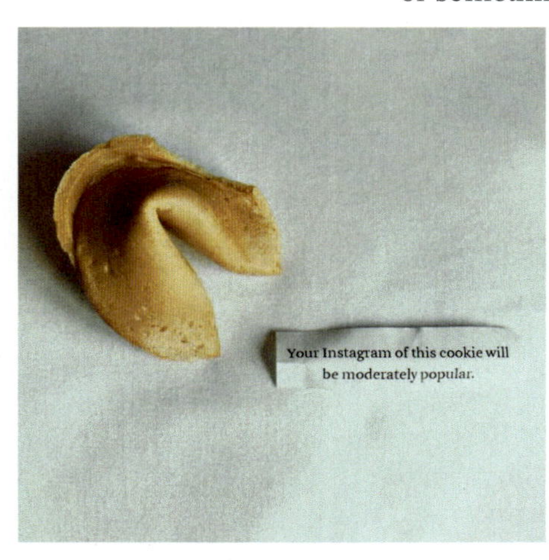

Your Instagram of this cookie will
be moderately popular.

I asked how they knew when someone liked them.

'There's a certain etiquette, certain signs, especially when it comes to liking photos,' Greta said. 'When a boy likes your [Facebook] profile pic or almost anything you post, it means that they're stalking you, too. Which means they have an interest,' said Zoe.

'If they like your Instagram pictures or favorite your tweets,' Padma offered.

'But the thing with social media is, if a guy doesn't respond to you or doesn't stalk you back, then you're gonna feel rejected and upset,' Melissa said.

'And rejection hurts,' said Padma.

'On Snapchat,' Melissa went on, 'I hate it when you send a picture of your face to a guy, and you say like, Hey, and they obviously see it, and it's like, Did I look ugly? Is that why you didn't respond?'

Annotation
79 forward confident; bold

'What if they were just busy or something?' I asked.

'That's no excuse,' said Melissa. The other girls laughed. 'No, really,' she said, 'because I feel like sometimes they don't respond because they know it'll make us feel insecure.' [...]

'But then if you ask them that, they say you're needy.' [...].

'Or "psycho,"' said Padma, frowning.

'Well, we are kind of needy,' Melissa said after a moment.

'I think social media makes girls more needy,' said Zoe. [...]

I asked them if they thought boys were as focused on social media as girls.

'Maybe not as much,' Melissa said. 'But they definitely are on it a lot 'cause they know we're on it and it's how they can talk to girls.'[...]

'Like when guys start a Facebook thing, they want too much,' said Padma. 'They want to get some. They try with different girls to see who would give more of themselves.'

'It leads to major man-whoring,' Greta said.

'They're definitely more forward to us online than in person,' Zoe said. 'Because they're not saying it to our faces.'

'Boys can be more confident online,' said Greta.

'That's completely true,' Padma said. 'If they tried to say the same things to us in person, there's a high possibility of them getting kicked in the balls!' Her eyes flashed.
943 Wörter

From: American Girls, *2017*

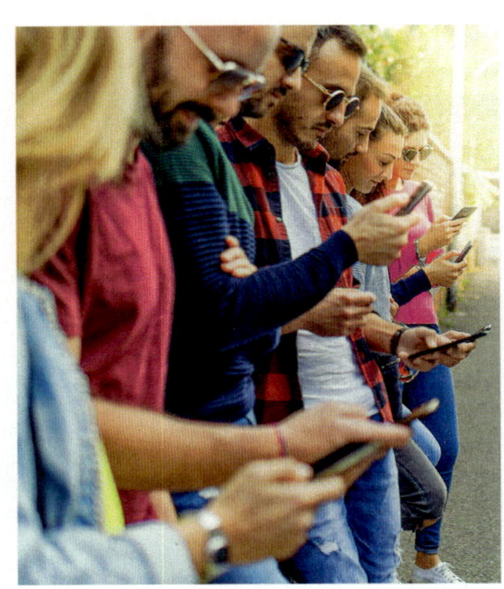

Comprehension

HA 1 * a Write eight sentences about the text: four true and four false. Make sure the order of true and false sentences is mixed up.

*** b** Exchange statements with a partner. Decide which ones are true and which ones are false. Rewrite the false statements from your partner to make them true.

Analysis

HA 2 ** Even though the text above is an example of non-fiction, it resembles a narrative text. Analyse how this impression is conveyed. ► WOB A9

HA 3 Examine the way the girls perceive social media. Give proof from the text.

► Support, p. 182

► Getting started (task 4 c)
Lernen App: Video on register

► SF 46: Having a discussion, p. 264

Language awareness

4 a The text includes quite a few filler words. Scan the text and note them down.

HA b Consider the effect of using filler words in this excerpt from a non-fiction text.

HA c *** Rewrite ll. 47–49 in a very factual, scientific style as you would expect to read in a work of non-fiction.

LÖS 4b
The text is more informal/conversation is more natural/authentic.

Beyond the text

5 Speaking Discuss the impact of social media on your life. Are the experiences described in the excerpt familiar to you? Decide whether the impact is more positive or negative. ► WOB: A5

Text 5

*** Addictive behaviour?

* • **Think** Think of a typical day in your life. Name the free time activities that take up most of your time.
Pair Compare your list with a partner. Together decide what the three activities you spend most of your time on are.
Share Share your results with your class. Discuss whether the activities run the risk of becoming addictive.

You are going to listen to an excerpt from an Australian podcast in which the impact of modern video games on Australian children is discussed.

Comprehension

Lernen App: Podcast (00:40–05:54)

► SF 40: Listening/Viewing for gist and detail, p. 253

► Check

► WOB: A6 Listening, pp. 20–23

Lernen App: Answer key for task 1

1 Listening (05:14 min.) Listen to the interview for the first time. Decide which of the statements below best summarizes the view of the guests. Das Interview sollte zweimal angehört werden.
1 Technology is similar to drugs as it is consumed, just like addictive substances.
2 Technology is worse than a drug as there is no escaping it.
3 Technology makes things possible and should be considered nourishment.

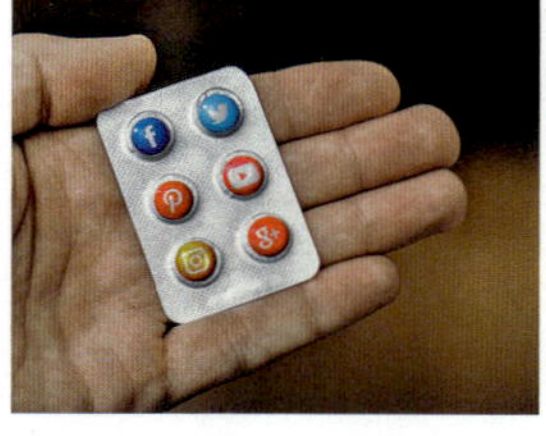

2 *** Listening Listen to the interview again and take notes on the following aspects:
1 the state of modern video games
2 Jocelyn's background
3 the comparison between technology and drugs
4 people's relationship with technology
5 technology as nutrition

► WOB: A6

Beyond the text

► SF 28: Argumentative writing, p. 236

HA 3 *** Writing *Comment on the following statement: Technology should be strictly controlled during young people's formative years.

► SF 43: Giving a presentation, p. 259

4 Speaking Prepare and give a three-minute-presentation discussing the question whether social media use can be compared to an addiction.

DIGI Präsentationen in PA üben; zwei SuS mit gegenteiliger Meinung präsentieren nacheinander → abstimmen, wer mehr überzeugt hat

DIGI digitale Visualisierungen nutzen

* Stress and how to cope with it

Marc Calmbach et al.

* • Talk to a partner about the following topics:
  1. Describe a place where you feel most comfortable. Explain why.
  2. Which situations are most stressful for you?
  3. What do you do if you are stressed?

Language help

The place I feel most comfortable is ... • My favourite place is ... because ... • I find situations in which I ... most stressful • Parents/school/siblings can be stressful when ... • When I'm really stressed I ... • The best thing to do when you are stressed is ... • What I find helpful in stressful situations is ...

You are going to read an excerpt from a study by the Bundeszentrale für politische Bildung *which examined the lives of teenagers aged between 14 and 17 in Germany.*

Stresserfahrungen sammeln die allermeisten Jugendlichen, vor allem in der Schule.

Die meisten Jugendlichen fühlen sich zumindest manchmal gestresst, einige sogar häufig bis ständig. Hauptauslöser dafür ist in zu erwartender Weise die Schule: Mehr als die Hälfte der befragten Jugendlichen empfindet zumindest zeitweise Stress in Bezug auf schulische Belange (Unterricht, Lernanforderungen, Probleme mit Lehrer*innen bzw. Mitschüler*innen). [...]

Auch Familie und Freund*innen können Stress bewirken (auf Geschwister aufpassen müssen, leidige Diskussionen mit Mutter und/oder Vater, unverhältnismäßige Erwartungen der Eltern, Probleme mit Freund*innen), allerdings in viel geringerem Maße. Einige Mädchen und Jungen berichten zudem von „Freizeitstress“. Überhaupt keinen Stress empfindet immerhin circa jede*r fünfte Befragte. Auffallend ist, dass an dieser Stelle der durch Social Media oder durch das Bewegen in virtuellen Räumen hervorgerufene Stress nicht genannt wird. Dies sprechen die Jugendlichen erst an, wenn sie speziell zu Aspekten rund um die Internet- und Smartphonenutzung befragt werden.

Musik ist wichtig für das Mood- bzw. Stressmanagement.

Zur allgemeinen Stressbewältigung setzen die Jugendlichen auf vielfältige Strategien. Unterschiede nach Bildung, Geschlecht und Lebenswelt zeigen sich dabei kaum. Besonders beliebt ist es, zur Ablenkung und Entspannung Musik zu hören, manche machen selbst Musik. Ebenfalls sehr populär ist es, sich eine Auszeit zu nehmen, das heißt: sich schlafen oder zumindest zum Ausruhen aufs Bett zu legen, eine bewusste Pause zu machen und einfach nichts zu tun. Das sind Momente, in denen Jugendliche ausgesprochen zufrieden sind mit ihrem Alltag [...]. Viele nutzen sportliche Aktivitäten, um herunterzukommen. Zudem spielt das soziale Nahumfeld eine wichtige Rolle: rausgehen und Freund*innen treffen, telefonieren, chatten, mit Familienmitgliedern reden. Die Mediennutzung und der Internetkonsum mithilfe des Smartphones, des Fernsehers oder des Computers dienen ebenfalls dem Stressabbau. Hier werden explizit Netflix oder Videos schauen, unspezifisches Surfen und (vor allem von den Jungen) Videogames spielen genannt. Allerdings können Social Media und Computerspiele wiederum Stress auslösend wirken [...].

Manche Jugendliche [...] versuchen außerdem, strukturiert und konzentriert die Stress auslösende Situation abzuarbeiten (vorrangig im schulischen Bereich oder bei überfülltem Terminkalender). Essen, trinken (kein Alkoholkonsum), rauchen, ein Buch lesen oder allein spazieren gehen werden seltener angeführt, um Stress zu kompensieren. Auch die Ausübung religiöser Praktiken erwähnen die 14- bis 17-Jährigen nur sehr vereinzelt als Stressbewältigungsstrategie.

361 Wörter

From: „Wie ticken Jugendliche? 2020, Lebenswelten von Jugendlichen im Alter von 14 bis 17 Jahren", Bundeszentrale für politische Bildung, *2020*

▶ SF 49: Mediating from German into English, p. 270
▶ Getting started
Lernen App: Video on mediation

HA **1** Mediating Speaking Your English-speaking friend is doing a project on teenagers and stress management. Record a message for them in which you explain the methods that help to reduce stress mentioned in the excerpt above.

▶ WOB: A7

DIF vorbereitende Notizen machen

Beyond the text

▶ SF 46: Having a discussion, p. 264

2 Speaking Discuss the impact of stress on teenagers' lives. Decide on the two most stressful factors and refer to ways they can be handled.

3 Reconsider the guiding question of this chapter. How would you answer it at this point?

Text 7

Lernen App: J.D. Salinger
▶ More info
▶ Getting started
Lernen App: Outsiders

Social conformity J.D. Salinger

* • Brainstorm songs, poems or films that deal with the topic of so-called outsiders and the reasons why they have been labelled as such.

JUDSON-ARIZONA
BOARDING - COLLEGE PREP. - COED
Fully accredited. Prep and General Courses. Healthful desert climate. Grades 1–12. Informal Western life. Small Classes. Remedial Reading. All sports. Riding. Art, music. Henry N. Wick, Dir., Judson School, Box 1569, Scottsdale, Ariz. 85252. Tel. 602-948-7731

Advertisement for the Judson Arizona boarding school, June 1971

*J.D. Salinger's famous *novel* The Catcher in the Rye *follows its protagonist Holden Caulfield on an odyssey through New York after he was kicked out of his boarding school, Pencey Prep. The following excerpt is the beginning of the novel.*

Where I want to start telling is the day I left Pencey Prep. Pencey Prep is this school that's in Agerstown, Pennsylvania. You probably heard of it. You've probably seen the ads, anyway. They advertise in about a thousand magazines, always showing some hot-shot guy on a horse jumping over a fence. Like as if all you ever did at Pencey was to play polo all the time. I never even once saw a horse anywhere near the place. And underneath the guy on the horse's picture, it always says: 'Since 1888 we have been molding boys into splendid, clear-thinking young men.' Strictly for the birds. They don't do any damn more molding at Pencey than they do at any other school. And I didn't know any-

Annotations
10 **mold sb.** shape sb.
11 **splendid** excellent; impressive
11 **strictly for the birds** *Das kann glauben, wer will.*

LÖS **Pre-reading**
- songs: Taylor Swift: *Anti-Hero,* Beck: *Loser,* Radiohead: *Creep* …
- films: *Billy Elliot – I will dance, Wonder, Requiem for a dream, Cool running, Saltburn* …
- poems: Edgar Allan Poe: *Alone,* William Wordsworth: *The Solitary Reaper* …

body that was splendid and clear-thinking and all. Maybe two guys. If that many. And they probably *came* to Pencey that way.

Anyway, it was the Saturday of the football game with Saxon Hall. The game with Saxon Hall was supposed to be a very big deal around Pencey. It was the last game of the year, and you were supposed to commit suicide or something if old Pencey didn't win. I remember around three o'clock that afternoon I was standing way the hell up on top of Thomsen Hill, right next to this crazy cannon that was in the Revolutionary War and all. You could see the whole field from here, and you could see the two teams bashing each other all over the place. [...]

Annotations
24 fencing *Fechten*
32 ostracize sb. exclude sb. from a group
35 good-by Salinger's own speeling of the word *goodbye*
41 flunk sth. fail sth.
42 apply oneself make an effort

The reason I was standing way up on Thomsen Hill, instead of down at the game, was because I'd just got back from New York with the fencing team. I was the goddam manager of the fencing team. Very big deal. We'd gone in to New York that morning for this fencing meet with McBurney School. Only, we didn't have the meet. I left all the foils and equipment and stuff on the goddam subway. It wasn't all my fault. I had to keep getting up to look at this map, so we'd know where to get off. So we got back to Pencey around two-thirty instead of around dinnertime. The whole team ostracized me the whole way back on the train. It was pretty funny, in a way.

The other reason I wasn't down at the game was because I was on my way to say good-by to old Spencer, my history teacher. He had the grippe, and I figured I probably wouldn't see him again till Christmas vacation started. He wrote me this note saying he wanted to see me before I went home. He knew I wasn't coming back to Pencey.

I forgot to tell you about that. They kicked me out I wasn't supposed to come back after Christmas vacation, on account of I was flunking four subjects and not applying myself and all. They gave me frequent warning to start applying myself-especially around mid-terms, when my parents came up for a conference with old Thurmer - but I didn't do it. So I got the ax. They give guys the ax quite frequently at Pencey. It has a very good academic rating, Pencey. It really does. [...]

Anyway, I kept standing next to that crazy cannon, looking down at the game and freezing my ass off. Only, I wasn't watching the game too much. What I was really hanging out for, I was trying to feel some kind of good-by. I mean I've left schools and places I didn't even know I was leaving them. I hate that. I don't care if it's a sad good-by or a bad good-by, but when I leave a place I like to know I'm leaving it. If you don't, you feel even worse.

631 Wörter

From: Catcher in the Rye, *2010 (first published in 1951)*

Banned book protest in Minnesota, U.S.A.

Vertiefungsmöglichkeiten:
Recherche/Referate zur Rezeptionsgeschichte von 'The Catcher in the Rye' (Zensur; *shootings*; Filmadaptionen)

Monument dedicated to J.D. Salinger's *Catcher in the Rye* in Lithuania

Comprehension

1 * Outline answers to the following questions:
HA 1 What do you learn about Holden Caulfield?
2 What kind of institution is Pencey Prep? What is special about it?
3 Why does Holden want to leave Pencey Prep?
4 What are the things he needs to do before leaving?

► WOB A9

Analysis

2 * Examine the *narrative perspective of the text and its effect(s) on the reader.

LÖS 2 first-person narrator from Holden's perspective → helps to make us see the school with his eyes and empathize with him

► Getting started (task 2)
Lernen App: Video on narrative perspective
► WOB: A9

3 Do either task **a** or **b**.

HA **a** *** Analyse the humorous style of the text. Give examples from the text as evidence.

b *** Challenge Analyse the style of the text. Give examples from the text as evidence. HA

Language awareness

► More language
Lernen App: Video about simple past and past progressive

4 **a** The text makes use of the progressive aspect. Read ll. 40–42 again, identify the progressive forms and explain why they are used. ► WOB: B1

HA **b** Write three sentences about your experiences at school using the progressive aspect.

Beyond the text

5 ***Quick write**: The excerpt conveys Holden's frustration with school and the feeling of not fitting in. Do you think these are relevant topics for young people? Why (not)?

► SF 38: Creative writing, p. 249

6 Writing Imagine Holden in twenty years. Write to his teacher Mr. Thurber in which you describe what his current life is like.

Text 8

What's on a teenager's mind?

* • Talk to a partner. Thinking about your own age group, what are typical conflicts that you are confronted with? Write down three of them and describe some typical situations when these problems arise.

Partner B: Go to p. 183, read the text and work on the tasks there.
Partner A: Read the text on the following page and do the tasks.

DIF Der Partner-B-Text bietet sich für leistungsstärkere SuS an.

The song Creep *by the English rock band Radiohead was released in 1992 and is still one of the band's most popular songs.*

Creep Radiohead

When you were here before
Couldn't look you in the eye
You're just like an angel
Your skin makes me cry
You float like a feather
In a beautiful world
I wish I was special
You're so fuckin' special

But I'm a creep
I'm a weirdo
What the hell am I doin' here?
I don't belong here

I don't care if it hurts
I wanna have control
I want a perfect body
I want a perfect soul
I want you to notice
When I'm not around
You're so fuckin' special
I wish I was special

But I'm a creep
I'm a weirdo
What the hell am I doin' here?
I don't belong here

She's running out the door (run)
She's running out
She run, run, run, run
Run

Whatever makes you happy
Whatever you want
You're so fuckin' special
I wish I was special
But I'm a creep
I'm a weirdo
What the hell am I doin' here?
I don't belong here
I don't belong here

167 Wörter

From: Pablo Honey, *1993*

▶ More info
Lernen App: Radiohead

Annotations
creep someone unpleasantly strange
8 **fuckin'** *(vulg)* (here) *verdammt*
10 **weirdo** unpleasantly strange person

Thom Yorke, singer and songwriter of the band Radiohead

Comprehension

1 Sum up the lyrics in not more than three sentences.

2 Outline the central conflict and the emotions depicted in the lyrics.

▶ SF 34: Writing a summary or an outline, p. 244
▶ WOB: A12

Analysis

3 Examine the *speaker and the addressee of the text. What do you learn about them? How are both roles used to get the message of the song across?

*** **4** Analyse elements of language and structure that underline this message.
rhetorische Mittel vorbereitend wiederholen

▶ SF 20: Reading and understanding poetry, p. 224
▶ WOB: A12 Poetry, pp. 38–39

Language awareness

*** **5** *Wish* and *want* are terms that are often used synonymously, although they are different. Reread the parts of the song that include these terms and note down an instruction for using each of them. ▶ WOB: B5

LÖS 5
- *want* → need to have something that is necessary or lacking
- *wish* → a more abstract or unrealistic desire / hopes or dreams that are hard to fulfil

Beyond the text

6 Present your results from the previous tasks to your partner.

7 Speaking Discuss which of the two texts better describes a conflict common to your age group and how the writer succeeds in conveying this concept.
▶ WOB: A5

▶ Getting started

▶ SF 43: Giving a presentation, p. 259
▶ SF 46: Having a discussion, p. 264
Lernen App: Video on giving a presentation

Lernen App: Video on adverbs

► SF 6: Essentials: language and study skills, p. 208

► More language (task 1)

► Check (task 1 a)

The following words can be an **adjective** as well as an **adverb** without any change of form:
daily • early • fast • good • hard • late • straight

Reactivate

Adjectives and adverbs both have a descriptive role but work in different ways. Adjectives describe nouns and pronouns more closely, whereas adverbs modify verbs, adjectives, complete sentences or even other adverbs.

1 Identifying adjectives and adverbs

HA **a** Read the text below and identify the adjectives and adverbs used in it.

Joan seems unhappy and stressed. She is writing her final exam tomorrow and is extremely nervous. She and some friends have studied excessively for the exam, but they are way more relaxed than she is. A few days ago, she dreamt that she was going to be late for the exam. Luckily, it was just a dream. To make sure nothing goes wrong, she has already packed her favourite bag carefully and meticulously.

HA **b** Using the text above, collect examples that show how adverbs can be formed. Add two more examples that are not used in the text.

Lernen App: Answer key for task 1a

HA 2 Irregular adverbs

Some adverbs have irregular forms and look exactly like adjectives. Take a look at the examples on the left, choose three adjectives and their corresponding adverbs and write six sentences in which adjectives and adverbs are used correctly.

DIGI Dokument digital teilen und die Mit-SuS Adjektive/Adverbien in den Sätzen bestimmen lassen.

► Check
Lernen App: Answer key for task 3
► WOB: B4

HA 3 Choosing an adjective or an adverb

Look at the following sentences. Choose the adjective or adverb to complete the sentences. Give reasons for your choice.

1 He is a … (marvelous/marvelously) singer.
2 Her poem was … (nice/nicely) written.
3 Our neighbour is such a … (nice/nicely) guy.
4 Bach's classical works were … (marvellous/marvellously) composed.

LÖS 3
1, 3 adjective describes noun
2, 4 adverb describes verb

► WOB: B4 Word order, p. 50
Lernen App: Answer key for task 4
► Check

1 Adverbs of frequency are usually placed before the main verb.
2 Adverbs of manner, place and time can often be found at the end of a sentence. They follow this rule: manner before place before time.
3 A sentence adverb modifies a whole sentence and is usually placed at the beginning of a sentence.

HA 4 * Adjectives and adverbs in a sentence

Put the words in the right order to create a sentence. Make sure to put the adjective and adverb in the correct place. Explain your choice.

1 incredibly / she / an / is / boxer / strong

5 Word order

There are certain rules for the position of adverbs in a sentence.

HA **a** Put the words below in the right order.
on Sundays / tells / luckily, / Emily / her stories / animatedly / at home / always

HA **b** Each adverb in the sentence above has a certain position. Match the rules 1–3 on the left with the respective adverbs from the sentence above.

► Check
Lernen App: Answer key for task 5

LÖS 5a
Luckily, Emily always tells her stories animatedly at home on Sundays.

LÖS 5b
1 always
2 animatedly at home on Sundays
3 luckily

Language awareness

6 Adjectives and adverbs in English and German

HA **a** Translate the German sentences below into English:

1 Sie hat den Test nicht ernst genommen.
2 Er ist komplett verrückt.
3 Die Erwachsenen sind laut.
4 Die Erwachsenen reden laut.

HA **b** * Using the sentences above, explain the differences in how adjectives and adverbs are formed in English and German.

Lernen App: Answer key for task 6 a
► Check

► WOB: B5

Work with words

Some verbs are followed by an adjective, not an adverb:

*1 Paul seemed **sad**.*
These verbs are called linking verbs: they link the subject of a sentence to a complement, here an adjective. This adjective describes the subject of the sentence more closely:

2 Despite the iceberg, the passengers stayed calm.
Examples of linking verbs can be found in the box on the right.

Some of these linking verbs can also be used as normal verbs. In that case, they are followed by an adverb and their meaning is different. Compare the following sentences:

1a	The flowers grew quickly.	The adverb *quickly* describes the verb *grow* (German for *grow*: *wachsen*) more closely.
1b	Tom grew angry.	The adjective *angry* gives more information on / refers to the subject of the sentence, Tom. (German for *grow*: *werden*) Here, *grow* is a linking verb.

7 Adjective or adverb?

a * Choose the correct option for the following sentences:
1 Don't try the cheese, it tastes ... (horrible/horribly)
2 We shouldn't eat animals – I feel ... about that. (strong/strongly)
3 The Ferris wheel turned ..., giving us a great view over the city. (slow/slowly)
4 The audience went ... when the band came on stage. (crazy/crazily)

LÖS 7a
1 horrible
2 strongly
3 slowly
4 crazy

HA **b** * Write four sentences using two different verbs from the box on the right. Two sentences should include adjectives, two adverbs.

Lernen App: Answer key for task 7
► Check

Examples of linking verbs are:
appear • be • become • feel • get • go • grow • look • prove • remain • seem • smell • sound • stay • taste • turn

Linking verbs that can also be used as normal verbs are highlighted.

Practise

HA **8 Using adjectives and adverbs**

Write a short text in which you describe how you handle stress and pressure. Use both adjectives and adverbs without making the text too artificial.

► Support, p. 184

► WOB: B5 Adjectives and adverbs, p. 51

Lernen App: Jennifer Clement
▶ More info

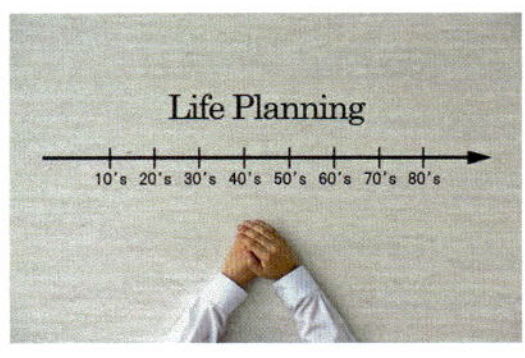

Annotations
17 tenderness fondness; affection
17 insignificant unimportant
31 eagle *Adler*

Forced to grow up
Jennifer Clement

* • Discuss what you consider as milestones of becoming an adult.

Below is another excerpt from the novel Gun Love. *Pearl's mum, Margot, has started a relationship with Eli, a stranger who settled in the trailer park some months ago.*

I heard everything from Noelle when she came to pick me up at school. I'd never seen her outside of the trailer park before except at church.

On the day of my mother's death, as I left the school building, Noelle walked toward me in her stiff, tiptoe Barbie-doll walk.

One cannot walk home alone, Noelle said.

Why?

Silence is also judgement, she said. A rabbit can be afraid of the moon. Death visits every house.

Just tell me, please. Just be clear.

A kid with a gun killed your mama. I heard everything. I saw everything.

At first I was quiet.

Did you hear me? Noelle said. Margot was shot. A kid with a gun killed your mama. Pearl, she's dead.

At first I was quiet. And then I was so grateful that my heart beat itself because I knew I would never be able to make it work if I had to do it. My heart's independent beats, beats that worked no matter what terrible thing had happened, made me feel tenderness toward my body and my insignificant life.

As we walked along the highway toward the trailer park, Noelle reached out and took my hand. I was fourteen years old, but I did not have to count how many people had held my hand before this moment. I didn't need math. Noelle's hand in mine felt so large compared to my mother's child-sized hand.

Many times my mother had said she hoped I would die before she did.

You won't be able to survive life without me, my mother explained. It will hurt so bad. There isn't even a song for it yet. Pearl, I hope you die first.

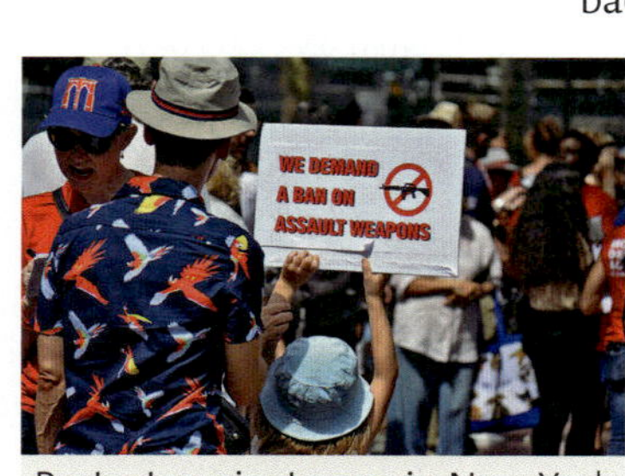

Protest against guns in New York

My mother was right. I should have died first.

Eli's down at the police station, Noelle said.

What's Eli got to do with this?

Nothing. Well, he sold the kid the gun and he was there when it all happened. Well, he didn't really sell it. It was a trade. That kid gave Eli his silver belt as a trade for the gun. And Eli was even wearing the belt when the cops took him away. It was fancy. It was silver with a gold eagle engraved in the center. [...]

I'm sorry, Noelle said. I wish I'd been your friend and now it's too late. Who knows where you're going to live now. It's afterward when we wish we'd been kind. I wish I'd baked you a cake and taken it to your car or let you use our bathroom to shower.

I didn't think of these things. I should have given you some of my dolls. I didn't really know that you and Margot mattered.

I stayed quiet. I listened to my heart. It beat as if every day were the same day.

I'm sorry, Noelle said again. I saw everything. [...]

There was a young woman dressed in a blue suit from Child Protective Services sitting inside the Mercury waiting for me. She was on the passenger side with the door wide open, filling in some forms on her lap. She didn't even know she was sitting in my bedroom.

As Noelle and I approached, the woman got out of the car.

She said, You must be Pearl.

I nodded.

I still couldn't speak. It was as if a superstition had taken over me, which I didn't even know I had. I thought, If I speak, all this will be true. I knew the words spoken would turn into the truth lived.

The trailer park was very quiet.

Most everyone is at the police station giving formal statements as to what they saw or heard, Noelle said. They already talked to me because I was the only person who witnessed it all. Life can surprise you.

And Eli? Well, he's not even considered a witness, Noelle said, as if she knew what I'd been thinking. He's part of the story. He got the kid the gun. What were they doing there hanging out at the swing anyway?

I wasn't speaking but I was placing Eli's name in my pocket like something I was going to chew on later.

597 Wörter

From: Gun Love, *2019*

Annotations

46 superstition irrational belief

52 witness sth. see a crime or incident happen

53 witness Zeug/in

Comprehension

1 a HA Summarize the excerpt above using the words from the box on the right that you think are necessary for a good summary. ► WOB: A9

b Exchange summaries with a partner. Justify your choice of words from **a**.

Lernen App: Video on writing a summary

► Getting started

belt • friend • school • mother • happiness • Mercury • Noelle • hamburger • trunk • gun • eagle • sunshine • swings • headmaster • cake • 14 • hands • Chevrolet • heart • banana • Eli

Analysis

2 Do either task **a** or **b**. See glossary entry *characterization for help.

HA **a** Characterize Noelle. Take into account what we are told about her, how she behaves and what she says.

HA **b** **Challenge** Characterize Noelle and Pearl.

► SF 31: Writing a character profile, p. 241

Language awareness

3 a Noelle regrets not helping Pearl and her mother in the past. Find the grammatical construction used by Noelle that conveys her regrets.

LÖS **3a**
'I wish … late.' (l. 32)

► Support, p. 184

HA **b** Using the same construction, write three sentences about possible regrets a teenager might have.

Lernen App: Video on giving a presentation

▶ Getting started

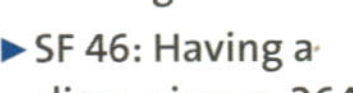

▶ SF 46: Having a discussion, p. 264

vorbereitendes Brainstorming im UG **Beyond the text**

*** **4** The word *initiation* can describe a transformation in which a person steps into a new role. Discuss to what extent the devastating murder of her mother could be the beginning of a transformation for Pearl into a new role. Present your findings.

▶ WOB: A5

Text 10

▶ More info

Lernen App: Paul Downs Colaizzo

Defining a generation Paul Downs Colaizzo

- Imagine you are invited to the Leaders of the Future conference. You are asked to deliver the opening speech about the role of your generation in today's world. Think of three issues you would like to talk about. Write them down. Present them in class and explain why you chose them.

The following speech is from a play called Really Really. *One of the protagonists, Grace, delivers the opening speech at the Future Leaders of America Conference.*

SCENE 5

An American Flag. A projection screen. Bizarre, tacky lighting. The sounds of a convention. Almost a carnival. This is a meeting for the Future Leaders of America.

GRACE Hello future leaders! It is my great honor to welcome you to the 36th Semi-Annual Future Leaders of America Conference. I am Grace Byrnes, your elected President, and I am going to say a couple of words before we begin our retreat. First of all, you'll have to excuse my hand. In an effort to be well-rounded, I misstepped and am now dealing with the consequences. I won't fully believe in equal rights until I see a man in a business skirt and heels. That said, I want to congratulate everybody here tonight and tomorrow for participating in these events. The people in this room represent a new generation. Growing up we were told, 'Don't worry about what others think of you.' And boy do they regret teaching us that one because now we are facing a generational vice. Research shows that amongst our peers the central concern for each individual is on the me. The I. The I. The me. Me. I. iPhone. MEphone. My turn. Me first. A line? I don't have to wait. A price? I don't have to pay. A test? I don't have to study. A generation of self-awareness and self concern – where they make what we want and what we want is more me. Facebook. Twitter. All social media. We are the members of a generation that has been dubbed Generation Me.

But as I stand here, in front of my peers, in front of the best and brightest and the most promising minds, I am forced to find the good in us. The good in me. The good in you. And at the end of my search, I have found our redeeming quality. The gem of this generation, and the upside to our selfishness, is the invincibility we espouse. Sure, we may consider that the rules do not apply to us, but for those of us still hungry to succeed in this world, our redeeming quality is that we look at obstacles in the same way. How do we do this? The successful members of Generation Me, the iGeneration, have a secret weapon. This weapon is composed of defiance and denial and

Annotations

6 **begin one's retreat** (here) start working
7 **well-rounded** (here) mature
13 **face a generational vice** meet an immorality of a specific generation
18 **dub sb./sth.** *(v)* give sb./sth. a name
21 **redeem** *(v)* save, rescue
21 **gem** treasure
22 **upside to sth.** positive aspect of sth.
22 **invincibility** *Unbesiegbarkeit*
22 **espouse** *(v)* assert
26 **defiance** disregard
26 **denial** rejection

greed, and yet is more precious than gold. The weapon, our weapon, is the desire and tendency to answer a simple question: What can I do to make this work? In any situation, what can I do to get what I want? Some people, after college, will move back home and sit in their parents' basements, blaming the unpredictable economy and the truly bizarre job market. That's how they will make this world work for them. But not us. The ones who refuse to take no for an answer. We will make our way in spite of the fact that the America this generation has been given is not the America that this generation was told we would get. Is this the land of opportunity? No. Now we're dealing with the land of strategy. Obstacles? We must see none. Dilemmas? They must be all the more fun. We will succeed. We just have to find a way. And if you don't want to be a victim of this mess, my advice is to find any way. So after the festivities of tomorrow end, and after we adjourn for another half of a year, I will be proud to be a representative of not only the Future Leaders of America, but more importantly of Generation Me. Like us or not, this is what we've got. Who knew hell and high water could be exciting! Thank you. And let's have fun tonight!

630 Wörter

From: Really Really, *2013*

Annotations
27 **greed** desire for getting more
38 **adjourn** [ə'dʒɜːn] *(v)* pause
41 **hell and high water** any great difficulty or obstacle

Info

The generation gap refers to differences in values, attitudes, beliefs and perspectives between older and younger generations. It is often the reason for conflict between these generations.

Comprehension

HA **1** Summarize how Grace describes her peer group, 'Generation Me'.

Lernen App: Video on writing a summary
► Getting started

Analysis

im Vorfeld das Thema *generation gap* besprechen

HA **2** ** Explain how Grace's speech addresses the generation gap.

HA **3** *** Examine how she makes her speech convincing.

DIF In PA können die SuS einander helfen.

► SF 18: Analysing speeches, p. 222
► Support, p. 184

Language awareness

HA **4** Analyse the use of personal pronouns in her speech. What effect do they have?

Beyond the text

CT **5** *** Speaking Think back to the issues you collected in the Pre-reading task. Using them, prepare and deliver your own speech about your generation at the Leaders of the Future conference.

DIF/DIGI PA ist möglich; Reden aufzeichnen und zur *self evaluation* nutzen

Lernen App: Video on preparing and giving a speech
► Getting started
► SF 44: Preparing and giving a speech, p. 262

Chapter task

1 * Talk to a partner. Has your opinion on the guiding question changed throughout the chapter? If so, how?

2 Choose between tasks **a** or **b**. Whichever task you pick, you should refer to your findings from dealing with the topic of this chapter.

a *** Speaking You are invited to a youth conference. Prepare a speech on the following topic: 'Teenage years – happy years?'

b *** Writing Write a poem on the following topic: Youth – a time of strain or gain? Present your poem in the context of a poetry slam.

Lernen App: Video on preparing and giving a speech
► Getting started (task 2 a)
► Info box, Different forms of poems, p. 41

DIGI digitale Poetry Slams zum Thema suchen und auswerten oder eine KI einen Text schreiben lassen und bewerten

▶ SF 16: Essentials: reading strategies and text types, p. 219

Poetry and you

1 * Work on your own and take some notes. Consider the following questions:
1 What expressions, words or names do you associate with poetry?
2 Do you like poetry? Why (not)? Collect arguments. ▶ WOB: A12

2 * Share your findings with a partner. Be prepared to present your ideas in class.

Maybe poetry plays a bigger role in your life than previously assumed. Quickly read the four texts below without going too much into detail.

▶ More info
Lernen App: Rupi Kaur

Text 1 Rupi Kaur

fall
in love
with your solitude

6 Wörter

From: milk and honey, *2015*

Lernen App: Kim Addonizio
▶ More info

Annotations
5 **idly** lazily
8 **gills** *(pl)* [gɪlz] *Kiemen*
13 **lure** *(n)* bait used for fishing

Text 2 ⁂ **Mermaid song** Kim Addonizio

for Aya at fifteen
Damp-haired from the bath,
you drape yourself
upside down across the sofa, reading,
one hand idly sunk into a bowl
of crackers, goldfish with smiles
stamped on.
I think they are growing gills, swimming
up the sweet air to reach you. Small girl,
my slim miracle, they multiply.
In the black hours when I lie sleepless,
near drowning, dread-heavy, your face
is the bright lure I look for, love's hook
piercing me, hauling me cleanly up.

82 Wörter

From: Tell me, *BOA Editions Ltd., 2000*

Lernen App: Gwendolyn Brooks
▶ More info

Annotations
5 **lurk** *lauern*
8 **thin sth.** mix a liquid with water to make it less strong

Text 3 **We real cool** Gwendolyn Brooks

The pool players.
Seven at the Golden Shovel.

We real cool. We
Left school. We

Lurk late. We
Strike straight. We

Sign sin. We
Thin gin. We

Jazz June. We
Die soon.

35 Wörter

From: Poetry, *1959*

Lernen App: Eminem
▶ More info

Annotation
7 **choke** (here) fail under pressure

Text 4 **Lose yourself** Eminem

[...] His palms are sweaty, knees weak, arms are heavy
There's vomit on his sweater already, mom's spaghetti
He's nervous, but on the surface he looks calm and ready
To drop bombs, but he keeps on forgettin'
What he wrote down, the whole crowd goes so loud
He opens his mouth, but the words won't come out
He's chokin', how, everybody's jokin' now
The clocks run out, times up, over, blow

Snap back to reality, oh there goes gravity
Oh, there goes Rabbit, he choked, he's so mad, but he won't
Give up that easy, no he won't have it, he knows
His whole back's to these ropes, it don't matter, he's dope
He knows that, but he's broke, he's so stagnant, he knows
When he goes back to this mobile home, that's when it's
Back to the lab again, yo
This whole rhapsody better go capture this moment
And hope it don't pass him

You better lose yourself in the music
The moment, you own it, you better never let it go
You only get one shot, do not miss your chance to blow
This opportunity comes once in a lifetime, yo [...] 197 Wörter

From: 8 Mile, 2002

Annotations
9 **gravity** *Schwerkraft*
12 **his whole back's to these ropes** (here) his back is against the wall (allusion to a boxing ring)
12 **dope** *(slang)* excellent
13 **stagnant** stiff; not flowing
16 **rhapsody** emotional piece of music with no formal structure

3 a Decide which of the texts are poems. Give reasons for your decision.

b * Which one of the texts do you like particularly well, which one don't you like at all? Discuss with a partner and give reasons.

c *** Read the definition of poetry below. Then go back to the four texts above and discuss whether or not they can be seen as poetry according to this definition. Give examples from the texts to support your decision.

Poetry is a literary genre based onx the interaction of rhythm and words. In poetry, words are chosen for their beauty and sound and are carefully arranged to present images and thoughts that might be too abstract to describe directly. A poem is a piece of rhythmical composition for creating pleasure with the help of delightful, imaginative, or elevated thoughts.

LÖS **3a**
All texts can be seen as poems as they are written in verse.

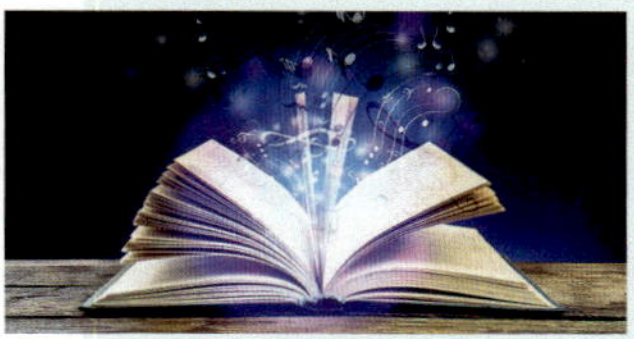

► WOB: A12

3b
Gedichte in vier Ecken des Klassenzimmers aufhängen, SuS positionieren sich bei ihrem Lieblingsgedicht → Austausch über Gründe in GA

DIF SuS in vier Gruppen aufteilen → jede argumentiert für ein Gedicht

Poetry – response, content, structure and tone

*Poetry is first and foremost about emotions. But to really grasp the meaning of a poem, a thorough knowledge of *stylistic devices and *rhyme schemes is necessary.*

4 Read the poem below. Note down in a ***quick write** how you feel about the poem. Give reasons.

Lernen App: Philip Larkin

► More info 

*** **This be the verse** Philip Larkin

They fuck you up, your mum and dad.
They may not mean to, but they do.
They fill you with the faults they had
And add some extra, just for you.

But they were fucked up in their turn
By fools in old-style hats and coats,
Who half the time were soppy-stern
And half at one another's throats.

Poet and author Philip Larkin, 1922–1985

Annotations
7 **soppy** sentimental; emotional
7 **stern** strict

Annotation
10 coastal shelf part of the sea near the shore where the water quickly becomes deeper

► WOB: A12

Man hands on misery to man.
It deepens like a coastal shelf.
Get out as early as you can,
And don't have any kids yourself.

89 Wörter

From: Poems, *2011*

5 It can often be helpful to start the analysis of a poem by focusing on the *speaker and the addressee of a poem. What does the poem reveal about them? Give evidence.

Lernen App:
Video on stylistic devices
Overview of stylistic devices
► Getting started

HA CT **6** The poem by Philip Larkin consists of three *stanzas. With a partner, name the main topic and feeling of each stanza. Also consider the language that is used.

7 The author makes use of an *anaphora. Identify the anaphora and analyse its effect.

LÖS 7
'They' (vv. 1–3) is repeated at the beginning of the poem: poem starts by stressing who is to blame for the children's faults (they = parents)

8 * a The poem has a specific *rhyme scheme. Choose the correct one below:
1 rhyming couplet: aa bb cc dd ee ff
2 enclosed rhyme: abba cddc effe
3 alternate rhyme: abab cdcd efef.

LÖS 8a
3

b Which role does the rhyme scheme play when it comes to analysing the poem? Examine its effect.

KV 3: This be the verse

HA **9** Taking your results from tasks **5–8** into account, what do you think is the message of the text? DIGI dLösungen auf digitaler Pinnwand notieren und vergleichen

LÖS 9
It is unfair to have children as parents always pass on their own faults, which has a negative impact on their children's lives.

Analysing a poem

Lernen App: William Butler Yeats
► More info

Annotations
2 nod *(v)* (here) slowly fall asleep
7 pilgrim person who makes a long and difficult journey
8 sorrow grief
10 murmur *(v)* say sth. quietly

*** **When you are old** William Butler Yeats

When you are old and grey and full of sleep,
And nodding by the fire, take down this book,
And slowly read, and dream of the soft look
Your eyes had once, and of their shadows deep;

How many loved your moments of glad grace,
And loved your beauty with love false or true,
But one man loved the pilgrim soul in you,
And loved the sorrows of your changing face;

And bending down beside the glowing bars,
Murmur, a little sadly, how Love fled
And paced upon the mountains overhead
And hid his face amid a crowd of stars.

96 Wörter

From: The Secret Rose, Love Poems of W.B. Yeats, *1990 (first published in 1893)*

10 In a group, analyse the poem by Yeats. Take everything into consideration that you have learned so far. The following tips might help you analyse the poem: Just look for the parts in the text that are highlighted in the same colour as the keywords below.

1 speaker
2 addressee
3 stylistic devices
4 rhyme scheme

► WOB: A12

Language help

The poem song consists of … stanzas. • The stanza is composed of/consists of … verses • Punctuation is/isn't used to … • The poem has a simple/complex sentence structure … • The poem deals with/addresses the topic of … • The tone in the poem is critical/humorous/sad/optimistic • The style of the poem is simple/complex. … • The stylistic devices … underline/suggest/emphasize …

Can songs be considered literature?

Poems are an integral part of literature, but what about song lyrics? Are songs poems in their own right and, therefore, also literature or something else?

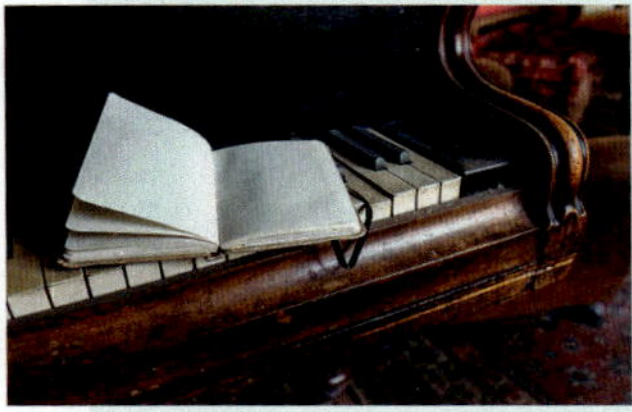

11 a **Think** Go back to the four texts on page 38–39. One of them is a song. Is it a poem nevertheless? Support your opinion by applying the knowledge and analysis skills you acquired in the Literature Lab to the lyrics.

b * **Pair** Discuss your results with a partner.

c * **Share** Present your findings in a group and discuss whether songs in general can be considered literature. Give more evidence from songs you know. Which additional features make songs still different?

Info

Famous U.S. singer-songwriter Bob Dylan was the first musician who was awarded the **Nobel Prize for literature** in 2016. His texts have been praised for their artful rhymes and their poetic word choice.

Creating poetry

12 a *** CT With a partner, write a poem about life as a teenager. If you want to, choose a specific form for your poem (see the Info box below).

CT b *** Present your poem to the class.

Die Gedichte können in einem Wettbewerb rezitiert werden.

Info

Different forms of poems

Haiku: consists of three short lines that do not rhyme; syllables are distributed between the three lines as follows: 5–7–5.
Acrostic: The first letters of each line can be read downwards to form a word, phrase or name.
Shape poem: Its words form a shape or picture and the image usually reflects the content of the poem.
Cinquain: consists of eleven words, distributed over five lines:
line 1: a noun
line 2: two words, often adjectives, that explain the functions of the noun
line 3: three words, more information about the noun
line 4: four words, further explanations about the noun
line 5: a one word synonym or any other reference for the noun

► WOB: A12 Poetry, pp. 38–39

Chapter 2
Individual and Society – Two Sides of a Coin

CT **1*** Describe the illustration.

► More language
Lernen App: Helpful words

2 a* **Think** Choose three words from the picture and explain in what way they are important to you. CT

CT **b** **Pair** Present your ideas to a partner. Together, examine in what way the words you chose relate to individual people or social groups.

CT **c** **Share** In class, discuss what idea of a society is presented in the illustration.

► SF 46: Having a discussion, p. 264

Language help

There is a connection between ... and ... • The combination of ... and ... suggests that ... • The link between... shows/underlines ... • Society is depicted/represented as ... through the use of ... / with the help of ...

LÖS **2b**
- words that may shape a person's identity (e.g. religion, language, gender, values)
- words signifying a unifying element that connects people in a society

CT **3** Take a look at the Chapter map on the right. How might the guiding question in the middle and the words in the boxes around it be related? What might they tell you about this chapter?

LÖS **2c**
- illustration and choice of the words show that groups/societies (i.e. countries) are shaped by individual people
- words relate both to individual people and social groups → group is comprised of individuals; individuals collectively form a group

LÖS **3**
- guiding question: central theme that connects texts and tasks leading to the chapter task
- the chapter focuses on how individuals form, determine and influence groups and vice versa

gender
society
religion
family
friends
culture
participation
involvement
language
ethnicity
values

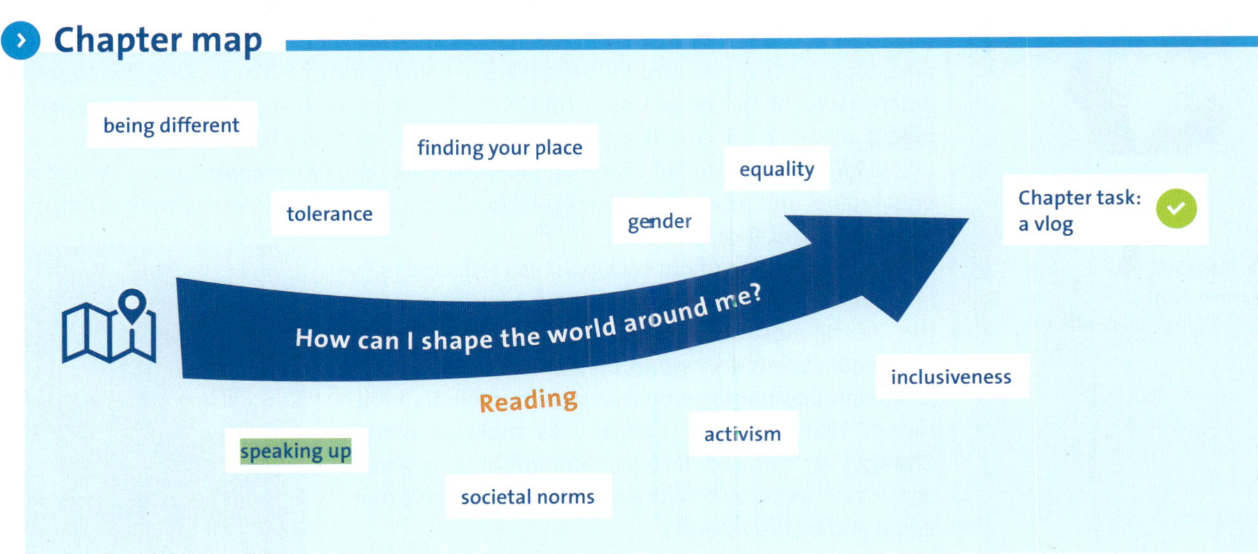

Lernen App: Useful vocabulary for the chapter

► More language 

Lernen App: Fulfilling your potential (00:04:27)

Fulfilling your potential

The shaping of an individual

It is widely acknowledged that a person's social and cultural background has a strong impact on their life. Our family, our surroundings, our country and even the region we grow up in all contribute to shaping our personalities in diverse ways. Factors such as religion, ethnicity, education, social status and gender also exert a significant influence on our lives, choices and level of success. Each specific environment – whether it is a small family in a remote rural area or a group of activists in a large and diverse metropolis – leaves its unique mark on an individual.

The demands of society

In most countries class barriers have become less restrictive over the last centuries and the introduction of compulsory education has led to greater educational opportunities in many parts of the world. Nevertheless, there is still injustice, discrimination and inequality both in advanced industrial societies and in the developing world. Material wealth, skin colour, ethnicity, gender, sexual orientation, age and disability may still influence a person's career opportunities and success in life. For example, girls in some parts of the world are excluded from secondary education; discrimination against Blacks may no longer officially exist but in reality people of colour are still discriminated against in many areas such as employment and housing; families living in poverty often have no access to healthcare; and disabled people are less likely to get the jobs they want because employers don't want to make an effort to accommodate them. People who come from privileged backgrounds (e.g. white heteronormative families without financial concerns) are rarely aware of the barriers others face just to get the opportunities privileged people take for granted.

Making a difference

If we want to make a difference in society, it's important, firstly, to question how unconsciously biased and prejudiced we ourselves might be, and, secondly, to stand up against discrimination and injustice whenever we can. There are many individuals and organizations who serve as role models and advocates for change, both locally and globally. In every community there are people fighting for a more inclusive society where everyone has equal opportunities. For instance, teenagers who are campaigning for action on climate change, women of all ages who are challenging social norms and inspiring others to fight for their independence, and movements campaigning for equal rights and promoting representation for all people regardless of their ethnicity or sexual orientation.

► More info
Lernen App: Gender-neutral pronouns

The transformation of our society is also reflected in the language we use. While the pronouns *he/his* and *she/her* are still most commonly used to talk about people, the gender-neutral pronoun *they/their* is becoming increasingly popular for people who are non-binary, which means that they don't identify as male or female. Changes like this and the sheer amount of activists and organizations show that there is a will to create a more equal and inclusive world.

481 Wörter

WOB: A1

1 Main ideas

HA CT **a** * The text gives examples of difficulties various groups face. Identify the groups and outline their situation.

b Describe what people are doing to change society as outlined in the text.

*** 2 Reflect

Find five concepts or ideas in the text that refer to the individual and society, e.g. education. Write two example sentences like the ones below for each concept.
Every individual receives a certain level of education.
A person's educational level may depend on his or her background.

HA 3 * Looking at pronouns

In the last paragraph the importance of pronouns is discussed. Check your knowledge of pronouns by filling in the missing pronouns and possessive pronouns.

1 This is my cat Mina. ... is my best friend.
2 'Have you seen Thomas? ... was supposed to be here at 6 p.m.'
3 Erin identifies as non-binary. ... are giving a talk at the conference about gender fluidity tomorrow.
4 'This dog seems lost. I guess ... is a stray.
5 George has found ... sister's backpack.
6 Someone has left ... coat behind. Hopefully, ...'ll come and pick it up soon.

► Check
Lernen App: Answer key for task 3

LÖS 3
1 She **2** He **3** They **4** it
5 his **6** their ... they

4 Chunk it! ► WOB: B8

a Find *collocations used in the text by matching the verbs in the left box with the noun phrases in the right box.

1	challenge
2	face
3	fulfil
4	have
5	leave
6	make

A	barriers
B	a difference
C	an impact on
D	a mark on
E	one's potential
F	social norms

b Use your dictionary to find more verbs that you can use with the nouns on the right. Struktur von Wörterbucheinträgen vorbereitend wiederholen DIGI Online-Wörterbücher oder Apps nutzen

Lernen App: Video about chunks
► Getting started

► Check
Lernen App: Answer key for task 4a

LÖS 4a
1F 2A 3E 4C 5D 6B

5 Text production

You choose Work on task **a** or **b**.

HA **a** ***Quick write**: Are you more of a group person or more of an individual?

b ** HA Analyse the cartoon in the context of the text on page 44.

CartoonStock.com

► SF 25: Analysing cartoons, p. 231

► WOB: A1 Reading for analysis, pp. 4–7

Info

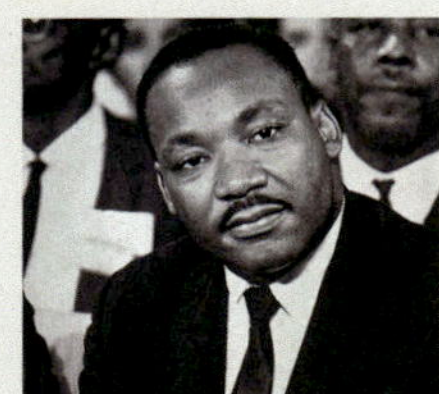

Martin Luther King (1929–1968) was an American pastor and peace activist. He used non-violent protests and civil disobedience to advocate for equal rights for African Americans. In 1968 King was assassinated, which led to riots in many US cities.

Lernen App: The March on Washington
► More info

Annotations

1 **score years** 20 years
1 **a great American** reference to President Abraham Lincoln
3 **Negro** African American (now considered offensive)
3 **sear sb./sth.** burn sb./sth.
4 **withering** that slowly destroys sth.
4 **captivity** state of being held prisoner
6 **manacle** *Fessel*
8 **prosperity** state of being rich
9 **languish** *(hier) verkümmern*
14 **wallow in sth.** enjoy sth. unpleasant
18 **creed** set of beliefs or principles
18 **we hold these … equal** quote from the Declaration of Independence
22 **swelter** be uncomfortably hot
27 **vicious** [ˈvɪʃəs] brutal
30 **every … together** quote from Isaiah 40:4–5 (Bible)
30 **exalted** (here) lifted up
31 **crooked** opposite of straight

*** I have a dream

Martin Luther King

Alternative: *quick write* mit dem Impuls *I have a dream*

* • If you were to give a speech with the title 'I Have a Dream', what dream(s) would you talk about? You could start like this: 'If I delivered a speech about my dreams, I would …'

Martin Luther King gave a famous speech in Washington, D.C., in 1963 at the March on Washington, which was part of the struggle to gain equal rights for African Americans by destroying the racism at the heart of U.S. society, particularly in the Southern States.

Fivescore years ago, a great American, in whose symbolic shadow we stand today, signed the Emancipation Proclamation. This momentous decree came as a great beacon light of hope to millions of Negro slaves who had been seared in the flames of withering injustice. It came as a joyous daybreak to end the long night of their captivity.

But one hundred years later, the Negro still is not free; one hundred years later, the life of the Negro is still sadly crippled by the manacles of segregation and the chains of discrimination; one hundred years later, the Negro lives on a lonely island of poverty in the midst of a vast ocean of material prosperity; one hundred years later, the Negro is still languished in the corners of American society and finds himself an exile in his own land. […]

Go back to Mississippi; go back to Alabama; go back to South Carolina; go back to Georgia; go back to Louisiana; go back to the slums and ghettos of the northern cities, knowing that somehow this situation can, and will be changed. Let us not wallow in the valley of despair.

So I say to you, my friends, that even though we must face the difficulties of today and tomorrow, I still have a dream. It is a dream deeply rooted in the American dream that one day this nation will rise up and live out the true meaning of its creed – we hold these truths to be self-evident, that all men are created equal.

I have a dream that one day on the red hills of Georgia, sons of former slaves and sons of former slave-owners will be able to sit down together at the table of brotherhood.

I have a dream that one day, even the state of Mississippi, a state sweltering with the heat of injustice, sweltering with the heat of oppression, will be transformed into an oasis of freedom and justice.

I have a dream my four little children will one day live in a nation where they will not be judged by the color of their skin but by content of their character. I have a dream today!

I have a dream that one day, down in Alabama, with its vicious racists, […] that one day, right there in Alabama, little black boys and black girls will be able to join hands with little white boys and white girls as sisters and brothers. I have a dream today!

I have a dream that one day every valley shall be exalted, every hill and mountain shall be made low, the rough places shall be made plain, and the crooked places shall be made straight and the glory of the Lord will be revealed and all flesh shall see it together.

This is our hope. This is the faith that I go back to the South with. […]

With this faith we will be able to hew out of the mountain of despair a stone of hope. With this faith we will be able to transform the jangling discords of our nation into a beautiful symphony of brotherhood.

With this faith we will be able to work together, to pray together, to struggle together, to go to jail together, to stand up for freedom together, knowing that we will be free one day. 559 Wörter

From: James M. Washington (ed.), A Testament of Hope. The Essential Writings and Speeches. Martin Luther King Jr., *1986*

Annotations
35 **hew sth. out of sth.** *(fml)* cut sth. large out of sth. using a tool
36 **jangle** *(v)* make an unpleasant sound

Info

In the speech, King uses the term ***negro*** repeatedly (cf. l. 3). At the time it was used as a common reference to Black people, but it often had racist connotations. Today, it is still used by some African Americans to underline shared identities. However, not all African Americans are comfortable using it. It should never be used by someone who is not Black.

▸ WOB: A1

Comprehension

HA **1** **a** * Briefly sum up the situation of African Americans as depicted by Martin Luther King in the first two paragraphs of his speech.
HA **b** * In your own words, list the various things that make up King's dream.

Tabelle anlegen lassen

Analysis

HA **2** **a** Identify the different parts of the speech.
HA **b** Examine how the structure of the speech helps to convince the audience.

3 Work on either task **a** or **b**.

a *** Find examples of the following *stylistic devices in the speech and analyse their use:
- *imagery
- *antithesis
- *repetition

b *** **Challenge** In his speech King uses various *stylistic devices. Identify them and evaluate their effect on the audience.

▸ SF 18: Analysing speeches, p. 222

▸ Getting started
Lernen App: Video on stylistic devices
Overview of stylistic devices

Bearbeitung auf eine bestimmte Zahl von Stilmitteln begrenzen (z. B. je drei), da die Dichte an Stilmitteln sehr hoch ist

Language help

arouse the interest of the audience • convince sb. • emphasize sth. • evoke emotions • illustrate sth. • make his point clearer • persuade sb.

*** **4** King was a minister in a Black Protestant church. Examine how his religious background can be seen in the language he uses.

DIGI vorbereitende Internetrecherche zu Kings biografischem Hintergrund

Language awareness

Lernen App: Video on will-future and going-to future

▸ More language

▸ WOB: B1 Tense and aspect, pp. 44–45

5 Examine the use of the future tense in the speech and explain why King uses it.

Beyond the text

HA CT **6** What are *your* dreams concerning a world worth living in? Think about different aspects (e.g. freedom, sustainable living, living together) and make a mind map and present it to your partner.

DIGI Mindmaps differenziert nach Neigung erstellen und gemeinsam an einer digitalen Pinnwand sammeln

▸ Getting started
Lernen App: Mind maps

Info

Martin Luther King is a **role model** for human rights activists worldwide. His peaceful resistance to segregation and his unforgettable speeches have shaped generations of activists – after all, most of the rights he was advocating for were passed into laws which significantly improved the lives of Black Americans.

► WOB: A1

HA **7** King was one of many people who throughout history have tried to change society. Look at the chart below. Describe and evaluate it, speculating about reasons for the changes that have taken place over time.

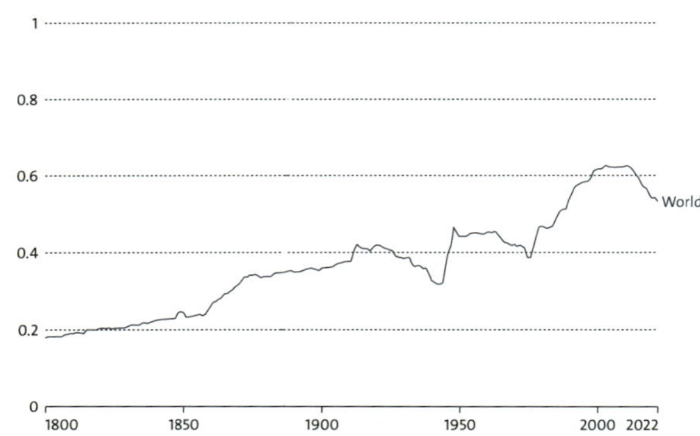

Source: OWID based on V-Dem (v13); Gapminder (V6); HYDE (V3.2); UN (2022)

Human rights based on the expert assessments and index by V-Dem, weighted by countries' populations. It captures the extent to which people are free from government torture, political killings and forced labor, they have property rights, and enjoy the freedoms of movement, religion, expression, and association. The variables ranges from 0 to 1 (most rights).

► SF 22: Analysing diagrams, p. 227

► Getting started
Lernen App: Video on analysing diagrams

Text 2

Info

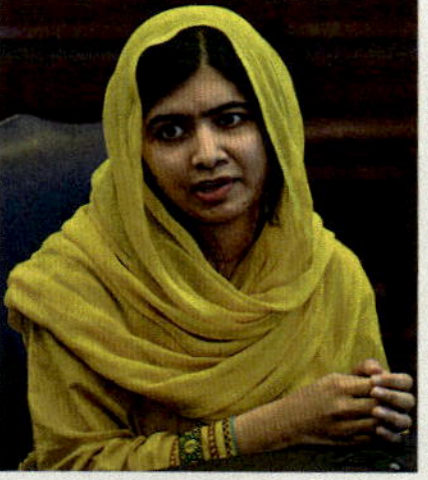

Malala Yousafzai was born in Pakistan in 1997. Her father was a teacher and ran a girls's school. In 2012 she was shot in the head by a Taliban after publicly talking about the right of girls to an education. She has remained in the UK following medical treatment for her injuries. In 2014 she was the youngest person ever awarded the Nobel Peace Prize. In 2020 she graduated from Oxford University.

DIGI Frage durch KI beantworten lassen und Ergebnisse anhand von Vorwissen beurteilen

Fighting for girls' education

Malala Yousafzai

Info

The role of religion in society

Religion often plays an important role in people's lives, regardless of where they live. However, there are differences in the ways religion is practised and perceived in urban versus rural areas. In urban areas, there tends to be more religious diversity, with a wider range of faiths and denominations represented. This can lead to greater tolerance towards different beliefs and practices, as well as a tendency towards more secularism.
In contrast, rural areas often have a more homogeneous religious landscape, with a dominant faith or denomination holding sway. Religion may play a more central role in community life, with more emphasis placed on shared rituals and traditions. In some cases, religious institutions may also be key social and cultural centers in rural communities.
Religion still plays a large role in people's lives – for good or bad. While a religion may give a sense of community and do charitable work, it can also restrict personal freedom or promote false information. In some Muslim areas, girls are forbidden to study while others are attacked for promoting education; in Christian communities in the Americas false information about Covid and vaccines was spread; in India, religious violence between Hindus and Muslims often breaks out. Religion can bring people together but also divide them.

215 Wörter

HA CT **1** Write down a list of advantages and disadvantages of living in a homogenous society.

HA CT • Discuss why it is important that every person regardless of gender, social background and place of birth receives a good education.

Malala Yousafzai is an activist who in 2019 founded the Malala Fund with her father to campaign for the right of every girl to 12 years of a good, free and safe education. The following text is from an interview with her.

UN News: **Tell us more about the new initiative the Malala Fund is carrying out to help girls' education in a number of countries.**

Malala Yousafzai: The Malala Fund started the Gulmakai Network, and the goal of this mission is to empower local leaders and some local activists. So we support them and we are already working in Pakistan, Afghanistan, Nigeria, and also the Syrian refugee areas. So we want to increase that investment and also support local advocates, as well as local girl advocates. So for that we have $3 million and we want to expand that group, redouble our efforts, and make sure we can give to as many local activists as we can because they are the real change-makers in their community, and when we empower them, through them, we can bring change.

UN News: **Specifically, how would you like to see this money used?**

Malala Yousafzai: We will invest in local leaders and local activists. These local activists speak out, locally, nationally; they campaign for girls' education. For example, in Nigeria, our activists, together with the Malala Fund, campaigned to ensure that the Nigerian Government increased education from 9 years to 12 years. So we succeeded in that campaign and it became part of the law. We are doing similar campaigning in Pakistan and Afghanistan. We are also including teachers' training. We are also including empowering other girls and helping them so they can also talk to leaders. It also includes e-learning and other improvements in the quality of education. So it's a vast project that covers many areas but our main goal is to empower local leaders.

UN News: **What are some of the things you observed in your efforts to promote girls' education during your travels?**

Malala Yousafzai: So this year I went on a Girl Power trip and I went to America, Canada, then Nigeria, Iraq, and Mexico, and in these places I met amazing and incredible girls and I heard their inspiring stories. In Iraq, I met a girl called Najla. She was 14 years old when she was wearing her wedding dress and she took off her high heels and she escaped from her wedding. She ran away. And later on, her village was captured by the extremist ISIS and she was actually attacked but she did not stop. She is still continuing her education, speaking out ... and she wants to be a journalist.

These are the stories that inspire me but my aim is to bring these stories into a global platform like the UN and allow these girls to meet their country leaders and local leaders so their voices can be raised. [...]

UN News: **What can men do to help achieve education for girls?**

Malala Yousafzai: Well, I think men have to do a lot. My father is an inspiration because his five sisters could not go to school. So, he decided he would allow his own daughter to go to school, to get her education, and then to raise her voice. When we started campaigning in Swat Valley, when terrorism started and girls' education was banned, there were many other girls who wanted to speak out but their parents, their brothers did not allow them. My father was the one who did not stop me.

We have to believe in girls, we have to believe in our sisters, in our daughters and allow them to be who they want to be. As my father says, you do not have to do

Annotations
1 **fund** (here) *gemeinnützige Organisation*
4 **empower sb.** give sb. the power to do sth.

Info

Charities and **volunteer work** play a huge part in creating a more equal, safer and tolerant world. For example, there are approximately 600,000 charities in Germany, and roughly 16 million Germans do voluntary work each year. Charities are dependent not only on the donations they receive, but also on the work of volunteers that support them. Many charities support developing countries by offering education, money or medical help, while others are dedicated to defend human rights and to create more equal and inclusive societies around the world.

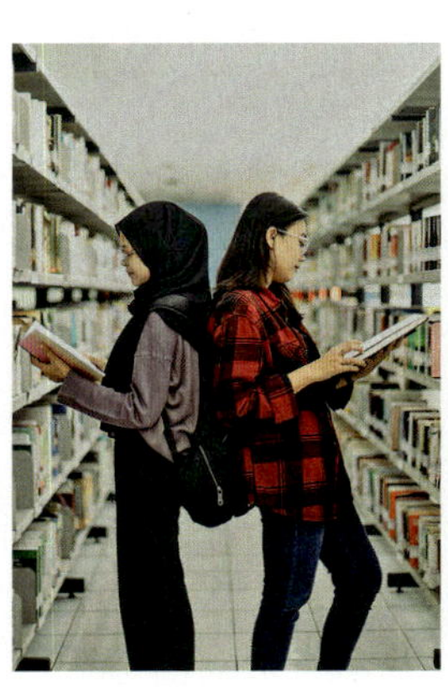

Annotation
48 **benefit sb.** be useful to sb.
51 **resilience** [rɪˈzɪliəns] ability to get strong again quickly after sth. bad happened

something, just do not clip their wings, just let them fly and let them achieve their dreams. So men have to come forward, they have to support women. It's better for the whole economy, better for each and every one of us. It will help the economy to grow even faster, it will improve the standards of living of each and every one of us, it would improve health. It also benefits the children because when women are educated, they are more likely to take care of their children, and their education, and their future. [...]

UN News: **You have shown tremendous courage, resilience. What within you gives you that power?**

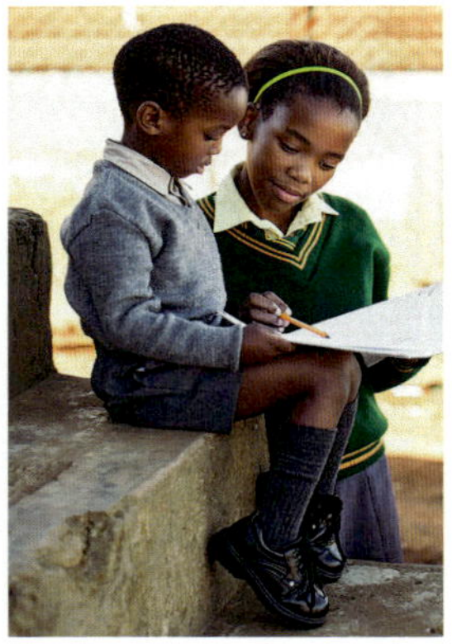

Malala Yousafzai: I have seen a lot in my life from terrorism, extremism, to then being attacked. And I was at the point where I had to make a decision [about] whether I want to continue my campaign for girls' education or not. And I've been away from my home in Pakistan for a long time. So going through all these situations in my life, I've learnt that, now surviving that attack, this life is for a purpose and that is for the education of children. It's only 70, 80 years that we live, and why not live it for a good purpose? Why not live it for a service that can help humanity, that can help the world? So I want to help as many girls as I can, to make sure they get quality education and achieve their dreams. 841 Wörter

From: 'INTERVIEW: In fighting for girls' education, UN advocate Malala Yousafzai finds her purpose', UN News, *5 October 2017*

arbeitsteilige Bearbeitung möglich

Comprehension

▶ WOB: A1 Reading for analysis, pp. 4–7

HA CT **1** Note down a key word or key phrase in each of Malala's answers. Explain your choice.

HA CT **2** Imagine you are going to give a presentation on the Malala Fund. Create a table or visualization that shows its aims, its methods, the places it works, the fields it works in and its achievements. DIGI Gestaltung mit Textverarbeitungsprogramm, Präsentationssoftware oder Designprogramm möglich

z. B. als Mindmap oder Tabelle

Analysis

Lernen App: Video on stylistic devices
▶ Getting started
▶ Support, p. 187

HA **3** *** In the interview Malala makes use of *stylistic devices. Find examples of the stylistic devices and explain why she uses them.

Language awareness

▶ More language
Lernen App: Video on indirect speech

4 **a** Imagine you are a reporter who is writing an article about Malala. How would HA you report her words in ll. 12–21?

HA **b** *** Explain why you rewrote her words in the way you did.
DIF Regeln der *indirect speech* und Merkmale des Berichts wiederholen, inkl. Verzicht auf *shift of tenses* bei noch geltenden Fakten

Beyond the text

Lernen App: Video on giving a presentation
▶ SF 46: Having a discussion, p. 264
▶ SF 43: Giving a presentation, p. 259
▶ Getting started
▶ WOB: A5 Speaking – presentation, pp. 16–17

5 In small groups, discuss acts of discrimination or inequality that you have witnessed and ways to overcome these forms of injustice. Methode: *think – pair – share*

HA CT **6** Speaking Imagine that you want to start a charity. What cause would your charity support? How would you try to make your charity known and find volunteers to support your cause? Prepare and give a short presentation that outlines the idea of your charity and how to promote it.
Präsentationen als *one minute talk* vorbereiten, Methode: Kugellager oder *milling around*

* A message for students

Barack Obama

HA • What do you expect your education to do for you personally?

HA • Why do you think the state pays to educate every person?

In a speech he gave at Wakefield High School while president of the USA, Barack Obama discussed the role of education and the obligations of teenagers.

Lernen App: Audio

Comprehension

1* **Listening** Listen to the audio. Match the areas of responsibility with the people responsible for that area. (04:13 min.)

1 teachers
2 parents
3 government
4 students

LÖS 1
1 AF 2 BCK
3 EHI 4 DGI

A inspiring students
B making sure students don't spend too much time watching TV
C making sure students stay on track
D paying attention to teachers
E supporting teachers and principals
F pushing students to learn
G putting in the hard work it takes to succeed
H setting high standards
I showing up to school
J turning around schools that aren't working
K making sure students get their homework done

► SF 40: Listening/Viewing for gist and detail, p. 253

► SF 18: Analysing speeches, p. 222

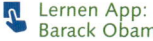

► More info Lernen App: Barack Obama

► Check Lernen App: Answer key for task 1

2* **Listening** Listen to the speech again. Name the three types of careers he suggests the students might have and the three school activities that might help them know that they should follow this path.

Lernen App: Answer key for task 2

► Check

► WOB: A6 Listening, pp. 20–23

3 **Listening** Note down what Obama says students learn from the following subjects:
1 science and math
2 history and social studies
3 all subjects

LÖS 3
1 knowledge and problem-solving skills
2 insights and critical-thinking skills
3 creativity and ingenuity

Beyond the text

HA CT 4*** **Intercultural communication** In the USA it is quite common to have a famous person come to a school and give advice to students who are graduating. Discuss whether such a practice would be good in Germany too.

arbeitsteilig Pro- und Kontra-Argumente vorbereiten und mündlich diskutieren, ggf. als amerikanische Debatte

► SF 12: Communicating across cultures, p. 213

CT 5 **Speaking** Obama gave this speech to a school with a diverse ethnic student population. Until the 1960s the school had been a segregated school for white students.
In small groups discuss how students' social, geographical and religious backgrounds may impact the education they receive and the expectations they may have of life. Present your strongest arguments.

Text von S. 44 zur inhaltlichen und sprachlichen Unterstützung heranziehen

► SF 46: Having a discussion, p. 264

► WOB: A5 Speaking – discussion, pp. 18–19

HA CT 6 Reconsider the chapter's guiding question in the context of Obama's speech. How would you answer it at this point?

Making a difference

LÖS Pre-reading
various reasons depending on the place of residence, e.g. discrimination, non-supportive environment, unstable political system, regional or geographical barriers, no access to healthcare, disabilities, no access to technology

- Having opportunities in life and control over your own destiny should be a fundamental human right that is universally accessible. However, not everyone has been given that right. Think of reasons why young people may not have the same opportunities in life and control over their destiny as you do.

Women Deliver is an organization that advocates for a world where young people are actively engaged in the decisions that affect their lives. Young people, especially young women, are encouraged to challenge norms, to speak up for equality and to make positive changes in their communities.

Comprehension

Auswertung im Kugellager oder als *milling around*

Auswertung mittels *peer feedback*

1 **a** * State which element of the infographic on p. 53 caught your eye first, HA and why.
HA **b** Outline the content, the central message and the main purpose of the infographic.

Analysis

▶ SF 24: Working with multimodal texts, p. 230
▶ WOB: A1 Reading for analysis, pp. 4–7

HA CT **2** *** Examine the layout and the structure of the infographic on p. 53 and analyse their effect.

Language help
headline • banner • column • row • at the top/bottom • in the top/bottom left/right corner • the upper/central/lower part consists of ... • separated by dotted lines • printed in bold/capital letters next to the text • provide the reader with figures / the percentage of ...

Language awareness

Lernen App: Answer key for task 3a
▶ Check
▶ WOB: B8 Collocations with prepositions, p. 56

LÖS 3a
1 for **2** to **3** for **4** from **5** for

SuS üben Umgang mit dem einsprachigen Wörterbuch

3 **a** HA CT The infographic contains several *collocations in which nouns or verbs are followed by a preposition. Find the prepositions that follow the following phrases:

1 have a need ...
2 face barriers ...
3 be a leading cause ...
4 be excluded ....
5 solutions ...

HA CT **b** Use the constructions above and make sentences about other teenage problems.

Beyond the text

DIGI Poster digital erstellen und an einer digitalen Pinnwand sammeln

4 **a** HA CT *** Create a poster in which you encourage young people to exercise their political rights by campaigning for issues which are important to them. Create slogans to support your message.

b Which of the issues you collected in **a** reveal a generation gap (cf. Info box p. 37) as the older generation does not seem as interested in them as your generation?

WITH **YOUTH,** *FOR* **YOUTH**

THE POWER OF YOUTH

Invest in Youth-Led Solutions for Gender Equality

YOUNG PEOPLE ARE CHANGING THE WORLD TODAY, CREATING THE REALITY OF TOMORROW.

SPEAKING UP | **DRIVING SOLUTIONS** | **CREATING CHANGE**

Yet, young people — especially girls and young women — **face barriers to health, rights, and opportunities.**

HEALTH

20 MILLION adolescent girls have an unmet need for **modern contraception**; complications in pregnancy & childbirth are a leading cause of death.

OVER 30% of all new **HIV infections** globally occur among young people aged 15-25.

Suicide is the third leading cause of death for adolescents aged 15-19.

RIGHTS

Legal restrictions and stigma contribute to **3.9 million unsafe abortions** annually among girls aged 15-19.

are married before the age of 18 every year.

15 MILLION girls aged 15-19 have been **forced** to have sex.

OPPORTUNITY

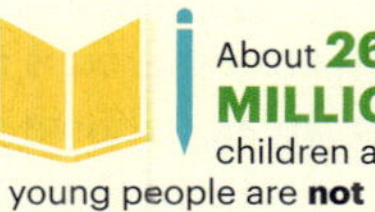

About **262 MILLION** children and young people are **not in school**.

21% of the world's youth were excluded from **employment, education, or training** in 2018.

In 2018, working youth were **twice as likely** to be living in extreme poverty than adults.

WOMEN DELIVER Updated March 2020. For data sources and definitions please visit www.womendeliver.org

From: Womendeliver.org, *2020*

Annotations
contraception methods of preventing pregnancy
abortion ending a pregnancy on purpose at an early stage
excluded from having no access to
adolescent *(adj)* developing from childhood into being an adult

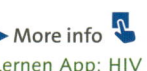

► More info
Lernen App: HIV

HA CT **5** * * * When you were doing task **4** on p. 52, you took it for granted that you have the right to campaign for issues which you consider important. Brainstorm reasons why you can take your right to campaign, to protest and to change things for granted. Then consider whether you are right to take them for granted.

Lernen App: Video on different models of democracy
► More info

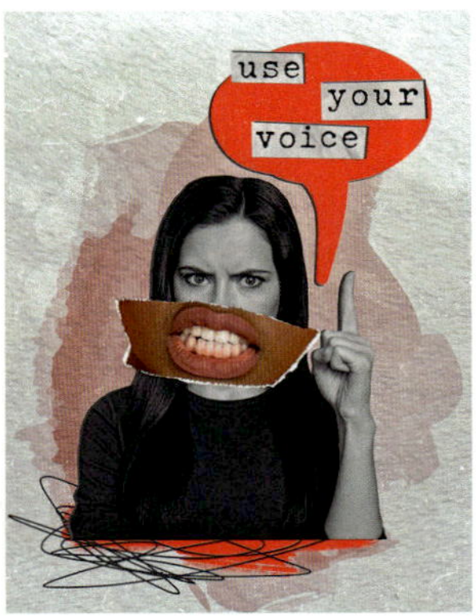

Fehlerquelle: Aussprache von *judicial* [dʒuˈdɪʃl]

Zusatz: Recherche und Kurzreferat über die Unterschiede zwischen *parliamentary democracy* und *presidential democracy*

Info

Living in a democracy

The word democracy has its origins in the Greek words 'demos' (people) and 'kratos' (power). At its core, democracy is about individual autonomy and equal rights for everyone. However, this can be challenging as a democracy needs to balance different and conflicting views. Therefore, compromise is an essential aspect of democracy, even if it means accepting a decision that does not align with your personal opinions. In a democracy, everyone has the right to vote and different political parties coexist. Additionally, every democratic state has some form of a constitution, laws, and a separation of powers between the executive, legislative, and judicial branches. Different models of democracy exist worldwide. For example, both the UK and Germany have parliamentary democracies, while the USA has a presidential democracy. A democracy functions most effectively when all of its citizens participate actively. Even if young people may not have the vote until they are 18 years old, they can get involved in political and social projects, thereby engaging in people power even before they are eligible to vote. For example, they can join protest groups to advocate for issues important to them. Democracy is not just about national politics but about making a change at a local level, such as in one's own school or community.

1 **a** * Read the text and collect key words for talking about 'democracy'.
HA Then arrange those terms in a mind map. DIF Kategorien/Unterthemen vorgeben
b With the help of your mind map explain the concept of democracy in your own words.

► WOB: A5

2 A democratic state has a separation of powers between the executive, legislative and judicial branches.
a **Partner A:** Go to page 185.
Partner B: Go to page 186.
b * * * Discuss the similarities of and differences between the UK and US systems of government.

► SF 23: Analysing visuals, p. 228
► SF 46: Having a discussion, p. 264
► WOB: A1 Reading for analysis, pp. 4–7

bei Bedarf Thematisierung des immer wieder kritisierten *First-past-the-post*-Systems in Großbritannien; online verfügbare Erklärfilme zum britischen Wahlsystem nutzen

HA **3** Due to its birth in Ancient Greece, democracy is often depicted as a temple held up by pillars. Look at the example on the right. From what you have read and what you know, evaluate the illustration and, if necessary, state what you would add or change.

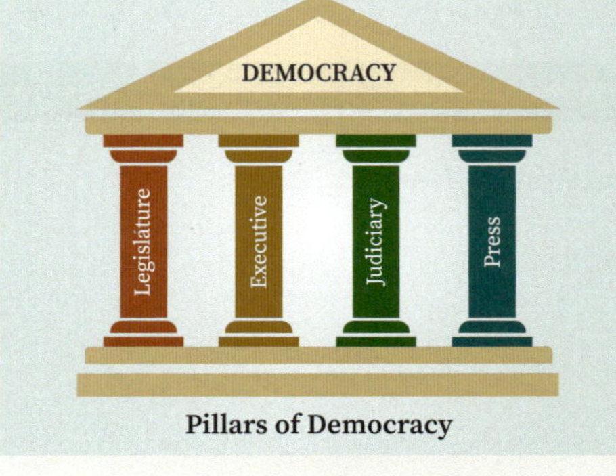

Pillars of Democracy

Reactivate

1 Your reading habits

HA **a** * What kind of reader are you? Describe your reading habits. The following questions may help you.
1 How much do you read?
2 Are you a fast/slow reader?
3 What kind of texts do you enjoy reading?
4 Which reading strategies do you use?
5 How do you approach reading texts in English?

HA **b** * The following terms describe useful reading strategies, which are helpful when training your reading skills. Find the matching explanations.

A extensive reading	1 reading sth. quickly in order to find important or specific information
B scanning	2 reading quickly through a text in order to get a general overview
C sensible guessing	3 a strategy of inferring the meaning of a word or phrase from its context or one's background knowledge
D skimming	4 reading as much as possible without necessarily picking up all the details.

HA **c** Explain when you might use each strategy.

2 Identifying text types

Knowledge of the text type can be helpful before you start to read a text.

HA **a** * List the following according to whether they are fictional or non-fictional texts.

advertisement – biography – drama – essay – newspaper article – novel – poem – short story – speech

HA **b** With a partner, discuss firstly, what the features (e.g. layout, use of photos) of each of the texts above might be, and secondly, what you might expect from each type of text.

Step ahead

3 Preparing for a reading task

HA **a** Before you read a text, look at all its elements to get an idea of what kind of text it is and what it is about. You can focus, for example, on the following:
1 length and structure (e.g. headings, paragraphs)
2 the beginning of the text
3 who wrote the text and when
Now write down all the information you can find out about the text on p. 56 without reading it (except for the first two paragraphs).

b Based on your findings, say what you think the text will be about.

► SF 16: Essentials: reading strategies and text types, p. 219

KV 4: Self Assessment: My reading habits

Lernen App: Video on skimming and scanning

► Getting started

► Check — Lernen App: Answer key for task 1b

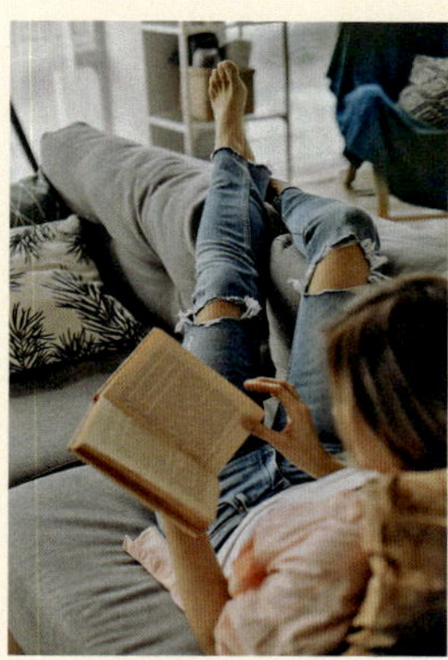

► WOB: A9

► Check
Lernen App: Answer key for task 2a

LÖS **2a**
fictional: drama, novel, poem, short story
non-fictional: advertisement, biography, essay, newspaper article, speech

► WOB: A1, A9

Zur Förderung der Lesemotivation kann Aufgabe 3c auch erst nach dem zusammenhängenden Lesen bearbeitet werden.

HA **c** Now read the text carefully. Make a table like the one below and fill it in with helpful information about the *characters, the *plot, the *setting and *narration. ► WOB: A9, A10

Characters: what we learn about the people	... ...
Plot: what happens	...
Setting: where the story takes place	...
Narration: how the story is told	...

Info

Angelica Gibbs (1908–1955) was an American writer of short stories. She was born in Baltimore, Maryland, and graduated from Vassar College. 'The Test' is her best-known story.

Annotations
- 8 **set** *(adj)* fixed, unmoving
- 12 **jumpy** *(infml)* nervous
- 15 **slatternly** *(adj)* dirty and untidy
- 16 **demeaning** *erniedrigend*
- 21 **slip sb. sth.** give sb. sth. (e.g. money) secretly

Fehlerquelle: Aussprache von *boulevard* ['bu:ləvɑ:d] (Z. 9)

Fehlerquelle: Aussprache von *dreary* ['drɪəri] (Z. 28)

Fehlerquelle: Aussprache von *maneuvering* [mə'nu:vərɪŋ] (Z. 61)

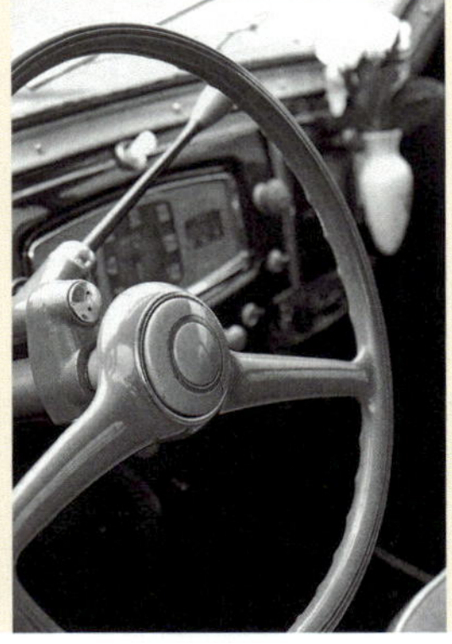

The test
Angelica Gibbs

On the afternoon Marian took her second driver's test, Mrs Ericson went with her. 'It's probably better to have someone a little older with you,' Mrs Ericson said as Marian slipped into the driver's seat beside her. 'Perhaps the last time your Cousin Bill made you nervous, talking too much on the way.'

'Yes, Ma'am,' Marian said in her soft unaccented voice. 'They probably do like it better if a white person shows up with you.'

'Oh, I don't think it's that,' Mrs Ericson began, and subsided after a glance at the girl's set profile. Marian drove the car slowly through the shady suburban streets. It was one of the first hot days in June, and when they reached the boulevard, they found it crowded with cars headed for the beaches.

'Do you want me to drive?' Mrs Ericson asked. 'I'll be glad to if you're feeling jumpy.' Marian shook her head. Mrs Ericson watched her dark, competent hands and wondered for the thousandth time how the house had ever managed to get along without her, or how she had lived through those earlier years when her household had been presided over by a series of slatternly white girls who had considered housework demeaning and the care of children an added insult. 'You drive beautifully, Marian,' she said. 'Now, don't think of the last time. Anybody would slide on a steep hill on a wet day like that.'

'It takes four mistakes to flunk you,' Marian said. 'I don't remember doing all the things the inspector marked down on my blank.'

'People say that they only want you to slip them a little something,' Mrs Ericson said doubtfully.

'No,' Marian said. 'That would only make it worse, Mrs Ericson, I know.'

The car turned right, at a traffic signal, into a side road and slid up to the curb at the rear of a short line of parked cars. The inspectors had not arrived yet.

'You have the papers?' Mrs Ericson asked. Marian took them out of her bag: her learner's permit, the car registration, and her birth certificate. They settled down to the dreary business of waiting.

'It will be marvellous to have someone dependable to drive the children to school every day,' Mrs Ericson said.

Marian looked up from the list of driving requirements she had been studying. 'It'll make things simpler at the house, won't it?' she said.

'Oh, Marian,' Mrs Ericson exclaimed, 'if I could only pay you half of what you're worth!'

'Now, Mrs Ericson,' Marian said firmly. They looked at each other and smiled with affection.

Two cars with official insignia on their doors stopped across the street. The inspectors leaped out, very brisk and military in their neat uniforms. Marian's hands tightened on the wheel. 'There's the one who flunked me last time,' she whispered, pointing to a stocky, self-important man who had begun to shout directions at the driver at the head of the line. 'Oh, Mrs Ericson.'

'Now, Marian,' Mrs Ericson said. They smiled at each other again, rather weakly.

The inspector who finally reached their car was not the stocky one but a genial, middle-aged man who grinned broadly as he thumbed over their papers. Mrs Ericson started to get out of the car. 'Don't you want to come along?' the inspector asked. 'Mandy and I don't mind company.'

Mrs Ericson was bewildered for a moment. 'No,' she said, and stepped to the curb. 'I might make Marian self-conscious. She's a fine driver, Inspector.'

'Sure thing,' the inspector said, winking at Mrs Ericson. He slid into the seat beside Marian. 'Turn right at the corner, Mandy-Lou.'

From the curb, Mrs Ericson watched the car move smoothly up the street.

The inspector made notations in a small black book. 'Age?' he inquired presently, as they drove along.

'Twenty-seven.'

He looked at Marian out of the corner of his eye. 'Old enough to have quite a flock of pickaninnies, eh?'

Marian did not answer.

'Left at this corner,' the inspector said, 'and park between that truck and the green Buick.'

The two cars were very close together, but Marian squeezed in between them without too much maneuvering. 'Driven before, Mandy-Lou?' the inspector asked.

'Yes, sir. I had a license for three years in Pennsylvania.'

'Why do you want to drive a car?'

'My employer needs me to take her children to and from school.'

'Sure you don't really want to sneak out nights to meet some young blood?' the inspector asked. He laughed as Marian shook her head.

'Let's see you take a left at the corner and then turn around in the middle of the next block,' the inspector said. He began to whistle 'Swanee River'. 'Make you homesick?' he asked.

Annotations

55 **flock** a group of animals

55 **pickaninny** [ˌpɪkəˈnɪni] *(infml, derog)* small, black child

65 **blood** *(infml)* man

68 **Swanee River** a song about a former enslaved person from Florida who longs for his old plantation

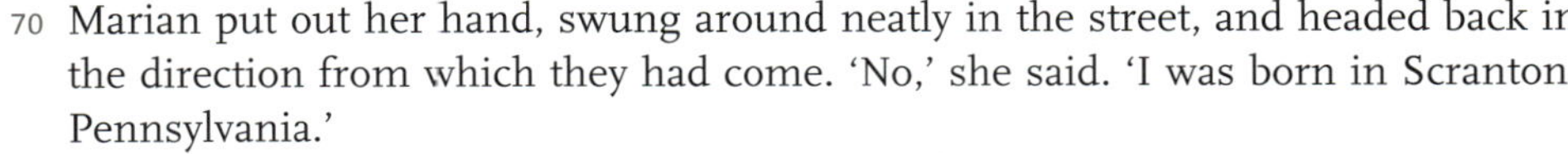

Marian put out her hand, swung around neatly in the street, and headed back in the direction from which they had come. 'No,' she said. 'I was born in Scranton, Pennsylvania.'

The inspector feigned astonishment. 'You-all ain't Southern?' he said. 'Well, dog my cats if I didn't think you-all came from down yondah.'

'No, sir,' Marian said.

'Turn onto Main Street and let's see how you-all does in heavier traffic.'

They followed a line of cars along Main Street for several blocks until they came in sight of a concrete bridge which arched high over the railroad tracks.

'Read that sign at the end of the bridge,' the inspector said.

'"Proceed with caution. Dangerous in slippery weather",' Marian said.

'You-all can read fine,' the inspector exclaimed. 'Where d'you learn to do that, Mandy?'

'I got my college degree last year,' Marian said. Her voice was not quite steady.

As the car crept up the slope of the bridge the inspector burst out laughing. He laughed so hard he could scarcely give his next direction. 'Stop here,' he said, wiping his eyes, 'then start 'er up again. Mandy got her degree, did she? Dog my cats!'

Marian pulled up beside the curb. She put the car in neutral, pulled on the emergency, waited a moment, and then put the car into gear again. Her face was set. As she released the brake her foot slipped off the clutch pedal and the engine stalled.

'Now, Mistress Mandy,' the inspector said, 'remember your degree.'

'Damn you!' Marian cried. She started the car with a jerk.

The inspector lost his joviality in an instant. 'Return to the starting place, please,' he said, and made four very black crosses at random in the squares on Marian's application blank.

Mrs Ericson was waiting at the curb where they had left her. As Marian stopped the car, the inspector jumped out and brushed past her, his face purple. 'What happened?' Mrs Ericson asked, looked after him with alarm.

Marian stared down at the wheel and her lip trembled.

'Oh, Marian, again?' Mrs Ericson said.

Marian nodded. 'In a sort of different way,' she said, and slid over to the right-hand side of the car. 1160 Wörter

From: The New Yorker, *15 June 1940*

Annotations
73 **dog my cats** expression of surprise
74 **yondah = yonder** (over) there

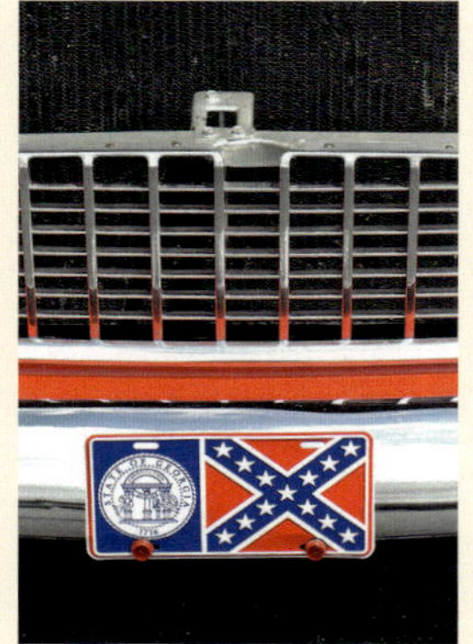

Lernen App: Video on working with closed text formats
► Getting started

► SF 2: Working with closed test formats, p. 201

Practise

Die Bearbeitung von Aufgabe 4 kann auch erst nach Aufgabe 5 erfolgen.

4 Dealing with closed-test formats

There are various types of closed-test formats which are designed to test your understanding of the general ideas in and the details of a text.

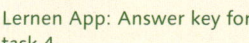

HA **a * Multiple choice**
Which of the following statements best summarizes the story?
- a The story explores the issue of racial discrimination.
- b The story deals with a conflict between a young black woman and a racist driving instructor during her second driving test.
- c The story is about a young black woman who repeatedly takes driving tests despite the racist behaviour of the driving instructors.

HA **b * Sentence completion**
Complete the sentences in 1–5 words using information from the text:
1. Mrs Ericson would like Marian to get a driving license so that she can …
2. Marian's driving skills are …
3. The inspector suspects that Marian wants to get a driving license in order to …
4. The inspector is surprised that Marian … the South.
5. The inspector … when he learns that Marian has a college degree.
6. After Marian's outburst the inspector …

c * Matching
Match the information about the characters with the names of the characters mentioned in the text.

1	the *protagonist of the short story	A	the first inspector
2	accompanied Marian to the first test	B	the second inspector
3	has not been happy with the white help	C	Marian
4	full of self-importance	D	Mandy-Lou
5	a name used to belittle the protagonist	E	Cousin Bill
6	puts the protagonist down all the time	F	Mrs Ericson

► Check
Lernen App: Answer key for task 4

LÖS **4a**
b

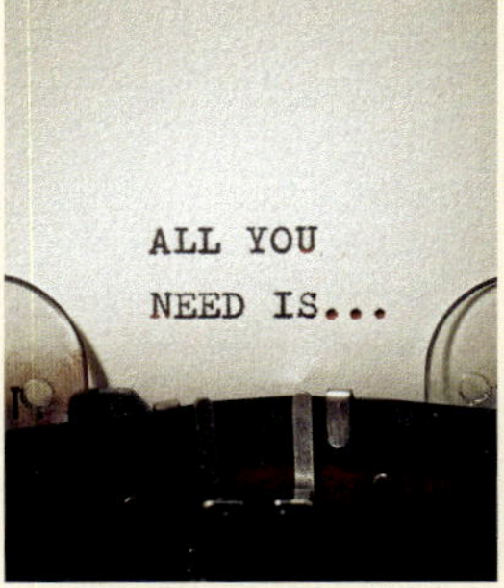

LÖS **4c**
1C 2E 3F 4A 5D 6B

Take another look

5 Reacting to the story

The main reason for reading a fictional text is for your own enjoyment, so discuss the following questions with a partner.
1. Did you like the story? Explain why or why not.
2. Explain why the story is called 'The Test' and not 'The Driving Test'.

► WOB: A5

Zur Förderung der Lesemotivation kann Aufgabe 5 unmittelbar nach dem ersten zusammenhängenden Lesen bearbeitet werden, z. B. als *Peer-to-peer*-Austausch.

6 Self-assessment

With a partner, create a *method card and mark the areas you need to practise more. Then fill it in with helpful strategies to improve your reading skills.

Method card – reading texts	
reading strategies	…
dealing with unknown vocabulary	…
understanding the plot	…
understanding the characters	…
understanding the setting	…
understanding the narration	…

► SF 15: Assessing yourself and giving feedback, p. 217

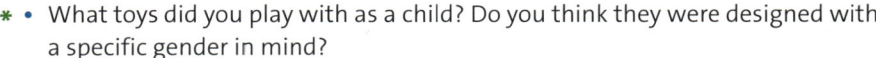

Kurzpräsentationen zu geschlechterneutralem Spielzeug vor oder nach Auseinandersetzung mit dem Text möglich (z. B. Barbie-Film, gesetzliche Vorgaben in verschiedenen Ländern)

The move to gender-neutral toys

Poppie Platt

SuS reflektieren auch die Merkmale von Spielwelten und Figuren in Computer-, Video-, und Handyspielen

HA * • What toys did you play with as a child? Do you think they were designed with a specific gender in mind?

Mr Potato Head is a popular U.S. toy consisting of a plastic model of a 'head' shaped like a potato, to which a variety of plastic parts can be attached, e.g. ears, eyes, a moustache, a nose.

The name's Potato Head. Mr Potato Head. Except it no longer is. The distinctive tuber-themed toy, with detachable eyes, nose, mouth, arms, hat and facial hair, has dropped the honorific. Potato Head has dispensed with formalities and become gender-neutral – and has caused no end of fuss on social media as a result.

U.S. toy company Hasbro announced last week that the 69-year-old family of Mr Potato Head toys, which became a 21st century children's favourite following a starring role in Pixar's Toy Story films, would henceforth be known as simply Potato Head, to 'promote gender equality and inclusion'. [...]

The truth is, however, toys have always been gender-neutral by nature. Children can choose to play with whichever products best ignite their imagination, creating a sense of fun that is hard to emulate as an adult – we all remember our favourite toys as children, whether that be a battered teddy-bear with holes in its padded belly, a plastic Action Man figure missing one arm, or piles of Lego bricks ready to be assembled into our very own Wonders of the World.

It is the marketing and branding strategies of toy companies that have for so long promoted gender stereotypes, and perpetuated ideas of there being certain toys for certain genders [...].

Jess Day, a campaigner with the group Let Toys Be Toys, which wants fewer gender stereotypes in the toy industry and successfully lobbied 15 UK retailers to remove gender-specific advertising and shelving, told the *Telegraph* that 'There is definitely an industry trend away from developing and marketing toys by gender.'

Day said: 'I don't think anyone really believes that a girl can't possibly want to play with a train, or a boy can't possibly want to play with a doll. And what do people think is going to happen if they do?'

'If you believe that there are general tendencies for boys and girls to want to play with different toys, then children don't need to be told which ones they're meant to want. Taking away these signs and labels allows children to choose freely, and has no downside.'

In addition to campaign groups like Let Toys Be Toys, reports and analysis from charities, academics and psychologists into the negative impact gendered toys can have on children's development have become more prevalent.

Annotations

- 3 **tuber** *Pflanzenknolle*
- 5 **honorific** title (e.g. Mr)
- 5 **dispense with formalities** (here) no longer use formal titles
- 14 **emulate sth.** try to do sth. as well as sb. else
- 16 **Action Man** toy action figure
- 22 **lobby sb./sth.** try to influence sb./sth. socially or politically
- 31 **downside** disadvantage
- 33 **charity** *Hilfsverein*
- 34 **prevalent** common, widespread

Fehlerquelle: Aussprache von *ignite* [ɪɡˈnaɪt] (Z. 13)

The Fawcett Society, a leading gender equality campaigning charity, warns that harmful gender stereotypes – often found in toys – are significantly limiting children's potential, as found in its landmark report from the Commission on Gender Stereotypes in Early Childhood.

Dr Christia Brown, a Professor of Developmental Psychology and Director of the Centre for Equality and Social Justice at the University of Kentucky, says that the impact toys have on children's development shows how important it is that they represent and appeal to all children, regardless of gender. The mixed response to Hasbro's announcement shows how divided society can be over certain issues, says Dr Brown, but also how willing and positive people are feeling towards the general trend of inclusivity.

Dr Brown said: 'I think that people forget sometimes that toys are profoundly important to children, and all toys are educational. They don't have to be special science toys to be educational – all toys teach different skills, they help children grow, they help children to envision themselves doing other things. Toys teach children about what the world is like, so they need to represent every part of the world to truly help them – by showing different careers and experiences that aren't limited by gender.'

Debates aside, companies increasingly adapting their marketing strategies to make products more inclusive will allow children to play more freely without worrying about enjoying the 'wrong' toys. 617 Wörter

From: Poppie Platt, 'From Potato Head to gender neutral dolls: the unstoppable rise of woke toys', telegraph.co.uk, *3 March 2021*

Annotations
- 37 **landmark** important; first of a kind
- 49 **envision sth.** imagine how sth. might be in the future
- 53 **sth. aside** regardless of sth.

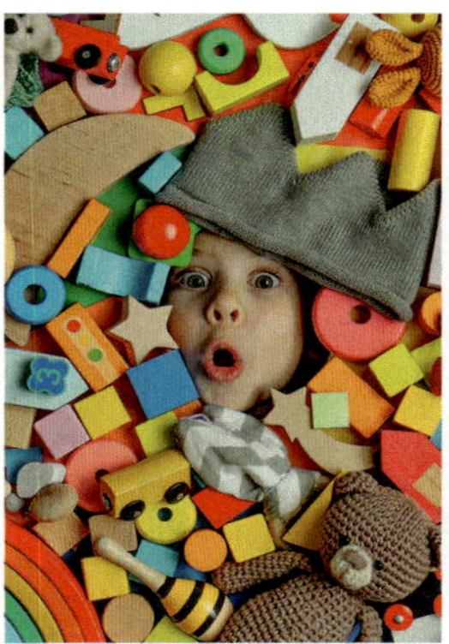

Comprehension

* **1** Complete the sentences in 3–10 words with ideas from the text. You may, of course, combine or summarize pieces of information.

1 The American toy manufacturer Hasbro has decided to …
2 Generally, the toy industry lately …
3 Children don't need to …
4 Dr Brown's main point is that …

LÖS 1
1 … rename Mr Potato Head toys as Potato Head toys / make Mr Potato Head toys genderless.
2 … has moved away from marketing toys by gender.
3 … be told which toys to play with.
4 … toys teach children about the world around them.

Analysis

*** **2** Examine whether the writer has an opinion on the subject she is writing about.

► WOB: A1 Reading for analysis, pp. 4–7

Language help

The writer expresses her own ideas / views / opinion… • The writer states / claims / suggests that… • The writer takes a (rather) neutral / balanced / objective / unbiased / subjective / biased view of the matter … • The writer supports / rejects … • The writer quotes … • The writer doesn't use quotes from …

LÖS 2
- ll. 12–17: 'The truth is …': clearly expresses her own view: toys are naturally gender neutral
- ll. 18–20: 'It is … genders': gender stereotypes are supported by marketing strategies
- all the sources quoted (Jess Day, Dr Christia Brown) are against gender labelling, all reports show that gender stereotyping of toys is damaging for children
- no quotes from people who oppose Hasbro changing the name of the toy
- ll. 53–55: 'will allow … toys': making toys gender neutral is better for children

Lernen App: Video on indirect speech
► More language

► Support, p. 187

DIF Passagen zum Umschreiben vorgeben

► SF 8: Working with dictionaries, p. 209

bei Bedarf Regeln für *indirect speech* wiederholen

Language awareness

3 **a** HA The author uses *direct and *indirect speech to let the opinion of experts be known. Find examples for this in the text.

b HA Name reasons for using direct and indirect speech in an article like this.

c CT HA Choose one example of direct and indirect speech from the text. Rewrite it into indirect or direct speech.

4 ** HA CT The title of the unabridged article is 'From Potato Head to gender neutral dolls: the unstoppable rise of woke toys'. Explain how you understand the term 'woke', and why the term has different meanings to different people.

Die relativ neue Bedeutung von *woke* (ein Bewusstsein für etwas haben) ist den SuS vermutlich geläufig, aber sehr unterschiedlich in die großen Wörterbücher aufgenommen. SuS vergleichen die Einträge für *woke* in verschiedenen (Online-) Wörterbüchern unter dem Aspekt von Sprachentwicklung und *register*.

Beyond the text

5 You choose Work on task **a** or **b**.

► SF 46: Having a discussion, p. 264

► SF 28: Argumentative writing, p. 236

a HA Speaking Collect arguments in the text in favour of gender-neutral toys. Then collect arguments against gender-neutral toys. Discuss the contrasting opinions. Together decide which argument is most convincing on each side. ► WOB: A5

Argumente ggf. arbeitsteilig vorbereiten (pro/kontra). Stärker formalisierte Formen der Debatte (z. B. amerikanische Debatte) ermöglichen eine breite Aktivierung.

b HA Writing Write a *blog entry in which you comment on the last paragraph of the article and discuss the need for gender-neutral toys.

Verbindung von *blog entry* und *comment*

DIGI *Blog entry* auf digitaler Pinnwand verfassen, Auswertung über Kommentarfunktion als *Peer-to-peer*-Feedback

► WOB: A2

Text 6

Educating people does have a lasting effect

- Does your school offer any extracurricular projects with organizations such as the police, social workers, media experts, etc.? Talk about your experiences.

Junge Ehrenamtliche des Aufklärungsprojektes „Wissen ist Respekt" aus dem Jugendzentrum *anyway* in Köln kämpfen gegen Homo-, Bi- und Transphobie auf dem Schulhof

Mittwoch, 9 Uhr morgens im Jugendzentrum. Eigentlich eine Uhrzeit, in der es gewöhnlich an einem solchen Ort noch sehr ruhig zugeht. Anders aber im *anyway*, dem einzigen Treff für schwule, lesbische, bisexuelle und trans* Jugendliche in Köln und Umgebung. 28 Schüler*innen haben in einem großen Stuhlkreis Platz genommen. Es wird getuschelt. Die Gesichter sind erwartungsvoll. Denn für sie gibt es heute einen ganz besonderen Schultag – ohne Lehrer, dafür aber mit Mica und Dominik. Die beiden Studierenden übernehmen den Unterricht. Auf dem Plan stehen nicht Mathe und Deutsch, sondern Aufklärung über sexuelle und geschlechtliche Vielfalt. In vielen Schulen kommt dieses Thema viel zu kurz oder gar nicht vor.

„Ich kann mich noch an meine Schulzeit erinnern. Da hatten wir eine Biostunde, wo es um Homosexualität ging", sagt Mica. „Aber meine Mitschüler*innen haben nur Klischeefragen gestellt: Sind alle Lesben hässlich? Haben alle Schwulen AIDS?". Für die mittlerweile 20-jährige Studentin war das damals eine frustrierende Erfahrung. Als sie merkte, dass sie auf Mädchen steht, hätte sie gern ernsthaft mehr über das Thema erfahren. Aber dafür war kein Raum und keine Zeit im Unterricht. Schlimmer noch: Nach ihrem Coming-out in der Schule mit 13 Jahren wurde sie nicht nur ausgegrenzt, sondern sogar körperlich von Mitschüler*innen angegriffen.

Wie reagierst du, wenn sich ein schwuler Mitschüler sich in dich verliebt?
Solche Erfahrungen machen leider noch zu viele Jugendliche, die schwul, lesbisch, bisexuell oder trans* sind. [...] Auch in einer vermeintlich toleranten Stadt wie Köln. Deswegen engagieren sich Mica und Dominik ehrenamtlich für das Aufklärungsteam „Wissen ist Respekt“ (WiR*), ein Angebot des Jugendzentrum *anyway*. Sie wollen Homo-, Bi- und Transphobie abbauen, ehe sie sich verfestigen und ehe Mitschüler*innen darunter zu leiden haben. An mehreren Vormittagen im Monat beantworten die Ehrenamtlichen deshalb die Fragen verschiedenster Schulklassen.

Zuerst klären Mica und Dominik über verschiedene Begriffe auf: Was bedeutet Coming-out? Was unterscheidet eine transsexuelle Person von einer Person, die Travestie macht? Mit den richtigen Definitionen im Gepäck locken Mica und Dominik dann die Schüler*innen aus der Reserve. Auf kleinen Zetteln stehen Fragen, die sie der Reihe nach vorlesen und offen und ehrlich beantworten sollen. Ein Schüler hat eine Karte gezogen, auf der geschrieben steht: „Wie würdest du reagieren, wenn sich ein Mitschüler des gleichen Geschlechts in dich verliebt?“ Ein schockierter Blick. Überforderung. Zunächst. Dann setzt das Nachdenken ein. Argumente werden ausgetauscht. Die Mitschüler*innen widersprechen und ergänzen sich. Dann die Erkenntnis: Das sind auch nur Gefühle, die jemand hat. Warum sollte man diese Person dafür verurteilen?

Dort helfen, wo Lehrer*innen an ihre Grenzen stoßen
„Die Schüler*innen sind in der Regel offen und respektvoll uns gegenüber“, sagt Dominik, 23 Jahre. „Aber es gibt immer ein bis zwei Schüler*innen, die sehr skeptisch sind und dem Thema erst einmal ablehnend gegenüberstehen.“ Um diese Schüler*innen geht es ihnen genauso wie jene, die vielleicht selbst einmal ein Coming-out haben werden.

Damit füllt WiR* eine wichtige Lücke an Schulen. Das weiß Jürgen Piger, Mitarbeiter des Jugendzentrums *anyway* und Leiter des Aufklärungs- und Antidiskriminierungsprojektes WiR*. Aus dem alltäglichen Kontakt mit Schulen weiß er, dass sich viele Lehrer*innen nicht trauen, das Thema im Unterricht anzugehen. Die Gründe dafür sind vielfältig. „Einerseits haben Lehrer*innen Angst, dass ihre Schüler*innen sie selbst für schwul oder lesbisch halten könnten. Andererseits haben auch viele Lehrer*innen noch ein Wissensdefizit bei dem Thema“, sagt Piger. Genau dort setzt WiR* an.

[...] Die mehr als 15 jungen Ehrenamtlichen sind Experten*innen auf ihrem Gebiet. In mehreren Workshops haben sie sich methodisch auf die Aufklärungsstunden vorbereitet. Und noch viel wichtiger: Sie stecken selbst in der Materie, da sie alle selbst schwul, lesbisch, bi oder trans* sind.

Am Ende folgt das Coming-out vor der Klasse
Das merken auch die Schüler*innen an diesem Vormittag ganz direkt. Denn kurz vor Mittag haben Mica und Dominik ihr großes Coming-out vor der Klasse. Danach beantworten sie anonyme Fragen,

die die Schüler*innen zuvor auf Zettel geschrieben haben. Wie habt ihr gemerkt, dass ihr homosexuell seid? Wie haben eure Eltern reagiert? Wie haben eigentlich zwei Frauen Geschlechtsverkehr? Die Fragen sind direkt, manchmal sogar intim. Aber Mica und Dominik wissen: Sie geben so viel Preis, wie sie selbst für richtig halten. „Man muss schon gefestigt sein, um sich vor fremden Schulklassen mehrmals im Monat zu outen“, sagt Dominik. „Aber es lohnt sich. Denn gerade beim Plaudern aus dem Nähkästchen können wir am glaubhaftesten vermitteln, dass es hier nur um menschliche Gefühle und nicht um etwas „Perverses“ geht.“

Natürlich wissen Mica und Dominik, dass sie nicht die Vorurteile und Klischees aller Jugendlichen an diesem Vormittag auflösen können. Aber sie regen zum Nachdenken an. „Ich bin überzeugt, dass Aufklärung nachhaltig wirkt“, sagt Mica. Und rückblickend auf ihre Schulzeit resümiert sie: „Für mich wäre es damals toll gewesen, so jemanden wie uns zu haben.“ 804 Wörter

From: „Ich bin überzeugt, dass Aufklärung nachhaltig wirkt“, anyway-koeln.de

Lernen App: Video on mediation
- ► Getting started 
- ► SF 49: Mediating from German into English, p. 270
- ► WOB: A7 Mediating, pp. 24–25
- ► SF 12: Communicating across cultures, p. 213

HA CT **1** Mediating | Intercultural communication You are taking part in an international seminar based around the question 'How can I shape the world around me?' Your team is concentrating on the role education and information play in shaping opinions. You come across this article on the website of an LGBTQ project. For your seminar's website you decide to write an article about the project and the motivation behind the involvement of the volunteers.
zunächst wesentliche Aspekte im Unterricht gemeinsam erarbeiten/strukturieren, passende englische Wendungen sammeln → zusammenhängenden Text als HA verfassen

Beyond the text

- ► SF 28: Argumentative writing, p. 236
- ► WOB: A2

HA CT **2** Writing Mica says, 'Ich bin überzeugt, dass Aufklärung nachhaltig wirkt'. Look back at the chapter's guiding question. Discuss how people like Mica can help to shape a more tolerant and respectful world.

Text 7

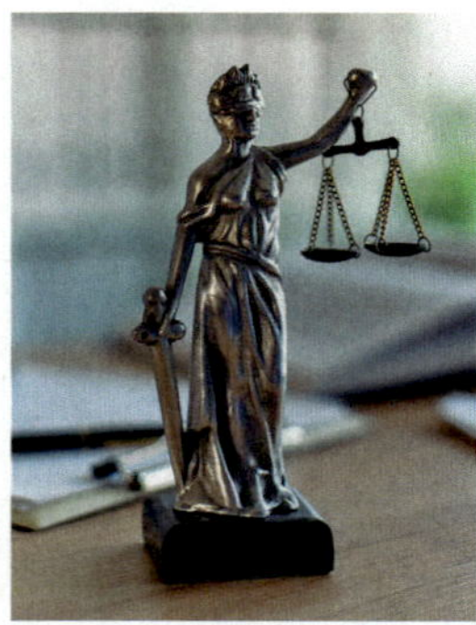

Begriff des *register*, verschiedene Sprachebenen und ihre Merkmale mit thematisieren

The interviewer (12:52 min.)

The short film you are going to watch is about a job interview. Thomas Howell has applied for a job as a solicitor in the pro-bono department of a law firm.

- Work in pairs. **Partner A** makes notes about the topics that might be discussed, while **Partner B** makes notes about the type of language that might be used. Present your ideas to each other. Compare your ideas with what happens in the film.

Language help

interviewer • interviewee • candidate /applicant • to apply for a job • the interviewer could/might ask ... • The interviewee is supposed to / should (not)... • They might (probably) talk about ... • the language used in an interview is usually ...

Lernen App: Short film

Comprehension

1 Viewing True or false? Correct the sentences if necessary.

1. James Dexter is conducting the job interview with Thomas Howell because his father wants to test the interviewee's open-mindedness.
2. Thomas Howell wants to leave his old job because the new job offers better career opportunities.
3. Paul Dexter is angry with his son James because James often interferes with the interviews.
4. Paul Dexter finally becomes aware of his son's talents and James is given more responsibility.

LÖS 1
1 false **2** false **3** true **4** true

Analysis

2 Viewing Analyse how Thomas Howell's feelings are expressed cinematically.

onkrete *tills* oder zenen orgeben

Language help

astonished • confused • easy-going • irritated • nervous • relaxed • serious • skeptical • thoughtful • uneasy

This is shown by a close-up of ... • A close-up / medium shot / long shot ... • underlines/emphasizes

DIGI SuS können konkrete Szenen arbeitsteilig an Tablets analysieren, selbst ein *still* auswählen und mit Hilfe von *Language help* und SF 41 beschriften.

Language awareness

3 Work on either task **a** or **b**.

a Find examples of typical interview phrases used by both the interviewer and the interviewee.

b Challenge Find examples of typical interview phrases used by both the interviewer and the interviewee. Add more phrases you might find useful. Act out a job interview using the phrases you found.

Zeitlimit und Regeln für die Notizen vorgeben

Beyond the text

HA CT **4** ** Do some research on the internet to find examples for inclusive workplaces in companies and firms and present some examples to the class.

HA **5** ** Writing Imagine you want to do an internship at the law firm in the film. Write a covering letter explaining why you would be a good candidate for a position at the firm.

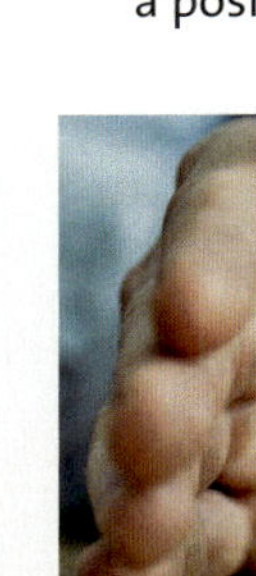

► SF 40: Listening/Viewing for gist and detail, p. 253

► Check (task 1)
Lernen App: Answer key for task 1

► Getting started (task 2)
Lernen App: Video on viewing skills

Annotations

solicitor (*BE*) a lawyer who prepares legal documents, advises people on legal matters, and can speak for them in a court

résumé (*AE*) (here) a record of your education and your former jobs which you send in when applying for a job; curriculum vitae

pro-bono department a department of a law firm that does legal work without asking for payment from the clients

senior (*adj*) (here) higher in rank

senior associate an employee who has a higher position and often leads teams in a firm

► SF 41: Analysing films, series and videos, p. 253

► WOB: A8 Viewing, pp. 26–27

DIGI mit den Suchworten *diversity, equity, inclusion* in Kombination mit Firmennamen suchen

► SF 13: Doing research, p. 214

► SF 36: Writing an application, p. 247

► WOB: B14

► SF 6: Essentials: language and study skills, p. 208

Reactivate

1 Understanding complex sentences

You may be able to write good texts comprising short sentences, but in order to improve your style you need to be able to formulate more complex sentences.

Info

In general you distinguish between **main clauses** and **sub(ordinate) clauses**.

HA **a** Fill the gaps in the following text using words from the box below. You may use all words more than once.

adjective • adverb • adverbial • because • compound • conjunction • defining • dependent • if • main • non-defining • relative • relative pronouns • subordinate • that • verb • when

Complex sentences are those that contain a ... clause as well as a ... clause. A ... clause is usually introduced by a linking word, also called a ..., e.g. ... , ... , ... and ... . Most ... clauses can come before, after or within the ... clause. There are different types of ... clauses, for example ... clauses and ... clauses.
An adverbial clause is introduced by a ... , for example *while* or *so that*. It is ... on the main clause and modifies an ... , a ... or another ... . There are different types of adverbial clauses depending on the information they convey.
A ... clause usually refers to a noun in the main clause but can also refer to the whole of the main clause. The words linking the ... clause to the ... clause are called ... . We generally differentiate between ... and ... relative clauses.
In English, and German too, you can also find so-called ... sentences where two ... clauses are coordinated by a ... .

► WOB: B6

► Check
Lernen App: Answer key for task 1a

LÖS **1a**
subordinate • main • subordinate • conjunction • because, if, that • when • subordinate • main • subordinate • adverbial • relative • conjunction • dependent • adjective • verb • adverb • relative • relative • main • relative pronouns • defining • non-defining • compound • main • conjunction

► Support, p. 187

► Check
Lernen App: Answer key for task 1b

► WOB: B11

HA **b** Complete the table of adverbial clauses with the conjunctions listed in the box below. Some conjunctions can be used for more than one type of adverbial clause.

after • although • as • as if • as soon as • because • before • by the time • even if • even though • everywhere • if • in case • just as • like • once • since • so that • though • till/until • unless • when • whenever • where • wherever • whether • while • while/whereas

Adverbial clauses of	Time	Place	Reason	Purpose	Contrast	Com-parison	Condition
Conjunctions	...	...	...	...	...	...	...

Language awareness

Info

Although **complex sentences** can improve your style, you need to take care. If a sentence is very long, it may be difficult to understand its meaning.

Subordinate clauses can improve your style. To use relative clauses appropriately, you have to differentiate between defining and non-relative clauses so as to avoid punctuation mistakes.

HA **2 Using relative clauses**

Decide whether the sentences below contain a defining or a non-defining relative clause. Add punctuation where necessary.

Defining relative clause: *This is the woman who looks after my cat when I'm away.*
Non-defining relative clause: *This is my best friend, who always looks after my cat when I'm away.*

1 The doctor examined my left leg which was hurting terribly.
2 My younger sister who has just completed an online course on ecology is coming to visit me on Monday.
3 The book that he is reading is of utmost importance for his thesis.
4 The pupil who sits in the last row always asks a lot of questions.
5 The students who had volunteered for the trial were brought in for further tests.
6 Berlin which is where my mum lives is the capital of Germany.

▸ WOB: B12

LÖS 2
defining: 3, 4, 5
non-defining: 1, 2, 6

Lernen App: Video on relative clauses
▸ More language

Info

A **defining relative clause** identifies who or what we are speaking about, whereas a **non-defining relative clause** just gives us more information about who or what we are speaking about. There is no comma before a defining clause, but there is one before and after a non-defining clause.

Work with words

HA **3 Working with adverbs**

The adverbs in the box can be used to introduce a new sentence related to the one that went before. Decide which sentence each adverb fits best.

consequently • furthermore • however • moreover • nevertheless

1 I would love to have a dog, but my girlfriend doesn't like dogs. ..., my landlord doesn't allow pets, so I doubt I'll get one.
2 The results of the trial were very promising. ..., we can't get our hopes up yet, as it is still early days.
3 There is little chance that we will succeed in changing the law. ..., it is important that we try.
4 Our product is not selling well. ..., we have decided on a completely different marketing strategy.
5 Learning Arabic will allow you to communicate with millions of people around the world. ..., it will look great on your CV!

▸ Check
Lernen App: Answer key for task 3

LÖS 3
1 Moreover
2 However
3 Nevertheless
4 Consequently
5 Furthermore

▸ WOB: B11

Practise

HA **4 *** Brush up your text**

Improve the following text by using adverbial and relative clauses.

Lara, Sian and Dylan are all politically active. They are meeting early on Saturday morning. They want to go to a conference about gender equality. The friends are excited. A lot of famous people are giving talks at the conference. They are some of the first attendees to arrive. The doors open. Sian enters first and grabs three seats in the first row. They can see everything from there. In preparation for the conference, they read most of the essays written by the speakers. Most of the essays were very progressive. They did not agree with the ideas in all of them.

▸ WOB: B6 Adverbs and adverbial phrases, pp. 52–53
▸ WOB: B12 Relative clauses, pp. 60–61

▸ WOB: B11, B15

► More info
Lernen App: Meiling Jin

World geography and the rainbow alliance

Meiling Jin

HA • Do you feel a strong attachment to your regional identity (e.g. a town, an area, a country)? What does this place mean to you?

HA • Many people have their roots in various places. Do you define part of your identity through the place where you live or come from (or perhaps where your parents come from)?

Peking is in China
As Kingston is in Jamaica
As Delhi is in India
As nowhere do we belong
You and I

And should we ever run away
Where shall we run to?
And should we ever fight a war,
Who shall we fight for
You and I?

At the end of the rainbow
Is a country of goodness
If we form an alliance,
Will we ever be free
To belong?

Or shall we always be carrying
Our ancestors' coffins in a bag?
Searching the globe
For a place to belong
You and I.

100 Wörter

From: Da Choong et al., eds., Black Women Talk Poetry, *1987*

Comprehension

► SF 20: Reading and understanding poetry, p. 224

► WOB: A12 Poetry, pp. 38–39

1 ***Quick write**: Describe your first impression of the poem, comparing the speaker's personal circumstances with your own.

* **2** Match the following nouns to the four stanzas of the poem. There are two more words than you need.
disorientation – fear – hope – insecurity – loneliness – rootlessness

LÖS 2
stanza 1: rootlessness
stanza 2: disorientation
stanza 3: hope
stanza 4: insecurity

Analysis

CT HA **3** Explain the title of the poem, taking the speaker's state of mind into account.

► Getting started
Lernen App:
Video on stylistic devices
Overview of stylistic devices

*** **4** Point out and explain how the following *stylistic devices are used in the poem. Analyse their effect.
*stanza – *speaker – *addressee – *rhyme – *repetition – *anaphora – *metaphor
Bearbeitung als Expertenpuzzle mit KV 5: Analysing the poem in jigsaw groups

Language awareness

*** **5** Analyse why the author uses two different forms of conditional clauses in the second and third stanza. **should** (stanza 2): formal expression, sounds more poetic than an if-clause, indicates an unlikely situation
will (stanza 3): if-clause type I refers to possible future action, suggests hope

Lernen App: Video on conditional sentences
▸ More language
▸ Support, p. 188
▸ WOB: A12

Beyond the text

6 A literary online magazine is asking for poems on the topic 'The World and Me' for its next issue.

You choose | Writing | Work on task **a** or **b**.

HA **a** Write a letter to the editor in which you explain why you think the poem 'World geography and the rainbow alliance' would fit the topic of the next issue.
▸ WOB: A2

b Write your own poem with the title 'The world and me', which you submit to the online magazine.

Lernen App: Video on writing a letter to the editor
▸ Getting started
▸ SF 37: Writing a letter to the editor, p. 248
▸ SF 38: Creative writing, p. 249

LÖS **6a**
criteria:
- personal salutation
- opening paragraph: reference to the article, purpose of the email
- short summary and interpretation of the poem
- explanation of how students relate the poem to the topic of the magazine
- closing: Yours sincerely / Best regards / Best wishes
- full name

▸ WOB: A4

Chapter task

In this chapter you have looked at many examples that show why it is important to shape the world around you.

1 HA **a** **Think** Look back at the various topics, struggles and causes that were discussed in this unit. Which of them was for you the most important one? Alternative: EA oder GA

HA **b** **Pair** With your partner, choose one issue presented in the chapter or, indeed, a completely new one that you would fight for.

HA **c** **Share** Present to the class the issue that you have chosen to campaign for. Ask your peers for further ideas to support your campaign.

HA **2** ** You have decided to initiate a campaign to fight for the issue which is very important for you. Create a short video message to post on your vlog in which you introduce your idea and try to convince other young people to join your campaign. gemeinsam Formate von Videobeiträgen in sozialen Medien besprechen und Kriterien festlegen

DIGI alternative Formate: *story, reel, in-feed-video …*

Info
A **vlog** (short for 'video blog') is a type of blog which is filmed, edited and put online by an individual. Vlogs are often shared on social media platforms and allow creators to connect with their audience on a more personal level.

▸ SF 43: Giving a presentation, p. 259

Drawing on your own experience

* **1** Discuss these questions with a partner:
1. Do you like going to the theatre?
2. Have you enjoyed the plays you've seen?
3. What do you remember about the atmosphere?
4. What makes a drama different from other forms of literature?
5. What do you think is the difference between watching a drama on stage and reading it?

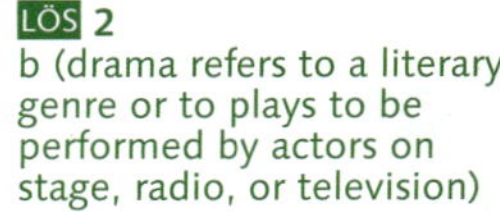
LÖS 2
b (drama refers to a literary genre or to plays to be performed by actors on stage, radio, or television)

Looking at elements of drama

2 Decide which of these statements best describes drama, and explain why.
- **a** Drama is the portrayal of fictional or non-fictional events through written dialogue.
- **b** Drama is the term for stories that are acted out before an audience.
- **c** Drama is used to describe a conflict between *characters on a stage.

► SF 16: Essentials: reading strategies and text types, p. 219

► Check 
Lernen App: Answer key for task 3

HA CT **3** * In a play the *characters use their words and movements to tell the story. There are different forms of communication by characters on the stage. Match the terms with the definitions.

*aside	a speech delivered by one of the characters alone on the stage, in which he or she reveals his or her thoughts, feelings or motives to the audience
*dialogue	a remark that is intended to be heard by the audience but unheard by the other characters
*monologue	a conversation that involves at least two characters
*soliloquy	a lengthy speech by just one character in the company of others

► WOB: A11

HA CT **4** In the script of a play the dramatist writes *stage directions to help the director and actors. Which of the following are the most typical functions of stage directions?
- **a** to describe a character
- **b** to explain what is happening to the audience
- **c** to tell the actors what to do on stage
- **d** to show what the scenery and costumes should look like
- **e** to explain what effect the lighting should have
- **f** to indicate the time and place of the action
- **g** to convey the thoughts of the characters
- **h** to say what objects should be on stage or used by the characters

Reading a script

Noughts and Crosses is a *play, which was adapted from Malorie Blackman's novel of the same name. It is set in a fictitious world ruled by the Crosses ('Daggers'), who live a privileged life and oppress the Noughts ('Blankers'), who are considered inferior. The two main characters Callum, a Nought, and Sephy, a Cross, have known each other since they were children. Callum is one of four Noughts who have recently been admitted to a school for Crosses called Heathcroft and so now attends the same school as Sephy.

In the excerpt below from *Act II, *Scene Twelve, Callum secretly visits Sephy in her bedroom after an incident at their school.

HA **5*** First, skim the excerpt and note down how the stage might look according to the stage directions.

[*Sephy touches Callum's cheek.*]
SEPHY I'm so sorry, Callum.
[*Callum pulls his head away.*]
CALLUM I don't want your ruddy pity.
SEPHY Stop it. Please.
CALLUM Why should I? Don't you want anyone to know YOU'VE GOT A BLANKER IN YOUR ROOM?
SEPHY Callum, don't.
CALLUM I want to smash you and every other Dagger who crosses my path. I hate you so much it scares me.
SEPHY I know you do. You've hated me ever since you joined Heathcroft and I called you a Blanker.
CALLUM And you've hated me for turning my back on you in the dining hall and letting you be beaten up by those girls.
[*Pause.*]
Then why is it that I think of you as my best friend?
SEPHY Because you know that's how I think of you. Because I love you. And you love me, I think.
[*Pause.*]
Did you hear what I said? I love you.
CALLUM Love doesn't exist – friendship doesn't exist between a Nought and a Cross.
SEPHY Then what are you doing in my room?
CALLUM I'm damned if I know.
[*Sephy sits on the bed. Callum sits alongside her, but some distance away. They are both very uncomfortable. They look at the floor. Then Sephy turns to Callum and offers her hand. He turns to her. She starts to lower her hand. He takes it and moves towards her. We hear the gentle sound of waves on the beach. They sit like this for a few moments. Then he kicks off his shoes and lies down on the bed, taking her with him. They hug.*]
Turn around.
[*Sephy does so. They spoon together.*]
Are you okay?
SEPHY Uh-hm.

Lernen App: Malory Blackman
► More info

► WOB: A11

Annotation
4 **ruddy** a mild swear word that shows that someone is annoyed

Selbst wenn die Regieanweisungen sehr sparsam sind, sollen die SuS ermutigt werden, zu überlegen, wie man sie umsetzen oder ausbauen könnte.

Annotation
47 **nod off** fall asleep for a short time

CALLUM I'm not squashing you?
SEPHY Uh-uh.
CALLUM You're sure?
SEPHY Callum, shut up.
[CALLUM *smiles.* SEPHY *turns to face him. They kiss.* SEPHY *pulls away.*]
Let's just get some sleep – okay?
CALLUM Okay.
[*They curl up.*]
Sephy?
SEPHY Mmm.
CALLUM Maybe we should go away together.
[SEPHY*'s nodding off.*]
SEPHY We'll talk about it in the morning.
[*Pause.*]

339 Wörter

From: Noughts and Crosses, *adapted from Malorie Blackman's novel by Dominic Cooke, 2008*

▸ WOB: A11

LÖS 6
c

HA **6** *Plot: Decide which of these sentences best sums up the excerpt.

a Sephy and Callum are quarrelling about an incident they were involved in.
b Callum has come to Sephy's room in order to express his anger.
c Sephy and Callum are confused about their feelings for each other.
d Callum declares his love for Sephy.

LÖS 7
Sephy: ashamed (v. 2) • gentle (v. 27) • considerate (vv. 11–12)
Callum: angry/hateful (vv. 9–10) • conflicted (v. 16) • considerate (v. 36)

HA **7** *Characters: Describe Sephy and Callum, using three adjectives for each character from the word bank below. Give evidence from the text to justify your choice.

aggressive • angry • apprehensive • ashamed • conflicted • considerate • desperate • determined • emotional • fearful • gentle • hateful • helpless • passionate • violent

SuS sprechen/spielen die Szene in Kleingruppen, zwei Personen lesen, die anderen beraten die Lesenden und dokumentieren die Umsetzung der *stage directions*.

HA **8** *** *Stage directions: Find out what kind of information the stage directions give. Draw a table like this:

Lines	Kind of information given in the stage directions
1	Action/emotion: tender, conciliatory gesture.
3	Action/emotion: anger must be shown through gestures and facial expression.

Acting out a script

SuS bearbeiten 9a und 9b in Kleingruppen im Anschluss an Aufgabe 8.

9 *** **a** In vv. 5–14 there aren't any stage directions. With a partner, think about how the *actors playing Sephy and Callum should show their emotions through gestures, facial expressions, tone of voice, position on stage, etc. Add as many stage directions as possible.

*** **b** Now act out vv. 5–14, using your own stage directions.

HA **10** In class, describe the *atmosphere in the excerpt, taking the words and actions into account.

11 In groups of two or three, analyse the changes in Sephy's and Callum's relationship as depicted in the excerpt. Then show these changes in a series of freeze frames.

Ergebnisse von Aufgabe 10 für die *freeze frames* verwenden, Entwicklung in 3 bis 4 Standbildern darstellen

Info

Freeze frame: Imagine you are watching the scene as a film and you press the pause button from time to time. The paused image is called a freeze frame. When analysing a literary text in class, creating freeze frames is an effective way of exploring characters, relationships and ideas.
You do need to follow some basic rules:

– Decide who will represent which character. You may also want to choose a director who oversees the process.
– Empathize with your character as much as possible, try to feel their feelings, to think their thoughts.
– Try out different postures, gestures, facial expressions.
– When presenting your freeze frame, stand still and do not talk.

exemplarische Präsentation angesichts der Vielzahl der Standbilder bei verschiedenen Gruppen

Examining conflict

12 The following nouns all belong to the word field of conflict.

argument • clash • confrontation • difference of opinion • disagreement • dispute • fight • quarrel

vorbereitend bearbeiten und zum Einstieg paarweise vergleichen

HA **a** Sort them according to their intensity. Look up the words you don't know in a dictionary.

HA CT **b** With a partner, choose three of the terms and discuss how each type of conflict might be performed on stage. Be prepared to present a very short dialogue illustrating them. einige Paare präsentieren, ohne den gewählten Begriff zu nennen; zuschauende SuS erraten ihn

► WOB: A11

HA **13** The famous Irish playwright George Bernard Shaw wrote 'No conflict, no drama' (in the preface to *Plays: Pleasant and Unpleasant*, 1898). Discuss whether you think he is correct. SuS bereiten stichwortartig Argumente vor → Diskussion im Plenum

Lernen App: George Bernard Shaw
► More info
► SF 46: Having a discussion, p. 264
► WOB: A11

In the following excerpt from Act I, Scene 7, Sephy is hiding in a cubicle in the girls' toilets to escape the problems that her friendship with Callum causes at school.

[*The Girls' Toilets.*
SEPHY *is in a cubicle.*]

SEPHY [*to audience*]. There is a proverb which says, 'Be careful what you wish for, because you might just end up getting it!' I never really knew what that meant until now. All those months helping Callum with his work so he'd pass the Heathcroft entrance exam, and we could go to the same school together, be in the same class together even. And now it had all come true. And it was horrible. Everything was going wrong. Well ... I couldn't hide in here forever. And who was I hiding from anyway? Well, all those people who'd been pointing and whispering as I walked past them in the school corridor, for starters – but mainly from Callum. I was

LÖS 13
pro:
- conflicts create tension
- conflicts can help to show character development
- conflicts are a part of life
- emotional impact of conflicts adds depth to a plot

con:
- a conflict may be too predictable
- sometimes people just want to be entertained
- too much conflict may seem unrealistic or artificial

Annotations
46 **knife sb.** injure or kill sb. with a knife
57 **horse manure** (here) nonsense

afraid to face him. If I didn't see him, I could pretend nothing between us had changed.
[*The school bell rings.*]
Okay! Here goes.
[SEPHY *opens the cubicle door. Three Cross girls,* LOLA, JOANNE *and* DIONNE, *confront* SEPHY.]

LOLA We want to have a word with you.

SEPHY And it has to be in here, does it, Lola?
[JOANNE *shoves* SEPHY.]

JOANNE About what you did yesterday.

SEPHY What's it to you?
[LOLA *slaps* SEPHY.]

LOLA I don't care if your Dad's God Almighty Himself. Stick to your own kind. If you sit with the Blankers again, everyone in this school will treat you like one of them.

JOANNE You need to wake up and check which side you're on.

DIONNE What d'you want to be around them for anyway? They smell funny and they eat weird food, and everyone knows that none of them are exactly close friends with soap and water.
[*The three girls laugh.*]

SEPHY What a load of rubbish. Callum has a wash every day and he doesn't smell. None of them do.
[LOLA, JOANNE *and* DIONNE *look at each other.* LOLA *pushes* SEPHY *down on the toilet.* SEPHY *tries to stand.* LOLA *pushes her down again.*]

LOLA We're only going to say this once. Choose your friends very carefully. If you don't stay away from those Blankers, you'll find you don't have a single friend left in this school.

SEPHY I bet none of you has even spoken to a Nought before.

JOANNE Of course, we have. When they serve us in shops and restaurants ...

DIONNE In burger bars!
[*They laugh.*]

JOANNE Besides, we don't need to speak to them. We see them on the news practically every other day. Everyone knows they're all muggers and they hang around in gangs and knife people and listen to crap music.

LOLA Look at the facts. It's on the news. The news doesn't lie.

SEPHY The news lies all the time. They tell us what they think we want to hear. The majority of Noughts are decent, hardworking people.

JOANNE Who told you that? Your dad?

LOLA I bet it was one of her Blanker friends. Blank by name and blank by nature.

SEPHY What are you talking about?

LOLA Blank, white faces with not a hint of colour in them. Blank minds which can't hold a single original thought. Blank, blank, blank.

SEPHY You ought to sell that horse manure worldwide. You'd make a fortune. Noughts are people, just like us. You're the ones who are stupid and ignorant and ...

[Lola *slaps* Sephy. Sephy *punches* Lola *in the stomach. She continues hitting* Lola. Lola *and* Joanne *grab one of* Sephy*'s arms.*]

Joanne Blanker-lover. You've had this coming for a long time.
[Dionne *beats up* Sephy.]

588 Wörter

From: Noughts and Crosses, *adapted from Malorie Blackman's novel by* Dominic Cooke, 2008

Annotation
62 You've had this coming. *Das war schon lange fällig.*

14 Work on the following tasks concerning the conflict in the play.

HA **a** 1 Look back at task **3** on p. 70 and explain the form of speech used by Sephy (vv. 1–18).
2 Explain why it is used here.

HA **b** The girls describe how they view the Noughts in this excerpt. What do we learn about one of the main differences between the Noughts and Crosses?

HA **c** Imagine you witnessed the scene from v. 20 on and later have to write a short report for the school's principal. Summarize the main events in not more than five sentences.

*** **d** The excerpt presents both a physical and a verbal conflict between the characters that results from the tensions and conflicts in their society.
1 Make two lists, one for the confrontation between the girls, and another one for the conflict between the two different social groups.

Conflict between the girls	Social conflict between Noughts and Crosses
they shove Sephy (v. 21)	Sephy should stick to her own kind (vv. 25–27)
....	...

2 Explain how these two levels of conflict might be used to push forward the conflict in the play.

HA **15** *** In a play there are usually five stages: *exposition, *rising action, *climax, *falling action and *resolution. Check each of the terms in the Glossary (p. 272ff.), then decide which stage the two scenes you have read belong to.

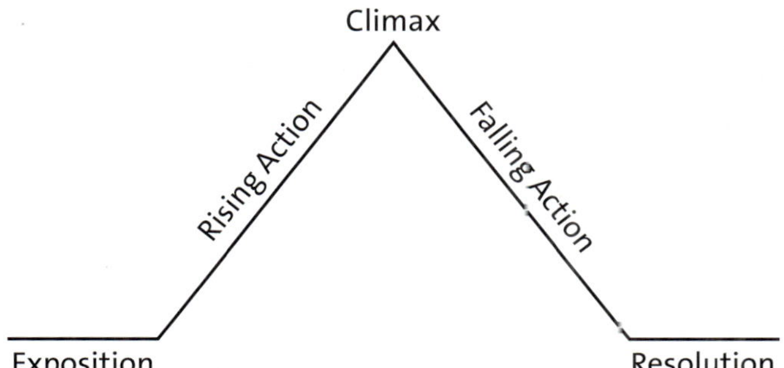

HA **16** *** Having read these two excerpts, assess why a theatre director decided to adapt the original novel into a play.

HA **17** Think of situations you know from your own personal life or from the news which would make a good play. Give a brief outline using the diagram in task **15** as a guide.

LÖS 14a
soliloquy; audience gains insight into Sephy's mind

LÖS 14b
- Crosses are not supposed to associate with Noughts (vv. 25–27, 37–38), they usually attend different schools
- Noughts are are dirty, smell, eat 'weird food', 'listen to crap music' (vv. 29–31, 47)
- Noughts usually do menial work, serve the Crosses (cf. v. 41)
- Noughts are all criminals (cf. vv. 45–46)

LÖS 14d (2)
- the relationship between Callum and Sephy could lead to difficulties for Sephy, as Crosses might ostracize her or even get violent with her
- Sephy might be forced to decide between the two groups
- the social difference might affect their relationship to such an extent that they split up

LÖS 15
excerpt 1 (Act II, Scene 12): takes place after excerpt 2; the two protagonists are assessing their feelings for each other → rising action
excerpt 2 (Act I, Scene 7): takes place before excerpt 1; Sephy is left to consider what she should do → rising action (not a climax as no dramatic change takes place)

► WOB: A11 Drama, pp. 36–37

Chapter 3
Literature and Media – Words in Motion

1) **Francisco Javier Arceo on Twitter/X @franciscojarceo** 'Popularity and usefulness are surprisingly uncorrelated on social media.' / Twitter/X
January 12, 2024 9 Wörter

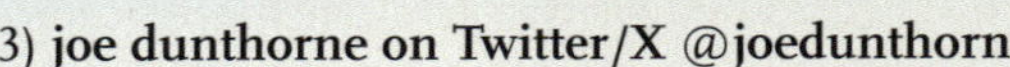
3) **joe dunthorne on Twitter/X @joedunthorne**

'I wrote about how one of my favourite childre[n] books, first published 1972, now reads like a nonf[ic]tion account of Jeff Bezos going into space – exce[pt] with environmentalist dinosaurs.' / Twitter/X
December 10, 2021 29 Wör[ter]

► More info

Annotation
Jeff Bezos In July 2021, the Amazon founder and billionaire went to space for 11 minutes on a rocket from his space company Blue Origin.

Lernen App: Stephen King and Joe Dunthorne

darauf achten, dass die Auseinandersetzung mit den Posts als stummes Schreibgespräch erfolgt

1 a Work in groups of three. Choose a different post (formerly known as tweet) each. On a piece of paper, write down your ideas and reactions in response to the post. After a minute, pass the paper, so that the next person can add their comments in response to yours. Do this until everybody has commented on every post. DIGI in einem *shared document* arbeiten

Language help

In my view ... • ... points out correctly that ... • I disagree/agree with the statement by ... • I am appalled/amused by ... • ... it is obvious that ... • ... reflects the idea that ... • is a perfect example of ...

DIGI Statements in einem *shared document* teilen

b *** Discuss your responses and agree on a common statement about all three posts from your group. Write it down, then compare your statements with the other groups in your class. DIF nur ein Statement zu einem der Posts verfassen

Lernen App: Writing a tweet

► Getting started

DIGI Posts digital aufbereiten und dem *Chapter Task Booklet* voranstellen

DIF KV 6: Predictions about the future of media and literature

2 a Write your own post about future changes in literature and/or the media that you predict. maximale Länge des Posts: 280 Zeichen

b Taking the posts and the keywords in the Chapter map into consideration, discuss with your partner how literature and media are reflecting our ever-changing world. Diskussion auch im Plenum möglich

LÖS **2a**
AI will be able to write books, plays, poems and screenplays just as well as a human author, so authors will lose their jobs.

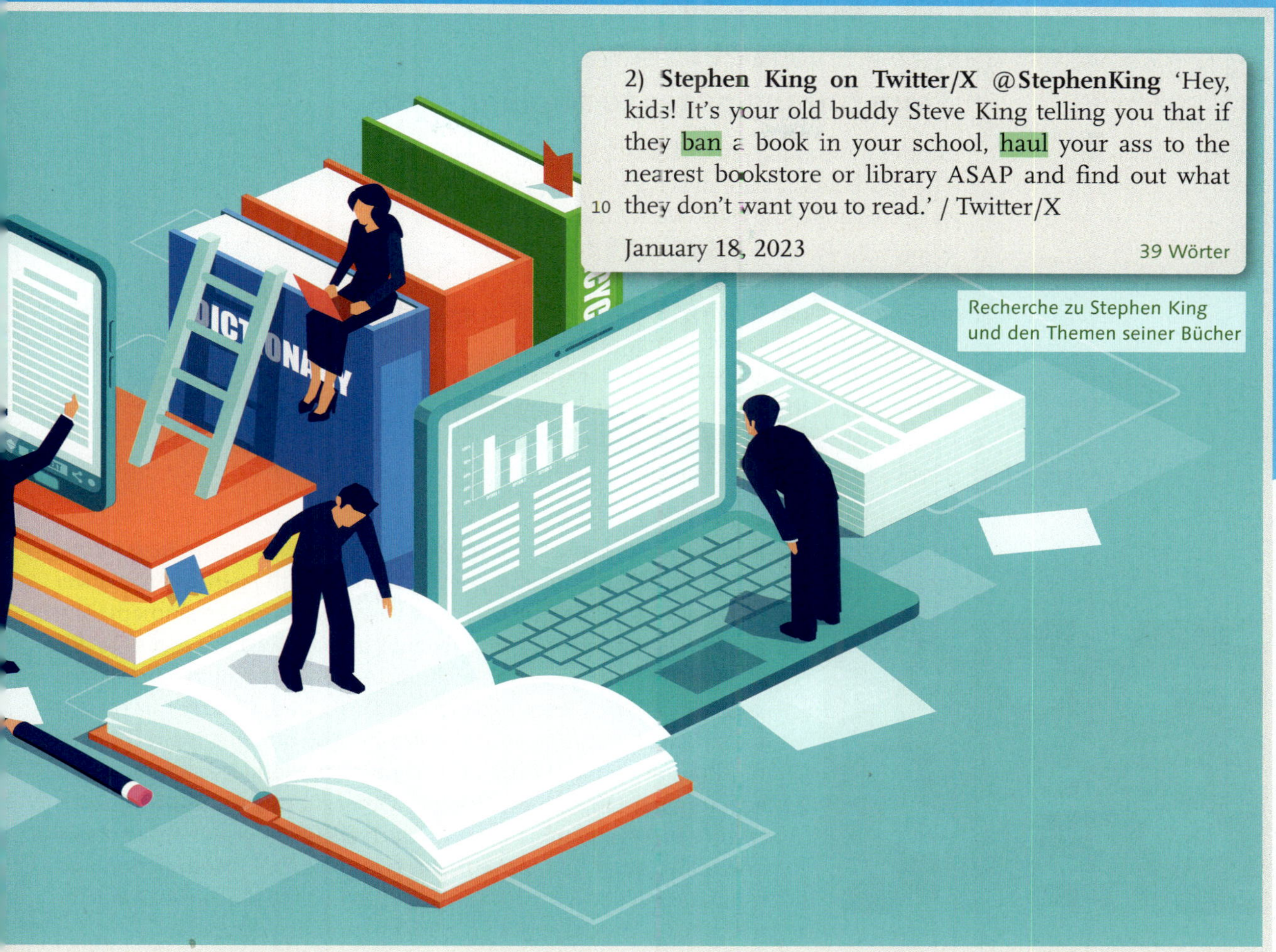

2) **Stephen King on Twitter/X @StephenKing** 'Hey, kids! It's your old buddy Steve King telling you that if they ban a book in your school, haul your ass to the nearest bookstore or library ASAP and find out what they don't want you to read.' / Twitter/X

January 18, 2023

39 Wörter

Recherche zu Stephen King und den Themen seiner Bücher

Chapter map

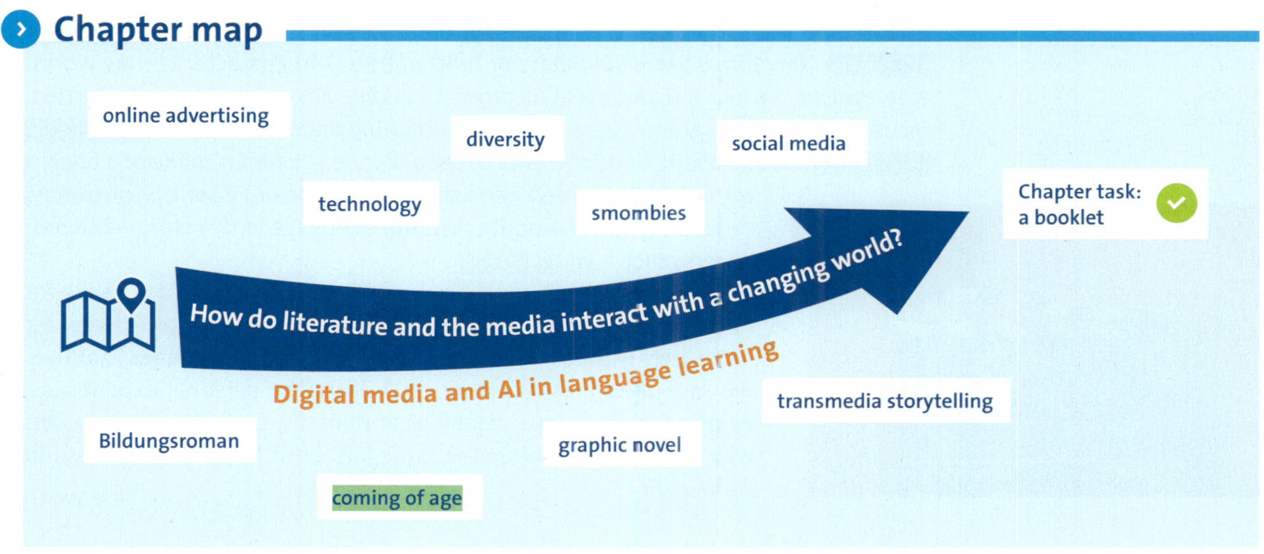

Lernen App:
Useful vocabulary for the chapter
▶ More language

Lernen App: From turning pages to scrolling feeds (00:03:55)

From turning pages to scrolling feeds

Stories have always been told

Human beings have always been storytellers. Even before there was written language, stories were passed down through oral tradition. The invention of the printing press allowed mass production of books, which increased literacy and made it easier to spread ideas to wider audiences. The culture and context of a community always had a big impact on the stories that were told – and vice versa.

A tradition of innovation

Storytellers have always experimented and pushed boundaries to create new forms, genres and perspectives. In addition to epic poetry and drama, the genre of the novel emerged in the 18th century as a new form of entertainment. The novel focused more on the individual, and allowed the reader to engage with ordinary, relatable characters on a personal level. Social issues and norms were explored and criticized. Changes in society due to industrialization and urbanization also brought about changes in literature and art. Early 20th century modernists experimented with fragmented, non-linear plots. Other literary forms of the 20th century include graphic novels, which combine visual elements of storytelling with text. Authors have also explored flash fiction and minimalist fiction, which has resulted in texts that achieve character and plot development within a limited number of words.

The influence of digitalization and technology

Brainstorming zu Beispielen für *transmedia storytelling*

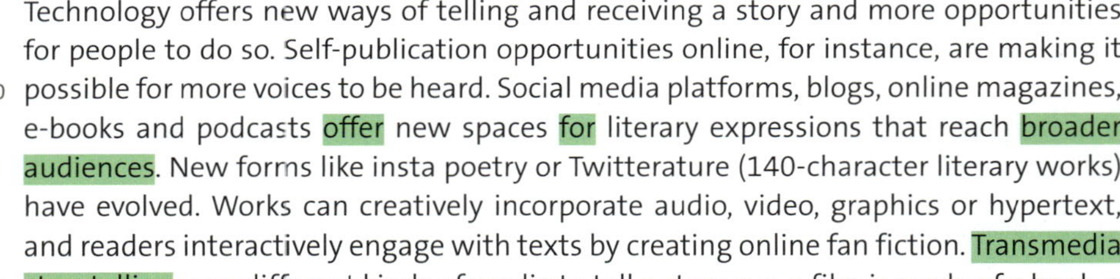

Digitalization has transformed many aspects of life, and literature is no exception. Technology offers new ways of telling and receiving a story and more opportunities for people to do so. Self-publication opportunities online, for instance, are making it possible for more voices to be heard. Social media platforms, blogs, online magazines, e-books and podcasts offer new spaces for literary expressions that reach broader audiences. New forms like insta poetry or Twitterature (140-character literary works) have evolved. Works can creatively incorporate audio, video, graphics or hypertext, and readers interactively engage with texts by creating online fan fiction. Transmedia storytelling uses different kinds of media to tell a story, e.g. a film is made of a book, a comic is transformed into a computer game or TV series. Consumers can choose their favourite medium to engage with a story – and producers reach a wide market.

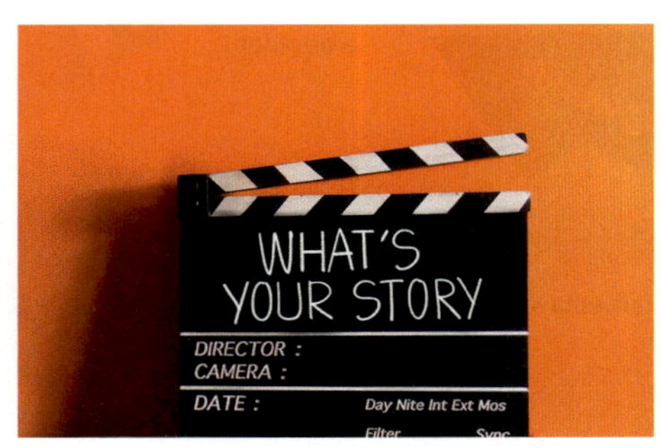

The latest advances in artificial intelligence (AI) make it possible for AI tools like ChatGPT to create content, e.g. stories or song lyrics, far more quickly than a human. Some authors fear this means that they will lose their jobs. However, as AI lacks the personal experiences, emotions and unique creativity of humans, texts produced in this way cannot (yet) achieve the same authentic levels of empathy and connection.

432 Wörter

1 Main ideas

KV 7: The way in which our stories have been told → neues Vokabular festigen (möglich als HA)

a Read the text and list at least five innovations in literature and the media.

b Compare your ideas with a partner and take turns explaining the innovations and their causes and effects to each other in your own words.

Lernen App: Answer key for task 1a

► Check

2 Reflect

DIGI Interessante Wörter/Konstruktionen an einer digitalen Pinnwand sammeln und laufend ergänzen

a Read the text again and write down:

1 One sentence that expresses a central idea of the text.
2 One phrase that was new to you.
3 One significant word you would like to keep in mind.

b Compare your notes with a partner and share your reflections about why you felt these words and phrases were the most significant or central ones.

3 Punctuation

a A sentence clause is a type of relative clause that refers to the entire main clause. It is separated by comma(s) and can be left out. Find two examples in the text. *Relative clauses* und *sentence clauses* erklären und Beispiele an die Tafel schreiben

b *** Write two more sentence clauses using information from the text. Pay attention to the correct punctuation.

Lernen App: Answer key for task 3a

► Check

► WOB: B12 Relative clauses, pp. 60–61

4 Chunk it!

a * Match words from the text to make meaningful collocations.

1 reach	A ideas
2 spread	B with a story/text/character
3 push	C content
4 engage	D elements
5 combine	E an audience
6 create	F boundaries

LÖS 4a
1E 2A 3F 4B 5D 6C

Lernen App: Video about chunks

► Getting started

► Check

► WOB: B8 Collocations with prepositions, p. 56

Lernen App: Answer key for task 4a

HA b Write new sentences with each collocation.

► WOB: B8

5 You choose Writing Literature and the media

Work on task **a** or **b**. Use as many collocations from **4** as possible.

HA a *** Write a poem or song about the transformation of literature and the media over time.

► Info box, Different forms of poems, p. 41

DIGI Schlüsselwörter und Auftrag in eine KI eingeben, danach SuS-Texte und KI-Texte vergleichen

DIF Bearbeitung ohne KI in PA

b *** Write a dialogue between an author HA and a computer scientist promoting a new AI tool in which they talk about the possibilities of AI for the world of literature and its limitations. Write about 150 words. If you like, you can act out your dialogue.

► SF 38: Creative writing, p. 249

Language help

absolutely important • I am totally convinced that … • I can assure you that … • There is no doubt that … • There is no denying the fact that … • Contrary to what people think, …

* Tech no language
Mack Exilus

vor der Recherche eigene Definitionen erstellen und vergleichen

- What are *smombies*, *phubbers* and *nomophobes*? Look at the illustrations and take a guess. Then research the three new words, so-called neologisms, and match each one to the correct picture. DIGI Begriffe mit den Smartphones als *freeze frames* festhalten → *smartphone dictionary* erstellen

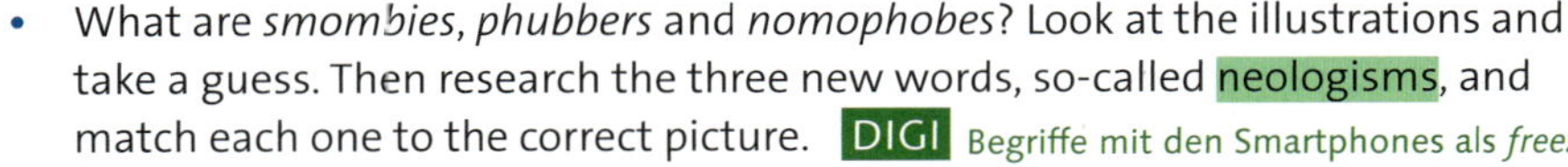

KV 8: New phone slang vocabulary

- What might a short play named *Tech no language* be about? Use the neologisms from the previous task to speculate.

Now read the one-minute play written by US-American therapist, actor and writer Mack Exilus.

Annotations
4 **get your bearings** acquire knowledge of your position relative to everything around or near you
5 **sluggish** moving more slowly than normal; inactive
7 **be wrapped up in sth.** give your entire attention to sth.
9 **respective** belonging to the separate people just mentioned
12 **trickle** (here) come or go slowly
12 **cluttered** full of sth. in an untidy way

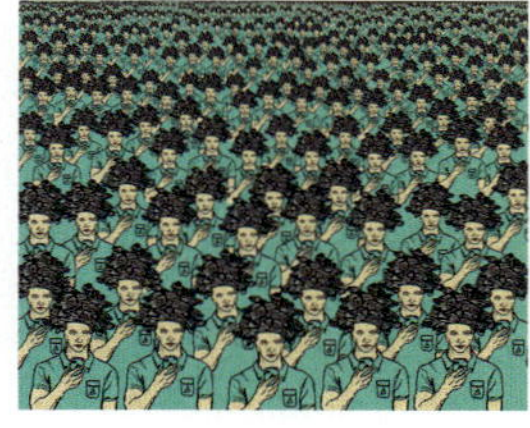

Note: there should be no dialogue throughout this piece. The main ACTOR should only use non-verbal actions to communicate with the TECH NO LANGUAGE ZOMBIES.

(An ACTOR walks on stage with a map in hand looking about trying to get his/her bearings. The ACTOR sees a group of kids walking sluggishly with portable video games in their hands. The ACTOR then tries to communicate with the kids, but they are so wrapped up in their video games they ignore him/her and continue to move around the space.)

(The ACTOR then sees a couple. They are both on their respective cell phones walking around, zombie like. The ACTOR tries to communicate with them and they too give him/her the cold shoulder. As this is happening, TECH NO LANGUAGE ZOMBIES begin to trickle onto the stage. The stage becomes cluttered with people on cell phones, texting, swiping their fingers on a tablet or iPad, listening to music on their huge headphones.)

(The ACTOR tries to get someone to help with directions. He is moving around the space much faster and with more intensity than the TECH NO LANGUAGE ZOMBIES. The ACTOR then gives up, becoming so frustrated that he/she stomps their foot. The TECH NO LANGUAGE ZOMBIES all turn and look at the ACTOR.)

(One of the TECH NO LANGUAGE ZOMBIES takes the map from the ACTOR and hands him/her a GPS. The ACTOR then goes into a zombie-like state.)

END

242 Wörter

From: One Minute Plays. A Practical Guide to Tiny Theatre, *2017*

Comprehension

* **1** Describe your spontaneous reaction to the play. You can use the phrases in the box for help.
► WOB: A11

Language help

The play made me feel ...
... appreciative • entertained • joyful • merry • thoughtful • reflective.
... ambivalent • confused • irritated • lost.
... angry • miserable • dreadful • critical.
What I found interesting • surprising • confusing was that ...
The play made me think of ...

DIGI erste Reaktionen auf das Stück in einem *shared document* festhalten

2 Read the play again. Then do task **a** or **b**.

a Answer the following questions.
1 What is it about?
2 Who are the characters and what are their relationships with one another?
3 What is the essential conflict or problem?
4 What is the meaning of the 'tech no language zombies' metaphor?

b Challenge Write a post of no more than 280 characters in which you summarize the play for your followers. Tell them what the play is about, who the characters are, what the essential problem is and what the 'tech no language zombie' metaphor means.

► WOB: A11

Analysis

► WOB: A11
► Support, p. 188

3 One striking feature of the play is the absence of verbal language. Analyse how silence and body language – including gestures (arms and legs), facial expressions (eyes and mouth), posture (i.e. the way you hold your body) – are used to contribute to the rising tension and the climax.

► More info
Lernen App: Non-verbal communication

Language Awareness

4 **a** HA Rewrite the second paragraph of the play and transfer the non-verbal communication into spoken words between the actors. DIF Bearbeitung in PA

b HA Describe how this version changes the effect and what function the silence had.

DIGI SuS tippen ihre Versionen und erstellen ein Booklet mit verschiedenen Versionen

Beyond the text

5 **a** Form groups of six. Each group prepares a staging of the play, based on their own interpretation. maximale Aufführungszeit: 1 Minute

► Support, p. 188

b Compare the different versions of the play. What made them similar and/or different? DIF bei der Gruppeneinteilung SuS verschiedener Leistungsniveaus mischen

DIGI Aufführungen filmen und alle Stücke zu einem Gesamtwerk zusammenschneiden → vor Bearbeitung von 5b ansehen

6 Think back to the guiding question. How would you answer it at this point?

DIGI Zwischenantworten als Audio aufnehmen und fortlaufend ergänzen → Audiocollage aus Reflexionen

Lernen App: A photo stimulus: Online activities

▸ Getting started 

How advertising haunts us

Jacqueline Hadasch

- ∗ **Think** Make a list of your online activities.
- ∗ **Pair** Compare your lists with a partner and note down the activities you have in common.
- ∗ **Share** In regard to the activities on your list, discuss the 'digital footprint' — i.e. traces of your digital activities and actions — you leave online. Discuss whether this could be dangerous.

▸ Support, p. 188

In her article from Süddeutsche Zeitung *Jacqueline Hadasch discusses the many ways of online advertising.*

Da ist zum Beispiel Frederic Luhede. Mit seinem Start-up Flow managt er Auftritte von Firmen in sozialen Netzwerken. Auf den ersten Blick ist Luhede dabei vor allem Gestalter: Der junge Mann aus Bad Tölz designt Fotos und Videos, um damit auf Facebook und Instagram Image-Kampagnen zu schalten. Aber Luhede ist auch Datenanalyst: Er kennt die Nutzer, die auf seine Onlineanzeigen klicken, recht gut. Zumindest weiß er, wie viele davon Frauen und Männer sind, wie weit sie von der werbenden Firma entfernt wohnen oder welche Privatinteressen sie haben. Und er weiß auch, welche Nutzer am Ende die Angebote kaufen.

Zu solchen Erkenntnissen verhilft ihm beispielsweise der sogenannte Business Manager von Facebook – eine spezielle Seite für Firmen, die sich auf der Plattform vermarkten wollen. Der Business Manager erlaubt es, Kriterien festzulegen, nach denen Facebook die Werbung nur bestimmten Personen zeigt. Wenn etwa ein Hotel, das Luhede betreut, Kunden zwischen 30 und 50 Jahren ansprechen möchte, die im Umkreis von 200 Kilometern von der Unterkunft wohnen und am liebsten Bio-Lebensmittel kaufen, kann er das mit wenigen Klicks entsprechend einrichten. Facebook zeigt die Werbung dann nur jenen Nutzern, auf die diese Merkmale zutreffen.

Das funktioniert, weil die Nutzer bereitwillig viel von sich preisgeben: Sie tragen ihr Geburtsdatum auf der Plattform ein, verraten per GPS ihren Standort und spendieren ein 'Gefällt mir' für bestimmte Seiten – von denen der Facebook-Algorithmus dann auf persönliche Vorlieben schließt.

Ein Großteil der Firmen hierzulande macht es sich zunutze, dass soziale Medien Werbung personalisieren können: Knapp 48 Prozent aller Firmen hierzulande schalten Anzeigen in sozialen Netzwerken. Die meisten Betriebe nutzen dafür Facebook oder Youtube. Das ergab eine Umfrage des *Deutschen Instituts für Marketing* von 2018. Für soziale Medien wiederum sind Werbeeinnahmen das wichtigste Geschäft. Facebook etwa hat 2018 55 Milliarden Dollar mit Werbung umgesetzt. Das sind knapp 99 Prozent des Gesamtumsatzes. Auch das zu Google gehörige Videoportal Youtube macht einen Großteil seines Umsatzes mit Werbung. 2018 waren das rund elf Milliarden Dollar. Um die Werbekunden anzulocken, wetteifern soziale Medien längst um den genauesten Werbealgorithmus, indem sie immer mehr Kundendaten sammeln und auswerten. [...]

Das führe teilweise zu gruseligen Erlebnissen, sagt Don Spaqi, Geschäftsführer der Werbeagentur Rpunktmedia. Zum Beispiel, wenn man Werbung für exakt die Schuhe erhält, die man vor drei Wochen gegoogelt hat. Wem so etwas passiere, dessen Daten wurden in der Regel nicht ohne Zustimmung ausgewertet. Meist habe man sogenannte Cookies akzeptiert, sagt Spaqi. Fordert eine Webseite dazu auf, ihre Cookies anzunehmen, erlaubt der Internetuser damit das Erstellen einer Textdatei. Die protokolliert und speichert sein Nutzungsverhalten während des Seitenbesuchs. Klickt jemand etwa zwölf Paar Schuhe durch, bevor er sich für einen Kauf entscheidet und legt dann eine Jacke in den Online-Warenkorb, bringt der Cookie das zu Protokoll. Er funktioniert wie ein kleiner Notizzettel, auf dem die Aktivitäten der Webseitenbesucher vermerkt werden. Dass Internetnutzer Cookies annehmen, sei kein seltener Fall, sagt Spaqi: 'Oft handhaben die Leute Cookies wie Allgemeine Geschäftsbedingungen – sie akzeptieren sie einfach, ohne sich groß zu informieren.' [...]

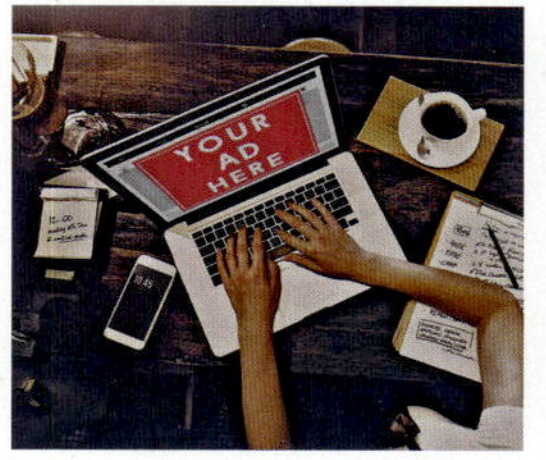

Werbetreibende wie Luhede und Spaqi helfen den Plattformen beim Datensammeln. Denn auch sie wollen ihre Anzeigen an die Menschen mit der größten Kaufwahrscheinlichkeit ausspielen. Schaltet Luhede eine Facebook-Werbung, testet er vorab eine Anzeige bei verschiedenen Zielgruppen. Facebook spielt die Anzeige für wenige Tage aus und zeigt Luhede im Business Manager, bei welcher Zielgruppe die Werbung am erfolgreichsten war. [...]

Das bedeute aber nicht, dass Werbung in sozialen Medien gleich auch einen Verkaufserfolg verspreche, sagt Björn Ivens, Professor für Vertrieb und Marketing an der Universität Bamberg. Obgleich der Anzeigenmarkt wachse und in Deutschland neben Konzernen immer mehr kleine und mittelständische Unternehmen Werbung in sozialen Medien schalteten, sei manchmal davon abzuraten. 'Produkte für Geschäftskunden etwa lassen sich effektiver auf Messen oder in Meetings bewerben', erklärt Ivens. [...] Ist die gewünschte Zielgruppe, etwa kleine Kinder, gar nicht in den sozialen Medien vertreten, sei die Litfaßsäule oder TV-Werbung immer noch eine effektive Werbemethode.

642 Wörter

From: 'Von Werbung verfolgt', Süddeutsche Zeitung, *August 11, 2020*

HA **1** Mediating | Intercultural communication An American friend of yours is writing a research paper on the impact of online advertising around the world. She has asked you for information about Germany. You summarize the article for her, and also tell her about the dangers referred to in it. Write an email to your friend.

DIGI Sprachmittlungen digital erstellen und evaluieren

Lernen App: Video on mediation

- ▶ Getting started
- ▶ SF 49: Mediating from German into Englisch, p. 270
- ▶ WOB: A7 Mediating, pp. 24–25

Beyond the text

2 Describe the cartoon. To what extent does it relate to the article?

"It's free, but they sell your information."

CartoonStock.com

DIGI Aussage des Cartoons in einem Satz formulieren und auf einer digitalen Pinnwand posten

- ▶ SF 25: Analysing cartoons, p. 231
- ▶ WOB: A1 Reading for analysis, pp. 4–7

DIGI mithilfe einer KI einen eigenen Cartoon zum Thema erstellen

Skills Lab: Digital media and AI in language learning

Schwerpunkt-Kompetenz Chapter 3: Digital media and AI in language learning

Reactivate

► Info box, Artificial intelligence, p. 165

Digital media has become a huge part of everyday life. In recent years, there has been a kind of revolutionary change since AI started being available to nearly everybody in many different contexts rather than being something that is solely developed and used by scientists.

1 Using digital media and AI in learning English

► WOB: B17

► Support, p. 189

DIGI digitales Dokument mit Links zu Beispielen und digitales Ranking erstellen

a * With a partner, collect forms of digital media and AI that you have come across in the context of school and learning. Note down situations in which these forms of media/apps/programmes, etc. were helpful or caused stress. Rate them according to their usefulness.

b * Discuss which of the functions from **a** are especially helpful while learning languages, in particular English. Present your ideas in class.

LÖS **1b**
- AI for research
- videos/podcasts for pronunciation and immersive experiences
- blog articles for sentence constructions, research and exposure to academic writing in English
- apps for vocabulary practice …

Step ahead

If used correctly, AI can be a game changer when it comes to language learning.

2 The ethics of using AI

► WOB A6

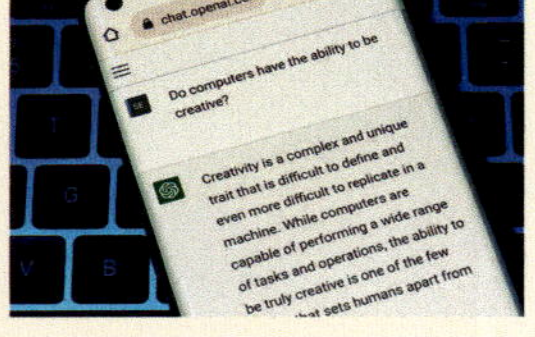

In the ABC Radio National podcast Life Matters *the participants discuss the question* Too Hard Basket: I use AI to do my job, should I tell my boss?

(03:48 min.)

a Listening Listen to the podcast and complete the sentences.

1 Kelly uses AI to …
2 She is getting more work done, but worries …
3 Comedian Lizzie believes that Kelly…
4 Simon is of the opinion that Kelly should …

► WOB: A6

b Check your solutions with a partner.

► WOB: A5

HA **c** The podcast is about the use of AI at the job. Is the situation different in the field of education? Discuss what you consider to be the biggest dilemma in using AI at school and think of ways to overcome that dilemma.

Practise

It can be tricky to get a feeling for working with AI and what is (ethically) right or wrong.

3 Evaluating AI texts

DIF je eine Einleitung in PA ansehen und sich mit einem Paar austauschen, das die andere Einleitung hatte

► WOB: B17

HA **a** *** Imagine that you have to write an introduction to this chapter. You use AI as a means to get a first idea of how to write the introduction. The two introductions below could be possible results. Read them and note down the good and bad aspects of these introductions.

1 'Words in motion – how literature and the media change over time' is a captivating topic that scrutinizes the development of language and communication by closer examining literature and media. This topic is contemplated by a profound examination of different forms of media and literature, as literature and media have evolved as well throughout the years and bear witness to the changes society experienced.

Schwerpunkt-Kompetenz Chapter 3: Digital media and AI in language learning

LÖS 3b
1 2
2 1 and 2
3 1 and 2
4 2
5 1

2 Words have multiple functions and carry several noteworthy characteristics – they can connect humankind, transcend barriers, and capture the soul of our shared knowledge and memories. Literature and media serve as means of distribution for words, and have continually developed and adapted throughout time, interdependently forming societal structures while being formed by them in return. In the course of this chapter we'll closer examine this interdependency while disputing the alterations these forms of media have encountered.

b Assess the quality of the given introductions by matching the following sentences with either AI text 1 or 2. Some items fit both introductions.

1 Mentions only part of the topic.
2 Uses rather complicated words.
3 Doesn't explain how the different subtopics relate to each other.
4 Doesn't explain the meaning of the topic.
5 Quotes the correct and full topic of the chapter.

▸ WOB: B17

4 Writing your own text

HA **a** ∗ On the basis of the texts from **3 a**, write your own introduction to this ∗∗ chapter. Avoid all the above-mentioned deficits and keep the aspects you like. Be careful not to copy anything one-to-one.

HA **b** Compare your introduction to the two introductions from **3 a**. What have you done differently or similarly? Have the two introductions helped you to write your own introduction? ▸ WOB: B17

DIGI Einleitung digital erstellen → dem *Chapter Task Booklet* voranstellen

Take another look

5 Feedback

DIGI Frage an KI weitergeben und deren Antwort ergänzen

a ∗ Evaluate your experience with AI in this Skills Lab. Choose two adjectives that describe your feelings best. Explain them.

b Discuss how working with AI could influence your language learning skills. Consider that the skills you acquire at school are not only relevant for school, but are needed in the future as well (work, travel, leisure time, ...). ▸ WOB: A5

HA **c** ∗ Fill in the table on digital aids for learning English.

Device	Usefulness yes / no	Have used it before	Will use it again
(AI) devices that create text			
tools that check spelling/grammar			
apps, etc. for vocabulary training			
digital quizzes/practice			
online collaborating devices			
pronunciation software			
translation programmes			
learning films			

Info

While **working with AI** you should always be aware of the following aspects:
– You don't know the origin of the material. It could be that you're stealing someone's intellectual property. Therefore, you should always ask yourself the question of whether it is right to use this content. Copy and paste is never the solution.
– You can't be sure the suggested content is correct. You should always double-check.
– Texts can include grammatical errors. Never take the results for granted.

Info

You can further your **experiences with AI** by trying to recreate task **3 a**. It is only possible to use AI if you formulate a task that can be answered by AI. How would you formulate a task that should generate an introduction to this chapter? It might be worthwhile to try it, but keep in mind that the time it takes you to formulate a task (often numerous trials are needed) could also be used to write an introduction on your own, especially as you always have to check the AI results for grammatical and factual correctness.

▸ WOB: B17 Digital media in language learning, p. 70

*** The hardships of an orphan   Charlotte Brontë

Partner B: Go to p. 189. **Partner A:** Read the Info box below and do the tasks.

Kurzpräsentationen zu den in der Infobox genannten Romanen möglich

▶ More info
Lernen App: Charlotte Brontë

Info

Bildungsroman

The *Bildungsroman* genre originated in Germany in the 18th century. It essentially refers to a *coming-of-age* or growing up novel, in which a young person's psychological character development and moral growth from childhood into adulthood is depicted. The young, and usually naïve, protagonist typically has some hardship and challenges to face on the physical or metaphorical journey to discover their true identity and reach maturity. There might be a conflict between social expectations and the character's own desires. Challenges in relationships, love, or educational and career pursuits might have to be faced. Usually, there is some emotional loss or disappointment at the start which is difficult to overcome. Famous examples of English *Bildungsromane* are *Great Expectations* (1861) by Charles Dickens, *The Catcher in the Rye* (1951) by J.D. Salinger, *Wuthering Heights* (1847) by Emily Brontë or *Jane Eyre* (1847) by her sister Charlotte Brontë – from which you will read an extract from the first chapter below. 157 Wörter

1 Decide on a total of ten words from the Info box to use as prompts which you can use to retell the content of the box.

2 Use your prompts to retell in your own words to your **Partner B** the information from the Info box above.

zusammenhängende Begriffe wie *character development* als ein Wort zählen

Ten-year-old Jane Eyre is an orphan whose parents have died. She has to live with her uncle's family, where she faces rejection by her aunt and cousins Eliza, John and Georgiana.

Annotations
- 3 **chiding** criticism for doing sth. wrong
- 3 **humbled** being made to feel you are not as important or good as you thought you were
- 4 **physical inferiority** state of being physically weaker than sb. else
- 13 **disposition** the natural qualities of a person's character
- 13 **sprightly** full of life and energy
- 18 **caviller** sb. who raises annoying objections or complains, often unnecessarily

[...] I never liked long walks, especially on chilly afternoons: dreadful to me was the coming home in the raw twilight, with nipped fingers and toes, and a heart saddened by the chidings of Bessie, the nurse, and humbled by the consciousness of my physical inferiority to Eliza, John, and Georgiana Reed.

The said Eliza, John, and Georgiana were now clustered round their mamma in the drawing-room: she lay reclined on a sofa by the fireside, and with her darlings about her (for the time neither quarrelling nor crying) looked perfectly happy. Me, she had dispensed from joining the group, saying, 'She regretted to be under the necessity of keeping me at a distance; but that until she heard from Bessie, and could discover by her own observation that I was endeavouring in good earnest to acquire a more sociable and childlike disposition, a more attractive and sprightly manner – something lighter, franker, more natural, as it were – she really must exclude me from privileges intended only for contented, happy, little children.'

'What does Bessie say I have done?' I asked.

'Jane, I don't like cavillers or questioners; besides, there is something truly forbidding in a child taking up her elders in that manner. Be seated somewhere; and until you can speak pleasantly, remain silent.' [...]

John Reed was a schoolboy of fourteen years old; four years older than I, for I was but ten; large and stout for his age, with a dingy and unwholesome skin; thick lineaments in a spacious visage, heavy limbs and large extremities. He gorged himself habitually at table, which made him bilious, and gave him a dim and bleared eye with flabby cheeks. He ought now to have been at school; but his mamma had taken him home for a month or two, 'on account of his delicate health'. Mr Miles, the master, affirmed that he would do very well if he had fewer cakes and sweetmeats sent him from home; but the mother's heart turned from an opinion so harsh, and inclined rather to the more refined idea that John's sallowness was owing to over-application, and, perhaps, to pining after home.

John had not much affection for his mother and sisters, and an antipathy to me. He bullied and punished me; not two or three times in the week, nor once or twice in a day, but continually: every nerve I had feared him, and every morsel of flesh in my bones shrank when he came near. There were moments when I was bewildered by the terror he inspired, because I had no appeal whatever against either his menaces or his inflictions; the servants did not like to offend their young master by taking my part against him, and Mrs Reed was blind and deaf on the subject: she never saw him strike or heard him abuse me, though he did both now and then in her very presence; more frequently, however, behind her back. [...]

[John] spent some three minutes in thrusting out his tongue at me as far as he could without damaging the roots: I knew he would soon strike, and while dreading the blow, I mused on the disgusting and ugly appearance of him who would presently deal it. I wonder if he read that notion in my face; for, all at once, without speaking, he struck suddenly and strongly. I tottered, and on regaining my equilibrium retired back a step or two from his chair.

'That is for your impudence in answering mamma a while since,' said he, 'and for your sneaking way of getting behind curtains, and for the look you had in your eyes two minutes since, you rat!

Accustomed to John Reed's abuse, I never had an idea of replying to it: my care was how to endure the blow which would certainly follow the insult. [...]

'You have no business to take our books; you are a dependent, mamma says; you have no money; your father left you none; you ought to beg, and not to live here with gentlemen's children like us, and eat the same meals we do, and wear clothes at our mamma's expense. Now, I'll teach you to rummage my book-shelves: for they *are* mine; all the house belongs to me, or will do in a few years. Go and stand by the door, out of the way of the mirror and the windows.'

I did so, not at first aware what was his intention; but when I saw him lift and poise the book and stand in act to hurl it, I instinctively started aside with a cry of alarm: not soon enough, however; the volume was flung, it hit me, and I fell, striking my head against the door and cutting it. [...]

799 Wörter

From: Jane Eyre, *1847*

Annotations

22 **stout** strong and thick
22 **dingy** dark and dirty
22 **lineaments** the typical features of sth.
23 **gorge yourself** eat a lot of sth.
24 **bilious** feeling sick as if you might vomit soon
29 **sallowness** state of having an unhealthy slightly yellow colour
30 **over-application** doing sth. to excess
30 **pine after sth./sb.** miss sth./sb. very much
33 **morsel** small piece of sth.
36 **menace** threat of causing harm
36 **infliction** act of making sb. suffer sth. unpleasant
36 **servant** person working in another person's house, e.g. cooking and cleaning for them
44 **totter** walk with weak unsteady steps
44 **equilibrium** balance
46 **impudence** rude behaviour that shows no respect
50 **endure sth.** put up with sth. that is painful or unpleasant
51 **dependent** child or other person who depends on sb. else for food, home money, etc.
54 **rummage** move things around while searching for sth.
58 **hurl sth.** throw sth. violently at sth./sb.

▸ WOB: A9

Comprehension

▸ SF 34: Writing a summary or an outline, p. 244

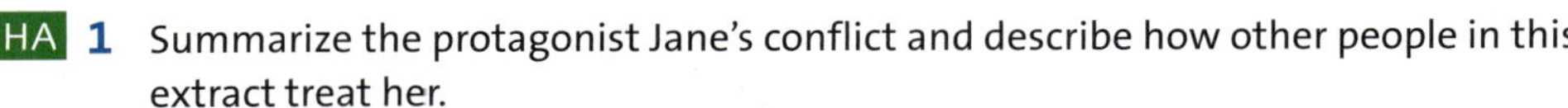

HA **1** Summarize the protagonist Jane's conflict and describe how other people in this extract treat her.

Unterschied zwischen direkter und indirekter Charakterisierung wiederholen → Support, p. 190

Analysis

▸ Support, p. 190

DIF PA **2** *** Analyse how direct and indirect *characterization is used in this extract to describe Jane and John.

▸ SF 19: Reading and understanding narrative texts, p. 223

HA **3** *** Analyse the language the author uses to show that Jane is unhappy and living in fear.

Language Awareness

HA **4** Some phrases in the text use old-fashioned words and expressions. Choose three and rewrite them in modern-day English. How does it change your impression of the text?

DIGI arbeitsteilig ein digitales Lexikon zu *old-fashioned phrases / modern phrases* erstellen

Beyond the text

▸ SF 46: Having a discussion, p. 264

5 Speaking Discuss how childhood difficulties, like experiences of bullying, can be overcome, and whether literary works can help people to feel less alone. Can reading literature help people deal with real world problems? Present the results of your discussion. ▸ WOB: A5

Text 4

DIGI 'graphic novels' als Suchbegriff eingeben und ‚Bilder' wählen → zahlreiche Beispiele

Looking back on childhood

Craig Thompson

- Together with a partner, find an example of a *graphic novel and write down all the elements it uses to tell the story. ▸ WOB: A3
- HA ***Quick write:** Write a short paragraph about how things that happen in childhood can have a lasting effect on a person's life and provide examples for your answers.

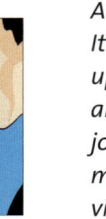

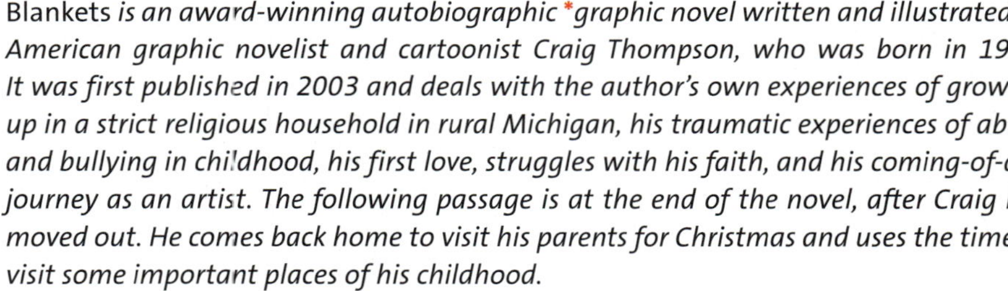

Blankets *is an award-winning autobiographic *graphic novel written and illustrated by American graphic novelist and cartoonist Craig Thompson, who was born in 1975. It was first published in 2003 and deals with the author's own experiences of growing up in a strict religious household in rural Michigan, his traumatic experiences of abuse and bullying in childhood, his first love, struggles with his faith, and his coming-of-age journey as an artist. The following passage is at the end of the novel, after Craig has moved out. He comes back home to visit his parents for Christmas and uses the time to visit some important places of his childhood.*

Unterschied zwischen graphic novels und Comics klären

KV 9: Features of graphic novels

From: Blankets, *2017*

Annotations
recess break time between lessons in school
shivers shaking movement of your body because of fear or fever
curfew time when children must be home in the evening
ground sb. punish a child or young person by not allowing them to go out with their friends for a period of time
vulnerable weak and easily hurt

Fehlerquelle: Aussprache von *curfew* [ˈkɜːfjuː]

Comprehension

▶ WOB: A3

▶ SF 34: Writing a summary or an outline, p. 244

HA **1** * Summarize what is happening in this extract in two sentences.

▶ Support, p. 190

HA **2** **a** Describe what makes Craig uncomfortable.
b Describe the relationship between Craig and his parents.

Analysis

Lernen App: Video on analysing visuals
▶ Getting started
▶ SF 26: Analysing graphic novels, p. 232
▶ WOB: A3 Analysing multimodal texts, pp. 12–15
▶ WOB: A3

HA **3** **a** In a *graphic novel, the pictures not only illustrate the written words but often tell their own story. Analyse how the visual narrative of the pictures is used to support or contradict the storytelling of the words in the thought bubbles.
DIF in PA vorbesprechen
b *** Examine how easy or difficult it would be to transfer the visual storytelling in the panels into written text only, and how the effect would change.
ein Panel auswählen und in einen Prosatext transformieren → Ergebnisse in PA tauschen und kommentieren

Language Awareness

▶ More language
Lernen App: Onomatopoetic words

HA **4** Rewrite the sentences that use capital letters and *onomatopoetic words into *prose. How does their effect change?

Beyond the text

5 Draw your own page of a graphic novel with 4–8 panels. Do task **a** or **b**.

HA **a** * Draw a story of a difficult moment in a person's childhood that is told in the form of a memory.

b *** Challenge Draw a story of a difficult moment from a person's childhood and use a variety of visual ways to express emotions (e. g. pictures, thought bubbles, speech balloons, font size, emanata ...). HA

DIGI Suchbegriff ‚Jane Eyre trailer' für genauere Informationen über Janes Geschichte
▶ WOB: A3, A9

HA **6** **a** * Compare the extract from *Jane Eyre* (1847) and the extract from *Blankets* (2003). Name universal and timeless issues relating to the lives of the two young people and identify similarities and differences.
HA **b** *** To what extent can both texts be considered *Bildungsromane*? Think back to the guiding question and include references to it in your answer.

Text 5

*** How to make a video game into a TV series

- * With a partner, discuss which opportunities and difficulties you see when a video game is transformed into a TV series.
- * Research what the video game / TV series *The Last of Us* is about and write down the most important key points of the plot and setting. HA

Now watch the video clip about the making of 'The Last of Us'. Before being adapted into a TV series, 'The Last of Us' was a popular computer game. It still has a huge fanbase today.

Lernen App: Video clip about the making of 'The Last of Us' (03:32 min.)

Comprehension

Lernen App: Answer key for task 1
► Check

1 Viewing Read the sentences below. Then watch the video and complete the sentences. ► WOB: A8

1 A surprising element of episode 3 is ...
2 The TV series deviates from the video game if ...
3 The biggest difference between the game and the show in this episode is ...
4 Contrary to Frank, Bill is described as ....
5 The last scene of this episode is emotional because ...
6 For the viewers, the emotion comes across because ...

Analysis

► SF 41: Analysing films, series and videos, p. 253
► WOB: A8 Viewing, pp. 26–27

2* Viewing Analyse the *cinematic devices used in this clip. What effects do they have?
* nur die Ausschnitte der Serie ansehen, Interview- und Making-of-Szenen außer Acht lassen

Beyond the text

Lernen App: Video on having a discussion
► Getting started
► SF 46: Having a discussion, p. 264
► WOB: A5

3* Speaking Discuss which audiences would prefer to watch the TV series and which audiences would prefer the video game, and whether you think that transmedia storytelling can help to reach new audiences. Present your conclusion.

4 a Together with a partner, brainstorm a list of points about how the streaming of TV series has changed the traditional television viewing experience.

HA b Individually, write a paragraph on the topic from **a** in relation to the guiding question, using your ideas from the brainstorming.

DIGI Punkte auf digitaler Pinnwand sammeln

DIGI/Alternative Video zur Frage erstellen

Language help

availability on-demand increases ... • binge-watching culture transforms ... • tailored to sb.'s interests • eliminates the need to ... • gives the freedom/ flexibility to ... • influenced storytelling ... • makes sth. more accessible ... • on a variety of devices ... • introducing interactive features ... • convenience ...

Chapter task

Imagine that the schoolbook authors have asked which texts you would like to see in this chapter.

HA **1*** Find a text of your choice that fits the topic of this chapter. Your text must be in English and could be a literary text, e. g. an extract from a *novel, a *short story, a *comic, a *graphic novel, a *play, a *poem, or song lyrics, but also a film *scene, a series, an *advertisement, a social media campaign, etc. It should be about a page long.

HA **2*** Write a paragraph in which you show how your chosen text interacts with a changing world and/or the time and society in which it was written.

HA **3*** Make a (digital) booklet out of all your class texts which complement this chapter and add one discussion question for each text. Alternatively, you can display your texts on posters and have a gallery walk.

DIGI Booklet digital mit Bildern und Deckblatt ausstatten

DIF Vorauswahl von Texten zur Verfügung stellen

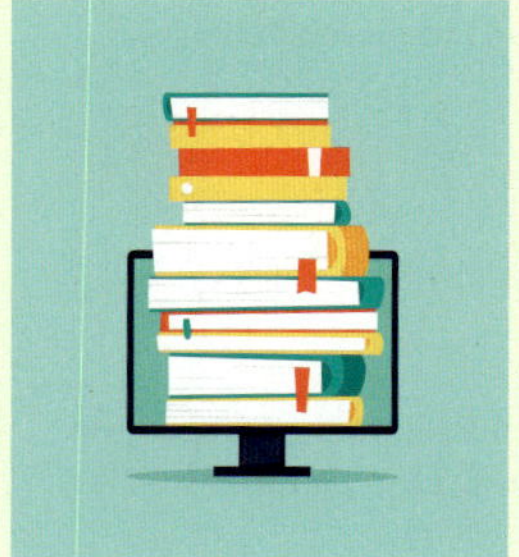

Chapter 4
Going Abroad: Expanding Perspectives – Confronting Privilege

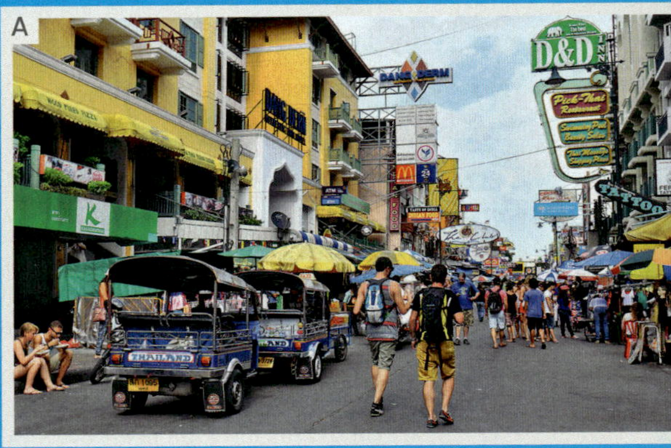

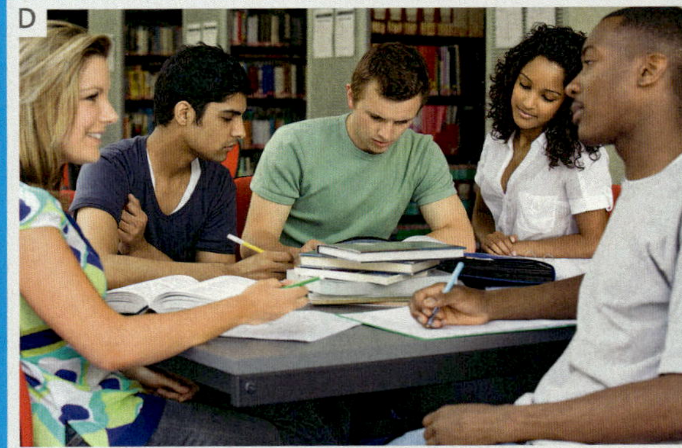

DIF einen Cluster vorgeben

DIGI Kooperationstools zur gemeinsamen Gestaltung

▸ Getting started
Lernen App: mind maps

1 a On your own, collect as many aspects you can think of regarding spending time in a foreign country after leaving school. Arrange your ideas in a *spidergram. Platz lassen für Erweiterung des *spidergram*

Alternative: *square*-Phase vorschalten

b * Compare your ideas with a partner. Add aspects if necessary.

DIGI leeren Bildrahmen für eigene Ideen bereitstellen

2 a * **Think** Look at the pictures of people spending time abroad and choose the one that most appeals to you.

DIGI Online-Wörterbücher nutzen

DIF ausgewählte Lexeme aus Lernwortschatz bereitstellen

b **Pair** Describe the picture you have chosen to a partner without saying which one it is. Your partner has to guess. Explain why it appeals to you. Together state what you would need to do to actually go on this trip of your choice.

Language help

The picture I chose shows/depicts ... • What you can see in the picture is ... • When I look at the picture, I ... • The destination/activity particularly appeals to me because ... • The activity I'd like to pursue is ...

zunächst Rahmenbedingungen klären (Dauer, Zeitpunkt, Alter)

CT **c** * **Share** In class, make a ranking chart of your favourite destinations for going abroad. Then share your ideas on what you need to do to go on the number one trip on your chart.

B

C

E

CT **3** **a** ⁂ Look at the aspects shown in the Chapter map. Speculate about their relevance to the chapter. Give a first answer to the guiding question.

b * Compare the Chapter map to your *spidergram in task **1**. Add important aspects.

Murmelphase, dann im Plenum besprechen

Chapter map

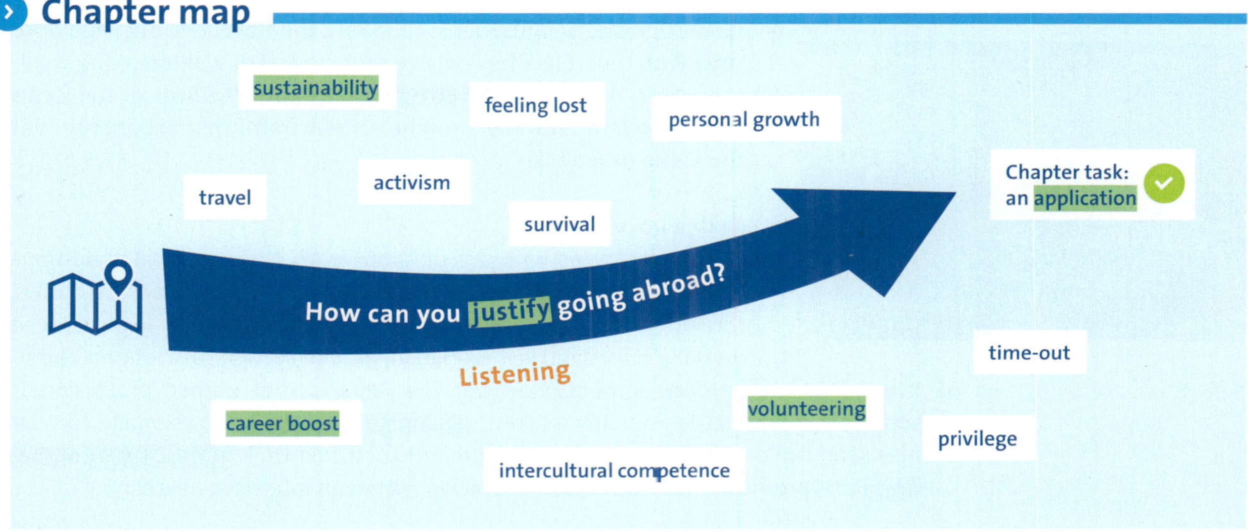

Lernen App: Going abroad in a globalized world (00:04:10)

▶ More language
Lernen App: Useful vocabulary for the chapter

Going abroad – then and now

The historical perspective

Travelling and going abroad after finishing school is not new. Even as far back as the 18th century young upper-class British people went on a so-called 'Grand Tour' of Europe in order to complete their education by visiting the famous landmarks of the Greek and Roman classical world and the Renaissance.

Einstiegsidee: freies Assoziieren ausgehend von den Bildern

Nowadays not just members of the upper classes, but also students from very different backgrounds either spend a year in a different country while still at school or take time out and travel the globe after completing their secondary education. Some even do both. For many, this is the icing on the cake and a reward for studying hard.

Motives for going abroad

Young people's motives for travelling differ vastly. Some seek adventure and look forward to getting away from the security of home, friends and family. Others hope to find themselves and enrich their lives or want to meet new people and form genuine friendships all over the world. Some opt for a trip with a social purpose. They decide to volunteer in disadvantaged and poverty-stricken communities in order to atone for global injustices. For others, backpacking, work and travel or starting university or a job abroad are the best options. Tragically, there are also global issues, such as war, famines, or environmental disasters, which force people to go abroad involuntarily. Forced migration to another country is often their only chance of survival or a better life.

Advantages and criticism

Young travellers predominantly speak of the benefits of going abroad, both for their personal development and sometimes even their choice of career. For example, employers claim that the wealth of experience 'gappers' gain while travelling helps to make them stand out from the crowd. You can also improve your language skills, learn a new language or improve one of the languages you studied at school. As English is the international lingua franca, you will encounter and learn to adapt to many different accents and varieties of English. Critics, however, argue that gap-year activities are purely egoistic and just serve to inflate the travellers' own ego or to spruce up their CVs. They believe that crowds of well-meaning westerners can never alleviate poverty or improve the lives of the locals they encounter. Travellers might benefit from their experience, but the locals never will.

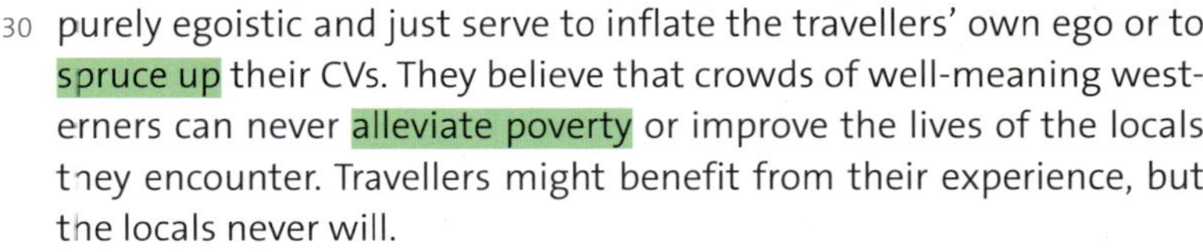

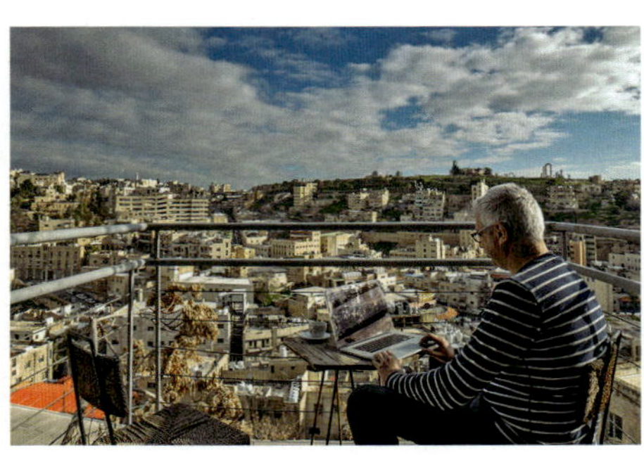

Taking up jobs abroad

Many employees who are unhappy with their pay and conditions leave their jobs to seek a better working environment abroad. Often, foreign companies offer a better work-life balance (e.g. reduced working hours and less workload) as well as high salaries and opportunities for career development. However, the departure of trained professionals sometimes exacerbates already existing workforce shortages. Occasionally companies send their employees to a branch abroad to sharpen their intercultural competence and promote exchange and cooperation within an international team.

476 Wörter

HA **1 Main ideas**

Outline how going abroad has changed over time according to the text.

2 Reflect

DIF *syntactic structures* vorgeben *(main, subordinate or relative clauses)*

a ✱ Decide which of the paragraphs was the most difficult for you to understand. ✱✱ Give reasons. Reconsider the vocabulary, content and sentence structure of the text.

HA b ✱ Go through the text again and collect five words or phrases that you would like to keep in mind. *spidergram* aus *Lead-in* um diese Wörter ergänzen

DIGI Auswahl in *wordcloud* visualisieren

3 *-ing* forms

In the text there are several *-ing* forms, which can be gerunds as well as participles.

HA a ✱ Find three sentences with *-ing* forms and rewrite the sentences without using an *-ing* form.

HA b ✱ Compare the original sentences with the rewritten ones. Which ones do you prefer?

HA c ✱ Name reasons for the *author's use of *-ing* forms.

Lernen App: Videos on gerunds and participles
▶ More language

▶ Check — Lernen App: Answer key for task 3a
▶ WOB: B7 Gerunds, p. 55
▶ WOB: B13 Participles, pp. 62–63

HA CT **4 Chunk it!**

The following nouns can be combined with both the verbs or the adjectives into *collocations that describe the effect going abroad can have. Form as many collocations as possible. Sometimes a verb or an adjective can be combined with more than one noun.

Lernen App: Video about chunks
▶ Getting started

▶ Check — Lernen App: Answer key for task 4
▶ WOB: B8 Collocations with prepositions, p. 56

Verbs	Adjectives	Nouns
acquire	beneficial	change
adapt to	better	experience
bring about	considerable	impact
develop	deep	understanding
experience	genuine	
feel	great	
gain	invaluable	
have	memorable	
make	mutual	
seek	profound	
show	strong	

L sollte darauf hinweisen, dass es viele mögliche Antworten gibt und nur die Gebräuchlichkeit einiger Verbindungen höher ist.

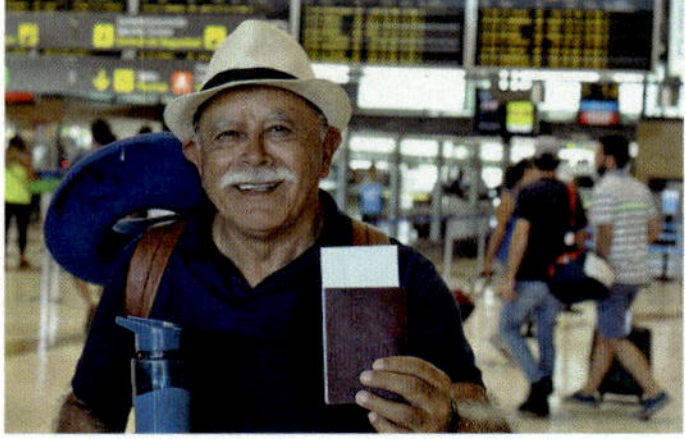

5 Text production

You choose Work on task **a** or **b**. Use as many collocations and useful phrases from **2** and **4** as possible.

CT a ✱✱✱ Speaking Give a one-minute presentation on the advantages of intercultural exchanges while travelling. ▶ WOB: A4

HA CT ✱✱✱ b What would a perfect 'gapper' be like? For an information leaflet on gap year travel, write a description of the perfect candidate.

▶ SF 43: Giving a presentation, p. 259

DIGI Cartoon über E-Book projizieren

► SF 25: Analysing cartoons, p. 231

DIF hilfreiche Vokabeln vorgeben *(formal dress, suit and tie, a hunched position, career path, benefits)*

What you can gain from going abroad

- Briefly describe the *cartoon below. What does it say about possible downsides of going abroad? ► WOB: A1

Vorgehen bei der Cartoon-Analyse kurz wiederholen

CAREERS COUNSELLOR
"Frankly – I don't see much chance of making a career out of backpacking!"
CartoonStock.com

The introduction to the travel guide The Big Trip *promotes the benefits of spending time abroad.*

There is only so much you can understand about the world from school, documentaries, the news, and your circle of friends on social media. There's no substitute for getting out there to see, hear, taste, touch and smell the realities of what the world is. And, most importantly, there is nowhere better to learn about yourself than from outside your comfort zone.

Travel in foreign lands, away from the securities of home, friends, and family, certainly has the power to take you there. Along the way you'll open yourself up to be enthralled, inspired, amused, amazed, bemused, enriched, empowered and – yes – even scared. It's a heady mix of emotions, but one that few people ever get tired of. When was the last time you heard of someone looking back at their life and wishing they'd travelled less?

The reason for this is that travel has the power to change your life for the better, often in ways you'd never imagined. For some travellers, such as Matt Phillips, it was coming to the stark realisation that fear was playing too large a role in his life. His lesson: dying wouldn't be his life's greatest tragedy, not truly living it would be. He has happily never looked back, and now travels the globe for a living while working for Lonely Planet. For others, it may be something as profoundly simple as finally grasping that wealth has nothing to do with a bank balance.

For many travellers it may be more practical, perhaps provoking an unexpected change of career: what starts out as a vacation ends up a vocation, a passion becomes a profession. Take the economics graduate who thought he was bound to work in an accountant firm but did a stint with a music distribution company during his gap year. He was so inspired he's been in the music business ever since. Similarly, Amanda Allen-Toland, who volunteered to work as a youth ambassador in Bangkok on an international development programme on AIDS, could not have predicted the positive impact her volunteering experience would have on her career. Upon returning home she moved on to work as a programme manager for the Asia Pacific Business Coalition on HIV/AIDS in Melbourne, Australia.

'It's paid dividends for me. It led me into an area I wanted to be in with a higher level of responsibility, excellent pay, and job satisfaction. It's the icing on the cake. My experience working and living in Thailand was so fantastic that even if my next role had been making fruit shakes, I'd do it all over again.'

Annotations
16 **heady** exciting
25 **grasp sth.** understand sth.
27 **vocation** *Berufung*

But it's not all about life-changing realisations or your career, […] you'll also gather friends and experiences that will be valuable for the rest of your life. Whenever someone mentions Kenya, you'll remember marvelling at the great wildebeest migration in the Masai Mara, or if you meet a New Zealander, Canadian or Scot you'll be able to regale them with stories of exploring their beloved mountains and meeting their fellow citizens. These intangibles will stay with you your whole life. 615 Wörter

Annotation
42 **wildebeest** *Gnu*

From: The Big Trip – Your Essential Guide to Gap Years, Sabbaticals and Overseas Adventures, *Lonely Planet, 2019*

Comprehension

HA CT **1** Outline the benefits of going abroad mentioned in the guidebook. Add keywords to your *spidergram from the beginning of the chapter.

Alternative: Aufgabe mündlich lösen, Visualisierung durch Symbole

DIGI Karten mit Vorteilen auf interaktivem Whiteboard hochladen

► WOB: A1

Lernen App:
Video on stylistic devices
Overview of stylistic devices

Analysis

HA **2** ** Analyse how the text promotes the idea of spending time abroad through
* 1 the choice of words
2 examples of people who have travelled
3 *stylistic devices
4 argumentative techniques.

Copy the table below and note down your results. Be prepared to present your table in class.

► Getting started
► Support, p. 190
► WOB: A1

DIGI arbeitsteilig bearbeiten und Ergebnisse auf digitaler Pinnwand präsentieren

	Quote/description/ explanation	Effect
Choice of words	...	...
Examples of people who have travelled	...	...
Stylistic devices	...	...
Argumentative techniques	...	...

DIGI Text projizieren, in dem die entsprechenden Wörter markiert sind

Language awareness

3 **a** In the first and the last paragraph of the excerpt, the personal pronoun *you* is used frequently. Explain what effect this has on the reader. Bear in mind that the text is an extract from a travel guide.

* **b** Rewrite one of the paragraphs without using the *you* and assess the different effect this has on the reader. ► WOB: A1

LÖS 3a
direct address: topic feels more personal, reader feels included and thus more inclined to identify with the idea

Beyond the text

CT **4** *** The guidebook promotes travel as an opportunity for self-discovery. Make a list of points that speak against going abroad especially to places far away. Include both private and global issues such as climate change and sustainability.

DIGI Nachteile den Vorteilen (Aufgabe 1) gegenüberstellen (andersfarbige Karten auf Whiteboard)

DIF für schnelle SuS: Online-Recherche und Präsentation zu Möglichkeiten des umweltverträglichen Reisens

LÖS 4
long-haul flights, high carbon footprint, add to global warming, personal reasons

Info

Travelling in times of global warming has taken on a new meaning. 5–8 % of global greenhouse gas emissions stem from tourism. Many who want to live more sustainably therefore completely avoid air travel. But while many people do not go on all-inclusive holidays at the beach, others refuse to give up their well-deserved summer holidays. So is travel a matter of conscience, or are new innovations needed to make sustainable tourism more appealing to all?

How to finance your term abroad

buzz group activity

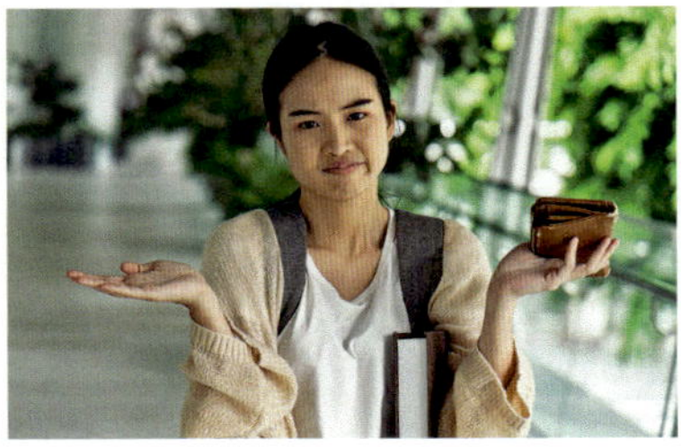

- Once they start university, many students have to manage without financial support from home. With a partner, discuss how you envision taking the step to financial independence and what worries you about this and what benefits you associate with it.

Studying abroad is a popular option among students from all countries. One of the biggest issues is how to fund the semester abroad. The following article outlines different options for German students.

Du möchtest im Ausland studieren, vielleicht sogar auf einem anderen Kontinent? Aber die Finanzierung hält dich davon ab? Kein Problem, in diesem Beitrag erfährst du, welche Möglichkeiten es gibt, dein Auslandssemester zu finanzieren.

Kosten über Kosten

Mit einem Auslandssemester sind neben den schönen Erfahrungen und Momenten auch viele Kosten verbunden. Die größten Ausgaben sind sicherlich die Studiengebühren und die Kosten für das Wohnen, die auf einen im Ausland zukommen. Doch dabei hört es nicht auf, je nach Land können auch die Flugtickets, Lebenshaltungskosten und Ausgaben für das Visum und Versicherungen sich schnell summieren. [...] Dennoch gibt es eine Vielzahl an Wegen, wie du dir deinen Traum vom Auslandssemester realisieren kannst.

Lernen App: Information about DAAD/Erasmus

► More info

Finanzierungsmöglichkeiten für dein Auslandssemester

[...] Stipendien sind eine super Möglichkeit, dein Auslandsstudium zu finanzieren. Hier lohnt es sich rechtzeitig über verschiedene Stipendien zu informieren und diese zu vergleichen. Je nach deinem Vorhaben und deinem Ziel, welches du im Ausland verfolgst, können unterschiedliche Stipendien passend sein. Studierst du auf Lehramt und möchtest ein Praktikum an einer schulischen Einrichtung im Ausland machen, eignen sich zum Beispiel das Stipendium Lehramt.International vom DAAD oder das Stipendium von Schulwärts. Es lohnt sich auf jeden Fall, sich rechtzeitig über Stipendienmöglichkeiten und deren Voraussetzungen sowie Förderungshöhe zu informieren. [...]

Neben Stipendien kann es sinnvoll sein, sich vorher von Deutschland aus einen Nebenjob zu suchen, welcher sich vom Ausland aus remote ausführen lässt. Hierbei sollte der zeitliche Aufwand, den der Nebenjob im Ausland neben dem Studium in Anspruch nimmt, abgewogen und nicht unterschätzt werden, denn im Ausland gibt es neben der Uni viel zu erkunden, was ebenfalls viel Zeit in Anspruch nimmt.

[...] Selbst wenn du kein BAföG beziehst, kann es sein, dass du einen Anspruch auf Auslands-BAföG hast. Hier solltest du mindestens ein halbes Jahr vorher beim zuständigen Amt für das Land, in welches es für dich gehen soll, einen Antrag auf Auslands-BAföG stellen, denn für Auslands-BAföG gelten andere Fördervoraussetzungen als für die Förderung deines Studiums in Deutschland.

[...] Bei einem Auslandspraktikum oder -Studium innerhalb und außerhalb der Europäischen Union fördert das Erasmus+ Programm Auslandsaufenthalte. Der Förderzeitraum liegt dabei zwischen zwei und zwölf Monaten. Je nach Land variiert hier die Fördersumme. [...]

Wie ich mir mein Auslandssemester finanziere.

Ich hatte ziemliches Glück mit der Finanzierung meines Auslandssemesters. Dank der Uni Oldenburg habe ich ein Stipendium über die Projektgelder des Programms Lehramt.International erhalten. Im Rahmen dieses Programmes können sich nämlich nicht nur Lehramtsstudierende zu Individualstipendien für Auslandspraktika bewerben, sondern auch Universitäten um lehramtsbezogene Fördergelder. Wenn Eure Uni hier gefördert wird, fragt nach, ob damit auch Stipendien für Auslandssemester finanziert werden. Dadurch wird bei mir ein Großteil meines Auslandsstudiums in Südafrika an der Nelson Mandela University finanziert.

Für das Lehramt.International-Stipendium zum Auslandspraktikum kann man sich als eingeschriebener Studierender im Lehramt beim DAAD für ein Stipendium zu einem Auslandspraktikum bewerben. Darüber hinaus muss bei der Bewerbung ein Sprachnachweis der englischen Sprache mit einem Niveau von mindestens B2 erfüllt werden (zum Beispiel in Form eines Cambridge oder TOEFL Tests). Nach Absprache kann dieser jedoch auch noch nach der Bewerbung nachgereicht werden. Zudem müssen der Bewerbung neben dem Antragsformular noch ein englischer Lebenslauf, ein Motivationsschreiben und eine Notenbescheinigung beigefügt werden. Allerdings geht es bei der Bewerbung nicht nur um die Noten, sondern die Motivation hinter dem Auslandssemester steht klar im Vordergrund.

Die Stipendienhöhe ist immer abhängig vom Zielland. In meinem Fall übernimmt das Stipendium:

- die Studiengebühren in voller Höhe, sodass ich nur noch circa 470 Euro Gebühren für die Administration zahlen musste,
- 1.725 Euro für die Flüge,
- eine monatliche Rate für die Lebenshaltungskosten von 1.010 Euro.

Zusätzlich zum Stipendium habe ich das Glück, dass ich meinen Nebenjob hier aus Südafrika remote ausführen kann, wodurch sich eine weitere Finanzierungsmöglichkeit für mich ergibt.

615 Wörter

From: 'Auslandssemester leicht finanziert', studierenweltweit.de, *21 October 2022*

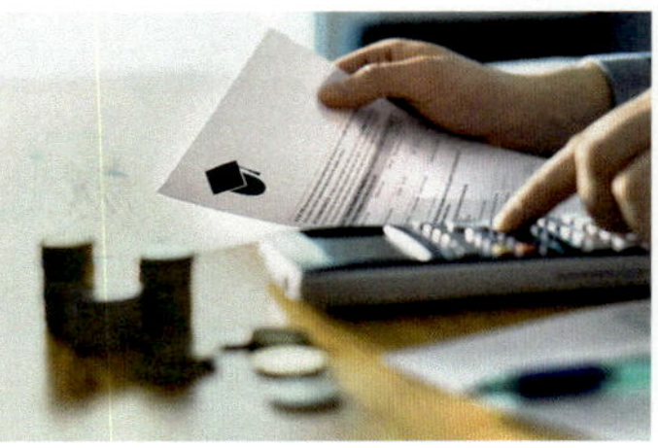

Lernen App: Video on mediation
▸ Getting started
▸ SF 49: Mediating from German into English, p. 270
▸ WOB: A7 Mediating, pp. 24–25

1 Mediating | Intercultural communication An email friend from the UK wants to do a term abroad and is researching different funding options. She asks what kind of funding is available for German students. You write her an email in which you explain the different financing options mentioned in the text above.

DIF Begriffe erklären (BAFöG, DAAD), Wörterbuch nutzen

Beyond the text

2 You choose | Speaking Together with a partner, work on either task **a** or **b**.

▸ SF 46: Having a discussion, p. 264
▸ SF 13: Doing research, p. 214
▸ WOB: A5

CT **a** Discuss how you can spend a term abroad in the most environmentally and climate friendly way possible. Present your ideas in class.

zuerst in EA reflektieren, dann Austausch

DIGI Ergebnisse in *wordcloud* sammeln

DIF Ideen auf Blättern visualisieren, im Plenum präsentieren

b *** Discuss countries you think might be interesting for a term abroad but cannot be considered due to global issues such as war, political tensions, or climate catastrophes. If necessary, do some research. Present your results to the class.

DIGI Internetrecherche, um Ideen durch Fakten abzusichern

DIF Kurzauswahl an Ländern vorgeben, in denen sich Auswirkungen der Erderwärmung zeigen

► SF 39: Essentials: listening and viewing, p. 252

► WOB: A6

Reactivate

1 Everyday listening

* a Do you like listening to audios, e.g. podcasts or audio books, in your free time? What is easy or difficult about listening in general and perhaps especially to audios in a foreign language?

PA bietet sich an → b Think of your past experiences with listening tasks. Which features distinguish listening at school from everyday listening?

2 Recollecting listening strategies

1. Read the task carefully.
2. Take notes, using abbreviations.
3. Don't try to understand every detail.
4. Make sure you have done all the tasks.
5. Try to anticipate what might be said.
6. Make sure you have done the tasks correctly.

* a There are some strategies that can help you with listening tasks. Copy the *method card below and match the strategies in the box on the left with the corresponding part of a listening task. ggf. *method card* aus der vorherigen Jahrgangsstufe weiterverwenden

DIGI Strategien per *drag and drop* in die Tabelle ziehen

KV 10: Method card

Method card – listening		
Pre-listening	While-listening	Post-listening
...	...	...

b *** Add further listening strategies that come to mind. Keep adding to your method card throughout the Skills Lab. DIGI Lernvideos zum *Listening* finden sich online

c * Apart from the differentiation between pre-, while- and post-listening, there is also a difference between listening for gist and listening for detail. With a partner, outline the characteristics of each and present them to your class.

d *** Which of the while-listening strategies you collected in tasks **a** and **b** are better suited to 'listening for gist', and which are better suited to 'listening for detail'?
den SuS bewusst machen, dass die Abgrenzung zum Teil fließend ist

Lernen App: Answer key for task 2a
► Check (task 2 a)

Lernen App: Video on listening
► Getting started (task 2 c)

DIF mögliche Lösungsaspekte durchmischt präsentieren und den Spalten zuordnen lassen

Step ahead

Pre-listening

CT 3 Preparing a listening task

Work in groups of three. Read the short introduction below and the tasks on p. 101 for the audio about high school in a different country. Then do the following pre-listening tasks.

- **Partner A:** Collect information about the text, such as general topic, text type, speakers ...
- **Partner B:** Try to anticipate ideas that could be presented and questions that might be discussed.
- **Partner C:** Focus on the while-listening tasks and make sure that you understand exactly what you are supposed to do.

Then exchange your results and be prepared to present them in class.

In the following interview, radio reporter Trevor Chappell is speaking about the experiences of high school students in a foreign country with Jason Heath, who is a representative of the student-exchange-organisation AFS, which organizes student exchanges and international volunteer programmes.

Info

In most listening tasks you are allowed to listen to the audio(s) twice. Sometimes the task refers to the **gist of the text, sometimes to details**. Read each task and its items carefully. Sometimes the task gives you instructions about what to do during the first or second listening. If not, decide whether you want to listen for gist or for detail during the second or first listening. You can also accomplish as much of the task as you want during the first listen and correct it or fill in any gaps during the second listen.

While-listening

4 Focus on listening

You are going to listen to the audio twice. Do the following tasks.

CT **a** * Listening Task 1: Listening for gist

Decide which of the following statements best describes the general content of the audio. Only one answer is correct.

1 The interview deals with the challenges faced by students at a high school in a different country.
2 The interview describes the situation exchange students find themselves in with their host families.
3 The interview explains how exchange students apply for the program and how AFS places them in the foreign country.

CT **b** Listening Task 2: Listening for detail (01:29 min.)

Note down the answers to the questions below to extract more detailed information from the audio. Write down 3–5 words for each question.

1 Why was the first meeting with his host family difficult for Jason, when he went to Germany as an exchange student?
2 What is expected of exchange students living with a host family?
3 According to Jason Heath, which families make the most suitable host families?
4 How old do you have to be to go abroad using the American Field Service (AFS)?
5 Which measures are taken by AFS to make sure that students and host family are 'a good fit'?
6 What can students, the agency and the host family do if there are any problems?

im Anschluss an die Aufgabe erneuter Blick auf die *Pre-listening*-Aspekte der *Method Card* (KV 10) und Evaluation, welche Strategien in Aufgabe 3 erfolgreich angewendet wurden

Post-listening

CT 5 *** Recapitulating the content

Explain why Jason Heath might want to talk about student exchanges on the radio program. Consider his personal experiences and his current position.

Practise

Now you will have a chance to practice your listening skills. You will hear a report titled 'Growing numbers of Chinese teens are coming to America for High School' by Josie Huang in which she describes the experiences of Chinese high-school students in the US.

6 Pre-listening

a Based on the title of the radio report, create a mind map on ...

- what information and questions you expect to hear in the report
- which other speakers apart from the reporter you expect to hear
- what different accents you expect to hear
- which words and phrases you expect to hear

Alternative: in GA bearbeiten

DIGI Mindmap-Programme verwenden

den SuS bewusst machen, dass es sich hier um Vermutungen handelt

► WOB: A6

► Check
Lernen App: Answer key for task 4a

Lernen App: Interview with Jason Heath (02:35 min.)

LÖS **4a**: 2

LÖS **4b**
1 handshake to say hello, different from Australia
2 help in their host family, obey their rules
3 families with young children (less jealousy)
4 15
5 international standards, team in every country, checks
6 talk with agency about problem, change family

► Getting started
Lernen App: Mind maps

Annotations
gaokao the national entrance exam for universities in China
Harvard, Princeton, Yale the top three universities in the US
UCLA, USC Californian universities that are also regarded as very good but not as good as Harvard, Yale, or Princeton

Lernen App: Answer key for task 7
► Check

Info

You can do tasks **a–b** during the first listen and **c–d** during the second listen. But you can also try to solve as many tasks as possible on the first try and add or correct your solutions during the second listen. Find the most suitable **strategy** for you.

CT **b** * Compare your mind map with your partner and discuss possible differences. Add aspects to your mind map where necessary.

7 Listening

Lernen App: Report by Josie Huang (04:34 min.)

Listening You are going hear the audio twice.

*** **a** Take notes of 5–7 words on … ausreichend Zeit geben, um Aufgaben a–d vorab zu lesen
1. the reasons that are mentioned as to why Chinese students come to the U.S.
2. the experiences that they have in the U.S.
3. the difference from the Chinese school system.

bei genügend Zeit Exkurs zur *gaokao*-Prüfung

*** **b** In one sentence, summarize the importance of the *gaokao* for Chinese students.

*** **c** Complete the following sentences in no more than 8 to 10 words:
1. Rich Chinese parents enrol their children in American High Schools because …
2. Chinese students at Arroyo Pacific Academy do not learn as much English as they should because …
3. The reason why most Chinese students do not go to public schools is that …

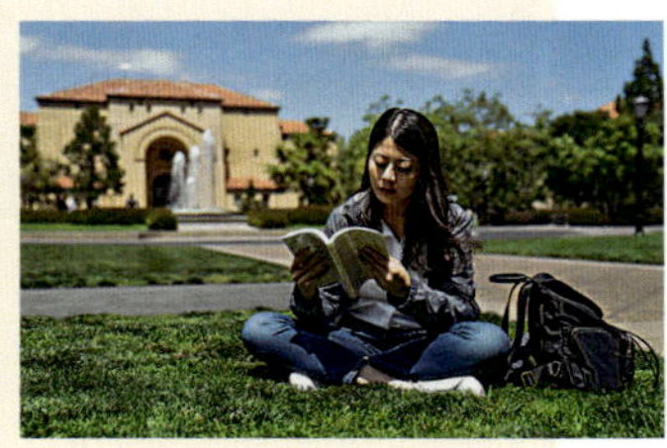

d Choose the right answer. Only one is correct.
Chinese students experience the American school system as being very different because …
1. they do not get as much homework as in China.
2. the teachers are not respected as much as in China.
3. students get to exercise more during classes in the US.
4. the teaching methods offer more freedom in the US.

LÖS 7b
gaokao: China's national university entrance exam that decides on where you will go to university and is regarded as very important for your future chances

LÖS 7d
… the teaching methods offer more freedom in the US

Take another look

Perspektive präzisieren (Anlass, Zielgruppe)

8 Focusing on content ***

Comment on Chinese parents' motivation for sending their children to a high school in the U.S.A.

verschiedene Formen des *argumentative writing* sind möglich (Kommentar, kurze Posts unter Online-Artikel)

9 Self-assessment

► SF 15: Assessing yourself and giving feedback, p. 217
► WOB: A6 Listening, pp. 20–23

Think about the pre-, while and post-listening tasks that you have completed. Add the aspects you should improve on to your *method card:

Method card – listening		
Pre-listening	While-listening	Post-listening
…	…	…
Aspects I can improve:		
…		

KV 10: Method card

→ Alternative: in den Ecken des Raumes und der Raummitte je ein Blatt mit Schlüsselwörtern aufhängen (z. B. *working with people, working with technology, working outdoors, dealing with numbers/figures*), SuS zu Positionierung und Austausch auffordern

How your professional career benefits from your experience abroad

Emma Sheppard

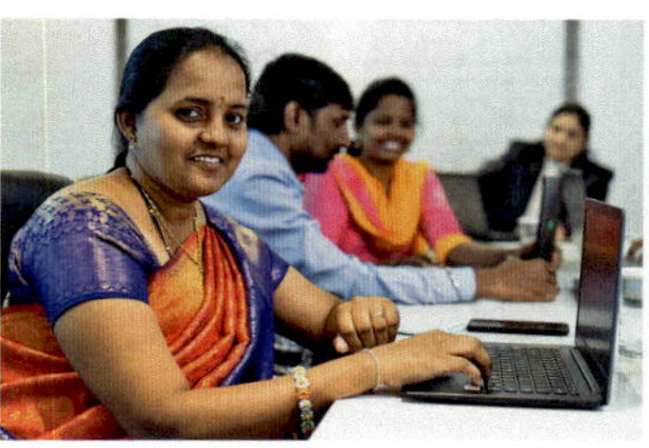

→ * • Do you already have an idea of what career you want to pursue later? What personal talents and skills do you have that make you enthusiastic about this profession? Share your future aspirations with the class.

A gap year can be a chance to gain experience that will have a lifelong impact on your personal career. The following text explains how to use your experience abroad to stand out in future job applications.

[...] Sophie Graham, a careers adviser for the National Careers Service says: 'The skills and experiences you gain can help you become ready for university and employment both academically and socially. Gap years can really boost those attributes employers are looking for.'

What you actually do during your gap year – whether it be travelling, working or volunteering – will depend on your own plans and the career that you eventually want to get into. Luckily Victoria McLean, founder of CityCV.co.uk, says there is no one answer: 'A gap year abroad can add language skills, an understanding of cultural differences and utilising your skills in whole new environments and situations.' [...]

Finding an internship in your chosen field can be a challenge, but the experts recommend being determined, speculatively contacting companies you admire and utilize any networks that you have. Lydia Fairman, owner of recruitment company Fairman Consulting adds: 'Take time to tailor [your email] to the company. Find a good person within to send it to (use LinkedIn or just pick up the phone and ask). Follow up a week or so later to check they've got it and be charming.'

Vicky McNeil-Kornevall, the co-founder of WorkingAbroad.com, says that volunteering in a field you're passionate about can also help set your application apart when it comes to bagging a dream job later: 'If it's cetacean research you are passionate about, and you can show that you have spent three months researching whales and dolphins in Patagonia for example, this will really stand out on your CV'. [...]

If a suitable internship or volunteering position proves elusive, there's no need to ditch the gap year plans, adds McNeil-Kornevall: 'Do something unusual and learn a skill that will make you stand out from the rest. Or learn a new language. Use the time wisely to do something constructive that will impress potential employers.'

Joe Hallwood, founder of Tefl Org UK agrees: 'Don't turn down any opportunities. It might not be something you're interested in doing right now but the skills you learn, experiences you have and people you will meet can all help shape your future career path. Travelling [itself] is a great way to learn a whole host of new skills – from a new language, to negotiation, to project management.'

Once you've returned home, how best to describe your adventure? Matt Arnerich, a writer for Inspiring Interns says that if you've spent time working or volunteering, the experience should be treated like any other job: 'Detail the organisation, the time spent there and your role to start with, and expand with the responsibilities you held and the skills you learned. Often what will really impress is the things that you achieved more than what you did day to day.'

Annotation

19 cetacean [sɪˈteɪʃn] indicative of the group of creatures that includes whales and dolphins

22 elusive difficult to find

Annotations
43 **sabbatical** a period of time when sb. stops working in order to travel or to study
44 **apologetic** feeling that you are sorry for doing something wrong

If you've been more focused on the travelling side, McLean adds that this should also take pride of place on your CV: 'Discussions about your gap year can give the reader a flavor of the kind of person you are. Good to talk about are things that show you are a strong individual – e.g. involvement in voluntary or community work – especially positions of leadership.' [...]

While gaps should be avoided in a CV if possible, Gregory says that candidates who have taken a gap year, career break or sabbatical should never shy away from talking about their experience. 'Never feel defensive or apologetic for your time out,' he says. 'It's a great experience, different from the ordinary, and out of the typical comfort zone. Try to show how your skills have developed as a result of the challenges you've experienced during that year.'

'You have some great stories to tell, but your best story is the one that shows what you can do next for your prospective employer.' 635 Wörter

From: 'How to make sure your gap year boosts your future career', theguardian.com, *09 June 2016*

Comprehension

Lernen App: Answer key for task 1
▶ Check

HA CT **1** Match the paragraphs (A–E) with a suitable headline (1–5)

Paragraph A: l. 1–10	1 Gain experience in your dream field
Paragraph B: l. 11–21	2 Tailor your CV
Paragraph C: l. 22–30	3 Think about what you want to get out of it
Paragraph D: l. 31–41	4 But don't apologise
Paragraph E: l. 42–49	5 Or do something unusual

LÖS 1
A3 B1 C5 D2 E4

▶ WOB: A1

HA CT
2 **Partner B**: Go to page 191 and do task **2**. **Partner A**: Summarize what advice the article gives on planning and selecting a gap year with a view to enhancing future career prospects. Take notes and exchange relevant facts with your partner later. DIF Austausch mit anderen SuS mit der gleichen Aufgabe (A/B), gemeinsame Ideensammlung

Analysis

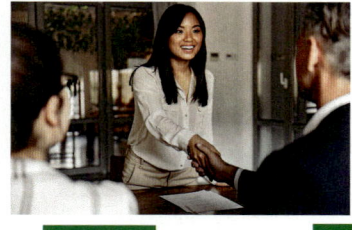

DIGI/DIF Textpassagen markieren und über E-Book einblenden

HA **3** *** Analyse how experts and their quotations are used in the text to convince the readers of the benefits of going abroad for their future careers.

Language awareness

Lernen App: Video on modal verbs
▶ More language

4 Analyse how the use of imperatives and modal verbs reinforces the advice to people who are interested in taking a gap year. ▶ WOB: A1

a Collect examples of imperatives and modal verbs from the text.
*** **b** Describe the effect of imperatives and modals on the reader.
*** **c** Rewrite a passage of text without using imperatives and modals.

DIF Modalverben in einer Textpassagen farbig markieren

- eine/mehrere Textpassagen gezielt auswählen (Z. 14–16 oder Z. 26–30)
- SuS darauf hinweisen, dass bei Zitaten in Analysen etc. der Text nicht verändert werden darf

LÖS 4b
- imperatives: reader is addressed directly and being told what to do, can make them feel more involved and more inclined to act
- modal 'can': shows a possible positive outcome if the advice is heard and the suggestions are followed

Beyond the text

5 You choose | Speaking Imagine you have taken a gap year after finishing school. Now you have returned and are taking the next careersteps. Prepare notes for an interview with either ...

► SF 45: Taking part in an interview, p. 263

► Support, p. 191

HA CT **a** * someone from the Human Resources department of a company you have applied to.

HA CT **b** * or the admissions tutor at the university of your choice.

Find a partner and do the interview. State how you have benefitted from your time abroad and how that could be useful for your future.

Text 4

DIGI Ergebnisse als *wordcloud* sammeln und projizieren

Arriving in a foreign country

Rachel Friedman

CT •* In a short buzz-group-activity, brainstorm what you have to do when you first arrive in a foreign country on your own. Decide which aspects or tasks you would find most challenging. Methode: Blitzlicht

*In the *novel* The Good Girl's Guide to Getting Lost *the American *first-person narrator, Rachel, decides to spend four months in Ireland. The following extract describes her arrival at the airport in Ireland.*

Street in Seoul, South Korea

Here are the facts of the present moment. It's 2002. I'm twenty years old. I've just embarked on four months in a foreign country alone. I'm carrying six hundred dollars in traveler's checks, money saved up from waitressing last semester. I booked two nights in a Dublin hostel before I left. Other than that, I've got no plan. And this greatly confounds me because I *always* have a plan. At least I used to be the kind of girl who always has a plan. [...]

I will myself through a revolving door and out into Ireland, where my bus is sunning itself. Three massive steps lead up into it, though there might as well be one hundred.

'You're grand', says the driver encouragingly, but I cannot see any graceful way to get myself plus Big Red inside.

I briefly consider splurging on a taxi, but it seems like an unnecessary indulgence when the bus is right here. It's cheap – and it's waiting.

Okay, I tell myself. You may very well be about to make a complete ass of yourself, but no one knows you. Come on. Get on the bus. Get. On. The. Bus. I put two feet on the first step and then turn back around to face my engorged red opponent. Twisting the suitcase sideways, I drag it awkwardly up onto the step with me. Only half of its girth makes it; for a moment we are in a perfect, precarious balance of bag and girl. Just as I am about to lose the battle to the overhanging weight, two steroidal angels reach down, and my suitcase floats the rest of the way back in. We shove it into the space designated for luggage, leaving enough room for someone else's small purse or maybe a small wallet.

► More info
Lernen App: Rachel Friedman

Annotations
- 5 **confound sb.** confuse or surprise sb.
- 7 **revolving door** *Drehtür*
- 12 **splurge** act of spending money on something unnecessary or extravagant
- 16 **engorge** become bigger
- 18 **girth** size

Annotations
24 **apprehension** worry
29 **indigestion** *Magenverstimmung*

I did it. I'm on a bus alone in a foreign country. For a fleeting second, I feel something surprising alongside the familiar emotions of confusion, doubt and apprehension. Later, I'll look back and recognize this rush of excitement as my first glimpse of what it means to travel alone in a faraway land: I can go anywhere. I can do anything. And the all-important: I can be anyone. Soon enough, I'll come to crave this feeling, seek it out and cultivate it, but right now it's an indecipherable sensation, quite possibly, I consider, indigestion. 399 Wörter

From: The Good Girl's Guide to Getting Lost, *2011*

Dublin Airport

▸ WOB: A9

Comprehension

1 **HA** Retell the arrival of Rachel in Ireland using the words and expressions below. Make sure that you do not copy complete sentences from the story but use your own words where possible. Alternative: KV 11: Comprehension

revelation • help • public transport • relief • first steps • luggage • struggle

Lernen App: Video on how to create a flow-chart
▸ Getting started
▸ SF 19: Reading and understanding narrative texts, p. 223
▸ Support, p. 191

Analysis

*** **2** Analyse the emotions the *narrator goes through in the course of the extract. Use a flow-chart to visualize her changing emotions and give evidence for your interpretations using suitable quotes from the extract. **DIGI** Flowcharts erstellen

*** **3** The *first-person narrator uses elements of humour to illustrate the struggle with her luggage. Analyse the means used to express this struggle and examine the effect it has.

LÖS 4a
- 'splurging ... taxi' (l. 12)
- 'about to ... yourself' (l. 14)
- 'steroid angels' (l. 20)

Lernen App: Video on formal/informal register
▸ Getting started 
▸ WOB: B14 Register, pp. 64–65

Language awareness

4 **a** The *style and *register of the text mirrors the fact that the narrator is a young adult. Find examples of *informal style and examine the effect this has.

*** **b** Rewrite some passages using a more formal register and analyse the effect this has. **LÖS 4b**
- I briefly consider spending money on a taxi. (l. 12)
- I am about to get embarrassed. (l. 14)
  → effect: less entertaining and light-hearted

Lernen App: Video on analysing a film
▸ Getting started
▸ SF 41: Analysing films, series and videos, p. 253

Beyond the text

5 In a group, do either task **a** or **b**.

*** **a** Imagine the *novel is made into a movie. Take notes on what the movie might look like. Add information about the cast, landscape, camera work, lighting, etc.
Passagen arbeitsteilig bearbeiten lassen

*** **b** **Challenge** Create a storyboard for the film version of the novel extract. Add initial ideas for short *dialogues or *monologues to appropriate scenes.
DIGI kostenlose Storyboard-Programme online verfügbar

Lernen App: How to create a storyboard

Schwerpunkt-Kompetenz Chapter 4: Listening

Reactivate

English is spoken today by millions of speakers around the world. But the way they speak English may differ greatly. That's because they use different varieties of English.

* 1 Two Englishes

You will certainly have encountered different varieties of English, starting with British and American English. With a partner, collect differences between the different varieties that you know. Think of pronunciation, grammar and/or vocabulary.

2 Why so many Englishes?

With a partner, outline what you know about why English is spoken in so many different countries, both as a native and non-native language.

Language awareness

English is used as a 'native' language, as a 'second official language' or a 'lingua franca', depending on who uses it.

3 Englishes throughout the world

a Read the Info box below and write a definition of the three terms 'native language', 'second official language' and 'lingua franca'.

b Complete the model of world Englishes on the right.

Info

The Englishes

In many countries, while English is not the mother tongue of most of the population, it serves as an important additional language. The historical or practical reasons for this vary, as does the exact role of English in these countries. In countries like the UK, the US or Australia, English is the native language. But there are lots of other countries in which English is not the native tongue, but where it is used as an official language, e.g. in education or government. Examples of this include India, Nigeria, Kenya, Malaysia, or Bangladesh. As a consequence, different forms of English have evolved, which are called varieties. But English is also widely used in other countries where it is not an official language but serves as a lingua franca. English has always been spoken by native speakers with different accents which are unique to specific regions. Whereas differences in pronunciation alone are called accents, regional differences involving vocabulary as well are called dialects. However, many other variants of the language have evolved. They differ from the standard form normally taught at school, in some cases because they are influenced by the first language of the (non-native) speakers. They are sometimes given names such as Singlish (Singaporean English), Chinglish, or Indish. This may sometimes make them difficult for outsiders to understand, but even if they differ from the standard, this does not necessarily mean that they are incorrect.

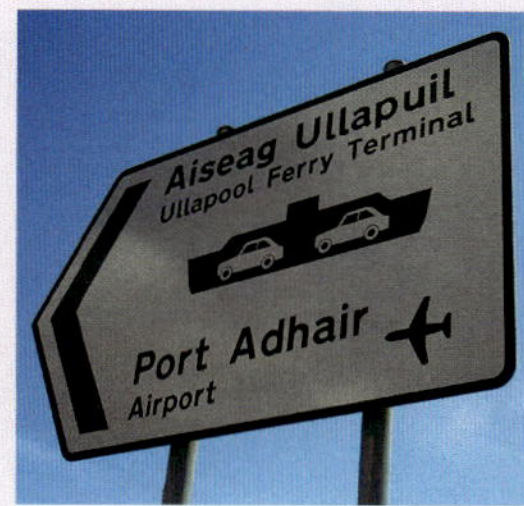

Bilingual ferry and airport sign in Scotland

► SF 6: Essentials: language and study skills, p. 208

► Support, p. 191

LÖS 2
- **historical reasons:** British Empire, colonial history of Great Britain
- **political reasons:** status of the US as a global superpower; use of English as a means of communication for speakers of different languages
- **entertainment industry:** dominance of the American entertainment industry (i.e. Hollywood)
- **linguistic reasons:** English may be easier to learn than some other languages

LÖS 3
- **native language:** language a person has been exposed to from birth or since very early childhood
- **second official language:** officially declared means of communication in a country with speakers of different languages
- **lingua franca:** language that is adopted as a common language between speakers of different languages

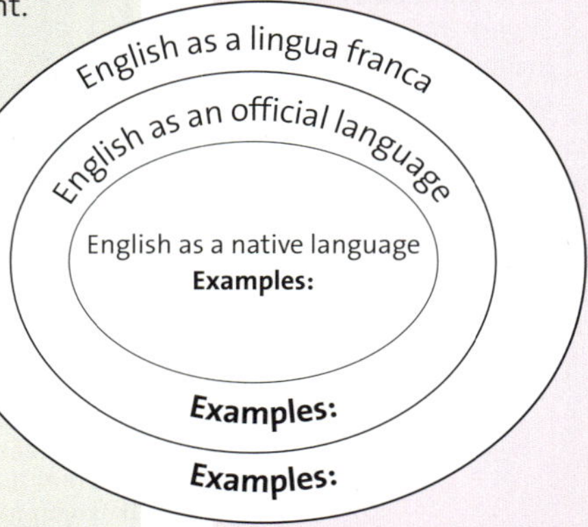

Schwerpunkt-Kompetenz Chapter 4: Listening

► Check
Lernen App: Answer key for task 4a

1. South African English
2. Scottish English
3. Indian English
4. Australian English
5. American English

Info

In our globalised world, it is common for non-native speakers to communicate in **English** in everyday life. Especially **in the workplace**, language barriers between international colleagues are broken down by using English as a lingua franca. Often, the English we hear in offices all around the world sounds different from standard English. Many non-native speakers tend to be influenced by pronunciation and idioms from their mother tongue. It is also not uncommon for misunderstandings to arise between native speakers because of dialects and accents. However, communication in English makes working in international teams or in foreign companies easier.

► SF 25: Analysing cartoons, p. 231

► SF 12: Communicating across cultures, p. 213

4 Identifying different accents

Lernen App: Different accents (02:09 min.)

When encountering Englishes from around the world, you will often have to deal with different accents, i.e. different pronunciation. beim Abspielen darauf achten, dass die Dateinamen für die SuS nicht sichtbar sind

a * Listen to the following five speakers of English who all read the first sentence of George Orwell's novel *1984*. Try to decide which speaker speaks which variety of English from the box on the left.

b * Add the varieties of English to the chart in task **3 b** if they are not already included.

c * Note down noticeable features for each variety you heard. Are there features which make a speaker particularly difficult to understand?
Alternative: Austausch in *buzz activity*

Work with words

5 Understanding different speakers of English

Intercultural communication As a group, do either task **a** or **b**.

a Make a list of useful strategies you can use whenever there are problems understanding your communication partner.

b * **Challenge** What can you do to facilitate communication? Think about sentence structure, choice of words, use of *repetition, your own pronunciation and objects or visualizations etc. Make a short video tutorial in which you give advice to your classmates.

HA 6 Mastering language barriers

Intercultural communication Explain the problem depicted in the *cartoon below.

"You Brits really crack me up. Biscuit instead of cookie and lorry instead of van. So tell me, when you just said 'You're fired', what's it mean in American?"

CartoonStock.com

LÖS 6
possible communication barriers between speakers of different 'Englishes', even between native speakers of English, so severe misunderstandings can occur

► WOB: A1

Practise

7 Asking for clarification

When communicating in international contexts you may face situations in which you will have to ask your partner for clarification. (01:04 min.)

a * Listen to the following dialogue. Describe the communication problem and note down the phrases the first speaker uses to ask for clarification. ► WOB: A6

KV 12: Mastering communication barriers

b Think of other phrases you can use to ask for clarification when you no longer understand the person who is speaking. ► WOB: A5
auch informelle Reaktionen erproben (*What? Huh?*)

LÖS 7b
- You mean…?
- I didn't quite follow, sorry.
- Could you clarify that for me, please?
- If I understand correctly, that means…?

The perks of working abroad

Laura Donnelly

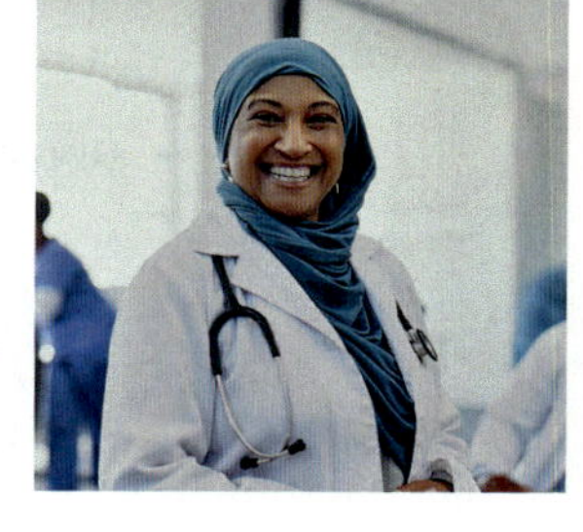

* • Generation X is generally said to have a strong work ethic. Do you think this also applies to your generation? What values are important to you in relation to your future profession? Discuss with a partner.

Many people who work in health care are leaving the UK to find work overseas. But why do so many healthcare professionals leave their home country to start anew on the other side of the world?

Doctors and nurses are abandoning the NHS to work in countries such as Australia, with overseas recruiters targeting those unhappy with pay and conditions in the UK.

Figures from the General Medical Council show the number of medics obtaining a certificate that allows them to work abroad has risen by 25 per cent in a year. Last year, there were 6,950 applications from UK doctors who are registered and licensed, up from 5,576 in 2021 – with around a quarter targeting Australia.

One of the country's largest acute hospitals has just offered 200 jobs after a recent recruitment drive, amid growing concerns about an exodus of healthcare workers from the UK.

It comes after a poll of 4,500 junior doctors in England found one in three intended to work abroad next year, with Australia and New Zealand the most popular destinations.

Senior medics said burnout, as a result of high pressures on NHS hospitals, and frustration with working conditions were among the key factors fuelling the trends. […]

Dr Adrian Boyle, president of the Royal College of Emergency Medicine, said: 'There are high levels of burnout so doctors are reducing their hours or they are leaving; basically we have the most amazing medical training programme for Australia,' he added. […]

St John of God Healthcare, a leading provider of acute hospitals, mental health facilities and community services in Australia, said it has just made 206 offers of employment to UK medical professionals, after a four-week recruitment drive in Britain.

Dani Meinema, group director of nursing and patient experience, said job applicants cited the main motivations as lifestyle, work/life balance, as well as salary and career development opportunities. Doctors and nurses from A&E units, oncology, intensive care, medical units and maternity services are among those recruited in the latest round. It comes as the NHS faces major workforce shortages, with more than 100,000 jobs – one in 10 – now vacant. Ms Meinema said the Australian way of life appealed to many medics who had trained in the UK, and struggled with the long hours and high stress. 'We can offer a different lifestyle, which in many places is centred on the beach, improved work-life balance and the chance to work in hospitals, many of them teaching hospitals that are renowned for acute clinical excellence and highly regarded patient-centred care.'

Lernen App: Generation labels
▶ More info 

Info

The media often refers to the differences between **Generation X** (born 1966–1980), **Generation Y** (born 1981–1995) and **Generation Z** (born 1995–2010). People who belong to these generations have been shaped by very different social developments, which mean they have different life experiences, plans and and priorities.

Annotations

1 **NHS (National Health Service)** Britain's public health service which is paid for by taxes
3 **the General Medical Council (GMC)** an organization keeping a register of qualified doctors
7 **acute (care) hospital** *Akutkrankenhaus*
8 **amid** in the middle of sth.
10 **poll** *(n)* a study in which people are asked for their opinions
26 **A&E unit (Accident and Emergency unit)** *Notaufnahme*
26 **oncology** the study and treatment of cancer
29 **vacant** unoccupied
30 **appeal to sb.** *(v)* interest sb.
33 **renowned** celebrated

Annotations
37 stint a period you spend working somewhere
42 cubicle a small, separate space with curtains or walls around it
54 flourish thrive

Dr Fergus Morris, 34, went from an NHS hospital in Staffordshire to work in Western Australia in 2015 and said he has not looked back. Dr Morris, now an A&E consultant, said he had planned a 12–month stint, but found the working conditions and standards of Australian hospitals, combined with higher pay, and an outdoors lifestyle, far superior to those in Britain. He said: 'Obviously the weather is nice and there's the surf and sea and sand; I thought it would make a break from working in the UK. But then there are so many other things; there are fewer patients waiting, you are able to see patients in a cubicle rather than a corridor. You get the time to examine patients properly, and to treat them, rather than just have to do everything so rapidly, and pass the patient on.' […]'I'm probably earning double what I would in the UK,' said Dr Morris, who works at two hospitals in Perth, including one run by St John of God Healthcare.

Info
The **Shadow Secretary of State for Health and Social Care** is a member of the political party in opposition who monitors the actions of the Secretary of State for Health and Social Care and comes up with alternative policies.

Charlie Massey, GMC chief executive said: 'We know that many doctors are not leaving UK practice because they have fallen out of love with medicine. Instead, they leave because they cannot tolerate the environments in which it is practised. Doctors who may otherwise have had long careers in this country are leaving the UK profession, talented individuals the system cannot afford to lose. At a time when patients face unprecedented waits for care, and healthcare professionals continue to be under immense pressure, we must do more to turn the tide of talented registrants leaving the NHS. If we want more doctors to flourish and grow their careers here in the UK, we must improve their working environments and make workplaces more inclusive and caring.'

Wes Streeting, shadow health secretary, said: 'The fact that so many doctors are seeking to work abroad shows that they have no confidence in this Government's ability to run the NHS. The British taxpayer has paid to train them and a mass exodus is the last thing we need.' […] 736 Wörter

From: 'NHS doctors abandoning UK for better pay and lifestyle overseas', telegraph.co.uk, *07 January 2023*

Comprehension

► WOB: A1
► SF 34: Writing a summary or an outline, p. 244

HA **1** Summarize in your own words why the UK is facing a major shortage of medical professionals.

Analysis

► WOB: A1

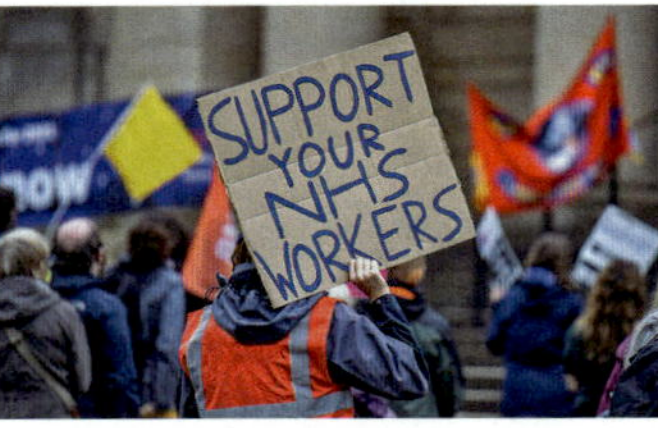

Lernen App: Videos on gerunds and participles
► More language
► WOB: B7 Gerunds, p. 55
► WOB: B13 Participles, pp. 62–63

HA **2** * Examine ways in which the *author emphasizes the seriousness of the problem.
* Analysekategorien vorgeben und arbeitsteilig bearbeiten lassen

Language awareness

3 The text includes several *-ing* forms. These can be gerunds as well as participles.

HA **a** * Scan the text and note down the *-ing* forms.

b * Together with a partner, collect everything you know about those two different forms. Identify one gerund and one participle from the forms you collected in **a**.

c * Speculate why the *author uses so many *-ing* forms.

DIGI Frage mithilfe einer DSGVO-konformen KI beantworten und Ergebnisse mit eigenen Vermutungen vergleichen

Beyond the text

4 You choose Work on task **a** or **b**.

HA **a** *** Writing Comment on the following statement: As there will be a shortage of around 307,000 nurses in clinical care in Germany by 2035 and the number of people in need of care is rising, community service should become compulsory for everyone. ▸ WOB: A2

DIGI Online-Recherche, ggf. auch per KI

b *** Speaking Intercultural communication Research working conditions in the UK. Pay special attention to sick leave, health insurance and paid time off. Compare them to working conditions in Germany. Present the results to your class. ▸ WOB: A4

▸ WOB: B14

HA CT **5** *** Writing You decide to train as a nurse after school. To gain some experience beforehand, you apply for a nursing internship at a New Zealand hospital. Write an application to the teaching hospital in Wellington in which you present yourself as a suitable candidate (cf. Info box on the right). Mention what kind of nursing you can see yourself doing in the future, e.g. working in the intensive care unit, in the paediatric ward, etc., and add why you are interested in the area you have selected. DIGI Abgleich des eigenen Textes mit einem durch KI formulierten Schreiben

6 How would you answer the guiding question of this chapter at this point?

Info

Typically, an **application** consists of a cover letter and a CV. In the former, you present yourself as a suitable candidate for the job. It is therefore important to use formal language and avoid mistakes. Show that you have researched the company and the open position. In the CV it is important to show who you are, what education you have received and what qualifications you have for the job ('Keep it short and simple').

▸ SF 28: Argumentative writing, p. 236
▸ SF 13: Doing research, p. 214
▸ SF 36: Writing an application, p. 247

Text 6

*** Who benefits from voluntourism?

Ossob Mohamud

Fehlerquelle: Aussprache von voluntourism [ˌvɒlənˈtʊərɪzəm]

** • The term *voluntourism* is made up of two individual words. Think about what those two words might be and guess what kinds of activities and trips might be subsumed under this term.

Language help

Voluntourism might be a blend of ... • *Voluntourism* is comprised of ... • I imagine that voluntourists ... • Typcial voluntourist activities could be ... • I guess that voluntourists choose destinations that ...

Lernen App: Portmanteau words

▸ More language
▸ SF 8: Working with dictionaries, p. 209

A very popular form of gap year experience is voluntourism. In the following texts, the pros and cons of voluntourism are examined.

Partner B: Go to p. 191.
Partner A: Read the following text on voluntourism; then do the tasks on p. 113.

I recently came across an interesting article questioning voluntourism and assessing whether it does more harm than good in communities of the global south. It reminded me of my own concerns with 'voluntourism' that originated in my college years in which I had participated in Alternative Spring Breaks. It was considered an alternative to what most college students did on their vaca-

Annotations
thrive flourish
6 **idle** lazy

LÖS **Pre-reading**
blend of 'volunteer' and 'tourism'; travel that gives travellers the chance to contribute money and/or time to projects in their destination country, i.e. medical help, education, building accommodations etc.

Annotations
10 **interspersed** *verteilt*
12 **self-congratulatory** praising yourself
12 **disingenuous** [dɪsɪnˈdʒenjuəs] not sincere
15 **vis-à-vis** [viːz ɑː ˈviː] in relation to
18 **presume** assume
20 **condescending** behaving as though you are superior to or more intelligent than others
21 **benevolent** *(fml)* generous
24 **alleviation** act of making sth. less severe
31 **clumsiness** act of doing sth. not smoothly or carefully
33 **inflate one's ego** enhance one's self-esteem
33 **spruce sth. up** improve the appearance of sth.
34 **genuine** real, authentic
38 **sprout** start to grow
40 **redemption** *(fml)* the act of saving or state of being saved from evil
41 **atone for sth** do sth. to show that you are sorry for sth.
41 **vacuity** lack of purpose
48 **disparate** different in some ways
48 **mutual** shared by two or more people
51 **advocate for sth.** support or argue for sth.
52 **subsidy** a grant or gift of money from a government or authority

tions: spending idle time by the poolside. The university-organised trips sent students to spend a week in disadvantaged and poverty-stricken communities to volunteer. This could take the form of teaching English at the local school, assisting in building and beautifying new homes for residents, or environmental cleanups. Interspersed throughout the week were also touristy getaways and souvenir shopping. Although I had memorable and rewarding moments, I could never shake off the feeling that it was all a bit too self-congratulatory and disingenuous.

Voluntourism almost always involves a group of idealistic and privileged travelers who have vastly different socio-economic statuses vis–à–vis those they serve. They often enter these communities with little or no understanding of the locals' history, culture, and ways of life. All that is understood is the poverty and the presumed neediness of the community, and for the purposes of volunteering, that seems to be enough. In my own experiences – also highlighted by the author of the article – this has led to condescending and superficial relationships that transform the (usually western) volunteer into a benevolent giver and the community members into the ever grateful receivers of charity. It makes for an extremely uncomfortable dynamic in which one begins to wonder if these trips are designed more for the spiritual fulfillment of the volunteer rather than the alleviation of poverty.

I couldn't help feeling ashamed at the excessive praise and thanks we received from locals and those on the trip alike. I cringed as we took complimentary photos with African children whose names we didn't know. We couldn't even take full credit for building the houses because most of the work had already been done by community members. In fact, if anything we slowed down the process with our inexperience and clumsiness. And how many schools in the west would allow amateur college students to run their English classes for a day? What had I really done besides inflate my own ego and spruce up my resume? I had stormed into the lives of people I knew nothing about, I barely engaged with them on a genuine level, and worst of all, I then claimed that I had done something invaluable for them all in a matter of five days (of which most of the time was spent at hotel rooms, restaurants, and airports).

An entire industry has sprouted out of voluntourism as it increases in popularity, possibly equal to the increase in global inequality. As the gap between rich and poor widens, [...] [t]he developing world has become a playground for the redemption of privileged souls looking to atone for global injustices by escaping the vacuity of modernity and globalisation.

But does this address the root institutional and structural causes of the problem? I do not mean to deny, across the board, the importance of the work voluntourists do. Volunteers in developing countries fund and deliver great programmes that would not happen otherwise, but the sustainability and the effectiveness of the approach is what I question. Time and energy would be better spent building real solidarity between disparate societies based on mutual respect and understanding. Instead of focusing on surface symptoms of poverty, volunteers and the organisations that recruit them should focus on the causes that often stem from an unjust global economic order. [...] How about having volunteers advocate for their home country to change aggressive foreign and agricultural policies (such as subsidy programmes)? This might seem unrealistic but the idea is to get volunteers to understand their own (direct or indirect) role in global poverty. The idea is to get volunteers truly invested in ending poverty, and not simply to feel better about themselves. 674 Wörter

From: 'Beware the 'voluntourists' doing good', theguardian.com, *13 February 2013*

► WOB: A1

Comprehension

HA CT **1** Summarize Ossob Mohamud's critique of voluntourism for your partner. Take notes only.
Liste, Mindmap, Cluster …

Analysis

► SF 34: Writing a summary or an outline, p. 244
► WOB: A1

2 Examine the effect the personal example has in Mohamud's article.

LÖS 2
- personal experience adds credibility to Mohamud's argument
- relates something she has seen herself and reflects on her experiences, draws conclusions and contextualizes them

Language awareness

► Support, p. 193
► WOB: A1

HA **3** The *author uses quite a number of sophisticated expressions such as 'condescending' (l. 20). Find further examples of sophisticated expressions and think about the effect Mohamud might want to achieve by using them.

SuS darauf hinweisen, dass Text B sich auf Text A bezieht.
Für Aufgabe 5 ist eine Sicherung der Argumente sinnvoll.

Beyond the text

Lernen App: Video on having a discussion

► Getting started
► SF 46: Having a discussion, p. 264
► WOB: A5 Speaking – discussion, pp. 18–19

4 *** Present your findings from **1–3** to your partner. Include especially arguments in favour of and against voluntourism.

5 You choose Gather relevant information from Ossob Mohamud's article, then work on task **a** or **b**.

a *** Speaking Discuss the pros and cons of voluntourism in a double circle using the information you have gathered so far. Partners A form the inner circle and partners B the outer circle. Partners A argue in favour of voluntourism, Partners B against it. Take three turns. After the third turn, come to a joint conclusion.

b In groups of four, discuss the question 'Who benefits from voluntourism?' on a placemat. Write your conclusion in the middle of the placemat.

DIGI digitale Durchführung der *Placemat activity* möglich

HA CT **6** ** Add the headline *voluntourism* to your mind map from p. 92 and fill in the positive and negative aspects that you collected for your discussion.

HA CT **7** *** Think back to the guiding question of this chapter. How would you answer it at this point?

Visualisierung des *double circle*, falls Methode noch nicht bekannt. L sagt an, welcher Kreis beginnt und wie der Kreis sich dreht.

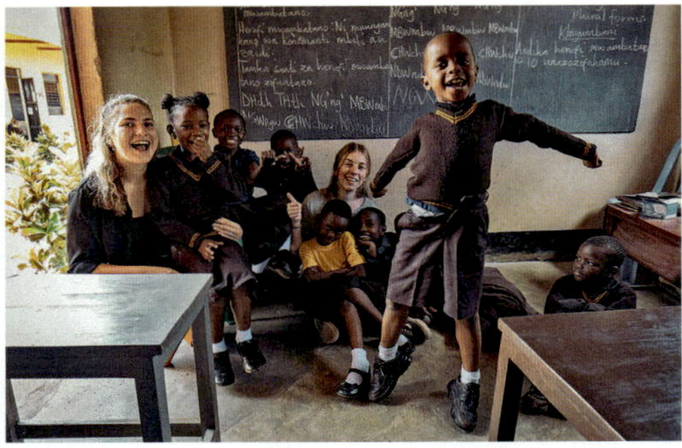

Experiences of a former voluntourist

- Before listening, talk with a partner about possible experiences you might have while doing voluntary work in disadvantaged and poverty-stricken countries.

You are going to hear the account of Pippa Biddle, an American former voluntourist who helped build a library in an orphanage in Tanzania a year before she graduated from high school. She talks about her experiences on the BBC World Service's Business Daily programme.

Alternative: SuS spekulieren über Erfahrungen der Person im Foto

► More info
Lernen App: The BBC World Service

► SF 39: Essentials: listening and viewing, p. 252

► Check
Lernen App: Answer key for task 1

► WOB: A6 Listening, pp. 20–23

Lernen App: Interview with Pippa Biddle (03:55 min.)

Comprehension

1 a CT Listening While listening to the interview for the first time decide which of the following statements best describes the general content of the audio.

1 On the whole, Pippa Biddle is positive about voluntourism but is critical of her organisation because it did not choose the right project and only had a financial interest.

2 Pippa Biddle wants to warn other voluntourists that they may take away local people's jobs, especially when they do construction work.

3 Pippa Biddle is of the opinion that voluntourism can never be a good option because voluntourists are not skilled enough and the organizations have a financial interest.

4 Pippa Biddle thinks that if voluntourists were better trained, they could offer skills support and thus benefit the local communities.

LÖS 1a: 3

b CT (02:02 min.) Listening Listen to the interview again and note down the answers to the questions below.

1 When going running, what did Pippa find out about the Tanzanian workers?

2 Why, in hindsight, is Pippa critical of her school's approach to voluntourism? Fehlerquelle: Aussprache von *hindsight* [ˈhaɪndsaɪt]

3 What is the difference between voluntourism and skilled aid work, according to Pippa, and which example does she give?

4 What is Pippa's suggested alternative to voluntourism?

LÖS 1b
1 The workers arrived early for work every day to secretly rebuild and correct what the volunteers had constructed, without the volunteers noticing. They were not late because they didn't care but because they needed a break.
2 They didn't want to adress the problem because they were focussed on their own students' needs and how they would benefit from the trip instead of the local community they were supposed to help.
3 Skilled aid workers, such as Doctors Without Borders, are highly trained. They work to help local people to develop necessary skills, whereas voluntourism overlooks this aspect. Voluntourism organisations are business organisations so they focus more on their financial gain.
4 People should focus on spending money locally and boost the local economy as normal tourists.

Beyond the text

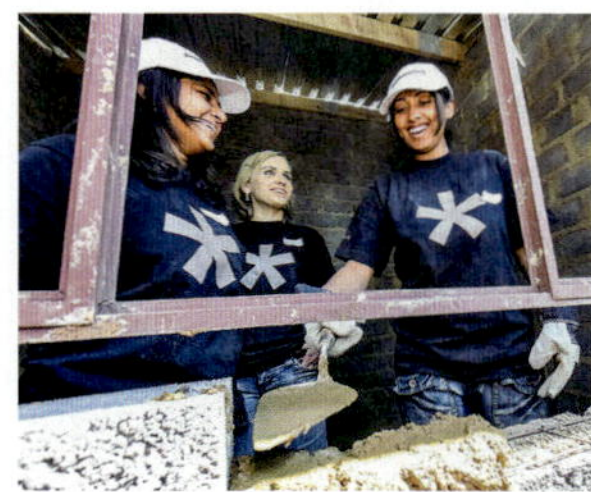

HA **2** * Go back to your *spidergram from page 92 and add aspects and examples that are mentioned by Pippa Biddle that you did not think of.

HA CT **3** *** Write a short response to Pippa Biddle's claim on her social media account that tourism is the only solution for unskilled travellers to 'give back'.

HA CT **4** * Discuss with your partner whether the criticism voiced in the interview has changed your view of going abroad after school. ► WOB: A5

HA CT **5** *** Think back to the guiding question of this chapter. How would you answer it at this point?

Alternative: SuS positionieren sich im Raum je nach Zustimmung/Ablehnung zu dem geäußerten *claim*

When the tourists flew in

Cecil Rajendra

► More info
Lernen App: Cecil Rajendra

* • Look at the two pictures and note down your spontaneous reaction to them. Then share your thoughts with a partner.

► SF 20: Reading and understanding poetry, p. 224

► WOB: A12 Poetry, pp. 38–39

The Finance Minister said
'It will boost the Economy
the dollars will flow in.'

The Minister of Interior said
'It will provide full
& varied employment
for all the indigenes.'

The Ministry of Culture said
'It will enrich our life ...
contact with other cultures
must surely
improve the texture of living.'

The man from the Hilton said
'We will make you
a second Paradise;
for you, it is the dawn
of a glorious new beginning.'

When the tourists flew in
our island people
metamorphosed into
a grotesque carnival
– a two-week sideshow

When the tourists flew in
our men put aside
their fishing nets
to become waiters
our women became whores

When the tourists flew in
what culture we had
flew out of the window
we traded our customs
for sunglasses and pop
we turned sacred ceremonies
into ten-cent peep shows

When the tourists flew in
local food became scarce
prices went up
but our wages stayed low

When the tourists flew in
we could no longer
go down to our beaches
the hotel manager said
'Natives defile the sea-shore'

When the tourists flew in
the hunger & the squalor
were preserved
as a passing pageant
for clicking cameras
– a chic eye-sore!

When the tourists flew in
we were asked
to be 'side-walk ambassadors'
to stay smiling & polite
to always guide
the 'lost' visitor ...
Hell, if we could only tell them
where we really want them to go!

245 Wörter

From: Bones and Feathers, *1978*

Annotations

7 **indigene** *Eingeborene/r*
13 **Hilton** a hotel chain
20 **metamorphose** change into sth. completely different
21 **grotesque** strange in a way that is unpleasant or offensive
27 **whore** *(derog)* a female prostitute
31 **custom** tradition; an accepted way of behaving or doing things in a community
36 **scarce** rare
43 **defile sth.** make sth. unclean
45 **squalor** dirty and unpleasant conditions
46 **preserve sth.** keep sth. as it is
47 **pageant** a public entertainment in the form of a procession or an outdoor performance of scenes from history
49 **eye-sore** an unpleasant or ugly building or object
52 **ambassador** a person who represents or promotes a country abroad

► WOB: A12

► Support (task 2), p. 193

► Getting started (task 2)

Info

There are many ideas that rethink different areas of **tourism in relation to environmental impacts**. For a start, the EU Commission has given away 70,000 Interrail passes to 18-year-olds. The train tickets allowed them to take train journeys in large parts of Europe within 30 days. There are also eco-travel portals that can help you travel more sustainably. The platforms select holiday accommodations according to certain criteria, including certificates in tourism (e.g. EU sustainability label), guest ratings (in terms of sustainability) and other sustainability criteria (e.g. green electricity, organic food, waste prevention).

Comprehension

1 Make a table in which you note down in the left column all the promises made before the tourists arrived, what actually happened in the right column, and the conclusion drawn by the locals below. Use your own words.

Lernen App: Video on stylistic devices
Overview of stylistic devices

Analysis

HA 2 Analyse the use of the *poem's structure and *stylistic devices to highlight the contrast between the promises and the reality of tourism.

3 The *tone of the poem is formal, except for one expletive. Identify the *verse and examine the effect this switch in tone has on the reader.

LÖS 3 The expletive 'Hell' (v. 56) shows the real emotions the locals hide behind their smiles for the sake of tourism and money. The use of a swearword underscores their anger.

Language awareness

4 The adverbial clause 'When the tourists flew in' is used repeatedly. Explain the effect this has on the reader. Replace as many of these *repetitions with a different sentence conveying the same meaning and analyse the effect this has.

► WOB: A5

Beyond the text

5 Speaking Intercultural communication Imagine you are a reporter at a press conference with the Finance Minister, the Culture Minister and the 'man from the Hilton'. In a hot-seat discussion, confront them with the realities of their promises. DIF Stärkere SuS entkräften in den Rollen der *officials* die Gegenargumente der *locals*.

CT 6 Speaking Discuss possibilities to make tourism more sustainable (cf. Info box on the left). Present your results.

DIGI Online-Recherche zur Vorbereitung

Chapter task

► SF 36: Writing an application, p. 247

Info

Don't forget to ...

- think about why you are suitable for this opportunity.
- mention the kind of volunteering work/ area of study you are applying for.
- bear in mind the criteria for a good application.
- make your application stand out.

video 1: 00:53 min.
video 2: 00:20 min.

You want to go abroad after school, but you are not yet sure of what what to do exactly. During your research, you come across an advertisement from IVHQ, an organization that arranges volunteer work abroad. You also find a field report from a German student who did a gap year in the US.

Lernen App: Ad and field report (videos)

1 Listen to Simon Birkenhead, Chief Executive at IVHQ, and Pascal, the German student at the Green River College in Boston. Choose the audio that you find more appealing based on whether you would prefer to work or study abroad. To be able to choose wisely: Möglichkeit geben, Videos während der Bearbeitung erneut anzusehe

- Note down the relevant information for each opportunity.
- Determine which opportunity best fits your skills and interests. ► WOB: A6

2 You choose Do either task **a** or **b**.

HA **a** Writing Prepare a convincing application for your preferred overseas experience by writing a CV and drafting the main part of your cover letter. ► WOB: B14

HA **b** Apply for your preferred overseas experience with a creative application video.

▸ WOB: A8

Approaching a film

1 a ∗ **Think** Make a list of the three films or series you like best and for each one, note down what you like best about it.

b ∗ **Pair** In a 'milling around activity' meet your classmates and talk about your favourite films or series and the reasons why you put them on your shortlist.

c **Share** Report the found criteria for good films back to the class.

LÖS 1c Agree together on the five most important criteria.
gripping story • action • strong characters you can identify with • romance • tension

Viewing and analysing a film

You are going to watch a short film called Run Rabbit *(2018).* (18:58 min.)

Lernen App: Video on analysing a film
▸ Getting started

▸ SF 39: Essentials: listening and viewing, p. 252
▸ SF 41: Analysing films, series and videos, p. 253

2 Based on the title, speculate about the *plot of the film.

3 The first part of a film usually serves to establish the situation and the main *characters. Lernen App: First 30 seconds of the film (video)

a Viewing Watch the first 30 seconds of the short film. Note down what you can see and what you can hear.
DIF visuelle und akustische Eindrücke aufteilen und die Notizen so reduzieren, ggf. Film zunächst ohne Bild abspielen

b In groups of three, exchange the emotions the *scene evokes in you. Collect the means used to trigger these reactions.

LÖS 3b
- threat, fear, stress, sympathy for the boys
- means: sounds (outside sounds, the boys' distressed noises), darkness in the room

c On the basis of your notes, what do you think the film will be about? Share your ideas with the class.

4 ∗∗∗ Viewing Now you are going to watch the end of the first scene until the title appears. What is the situation depicted in the scene? Explain Tarek's reaction.

Lernen App: First scene (video)

LÖS 4
New Year's celebration in New Zealand (accent), seems to have triggered memories of war-like situations in the boys

5 ∗ Viewing Watch the rest of the short film. In a *quick write note down your first reaction to the short film.

Lernen App: Rest of the film (video)

6 a After having watched the whole short film finish the sentences to summarize it.

1 Tarek is a refugee who is now ...
2 In his host family he struggles with ...
3 When he meets some local teenagers ...
4 At a sheep shearing station he ...
5 His host father finds out that ...
6 In the local Easter rabbit hunt, Tarek ...
7 After having shot three rabbits ...
8 Tarek leaves the green and ...
9 At the end of the film ...

▸ Check
Lernen App: Answer key for task 6a

∗ b Go back to task **1** and your speculations about the *plot. Did they prove true? How do you explain the title of the film?

∗ **7** Do some quick research on the Easter rabbit hunt in New Zealand. Using this information, explain the killing of rabbits shown in the short film.

▸ SF 13: Doing research, p. 214

HA **8** ∗∗∗ Writing Write down a short character profile for Tarek, collecting all the information you can get from the film.

▸ SF 31: Writing a character profile, p. 241

DIF Kategorien vorgeben, z. B. *general information, behaviour/character traits, emotions/ideals*

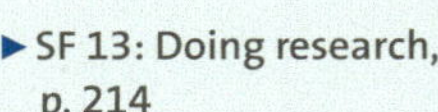

DIGI Unter dem Suchbegriff *Central Otago Great Easter Bunny Hunt* finden die SuS treffgenaue Informationen.

► WOB: A8

Film techniques and their effects

The fact that Tarek and his brother are strangers in New Zealand is illustrated cinematographically throughout the film. These cinematic techniques are going to be the focus of analysis in the following.

HA **9** *** The camera work determines what we see in a film. To make yourself familiar with some of the key terms of camera work, match the terms and their explanations (A–J) with the film stills (1–10).

- **A** **Extreme close-up:** shows a small object or part of an object in detail that is relevant to the story.
- **B** **Close-up:** gives a full view, usually of a human face, to reveal emotions.
- **C** **Medium shot:** shows the upper body part of one or more persons to display facial expressions and gestures.
- **D** **Full shot:** gives a full view of a person's body and not much else.
- **E** **Long shot:** provides a view from a distance to establish a *setting (establishing shot).
- **F** **High-angle shot:** the subject or object is seen from above (camera looking down) thus appearing smaller (and often less important).
- **G** **Low-angle shot:** the person or object is seen from a low-level position (camera looking up) thus making what is shown appear more important.
- **H** **Eye-level shot:** the camera is positioned at about the same level as a person or object that is shown.
- **I** **Over-the-shoulder shot:** the camera is placed just behind one person so that their shoulder is in the frame while you are looking at other people or other action that is taking place.
- **J** **Bird's eye perspective:** an extreme form of high-angle shot (e.g. taken from a helicopter, a drone, or an airplane).

► Check
Lernen App: Answer key for task 9

LÖS 9
A8 B5 C9 D2 E1 F3 G10 H6 I4 J7

1

2

3

4

5

6

7

8

9

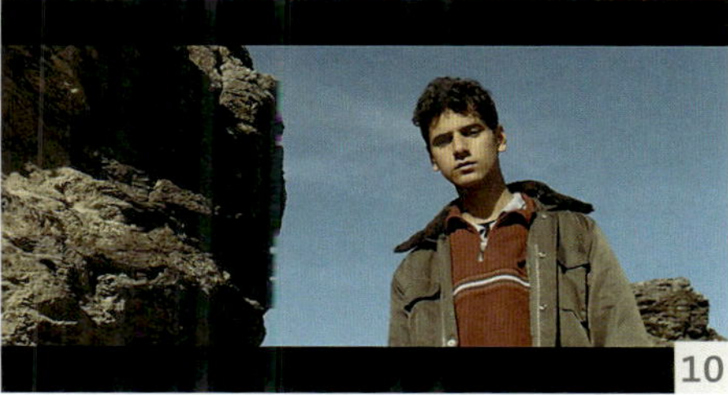
10

▸ WOB: A8

- Lernen App: 'Prayer scene' (video)
- Hinweis, dass bei der Analyse filmischer Mittel deren Wirkung erklärt werden muss

10 *** Viewing Watch the 'prayer scene' and collect the means used to portray Tarek and his brother as strangers in the host family.

11 Viewing Work with a partner and watch the 'dinner scene'.

a *** Analyse, how Tarek's emotional state is presented in the 'dinner scene'. **Partner A** focuses on camera work, **Partner B** focuses on the sound level (cf. Info box on the right).

b * Present your results to your partner and discuss, the extent to which the visual and the acoustic level complement and/or contrast with each other.

Language help

Tense/joyful/melancholy/aggressive/intimate/hectic • loud/high/low/deep/shrill voices • shouting/whispering/screaming/chattering people • mellow piano/violin music • low background music • fading sounds • gradually getting louder • deafening noise • ear-splitting/muffled sounds • subdued/hushed voices • hardly perceptible • a sharp contrast between the pictures and the sound • a voice offscreen • the sound mirrors ... • the sound provides a contrast to ... to fit ...

Info

Different kinds of **sound-effects** can contribute towards the overall effect of a film. They can ...
- illustrate and support the message of the sequence in question, or they could provide a stark contrast, e.g. in order to confuse or mislead the viewer or to make the audience more attentive.
- be used to let the audience find out more about the place, time and cultural setting of the film's story.
- evoke and intensify the viewer's feelings while watching, also creating tension or relief.
- structure the film by either illustrating breaks or by highlighting the continuity of the action.

12 Work with your partner from assignment 11.

a *** Viewing Watch the scene in which Tarek meets the local teenagers and examine how Tarek's role as an outsider is conveyed cinematographically.

Hinweis, dass Partner A auf *sound level* und Partner B auf *camera work* fokussieren soll

Lernen App: Scene with Tarek

▸ WOB: A8

*** b Present your results to your partner and agree on the three most relevant cinematic devices, also specifying their effects on the viewer.

Film technique	Effects on viewer
...	...

KV 13: Viewing grid (Sheep-shearing scene)

DIGI *viewing grid* über ein kollaboratives Tool gemeinsam ergänzen

Lernen App: 'Sheep sharing scene' (video)

When working with films it makes sense to use a viewing grid in order to note down and structure your observations. For the following scene, you will work with this type of viewing grid.

13 Work in groups of four.

a *** Viewing Watch the 'sheep shearing scene'. Analyse how Tarek feels in this scene and how this emotional state is conveyed cinematographically. Copy the viewing grid below and decide which group member will focus on which aspect.

b ** Exchange your findings and note down your partners' results in your own viewing grid. Be prepared to present a short summary of your combined analysis in class.

Viewing grid			
Camera range	Effect created	Camera movement & camera angle	Effect created
...	...	...	...
Sound	Effect created	*Setting/colours/ lighting	Effect created
...	...	...	...
Overall effect created in this scene using cinematic devices: ...			

HA c * Tarek does not converse with the other sheep shearers, as he cannot speak English. Write down what he would say if he could make himself understood before leaving the sheep shearing station.

Lernen App: 'Easter rabbit hunt' (video)

KV 14: Viewing grid (The Easter rabbit hunt)

14 *** Viewing Watch the scene depicting the 'Easter rabbit hunt'. Note down how Tarek's inner development is portrayed in the scene. Focus on camera range, camera perspective, sound and editing. Remember to also note down the overall effect created in this scene by all these cinematic devices. You may create a new viewing grid for this task.

Alternative: lineare Sicherung der kombinierten filmischen Mittel

Taking a closer look

15 You choose | Writing | Do either task **a** or **b**.

HA **a** *** Write an analysis of the 'Easter rabbit hunt scene', explaining how Tarek's inner conflicts are portrayed cinematographically.

HA **b** Write Tarek's interior monologue after having rescued the rabbit. Bear in mind what you have deduced about his former experiences and his background.

Lernen App: 'Easter rabbit hunt' (video)

Film lässt biografische Hintergründe im Dunkeln → Antworten sind Vermutungen

Info

Forced migration

Whereas a gap year, a semester or job in a foreign country provide you with mostly positive, sometimes luxurious chances, there are situations where people have to leave their home area or homeland involuntarily. This is called forced migration or forced displacement. Reasons include threats from the government or terrorist groups, environmental disasters, religious or ethnic persecution, famine or drought. So it is due to forces beyond their control that refugees and internally-displaced persons (IDPs) have to move either within their home countries or between countries. In the past decade the global refugee crisis has more than doubled in scope, meaning that 1.2% of the global population have been in search of a better, safer life away from home. Many of these people are refugees from countries like Eritrea, Somalia, Sudan, Afghanistan, Ukraine or Syria.

*** **1** What information from the Info box is reflected in the film 'Run Rabbit'? Consider possible reasons for the migration and how it influenced the characters' perspective of their new surroundings.

LÖS **1**
Tarek might have come from a country in war, from a place where he was persecuted or where people suffered for different reasons (poverty, environmental catastrophe, etc.). He can use a gun, which suggests former experiences with violence or a need to protect himself. He and his brother do not speak English and are very young, which suggests involuntary displacement rather than going abroad to find a new life.

Fehlerquelle: Aussprache von *drought* [draʊt] (Z. 6)

Beyond the film

► WOB: A5

16 Drawing on your impressions of the film, discuss how you could try to help Tarek and other migrants cope with their new surroundings.

SuS mit Migrationsgeschichte können ggf. individuelle Erfahrungen mit der Lerngruppe teilen. Um die Aufgabe zu entpersonalisieren, kann alternativ auf die Jugendlichen im Film fokussiert werden: *What could help Tarek to cope with his new surroundings?*

► SF 13: Doing research, p. 214

17 You choose | Do either task **a** or **b**.

HA **a** *** Research how other films, poems or songs depict people who have to go abroad involuntarily. How effectively do they use *cinematic devices or *stylistic devices to convey their message? Be prepared to present your findings to the class. ► WOB: A8

DIGI Suchbegriffe: *refugee poems and songs, films about refugee experience*

b *** HA CT In a world of forced migration is it justifiable to travel the world, do a gap year or spend a semester abroad for one's own personal fulfilment? Comment on the issue.

► WOB: A2

► WOB: A8 Viewing, pp. 26–27

Chapter 5
Global Challenges – Opportunities or Disaster for the Blue Planet?

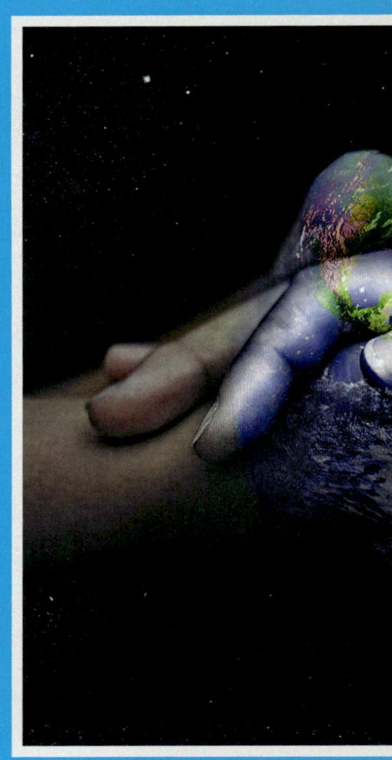

PA möglich — DIF als *scaffolding* gesammeltes Vokabular bereitstellen

▶ SF 23: Analysing visuals, p. 228

DIGI Sammlung über ein digitales Tool empfehlenswert

HA CT **1** a * Choose one of the two pictures and write down what comes into your mind when you look at it.

b * Find someone who has chosen the other picture. Tell each other about your reaction to the picture you have chosen. Name reasons.

fächerübergreifende Bezüge zu Politik und Geografie

DIGI Ranking mithilfe eines digitalen Tools möglich. SuS sollen priorisieren, so dass der Fokus auf den Lösungsansätzen liegt.

HA CT **2** a * **Think** What would you consider the most prominent challenges your generation is facing?

HA CT b * **Pair** Form small groups in which you compare and discuss your ideas. Agree on the five greatest challenges and rank them in order of importance.

HA CT c * **Share** Present your findings to the class. Agree on steps that could be taken to deal with the challenges of the future.

▶ More language Lernen App: Opportunity or burden – helpful words and phrases

DIGI erstes Meinungsbild durch Abstimmung mit einem digitalen Tool oder durch Positionierung im Raum

HA **3** a *** A world of opportunity – or a crushing burden: Which of these phrases best describes your attitude to the world you live in? Make notes so that you can present your views.

CT b * Speaking Find someone who has chosen the opposite point of view from yours. Each of you presents their viewpoint in a short speech in front of your class.

CT c * Discuss the arguments you have just heard. Which side do you find more convincing? Die Abstimmung kann am Ende des Kapitels wiederholt werden.

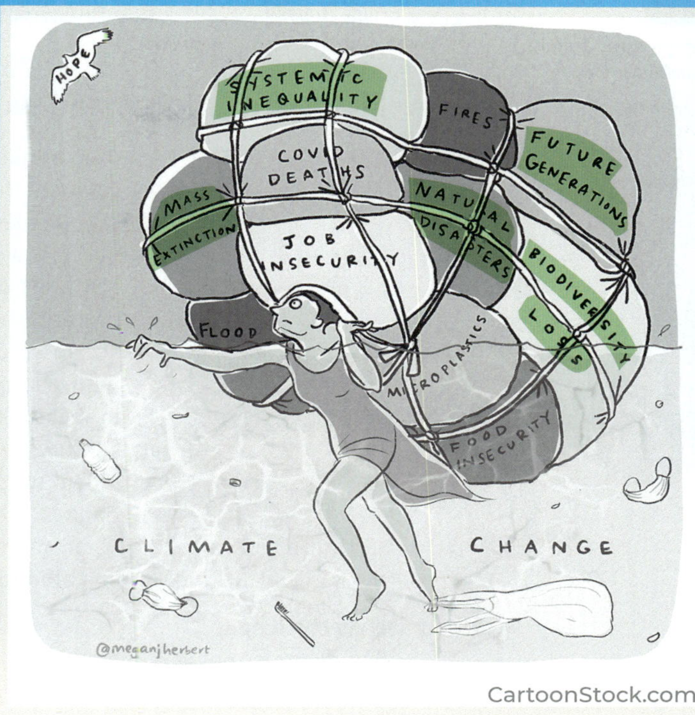

4 a * Take a look at the Chapter map below. With a partner, speculate about how **CT** the chapter might answer the guiding question in relation to the keywords surrounding it.

Die *guiding question* des Kapitels wird hier mit der *Chapter map* eingeführt und auf den Seiten 135 und 145 erneut reflektiert und beantwortet.

CT b * Do you think that there are concrete solutions for the problems of tomorrow? Share your fears and hopes with your partner.

DIGI Abstimmung über digitales Tool möglich

Die SuS reflektieren das Thema auf einer emotionalen Ebene *(hopes and fears)*.

Chapter map

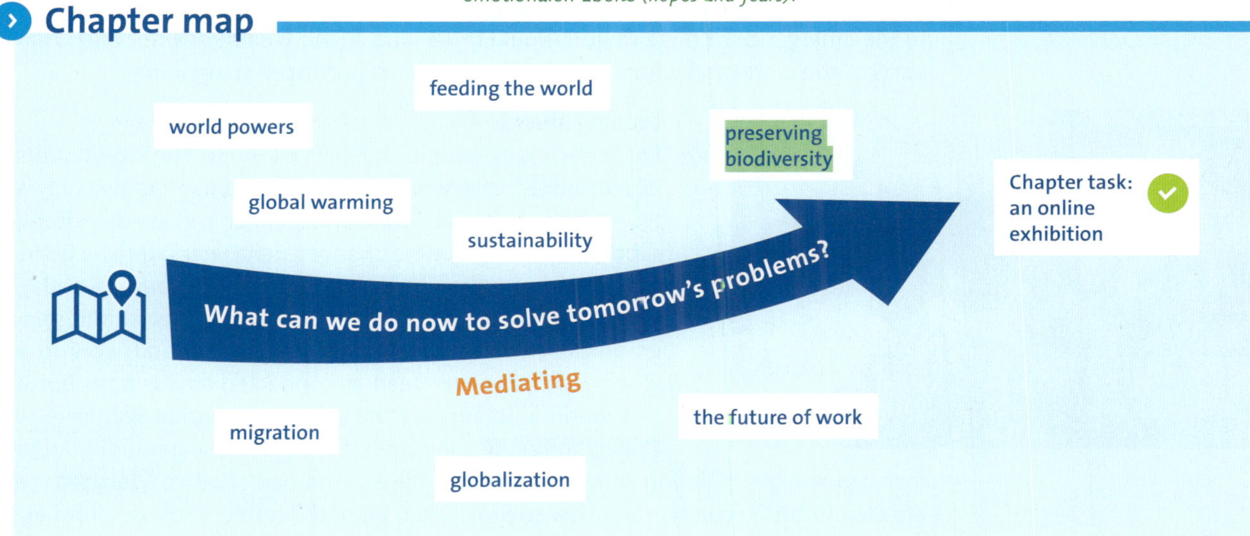

Lernen App: Useful vocabulary for the chapter

► More language

Lernen App: Living in a globalized world (00:03:36)

Living in a globalized world

Our shrinking world

For more than 2000 years, our world has steadily been growing smaller. Migration, trade, and intercultural exchange have always been the motors of human progress. In recent centuries, improvements in shipbuilding, navigation, transportation and communication have accelerated this process and made our world more connected than ever before in human history. We can fly from London to New York in less time than it took to travel from London to Birmingham in the 18th century. Internet connections put the world at our fingertips, global supply chains bring raw materials and manufactured goods to consumers all around the world, and skilled workers move to the country that offers the best working conditions. Opportunities for living, studying and working abroad are greater today than they have ever been.

New challenges

This progress has come at a price. Improvements in medical care and sanitation have led to rapid population growth. Eight billion people and the unjust distribution of resources place a strain on our ability to feed, house and educate everyone. Energy from fossil fuels produces carbon dioxide, and CO_2 emissions are responsible for climate change. The resulting floods, droughts and heat waves are often deadly and provoke mass migration of people fleeing from hunger and death. The exploitation of natural resources leads to the decline of biodiversity when species lose their natural habitat, and it may be responsible for the outbreak of global pandemics. Globalization in the economic sense can empower individuals to take advantage of new opportunities, but it has also led to the emergence of huge multinational firms who create wealth only for particular parts of the world and whose global influence is often difficult to regulate.

Fehlerquelle: Aussprache von *drought* [draʊt] (Z. 27)

Fehlerquelle: Aussprache von *exploitation* [ˌeksplɔɪˈteɪʃn] (Z. 28)

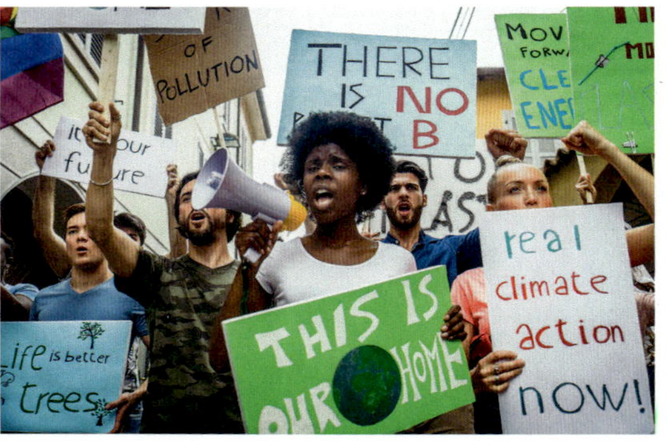

Looking ahead

For some young people starting out in life, the world offers opportunities that would have sounded like fantasy only a few decades ago. A Swedish teenager refuses to attend school to protest climate change, and a year later she is the figurehead of a worldwide movement. The youth of today, especially those who have the privilege of social and geographical mobility, have the chance to live and work in a world that has never been as connected as it is now. But if this world is to survive, the young generation will have to find solutions to the problems they have inherited: how to feed a growing population without destroying the environment, how to deal with the effects of climate change, and how to protect our planet's limited resources from exploitation and destruction.

HA CT **1 * Main ideas** arbeitsteilige Bearbeitung in Kleingruppen möglich

Copy and complete the outline below:

I. Our shrinking world
  a. Transportation
  b. ...

II. ...

LÖS 1
I. Our shrinking world: **a.** Transportation **b.** Flow of information and goods **c.** Work migration
II. New challenges: **a.** Population growth **b.** Strained resources **c.** Wealth gap
III. Looking ahead: **a.** Chances for the young generation **b.** Problems to tackle

2 Reflect

Lernen App: Answer key for task 2a ▶ Check

HA CT **a *** Find the matching word or phrase in the text for each of the following:

1 *Lieferketten*
2 *Arbeitsbedingungen*
3 *Rohstoff*
4 *einen Vorgang beschleunigen*
5 *eine Möglichkeit bieten*

HA CT **b *** Create a quiz similar to the one above. Give it to your partner and do the quiz your partner has prepared. DIGI Quiz digital oder per KI als Wortsuchrätsel erstellen

DIF Wörterbuch nutzen

HA CT **3 * Word formation**

Lernen App: Answer key for task 3 ▶ Check

Copy the table below and fill in the missing words that can be formed from the nouns from the text. Use a dictionary if necessary.

▶ SF 8: Working with dictionaries (print and online), p. 209

Hinweis auf Lerntechniken für Vokabular (Wortfamilien)

Noun	Verb	Adjective
challenge		
destruction		
migration		
movement		
population		
progress		

Info

New words are created through the process of **word formation**. This can, for example, be done through compounding, in which two or more different words are added to create a new one (tooth + brush = toothbrush). Another process, derivation, involves adding a suffix or prefix to an already existing word (dark + -ness = darkness). Conversion is when a word changes its word class ('It was a good read.' / 'She is reading.'). There are other processes like blending (motor + hotel = motel), abbreviation (veterinary -> vet) or clipping (advertisement = ad) through which new words are formed.

4 Chunk it!

zusätzliche Übung: KV 15: Collocations and phrasal verbs

Vokabeln mit zugehöriger Präposition als *chunks* lernen

HA CT **a** In each of the following sentences, a preposition is missing. Consult the text again if you are unsure. Fill in the preposition.

Lernen App: Video about chunks

1 Our lifestyle has come ... a high price.
2 We must find a solution ... the problem soon.
3 There have never been more opportunities ... living abroad.
4 Improvements ... health care have contributed to population growth.
5 We will have to deal ... the consequences of our lifestyle.
6 Rain forests must be protected ... further destruction.

b Choose three *collocations from task **a** and write a sentence with each of them. Swap exercises with your partner and give each other feedback.

▶ Getting started

▶ Check Lernen App: Answer key for task 4a

▶ WOB: B8 Collocations with prepositions, p. 56

DIGI Online-Wörterbuch nutzen

HA CT **5 Speaking about connectedness**

Lernen App: Video on preparing and giving a speech ▶ Getting started

Speaking Does the world need more connectedness, or perhaps less? Make notes on your ideas, and then present them to your class in a brief speech.

▶ SF 44: Preparing and giving a speech, p. 262

DIGI Reden aufnehmen DIF alternativ Podcasts erstellen

Lernen App: Video on how to create a flow chart

► Getting started

Globalization: How does it work? Alex Gray

- **Partner B:** Go to p. 194. **Partner A:** Read the text in the Info box below and take notes.
- HA Share the most important points with your partner. Together, note down the most crucial developments in the British Empire and the United States that contributed to globalization in a form that you prefer, e.g. a table, a mind map, a flow chart, etc.

DIGI digitale Mindmaps oder Pinnwände zur Sammlung der Ergebnisse nutzen

Seizure of the Greek islands of Delos and Mykonos by the British

fächerübergreifender Bezug (Geschichte, Geografie)

Info

The first truly global empire

Empires that stretch across more than one continent have existed for thousands of years. The Chinese, the Greeks under Alexander, and the Arabs, for example, all created cultural and trading empires that extended far beyond their land of origin. From the 16th century onwards, a small island on the western edge of Europe rose to become the centre of the largest empire in the world. Living on an island meant that the English had always been a seafaring people. By 1600, England had become the leading maritime power in Europe. British merchants, protected by a powerful navy, engaged in trade in the Middle East, Asia and Africa. As the century progressed, Britain founded colonies across the globe, especially in India, Africa and North America. These colonies were plundered and exploited to provide raw materials for British factories. Where labour was scarce, such as in North America, British landowners enslaved people in Africa and transported them to work on cotton and tobacco plantations. By the 19th century, London had become the centre of a worldwide empire without parallel in human history, all at the expense of the indigenous populations of the countries the British colonized.
Two developments dealt a death blow to the British Empire. One of these was the emergence of nationalism. Peoples around the globe rejected the idea of being ruled by a foreign power. They wanted to bring an end to the violent era of British domination as well as the extraction of their country's resources for the benefit of others rather than themselves. One by one, the former colonies gained independence, sometimes by peaceful means, sometimes through bloody conflict. The other was the rise of rival industrial powers, especially Germany and the United States, that successfully challenged Britain's status as the leading producer of manufactured goods. The 20th century witnessed the end of both the British Empire and Britain's role as a major centre of manufacturing.

324 Wörter

Lernen App: NGOs

► More info

The text below is from the website of the World Economic Forum, an international NGO best known for its annual meetings in Davos (Switzerland), where political, academic and business leaders meet to discuss issues of global importance.

[...] In simple terms, globalization is the process by which people and goods move easily across borders. Principally, it's an economic concept – the integration of markets, trade and investments with few barriers to slow the flow of products and services between nations. There is also a cultural element, as ideas and traditions are traded and assimilated.

Globalization has brought many benefits to many people. But not to everyone.

To help explain the economic side of globalization, let's take a look at the well-known coffee chain Starbucks.

Annotations
5 **trade sth.** buy and sell sth.
5 **assimilate sth.** make sth. part of sth. else

The first Starbucks outlet opened its doors in 1971 in the city of Seattle. Today it has 15,000 stores in 50 countries. These days you can find a Starbucks anywhere, whether Australia, Cambodia, Chile or Dubai. It's what you might call a truly globalized company.

And for many suppliers and jobseekers, not to mention coffee-drinkers, this was a good thing. The company was purchasing 247 million kilograms of unroasted coffee from 29 countries. Through its stores and purchases, it provided jobs and income for hundreds of thousands of people all over the world.

But then disaster struck. In 2012, Starbucks made headlines after a Reuters investigation showed that the chain hadn't paid much tax to the UK government, despite having almost a thousand coffee shops in the country and earning millions of pounds in profit there.

As a multinational company, Starbucks was able to use complex accounting rules that enabled it to have profit earned in one country taxed in another. Because the latter country had a lower tax rate, Starbucks benefited. Ultimately, the British public missed out, as the government was raising less tax to spend on improving their well-being. [...]

We might think of globalization as a relatively new phenomenon, but it's been around for centuries.

One example is the Silk Road, when trade spread rapidly between China and Europe via an overland route. Merchants carried goods for trade back and forth, trading silk as well as gems and spices and, of course, coffee. (In fact, the habit of drinking coffee in a social setting originates from a Turkish custom, an example of how globalization can spread culture across borders.) [...]

Globalization has speeded up enormously over the last half-century, thanks to great leaps in technology.

The internet has revolutionized connectivity and communication, and helped people share their ideas much more widely, just as the invention of the printing press did in the 15th century. The advent of email made communication faster than ever.

The invention of enormous container ships helped too. In fact, improvements in transport generally – faster ships, trains and airplanes – have allowed us to move around the globe much more easily. [...]

Globalization has led to many millions of people being lifted out of poverty.

For example, when a company like Starbucks buys coffee from farmers in Rwanda, it is providing a livelihood and a benefit to the community as a whole. A multinational company's presence overseas contributes to those local economies because the company will invest in local resources, products and services. Socially responsible corporations may even invest in medical and educational facilities. [...]

While some areas have flourished, others have floundered as jobs and commerce move elsewhere. Steel companies in the UK, for example, once thrived, providing work for hundreds of thousands of people. But when China began producing cheaper steel, steel plants in the UK closed down and thousands of jobs were lost.

Workers sorting coffee beans in Rwanda

Annotations

- 13 **supplier** *Lieferant*
- 14 **purchase sth.** [ˈpɜːtʃəs] buy sth.
- 21 **accounting** *Buchhaltung*
- 23 **miss out** not profit or benefit from sth.
- 27 **Silk Road** network of trade routes between Asia and Europe that were active from the second century BCE until the mid-15th century
- 29 **gem** precious stone
- 33 **leap** (here) progress
- 36 **advent** [ˈædvent] coming into being
- 42 **livelihood** way of making a living
- 47 **flourish** perform well, grow
- 47 **flounder** perform badly
- 49 **thrive** perform well
- 51 **plant** *(n)* factory

Info

Worldwide, around two billion cups of **coffee** are consumed every day. Most of the beans used to make this drink come from countries in Asia, South America and sub-Saharan Africa. Unfortunately, the growing demand for the product, combined with a drop in prices, often leads to rising child labour rates and precarious working conditions for local farmers as well as to agricultural practices which are harming the environment.

Every step forward in technology brings with it new dangers. Computers have vastly improved our lives, but cyber criminals steal millions of pounds a year. Global wealth has skyrocketed, but so has global warming.

While many have been lifted out of poverty, not everybody has benefited. Many argue that globalization operates mostly in the interests of the richest countries, with most of the world's collective profits flowing back to them and into the pockets of those who already own the most.

Although globalization is helping to create more wealth in developing countries, it is not helping to close the gap between the world's poorest and richest nations. Leading charity Oxfam says that when corporations such as Starbucks can legally avoid paying tax, the global inequality crisis worsens.

Basically, done wisely (in the words of the International Monetary Fund) globalization could lead to 'unparalleled peace and prosperity'. Done poorly, 'to disaster'.

710 Wörter

From: 'What is globalization anyway?', www.weforum.org, *10 January 2017*

Comprehension

▸ WOB: A1

DIF *research project* zum WEF

DIGI Notizen auf Tablets austauschen oder gemeinsam an einem geteilten Dokument arbeiten

HA CT **1** **a*** Outline the information presented in the text by dividing it into sections and formulating the question that is answered in each section.

CT **b*** Compare outlines with your partner. Make changes if needed.

HA CT **2** List the benefits and drawbacks of globalization as presented in the text.

DIF Ranking der genannten Faktoren erstellen

Analysis

▸ WOB: A1

▸ Support, p. 194

▸ SF 17: Reading and understanding non-fictional texts, p. 221

HA CT **3*** Analyse the *author's attitude with regard to the topic of globalization. Find examples and passages from the text that prove your point.

DIF Darstellung aus anderer Sichtweise schreiben: *Write a commentary for the newspaper of a protest group at the WEF annual meeting in Davos.*

Language Awareness

▸ WOB: A1

DIF Liste mit Stilmitteln bereitstellen

DIF Formulierungshilfen für die Textanalyse vorgeben

HA **4** **a** In the last part of the text (ll. 47–64), the author frequently writes sentences that contrast positive and negative aspects. Point out examples and identify the techniques the author uses.

HA **b** Describe the effects these techniques evoke.

Beyond the text

Lernen App: Video on presentations
Video on having a discussion

▸ Getting started

▸ SF 43: Giving a presentation, p. 259

▸ SF 46: Having a discussion, p. 264

DIGI/DIF Umsetzung als Kurzfilm (fiktives Interview) oder Podcast

▸ WOB: A4

5 You choose | Speaking With a partner, do either task **a** or **b**.

HA CT **a*** Discuss the influence of globalization on your everyday life, e.g. transportation, entertainment, shopping ... How would your life change if from one day to the next all the effects of globalization were undone? Prepare a presentation in which you present your vision of a life without globalization.

HA CT **b*** Discuss the pros and cons of globalization. Each of you presents one side. Together decide which of your arguments is the strongest for each side.

▸ WOB: A5

DIGI Aufnahme als *radio show*

* Digital nomads

Umsetzung als *cocktail party* möglich: SuS gehen im Raum umher und sprechen mit unterschiedlichen Partner/innen

* • Can you imagine a lifestyle where you are permanently on the move, without a home of your own? Compare your reactions.

You are going to watch a video about 'digital nomads', i.e. people who have jobs they can do from anywhere with a Wi-Fi connection.

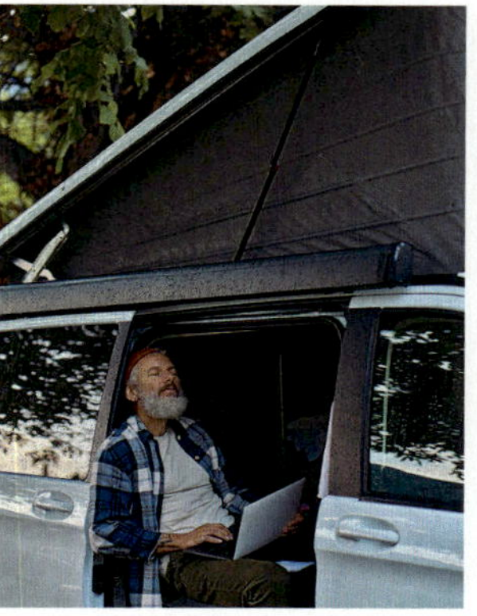

Lernen App: Video on digital nomads (04:57 min.)

Comprehension

HA **1** * The words in the left column of the table below are all used in the video. Before watching the video, match them to the meanings on the right. After you have watched the video, check whether you've matched them correctly.

1	entrepreneurial	a	being able to work anywhere
2	millennial	b	place where you can work on your own
3	corporate life	c	business minded
4	remote worker	d	do sth. before others do it
5	coworking space	e	accept sth. as good
6	contractor	f	person born between the early 1980s and the mid-1990s
7	commission	g	the lifestyle within a large firm
8	location independence	h	sb. who has a contract to provide goods or services for a firm
9	be ahead of the curve	i	someone who works outside a firm
10	embrace sth.	j	money paid to you for your work

► Check Lernen App: Answer key for task 1

DIF Wörterbuch nutzen

SuS korrigieren einander in PA

2 **a** * Viewing In the video, two digital nomads, Erick Prince and Mike Holp, HA are presented. Work with a partner and each choose one of the two people. While watching, make notes on

bei Bearbeitung als HA beachten, dass das Video online mit Untertiteln verfügbar ist

1. how they make a living.
2. why they chose to become digital nomads.
3. the advantages of their current lifestyle.

b * Compare notes with your partner. Talk about the points you are unsure about.

► SF 40: Listening/Viewing for gist and detail, p. 253

DIF Mike Holps Anteil im Video ist kürzer und einfacher

Lösung als Venn-Diagramm möglich

3 * Viewing Now watch the video a second time. Make notes on the following aspects:

HA
1. the advantages of being a digital nomad
2. what you need to make a living as a digital nomad

DIF geeignet zur erneuten Umwälzung des Vokabulars oder zur Vertiefung zu Hause

Analysis

HA **4** Analyse the cinematic devices used and describe the effect(s) they have.

ggf. arbeitsteilig in Sequenzen bearbeiten DIF in PA oder Kleingruppen bearbeiten

► SF 41: Analysing films, series and videos, p. 253

► WOB: A8 Viewing, pp. 26–27

Beyond the text

5 You choose Writing Do task **a** or **b**.

HA **a** * Digital nomad – an attractive lifestyle choice for you? Write a personal statement.

HA **b** 'By 2050 most people will be remote workers.' Do you agree? Write a *comment. kreative Variante: *Write a diary entry as a digital worker in 2050.*

DIGI alternativ Blog erstellen

► SF 28: Argumentative writing, p. 236

► WOB: A2 Writing, pp. 8–11

Schwerpunkt-Kompetenz Chapter 5: Mediating

Lernen App: Videos on tenses in English

► SF 6: Essentials: language and study skills, p. 208

► More language

► Check
Lernen App: Answer key for task 1

Reactivate

When you talk or write about developments and trends, you often need to refer to the past and the present. Most English verbs have eight different forms that can be used for that:

simple present	present progressive
present perfect simple	present perfect progressive
simple past	past progressive
past perfect simple	past perfect progressive

1 Looking at different verb forms

In sentences 1–8, different forms of *wait* are used. Match the sentences to the tenses and aspects mentioned in the box on the left.

1 I waited ten minutes for the bus to arrive.
2 How long have you been waiting here?
3 I had been waiting for over an hour when the bus finally arrived.
4 Hi, it's me. I'm still waiting for the bus.
5 I never wait longer than five minutes for a bus.
6 I was waiting for the bus when I saw Ahmad leave the shop.
7 Have you ever waited for something to happen that never did?
8 Lisette said that she had waited until 11 pm for Ben to phone her.

A simple past
B present perfect
C present perfect progressive
D past progressive
E past perfect
F simple present
G past perfect progressive
H present progressive

DIGI/DIF bei Bedarf mithilfe von Lernvideos Regeln wiederholen und an der Tafel sammeln

Language awareness

2 Comparing the use of tenses in German and English

► WOB: B1

DIGI in PA an einem geteilten Dokument bearbeiten; LuL stellen zum Abgleich eine Formentabelle zur Verfügung

HA **a** Translate the sentences from task **1** into German and compare the use of tense and aspect in English and German.

HA **b** Note down the differences in a form that suits you best and helps you to remember them, e.g. table, mind map ...

Work with words

3 Adverbs, adverbial phrases and question words

In English, certain verb forms are often used together with certain adverbs, adverbial phrases or question words.

► WOB: B1

► Check
Lernen App: Answer key for task 3a

HA **a** ∗ Copy and complete sentences 1–6 with the verb in brackets.
1 When (you / hear) about the accident?
2 Max (play) video games since three o'clock.
3 We (move) to Abu Dhabi four years ago.
4 How long (you / live) here?

LÖS 3a
1 did you hear
2 has played
3 moved
4 have you lived / have you been living

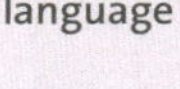

Schwerpunkt-Kompetenz Chapter 5: Mediating

5 I (not see) Kevin yet this morning.
6 We (be) best friends since kindergarten.

LÖS 3a
5 have not seen 6 have been

HA b * Collect adverbs, adverbial phrases and question words that are frequently used with a particular tense and/or aspect.

DIGI/DIF bei Bedarf Aufgabe 3b vorziehen und vor der Bearbeitung von 3a *signal words* als Tabelle an einer digitalen Pinnwand sammeln; Lernvideos nutzen

Practise

HA 4 Going abroad

Decide which form of the verb in brackets must be used in each of the following sentences.

1 People (never be) more mobile than they are today.
2 Every year, millions of people (travel) abroad for various reasons.
3 Some of them are tourists who want to visit places they (dream) about for years.
4 Others (leave) their homeland in search of a better life.
5 The number of migrants worldwide (rise) steadily for years.
6 Perhaps you (think) about going abroad after finishing school.
7 Many universities (offer) the chance to spend time abroad.
8 'Work & travel' is another possibility that (become) extremely popular in recent years.

► Check Lernen App: Answer key for task 4
► WOB: B1

HA 5 Correct verb forms

SuS korrigieren sich gegenseitig

Complete the sentences with the correct form of the verbs in brackets.

1 In the late 16th century, improvements in shipbuilding (make) it possible for ships to sail around the world and return safely.
2 In the course of the century, the major seafaring nations of Europe – Spain, Portugal, England and the Netherlands – (become) bitter rivals in the struggle for new markets.
3 By 1800, Great Britain (defeat) the competition and (be) now master of a worldwide empire.
4 Even though England (lose) its American colonies in 1781, it still (possess) colonies in Canada, Africa, India, China, Australia and New Zealand.
5 In Australia, for example, immigrants from England (look after) sheep they (bring) to Australia from the mother country.
6 Ships (transport) the sheep's wool to factories in England, where it was spun into cloth.
7 Other machines (make) clothes from the cloth.
8 Ships (bring) some of these clothes back to Australia, where the colonists (buy) them.
9 This system (make) British merchants – and indirectly Britain itself – rich and powerful.
10 In some parts of the British Empire, however, people (rebel) against a system that (make) them poor and others rich.
11 In India, for example, Gandhi (teach) his followers how to spin their own cotton to make cloth.
12 This (be), of course, against the law, and explains why the spinning wheel (become) a symbol of the independence movement in India.

Lernen App: Answer key for task 5
► Check

LÖS 5
1 made
2 were becoming/became
3 had defeated … was
4 had lost … possessed
5 were looking after … had brought
6 transported
7 made
8 brought … bought
9 made
10 were rebelling/rebelled … made/was making
11 taught
12 was … became

► WOB: B1 Tense and aspect, pp. 40–43, pp. 46–47

DIGI/DIF ergänzende digitale Präsentation zum Thema erstellen

Five arguments for biodiversity

Julie Shaw

Natural pond in a nature reserve in the Netherlands.

- What do you think of when you read the word *biodiversity*? Why might someone think it necessary to present arguments in favour of biodiversity?

Currently, more than 1 million species are at risk of extinction. This threatens not only the health of the planet, but also that of humans. The following five reasons show why biodiversity is necessary for the stability of the planet.

[...] 1. **Wildlife support healthy ecosystems that we rely on.**
Conservation researchers Paul R. and Anne Ehrlich posited in the 1980s that species are to ecosystems what rivets are to a plane's wing. Losing one might not be a disaster, but each loss adds to the likelihood of a serious problem.

Whether in a village in the Amazon or a metropolis such as Beijing, humans depend on the services ecosystems provide, such as fresh water, pollination, soil fertility and stability, food and medicine. Ecosystems weakened by the loss of biodiversity are less likely to deliver those services, especially given the needs of an ever-growing human population.

One example of this is Kenya's Lake Turkana – the world's largest desert lake, a habitat for a variety of wildlife including birds, Nile crocodiles and hippos and a source of food and income for about 300,000 people. The lake is under heavy pressure because of overfishing, cyclical drought, changing rainfall patterns and the diversion of water by upstream developments, and these changes are leading to a loss of biodiversity, declines in fisheries' yields and a reduced ability to support humans. Without conservation methods in place, this could be the fate of many more ecosystems.

2. **Keeping biodiverse ecosystems intact helps humans stay healthy.**
Research indicates that there is a close link between disease outbreaks and the degradation of nature.

Seventy percent of emerging viral diseases have spread from animals to humans. As the global wildlife trade continues and development projects expand deeper into tropical forests, humans are increasing their exposure to wild animals – and the diseases they may carry. For example, the COVID-19 pandemic can likely be sourced to a wild animal and fish market in Wuhan, China. This shows that we must take care of nature to take care of ourselves. [...]

3. **Biodiversity is an essential part of the solution to climate change.**
In a landmark study published in 2017, a group of researchers led by Bronson Griscom, who researches natural climate solutions at Conservation International, discovered that nature can deliver at least 30 percent of the emissions reductions needed by 2030 to prevent climate catastrophe. Protecting biodiversity plays a crucial part in achieving these emissions reductions.

The destruction of forest ecosystems is responsible for 11 percent of all global greenhouse gas emissions caused by humans, so conserving forests would stop the release of these gases into the atmosphere. Trees and plants also store carbon in their tissue, making it even more necessary to protect them.

Some ecosystems, such as mangroves, are particularly good at storing carbon and keeping it out of the atmosphere – where it contributes to climate change. Forests and wetland ecosystems provide crucial buffers to extreme storms and flooding

Annotations
- 2 **posit sth.** claim that sth. is true
- 3 **rivet** *Niete (beim Maschinenbau)*
- 4 **likelihood** *Wahrscheinlichkeit*
- 6 **pollination** *Bestäubung (von Blüten)*
- 6 **soil** *(Erd-)Boden*
- 6 **fertility** *Fruchtbarkeit*
- 13 **drought** [draʊt] lack of rain
- 13 **diversion** *Entnahme, Ableitung*
- 14 **upstream** *stromaufwärts*
- 15 **decline** *Rückgang*
- 15 **yield** *Ertrag*
- 19 **degradation** damage
- 20 **emerge** become known
- 22 **exposure** contact
- 24 **source sth.** *etwas bis zur Quelle zurückverfolgen*
- 26 **essential** necessary
- 27 **landmark** *(adj)* major, very important
- 30 **crucial** [ˈkruːʃl] important
- 35 **tissue** [ˈtɪʃuː] *Gewebe*
- 38 **buffer** *Pufferzone*

Fehlerquelle: Aussprache von *Beijing* [ˌbeɪˈdʒɪŋ] (Z. 5)

Fehlerquelle: Aussprache von *drought* [draʊt] (Z. 13)

related to climate change. These ecosystems are complex, which means they function best, and are more resilient to the effects of climate change, when all the pieces of the ecosystem are in place – meaning the biodiversity is intact. […]

4. Biodiversity is good for the economy.
At least 40 percent of the world's economy and 80 percent of the needs of the poor are derived from biological resources.

Altogether, the food, commercial forestry and ecotourism industries could lose US$ 338 billion per year if the loss of biodiversity continues at its current pace. Around 75 percent of global food crops rely on animals and insects such as bees to pollinate them, but many of these pollinator populations are in decline – which could put more than US$ 235 billion of agricultural products at risk.

Meanwhile The Economics of Ecosystems and Biodiversity (TEEB) initiative estimates that global sustainable business opportunities from investing in natural resources could be worth US$ 2 to 6 trillion by 2050.

Millions of people also depend on nature and species for their day-to-day livelihoods. This is particularly true for struggling communities in developing countries, who often turn to high-biodiversity ecosystems as their source of food, fuel, medicines and other products made from natural materials for their own use and as sources of income. Nature-related tourism is also a significant income generator for many people as well.

5. Biodiversity is an integral part of culture and identity.
Species are frequently integral to religious, cultural and national identities. All major religions include elements of nature and 231 species are formally used as national symbols in 142 countries. Unfortunately, more than one-third of those species are threatened, but the bald eagle and American bison are examples of conservation successes because of their role as national symbols. Ecosystems such as parks and other protected areas also provide recreation and a knowledge resource for visitors, and biodiversity is a frequent source of inspiration for artists and designers.

778 Wörter

From: 'Why is biodiversity important?', www.conservation.org, *17 May 2021*

Annotations
40 resilient *widerstandsfähig*
44 be derived from sth. *von etwas abgeleitet sein*
46 pace speed
47 food crops plants that are grown to be eaten
53 livelihood existence
54 struggling disadvantaged
59 integral to sth. very important for sth.
65 recreation *Erholung*

Flag of Dominica, an island nation in the Caribbean

Comprehension

HA **1** * Organize the information presented by the *author in two lists: benefits of biodiversity – consequences of loss of biodiversity.

Analysis

2 Do either task **a** or **b**.

HA **a** * The author uses a number of *stylistic devices to make her text more effective. Find an example of each of the following stylistic devices and examine its effect.
1 *analogy
2 *enumeration
3 example(s)
4 *contrast

HA **b** * Challenge Analyse the *stylistic devices the author uses. What effect(s) do they have?

Lernen App:
Video on stilistic devices
Overview of stilistic devices
▶ Getting started 

▶ WOB: A1 Reading for analysis, pp. 4–7

vorbereitend Stilmittel wiederholen oder auf *glossary* (pp. 272–288) verweisen

Language awareness

▶ WOB: B7 Gerunds, p. 55
▶ WOB: B13 Participles, pp. 62–63

DIGI vorbereitend mithilfe von Erklärvideos *gerund* und *participle* besprechen → gemeinsam abgleichen

CT **3 a** The author uses a number of terms from the field of biology. They are often combined with gerunds or participles (*-ing* forms). Together with a partner, collect as many of these combinations as you can find.

CT **b** Each of you identifies at least one gerund and one participle from the terms you collected in **a**.

c * Speculate why the author uses scientific language. DIF vorbereitend Merkmale von *scientific language* wiederholen

DIGI/DIF Aufzeichnung der Rede erlaubt wiederholte Versuche und den Einsatz zusätzlicher Effekte

Beyond the text

▶ Getting started
▶ SF 44: Preparing and giving a speech, p. 262
▶ SF 35: Writing a formal letter or email, p. 245

auf Argumente aus Aufgabe 1 zurückgreifen

4 You choose Do either task **a** or task **b**.

HA CT **a** Speaking Choose the most important argument for biodiversity from the text and defend your choice in a short speech.

HA CT **b** * Writing A forest near your home * has been chosen as the site of a * shopping centre. Write an email to the local newspaper stating your opinion.

Lernen App:
Video on preparing and giving a speech
Video on writing a letter to the editor

Text 4

Feeding the world

Lernen App: Video on food production (04:43 min.)

* • You are going to watch a video with the title 'What is the environmental impact of feeding the world?'. What issues do you expect it to deal with? DIGI erste Ideen in *word cloud* sammeln

Watch the video from the series 'Our hungry planet: food for a growing population'.

DIF Video stoppen oder mehrfach ansehen

Comprehension

▶ SF 40: Listening/Viewing for gist and detail, p. 253
▶ WOB: A8 Viewing, pp. 26–27
▶ Check

Lernen App: Answer key for task 2a

LÖS 2a
1 larger global middle class
2 environmental changes and habitat destruction
3 Africa
4 meat production
5 a lot of water
6 reduce our use of land and water
7 food deserts
8 goes to waste

HA CT **1 a** * Viewing After watching the video for the first time, write down all the arguments you can remember that are connected with food production.

CT **b** Compare lists with a partner. Add missing arguments to your list.

HA CT **2 a** Viewing Watch the video a second time. Write down the completion of the statements 1–8 below on a separate piece of paper.

1 By the year 2050 there will be a ...
2 Food production is a major cause of ...
3 Land needed for growing food and raising animals takes up as much land as ...
4 Three-fourths of all agricultural land is currently used for ...
5 Meat production (especially beef) also requires ...
6 Eating vegetables instead of meat can help ...
7 Places where you can't buy healthy foods are called ...
8 About one third of food production ...

CT **b** * Compare results with your partner. Make any necessary additions or corrections.

Lernen App: Video on analysing a film
► Getting started

Analysis

3 Do either task **a** or **b**.

DIF Verbesserungsvorschläge machen oder selbst ein Video aufnehmen

HA CT **a** The video uses various visual means to underline its message. How effective do you find this use of the visual medium? Name reasons for your opinion.

HA CT **b** Challenge Analyse the use of visual means in this video and name the ones you find most effective. Give reasons for your opinions and suggest other cinematic devices that might have helped to bring across the message of the video.

► SF 41: Analysing films, series and videos, p. 253

► Support, p. 194

DIGI Kampagne (Video oder Podcast) zum Thema erstellen

DIF Text von einer KI verbessern lassen → überprüfen, ob der neue Text noch inhaltsgleich ist

Beyond the text

HA CT 4 Writing Write a *letter to your school administration and comment on your school's idea to ban meat products from the school cafeteria. Refer to the Info box on the right to include arguments concerning your school's environmental footprint.

► SF 28: Argumentative writing, p. 236

► WOB: A2 Writing, pp. 8–11

HA CT 5 Describe the *cartoon below and analyse its message. Relate it to the previous tasks. ► WOB: A1

► SF 25: Analysing cartoons, p. 231

"Tell us that really scary story again...the one about how they make chicken nuggets!"

DIGI mithilfe eines KI-Bildgenerators unter Verwendung präziser *prompts* ein möglichst ähnliches Bild kreieren

Info

The environmental footprint refers to the impact a company, a society or an individual has on the environment. It measures the amount of natural resources a person or society uses and the emissions or waste they generate to maintain a certain lifestyle. The environmental footprint differs greatly from country to country and even between the inhabitants of one country. The richer someone is, the more likely it is that they exceed the available resources and produce harmful emissions, thus damaging the world. A lot of things influence our environmental footprint including the things we eat and how we dress and travel. Almost all developed countries live above their limit and use way more resources than are available.

6* How would you answer the guiding question of this chapter at this point?
Die hier erstellten Notizen können später für die Bearbeitung der *Chapter task* weiterverwendet werden.

► SF 48: Essentials: mediating, p. 269
► WOB: A7

DIGI/DIF Ein (digitaler) Spickzettel mit den wichtigsten Regeln kann hilfreich sein. Im Lauf der Bearbeitung des *Skills Lab* gleichen die SuS weitere Aspekte im Austausch ab und ergänzen den Spickzettel.

Info

You **paraphrase** when you explain something instead of translating it. For example, you don't know what a *Brötchentaste* is in English, so you write 'a button on a parking meter that permits short-term parking'.

Reactivate

1 Recollecting mediation strategies

HA **a** * The statements below are all false. Rewrite them to make them correct:
1 Mediating is another word for translating.
2 A solution to a mediation task must be the same length as the original.
3 Your text must be written in the same text type as the original one.
4 You can add your own ideas to your solution if you want.
5 You mustn't leave out any information from the text.
6 Your text should be in the same style as the original.

b * Compare solutions with your partner. Discuss any points you disagree on.
c * Add further points to remember that you think are important.

* 2 Helpful advice

Discuss which of the following tips you find helpful and why.
1 Read the given text more than once to make sure you understand it.
2 If you are working with a printout, use a text marker to mark the parts of the original that are relevant for your task.
3 Make notes on the relevant information from the given text. Decide whether you want to write your notes in German or in English.
4 If you can't find an exact English equivalent for a German term, you can paraphrase it.
5 A bilingual dictionary can be useful, but don't waste time looking up every word—concentrate on the important aspects.
6 You don't need to precisely follow the order of the original text in your own text.
7 It may be necessary to explain cultural differences to your addressee (e.g. that a German *Kindergarten* isn't the same as an American kindergarten).

Step ahead

Mediating not only means transferring ideas from one language to another, but often also changing the text types and adapting ideas for a specific addressee.

HA * 3 Examining the task

Examine the aspects you have to focus on if you do the task below.

> Your American cousin writes you to tell you about a school project she started after the droughts and forest fires in California happened. The aim of the project is to find innovative methods of dealing with climate change. You come across the text on p. 138. Summarize the relevant information for her in an email.

4 Examining text types

▸ WOB: A7

HA **a** * Compare the original text and the text you are to write by copying and filling out the table below:

	Original text	My text
Topic	...	...
*Text type	...	...
Addressee	...	...
*Style	...	...

LÖS 4b
- reason why you are writing/ what you are referring to (school project and information from article you found)
- relevant information from the article
- standard elements of an email (personal greeting, closing, writer's first and last name)
- possibly include emotions and exclamations to underline feelings
- write from a first-person perspective

HA CT **b** * Together with a partner decide which features your email must contain.

Merkmale einer informellen E-Mail kurz wiederholen

5 Paraphrasing words

HA **a** * Examine the following phrases and paraphrase them in English.

1 Wiederaufforstung
2 Wurzelwerk
3 Ernteerträge
4 Hungersnöte
5 Nahrungsmittelhilfe
6 Überflutung

HA **b** * Decide whether you need them for your mediation task at all. Add terms you think you do need and paraphrase them.

DIF Mediation ohne Wörterbuch erstellen und unbekanntes Vokabular umschreiben

Practise

6 Writing

Now write your mediation text according to the task given on p. 136. Use all the information you gathered in the exercises to improve your text.

DIGI in PA oder GA an einem geteilten Dokument bearbeiten

Take another look

7 Peer assessment

An dieser Stelle kann KV 16: Peer assessment (Feedbackbogen zur Mediation) behandelt werden.

Swap texts with your partner. Compare them and give each other feedback.

▸ SF 15: Assessing yourself and giving feedback, p. 217

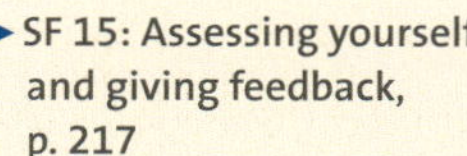

HA

8 * Self-assessment

On the basis of your partner's feedback, create a *method card and write down strategies for mediation tasks. Decide for each strategy whether you are already good at it or if you need more practice.

Method card – mediating	
What I am good at	What I need to practise
...	...

DIGI *method card* digital erstellen und ergänzend zum digitalen Spickzettel (▸ Aufgabe 1b) verwenden

▸ WOB: A7 Mediating, pp. 24–25

Greening the desert

S. Holten

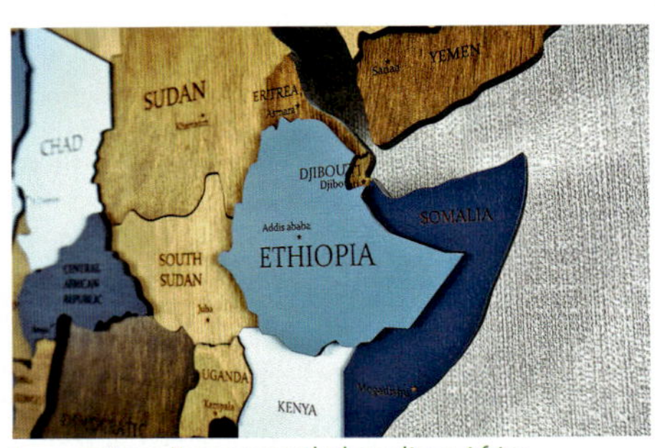

Lernen App: Recommended reading: Africa Is Not a Country
▶ Getting started

Lernen App: The Right Livelihood Award
▶ More info

fächerübergreifendes Lernen (Geografie); bloße Reproduktion von Vorurteilen über afrikanische Länder sollte vermieden werden

CT ✱• What images come to mind when you think of the challenges the African continent has to face? Compare your ideas.

You are going to read about an Australian agronomist who won the Right Livelihood Award in 2018 for a discovery he made while working in Africa.

Wir fahren nach Südäthiopien in die Region Humbo. Etwa sechs Stunden dauert die Fahrt von Addis Abeba aus. Vor vielen hundert Jahren war Äthiopien ein grünes Land, heute sind viele Regionen völlig vertrocknet. [...] Oft sehen wir tiefe Gräben von drei und mehr Metern Tiefe, die der Regen und die Fluten in die Erde gefressen haben. Hier und da stehen einzelne Bäume auf grauen, von der Sonne ausgedörrten Äckern. Rinder und Ziegenherden drängen sich im Schatten. Die Hitze lässt die Luft über dem Boden flimmern.

Tony Rinaudo, Experte für Wiederaufforstung und Landwirtschaft bei World Vision, begleitet uns. Seit mehr als 30 Jahren kämpft er unermüdlich, um verödete Gebiete wieder zum Leben zu bringen [...]. Zunächst versuchte er zu Beginn der 80er Jahre in Niger Millionen Bäume neu anzupflanzen, aber die meisten gepflanzten Bäume gingen wieder ein.

[...] Doch dann wurde Tony in einer abgerodeten Region auf intaktes Wurzelwerk aufmerksam und begann damit zu experimentieren, aus den Wurzeln neue Bäume zu ziehen. Anfangs stieß er auf viel Skepsis [,] als er versuchte, die Bauern in Niger zu überzeugen, ein kleines Gebiet Ackerboden abzusperren und zu schützen. Niemand wollte ihm glauben, dass eine so einfache und preiswerte Methode Erfolg haben könnte. Die Bauern nannten ihn den verrückten weißen Bauern, der immer nur Unsinn erzählt. Nur weil Tony ein gutes Verhältnis zu der Dorfbevölkerung hatte, vertrauten sie ihm und versprachen, ihn bei seinem Experiment zu unterstützen.

Schon nach einem Jahr zeigten sich Erfolge. Aus den Wurzeln waren wieder kleine Bäume und Sträucher gewachsen. Bis heute konnte mit Hilfe der von den Bauern selbst durchführbaren Renaturierung (Farmer managed natural renaturation – kurz FMNR) in Niger ein Gebiet von mehr als fünf Millionen Hektar regeneriert werden. Wüsten wurden wieder grün, und die Bauern, die die FMNR-Methode auf ihren Äckern anwandten, konnten bis zu doppelt und dreifach so hohe Ernteerträge einfahren wie vorher. [...]

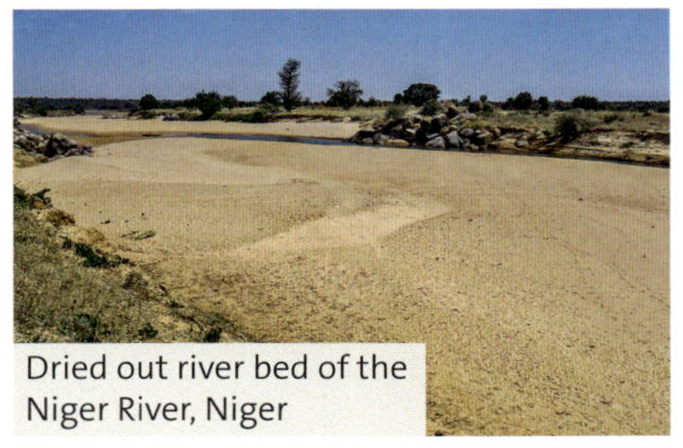
Dried out river bed of the Niger River, Niger

„Als ich damals in Niger durch die Wüste fuhr, war ich kurz davor zu verzweifeln", erklärt Tony. [...] „Doch als ich aus meinem Auto stieg, um Luft aus den Reifen zu lassen, damit ich besser durch den lockeren Sand fahren konnte, sah ich kleine Büschel mit grünen Blättern überall aus dem Boden ragen. Als ich tiefer grub, erkannte ich, dass unter diesen Büscheln ein riesiges Wurzelwerk, ein unterirdischer Wald vorhanden war. Dies öffnete mir die Augen."

Das Erlebnis in der Wüste Nigers ließ Tony nicht mehr los. Als Verantwortlicher für World Vision-Projekte in Äthiopien startete er

2004 in der Humbo Region mit ersten Workshops, um FMNR bekannt zu machen. Auch hier stießen er und die Kollegen anfangs auf Skepsis, da die Bauern zunächst dachten, World Vision wolle ihnen das Land wegnehmen. Doch die Lage in Humbo war so verzweifelt – mehr als 20 Jahre lang kam es in der Provinz immer wieder zu Hungersnöten. [...] Daher ließen sich einige Bauern erweichen und halfen Tony, ein kleines Stück Land zu schützen und zu pflegen.

Als wir Humbo erreichen, können wir unseren Augen kaum trauen. Nach der Fahrt durch trockene Regionen sehen wir hier ein grünes Paradies. Wo zuvor nur karge Hügel zu sehen waren, bedeckt nun dichter Wald die sanfte Landschaft. Bauer Ergene ist mit den Mitgliedern seiner Kooperative verabredet, da heute die Bäume beschnitten werden müssen, damit sie groß und kräftig werden. Ergene erzählt, wie es war, bevor der Wald wieder wuchs: „Vor FMNR waren die Hügel sehr trocken. Erosion war ein großes Problem. Immer wenn es regnete, gab es große Überflutungen. Riesige Felsbrocken rollten den Berg hinab und zerstörten unsere Ernten. Manchmal blieb der Regen komplett aus, dann vertrocknete das Korn. Ohne Nahrungsmittelhilfe wären wir hier alle verhungert."

Farmland in rural Ethiopia

Heute erntet Ergene eine Vielfalt an Gemüse- und Obstsorten, wie Mangos, Bananen, Papayas, Kartoffeln, Sorghum, Kaffee, Sojabohnen und Mais. Seine zehn Kinder gehen alle zur Schule, die älteren besuchen inzwischen die Universität. Früher mussten die Kinder weite Wege laufen, um Brennholz und Wasser für die Familie zu holen. Zeit für die Schule gab es oft nicht. [...]

Der Wald hat das Leben der Menschen in Humbo nachhaltig verbessert. [...] Heute kauft sogar das World Food Programm in der Region ein, um in anderen Teilen Afrikas Menschen zu helfen, die von Hungersnöten bedroht sind. „Niemand auf der Welt müsste hungern", sagt Tony. „Durch FMNR können riesige Teile der Erde wieder begrünt werden. Die Menschen müssen nur die Augen öffnen. Überall wachsen Bäume unter der Erde." [...]

711 Wörter

From: ‚Tony Rinaudo – der verrückte weiße Bauer', worldvision.de, 21 September 2016

1 You choose | Mediating | Do either task **a** or **b**.

Lernen App: Video on mediation
Video on preparing and giving a speech

HA CT **a** * Writing You belong to a student group that is preparing a presentation called '10 simple ways to save our planet'. Your task is to write a text describing the method Tony Rinaudo discovered in Niger. Write a suitable text of about 250 words.

DIGI Texte in einem zweiten Schritt digital präsentieren

HA CT **b** Speaking Your student environment club is taking part in a campaign to nominate five 'Green Global Heroes', people who have made a contribution to preserving our planet. Based on the information from the text, prepare a short speech in which you recommend Tony Rinaudo as a nominee.

DIF Präsentation in PA oder GA erstellen

▶ Getting started
▶ SF 49: Mediating from German into English, p. 270
▶ WOB: A7 Mediating, pp. 24–25
▶ SF 44: Preparing and giving a speech, p. 262

Beyond the text

HA CT **2** *** Speaking There are many African initiatives that try to fight the damage to the environment caused mainly by Western demand for agricultural products. Research some initiatives and present the one you find most interesting to your class.

Lernen App: Information about several African environmental activists

▶ WOB: A4

Lernen App: African initiatives

▶ Getting started
▶ SF 13: Doing research, p. 214
▶ SF 43: Giving a presentation, p. 259

Global migration

CT *• Which countries do most migrants come from? Which countries do they migrate to, and for what reasons? Speculate.

The graphs below show you the five most important countries of origin of migrants and the five most important countries of destination in 2020.

fächerübergreifendes Lernen (Politik, Geografie); Reproduktion von Vorurteilen sollte vermieden werden

Die SuS werden ihre Antworten vermutlich zuerst auf Deutschland beziehen.

Citizens living abroad (2020)

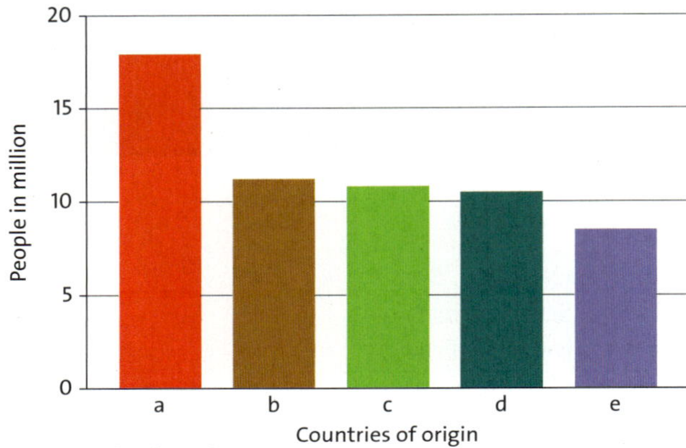

Number of migrants living in this country (2020)

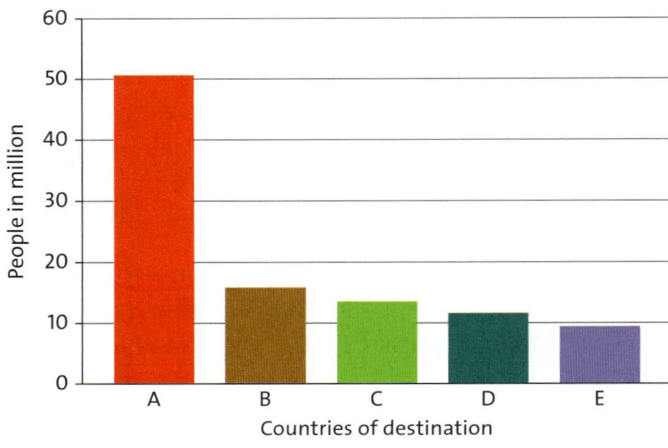

From: United Nations

Lernen App: Video on analysing diagrams

► Getting started

DIGI Umsetzung als digitales Quiz möglich

Comprehension

CT **1** * **a** In the table below, you find the names of the five main countries of origin and destination (in alphabetical order). Match the countries of origin to columns a–e and the countries of destination to columns A–E.

► Check — Lernen App: Answer key for task 1

Hier wird der Blick auf die weltweite Migration gelenkt. Daher werden andere Länder in den Fokus kommen als beim *Pre-reading*.

Countries of origin	China • India • Mexico • Russia • Syria
Countries of destination	Germany • Russia • Saudi Arabia • UK • U.S.A.

► WOB: A1 Reading for analysis, pp. 4–7

CT * **b** Compare your ideas with the real ranking of the countries involved. Together with your partner, speculate on what makes a country attractive or unattractive.

DIF aktuellere Zahlen recherchieren und präsentieren

DIGI/DIF digitale Pinnwand mit Ergänzungen zu Stichworten auffüllen; Pinnwand mit Annotationen dazu ergänzen, warum diese Faktoren wichtig sind

Beyond the text

HA CT **2** * **a** The reasons why people migrate can be divided into push and pull factors. Sort the words in the box below into two lists:

corruption • crime • discrimination • educational opportunities • employment opportunities • financial security • higher wages • famine • language • living standard • military duty • natural disasters • personal freedom • political oppression • poverty • social climate • war

Info

Push factors are reasons why people decide to leave their country of birth.
Pull factors are reasons why migrants choose one country over another.

CT **b** Discuss the ones you are not sure about in class.

Einige Begriffe *(living standard, social climate)* sind ohne Zusatz nicht eindeutig.

DIF Begriffe in eine Rangfolge bringen und Entscheidung begründen

The age of mass migration

Lernen App: Interview with Dr. Khanna (07:28 min.)

CT • Think about the driving forces of migration worldwide. Do you think there might be new or different drivers of migration in the future? Methode: *think – pair – share*

You are going to hear an interview with Dr. Parag Khanna, a global strategy expert, on the future of migration. The interview was broadcast by ABC Radio (Australia) in 2021.

Displaced Germans waiting in Berlin's Anhalter Bahnhof station, 1945

Comprehension

1 Listening (HA, CT) While listening, decide which of the following statements are correct.

1 Dr. Khanna believes that the age of mass migration began thousands of years ago.
2 Khanna says that migration was actually higher in the past than it is today.
3 Khanna feels optimistic about the future of mass migration.
4 Khanna praises Germany and Canada for the way they handle migration.
5 Khanna believes that it is senseless to try to regulate migration.
6 Khanna thinks that having an immigration policy that considers the country's needs is best.
7 Khanna says that most refugees don't travel large distances.
8 Khanna emphasizes the danger of populist backlash if a country opens its borders to refugees.

▶ Check
Lernen App: Answer key for task 1

▶ SF 40: Listening/Viewing for gist and detail, p. 253

▶ WOB: A6 Listening, pp. 20–23

2 Listening (HA, CT) Listen to the interview a second time. Correct the false statements from task 1.

Beyond the text

3 You choose | Intercultural communication Do either task a or b.

a (HA, CT) Writing Research Australia's history of migration and comment on the following statement: Migration is a central element of Australia's national identity.
▶ WOB: A2

b (HA, CT) Speaking Do some research on Australia's migration programme and prepare a short presentation in which you explain how it is supposed to contribute to solving some of the government's problems, e.g. widespread workforce shortages and an ageing population.
▶ WOB: A4

DIGI/DIF Präsentation digital erstellen/als Podcast gestalten

▶ SF 23: Doing research, p. 214

▶ SF 28: Argumentative writing, p. 236

▶ SF 43: Giving a presentation, p. 259

▶ SF 12: Communicating across cultures, p. 213

Lernen App: A photo stimulus: Australian customs and traditions

▶ Getting started

4 a (HA) Intercultural communication In groups of 3–5, collect everything you can remember about customs and traditions of Australia. Include a quick internet research if needed.

b (CT) Then agree on three customs or traditions you find most interesting or unusual.

c (CT) In class, collect the customs and traditions that the groups settled on and decide which of them could be most confusing or strange to new people coming to the country. DIF *mini-presentations* erstellen

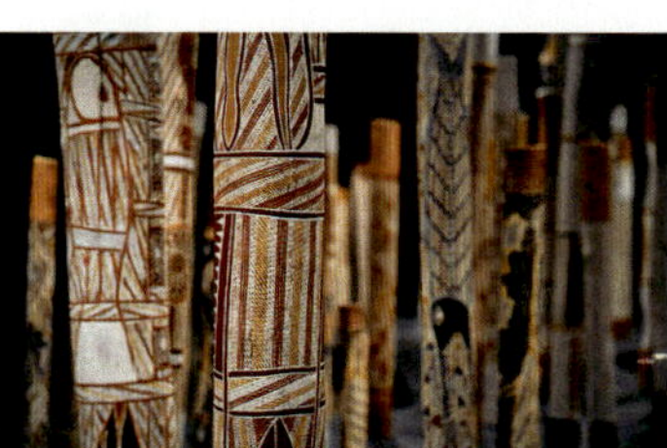
Didgeridoos (also called yidaki, mandapul or mako), traditional aboriginal instruments

Lernen App: Wang Ping
▶ More info

▶ SF 20: Reading and understanding poetry, p. 224

Annotations
2 **fade** slowly disappear, vanish
4 **scar** mark left on the skin by a wound that has healed
4 **proxy war** *Stellvertreterkrieg*
5 **carnage** *Gemetzel*
5 **genocide** *Völkermord*
6 **incinerate sth.** burn sth. to ashes
6 **mushroom cloud** cloud formed by the explosion of an atomic bomb
12 **laundromat** *Waschsalon*
12 **bodega** small shop that sells everyday goods
14 **ancestors** family members who lived before you
15 **spine** *Rückgrat*
17 **orphan** child without parents
20 **chant** speak in a rhythmic or repetitive way

▶ WOB: A12 Poetry, pp. 38–39

Fehlerquelle: Aussprache von *drought* [draʊt] (Z. 5)

Fehlerquelle: Aussprache von *genocide* [ˈdʒenəsaɪd] (Z. 5)

Info

The term **speaker** or **lyric voice** is used for the invisible 'person' who 'speaks' the words of a poem. The lyric voice may refer to itself as 'I' (or 'we') or may remain invisible. It should not be equated with the poet, who may or may not share the thoughts and feelings of the lyric voice.

* * * Things we carry on the sea

Wang Ping

Umsetzung als *word cloud* zeigt die Häufigkeit der genannten Begriffe

CT * • Imagine you had to leave your homeland forever. What would you take with you?

*You are going to read a *poem by Wang Ping, a Chinese-American author who grew up on a small island in the East China Sea. After studying English at the University of Peking, she left China in 1985 for the U.S., where she has lived ever since.*

we carry tears in our eyes: good-bye father, good-bye mother
we carry soil in small bags: may home never fade from our hearts
we carry names, stories, memories of our village, our civilization
we carry scars from proxy wars of greed
we carry carnage of mining, droughts, floods, genocides
we carry dust of our families incinerated in mushroom clouds
we carry our islands sinking under the sea
we carry our hands, feet, bones, hearts and best minds to start
a new life

we carry diplomas: medicine, engineer, nurse, education, math,
poetry, even if they mean nothing to the other shore
we carry railroads, plantations, laundromats, bodegas, taco trucks,
farms, factories, nursing homes, hospitals, schools, temples...
built on our ancestors' backs

we carry old homes along the spine, new dreams in our chests
we carry yesterday, today and tomorrow
we're orphans of the wars forced upon us
we're refugees of the sea drowning in plastic wastes
we came from the same mother in Africa
our tongues carry the same weight as we chant

爱 (ai), حب (hubb), ליבע (libe), amour, love
平安 (ping'an), سلام (salaam), shalom, paz, peace
希望 (xi'wang), أمل ('amal), hoffnung, esperanza, hope, hope, hope
as we drift ... from dream to dream ... sea to sea ...

195 Wörter

From: My Name is Immigrant, *2020*

Comprehension

HA CT **1** Describe the role of the *speaker.

HA CT **2** Point to push and pull factors (c.f. Info box. p. 140) named in the poem.

Analysis

HA CT **3** **a** * * Work with a partner. One of you examines the relationship of the *speaker to the past. The other examines the relationship of the speaker to the future.

CT **b** Compare your results and draw conclusions.

► WOB: A12

4 You choose Do task **a** or **b**.

HA **a** The poet makes frequent use of *enumeration. Point to examples and explain their effect(s) on the reader.

HA **b** In the last *stanza, the poet uses other languages. Examine the effect produced and its relationship to the poem as a whole.

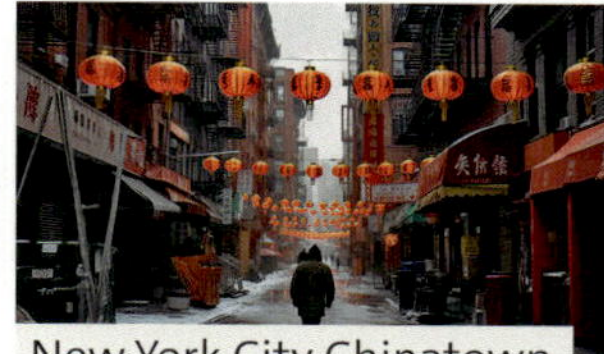
New York City Chinatown

Language Awareness

5 **a** * The language of poetry is different from the language we use in every-day life.
HA * Examine l. 15 closely. Analyse how the language used here differs from everyday language.

b Together with your partner, discuss possible interpretations of this sentence.

► WOB: A12
► Support, p. 195
auf glossary (pp. 272–288) verweisen

DIF Gedicht in anderes *register* oder andere Textform umschreiben (z. B. moderner Jugendslang, *news report*)

Beyond the text

HA **6** *** Intercultural communication Writing Your class is preparing a multi-media presentation on the topic of 'migration'. Wang Ping's poem is one of the texts that is under consideration. Write a *comment in which you explain why you think this poem should or should not be used in the presentation.

► SF 28: Argumentative writing, p. 236
► WOB: A2 Writing, pp. 8–11
► WOB: A12

Text 9

*** Young climate activists

Casey Ruairi

DIGI Ideensammlung in *word cloud*

CT ••*In recent years climate protest has become a worldwide youth movement. What motivates young people to demonstrate for the environment?

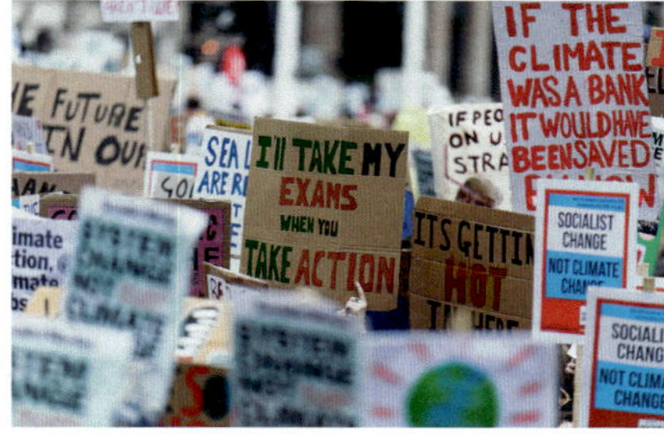

The global fight against climate change is being led by teenagers. Al Jazeera, the first independent news channel in the Arab world, has therefore interviewed young activists about their work, the impact of climate change on their hometowns and their future expectations.

More than three years have passed since the solitary protest of Swedish teenager Greta Thunberg quickly grew into a youth climate movement of unprecedented size. Millions have participated in climate strikes in more than 150 countries as part of the Fridays for Future movement, demanding governments take the action necessary to limit global heating to 1.5 degrees Celsius (2.7 degrees Fahrenheit) and ensure a just and equitable transition away from fossil fuels. Teenagers and young adults are now some of the most prominent figures in the global debate around climate change. As world leaders are set to negotiate further emissions targets and economic measures at the COP26 in Glasgow, their demands are louder than ever. […]

Yurshell Rodriguez

'I know what is being done on the front line of climate change,' says Yurshell Rodriguez, 26, who comes from the Colombian island of Old Providence, in the Caribbean. 'I can say that I know it in my bones. I feel it. I lived it.' Rogriguez's home,

Annotations
1 **solitary** done alone
2 **unprecedented** without equal in the past
6 **equitable** fair
8 **negotiate** *verhandeln*

Fehlerquelle: Aussprache von *Fahrenheit* [ˈfærənhaɪt] (Z. 5)

Fehlerquelle: Aussprache von *Caribbean* [kəˈrɪbiən] (Z. 12/13)

Info

The **United Nations Framework Convention on Climate Change**, which entered into force in 1994, brought together 198 countries with the goal of reducing human impact on the global climate. Each year, a conference of all parties (**COP**) to the convention is held in one of the member states to review global progress and formulate new goals.

Annotations

- 14 **wipe sth. out** destroy sth. completely
- 22 **capture sth.** *etwas (chemisch) binden*
- 23 **landmark case** *Gerichtsfall von grundsätzlicher Bedeutung*
- 27 **divide** *(n)* gap; difference
- 27 **paramount** *(adj)* very important
- 34 **flare** *(v)* burn
- 34 **extraction** *Gewinnung*
- 34 **culprit** person or agent responsible for sth. bad
- 35 **acidification** *Übersäuerung*
- 40 **advocate** *(v)* **for sth.** work for sth. (e.g. a goal); support sth.
- 43 **assent** Zustimmung
- 49 **devise sth.** work sth. out
- 50 **elevate sth.** make sth. more visible
- 50 **marginalise sb.** ignore sb. and their interests
- 56 **water sth. down** make sth. less radical

like many of her neighbours', was wiped out when Hurricane Iota struck the island in late 2020, causing widespread damage to homes, schools and sanitation facilities. 'Having to rebuild your entire community, after such a profound trauma, for me has been the most challenging thing in the world: being a climate activist but also being a climate victim.' A member of the Indigenous Raizal community, she has been involved in environmentalism since her childhood, and wants to do everything she can to protect the island's coral reef, the third-longest in the world. An environmental engineer, she wrote her thesis on the role of the seagrass around Old Providence in capturing carbon dioxide. In 2018, she was part of a group of young activists that won a landmark case against the Colombian government for its failure to halt deforestation in the Amazon rainforest. On a trip to Spain during COP25, Rodriguez was left unimpressed by the heavy corporate presence of businesses such as Coca Cola, yet inspired by the dynamism of the youth movement, which met separately at a different location. Bridging this divide is paramount for the youth movement, she believes. 'We're not getting that attention from our politicians or our decision-makers. So we are making them look at us, making them listen to us. We're not going to stop being vocal. Because if we stop, we lose.' [...]

Kelo Uchendu

When Uchendu, 25, visited the Niger Delta a few years ago, he wondered why acid rain was so much more common there than in other parts of Nigeria. He began his own research, learning not only that gas flaring during oil extraction was the culprit, but also about other issues like ocean acidification, which pointed towards the effects of climate change on Nigerian communities. Education is a key focus of his activism, and he wants climate change to become a key part of the curriculum. 'For most people who learn about climate change, believe me, they don't learn it from school,' he says. In 2018, he founded the Gray2Green, an organisation dedicated to mobilising young people to advocate for sustainable climate policies, and has recently been working with a member of the Nigerian House of Representatives to influence the country's landmark climate bill, which is currently awaiting presidential assent. 'I feel that this is the right time for young people to start taking leadership, trying to sit at the table, to make meaningful contributions in the decision-making processes. To try to influence policies, to try to build solutions.' Uchendu was a coordinator with Mock COP, a youth-led online conference held last year in place of the COP26, which was delayed until this year because of the pandemic. As many as 330 activists from 142 countries, mostly representing the Global South, devised a treaty that they will use to lobby for more radical action during negotiations in Glasgow. 'The Mock COP focuses on elevating the voices of marginalised communities who have been historically neglected in the decision-making processes and the negotiation processes,' says Uchendu. The agreements set in the COP26 summit have always been determined primarily by industrialised nations and their strong lobbying influence, he says. But younger activists are not keen on compromises. 'One thing I've seen working with decision-makers is that ... there's a lot of this temptation to water down actions to make everybody feel comfortable, which is not something that you see often with the youth movement.'

740 Wörter

From: 'Young Climate Activists and the Battle to Avert Catastrophe', www.aljazeera.com, *03 November 2021*

DIF Rodriguez mit weiteren bekannten Aktivistinnen vergleichen (z. B. Greta Thunberg, Malala Yousafzai)

Comprehension

HA CT **1** Describe the relationship between Rodriguez' biography and her climate activism.

HA CT **2** Outline how Uchendu became involved in the climate movement in Nigeria.

► WOB: A1

Analysis

HA CT **3** Compare what Rodriguez and Uchendu say about youth climate activism. List the points on which they agree and the points where they differ.

für PA geeignet; Darstellung der Ergebnisse als Venn-Diagramm bietet sich an

Language awareness

HA CT **4** *** Examine the use of direct quotes in Ruairi's article. Show how the use of direct speech supports the message of the text.

Beyond the text

Lernen App: Podcast (04:23 min.)

► WOB: A7
► Getting started
► SF 40: Listening/Viewing for gist and detail, p. 253
► SF 49: Mediating from German into English, p. 270
Lernen App: Video on mediation

CT **5** *** Mediating **Partner B**: Go to page 195 and do task **5**. **Partner A**: Listen to the first part of the podcast. Then tell your partner in English what Luisa says about the 'Fridays for Future' movement and the term *activist*.

HA CT **6** Imagine you belong to an environmental activist group that is going to take part in a protest demonstration. Choose one of the slogans on the right for your poster. Say what you think it means and why you chose it. DIF eigenen Slogan erfinden

1. The climate is changing—why aren't we?
2. There are no jobs on a dead planet.
3. If you aren't part of the solution, you're part of the pollution.

CT **7** * How would you answer the guiding question of this chapter at this point?

► WOB: A4

DIGI digital gestützte Darstellung als *virtual gallery walk* präsentieren

Info

Greenwashing

A lot of people are trying to minimize their impact on the environment by adjusting their lifestyle, but making sustainable choices is not always easy. In order to appeal to customers, corporations are now using greenwashing, a marketing tactic, to make products or entire brands appear more eco-friendly than they really are. In recent years many companies have been criticized for spending more money on greenwashing than actually becoming more sustainable and really decreasing their negative impact on the environment.

HA CT **1** Climate activists are demanding change and greenwashing seems to be the solution for a lot of brands. Do some research on the characteristics of greenwashing. Present your findings to your class.

► SF 13: Doing research, p. 214

Chapter task

You have learned about some of the challenges that will confront your generation.

*** HA As a class, prepare an online exhibition which presents some of the global issues you have read about in this chapter, along with ways your generation can contribute to solving them. You may include graphs and charts, *cartoons and photos as well as short informational texts. DIGI Nutzung einer digitalen Pinnwand mit ortsunabhängigem Zugriff empfehlenswert

► SF 13: Doing research, p. 214

Your reading experience

DIF In jeder Gruppe sollten SuS vertreten sein, die gerne lesen. Leistungsstarke SuS können einen Kurzvortrag zum Thema *Why reading is important* halten.

▶ WOB: A9

▶ SF 16: Essentials: reading strategies and text types, p. 219

1 **a** * Discuss in small groups why you enjoy or don't enjoy reading *novels.
b * Collect the reasons named in two groups.

science fiction • romance • historical novel • fantasy • dystopia • coming-of-age novel • mystery • detective novel • utopian novel

2 **a** The box on the left contains names of popular *genres of the novel. Explain how they differ from each other. arbeitsteilige Bearbeitung möglich
b * Compare with your partner: Which of these genres do you like? Are there genres you don't like? Give reasons. DIF Lieblingsgenre mit Beispielen und Lesetipps präsentieren

Terms for analysis

DIF bei Bedarf auf das *glossary* (pp. 272–288) verweisen

Lernen App: Answer key for task 3
▶ Check

*atmosphere • *characterization • *narrative perspective • *narrator • *plot • *setting • *style

HA **3** *** Match the terms in the box on the left to the definitions A–G below.

A the person who tells the story
B the structure of events in a literary text
C the time and place of the story in a literary text
D the feeling or mood that is created by the story
E the way in which the author presents the *characters to the reader
F the particular way in which a text is written, e.g. formal or informal
G the point of view from which a story is told

Looking at the *narrative perspective

Lernen App: Answer key for task 4
▶ Check 

A *omniscient narrator
B figural narrative situation
C *third-person narrator
D *first-person narrator

4 The narrative perspective influences how the reader perceives a story, since different types of narration allow different insights into the *plot.

HA **a** *** Match the names of the narrative perspectives (A–D) from the box on the left to their description below.

Wiederholung der Terminologie, ggf. unter Bezugnahme auf den Deutschunterricht

1 The narrator is a character in the story and presents the *action through their eyes. They only know what they think and feel. Readers tend to identify with the narrator.
2 The narrator knows the feelings and thoughts of every character. They can look into the past, tell the reader about the present and also anticipate the future.
3 The narrator refers to the characters from outside the story and uses *he*, *she*, *they* or their names. The narrator is not a character in the story.
4 The narrator slips into one character and tells the story from that person's perspective and thus sees the world only through the eyes of the chosen character.

LÖS 4
1D 2A
3C 4B

GA **b** *Comment on the effect of each narrative perspective.

Lernen App: Helon Habila and *Oil on Water*
▶ More info 

*** Childhood memories Helon Habila

You are going to read an excerpt from a novel called Oil on Water. *It is about a Nigerian journalist named Rufus (who is also the narrator) who goes on a trip to the Niger Delta in search of a British woman who has been kidnapped.*

While I was on my way back to Chief Ibiram's front room, the men returned. I passed them hauling their canoes out of the shallow water and tying them to the house stilts; others carried the day's catch in plastic buckets and wicker baskets, and, from what I could see, it wasn't bountiful. The boy and the girl took from the

Annotations
2 **haul sb./sth.** pull sb./sth.
3 **wicker** *Korbgeflecht*
4 **bountiful** plenty

boat a basket with a handful of thin wiggling fishes at the bottom. The kids stopped on the veranda when they saw me, waiting for me to speak, standing side by side with the basket on the floor between them, and behind them the sun was huge and dying, spilling orange and red and rust on the shallow river and the mangroves.

▸ WOB: A9

Mangrove trees

– Smile.

They smiled. I clicked. I wanted to talk to them, but I couldn't think of anything to say. I had known the boy for a couple of days now, and in that time I had never heard him say much, only answers to his father's questions or commands, and mostly they never talked at all; each seemed to have an instinctive understanding of what the other wanted.

– When I was a boy, me and my sister, we used to catch crabs. They looked at each other. – No crabs here now. The water is not good.

The girl, whose name was Alali, was more willing to talk. The boy only nodded with his head lowered, a fixed smile on his lips. I wanted to tell them about my childhood in a village not too far away from here. I realized how very much like theirs my childhood must have been. Barefoot and underfed we may have been, but yet the sea was just outside our door, constantly bringing surprises, suggesting a certain possibility to our lives. Boma and I used to spend the whole night by the water, catching crabs, armed with sticks and basket, our hands covered in old rags to protect our fingers from the scissor-sharp claws. We usually sold our catch to the market women, but sometimes, to make more money, we took the ferry to Port Harcourt to sell to the restaurants by the seafront. That was how we paid our school fees when our father lost his job.

376 Wörter

From: Oil on Water, *2010.*

HA **5 a** Take notes on ways in which the narrative perspective is linked with the content of the text above. darauf achten, dass SuS präzise Textbelege für ihre Beobachtungen geben

b * Compare notes with your partner.

Read the text below and do task **6** *and* **7** *on the following page.*

Rufus was on his way back to Chief Ibiram's front room when the men of the village returned from their fishing expedition. He passed them as they were hauling their boats onto the shore and unloading the meagre catch. Rufus noticed a boy and a girl carrying between them a basket with a few wriggling fish at the bottom. They stopped when they saw the stranger watching them.

Rufus reached instinctively for his camera. 'Smile' he said.

The kids smiled for him. Maybe he was a tourist and would give them a few coins.

After he had taken the photo, Rufus stood watching them, trying to think of something to say.

'When I was a boy, me and my sister, we used to catch crabs.'

The girl looked to her brother, who was staring at the ground in embarrassment. As usual, he was not in the talking mood. 'No crabs here now. The water is not good,' she replied.

► WOB: A9

Rufus thought back wistfully to his childhood, when he and his sister Boma had spent their nights on the beach catching crabs to sell at the market. They had needed the money to pay for their school fees after their father had lost his job. But in retrospect it now seemed to him like a lost paradise. 216 Wörter

auf präzise Textbelege achten

LÖS 6b omniscient narrator: knows feelings and thoughts of different characters (cf. ll. 7, 14–17)

Beschreiben der Wirkung kann für weniger geübte SuS schwierig sein → genaue Textarbeit wichtig, um zu erklären, wie z. B. Atmosphäre erzeugt wird

HA **6** a Make notes on the changes in the way the episode is told.
HA b * Analyse the perspective the story is told from. Point to evidence from the text.
c Compare the two texts. How do they differ in the effect they produce.

7 *** Discuss possible reasons for the author's choice of narrative perspective.

*Read another excerpt from the same novel and work on task **8** and **9**.*

While travelling in the jungle in search of the kidnapping victim, Rufus's colleague Zaq falls seriously ill. He sends Rufus back to Port Harcourt to get help from Beke Johnson, the editor-in-chief of the newspaper Zaq works for.

The office was next to a dump site, and facing it across the road was a police barracks. From the office's dim and miserable interior one could hear the bugle calling the men to the parade ground, and one could smell the dump site. I found Beke Johnson eating from a lunch box on his desk; the box gave up a strong smell of burned palm oil and onions. A square red stain sat in the centre of his blue tie. The office was narrow and long, like a corridor, and his desk was at one end, near the window that faced the barracks. On the table were files spilling out papers, an old computer, a stapler and a stone paperweight, all jostling for space with the lunch box. He ate with a loud, wet sound, his mouth open. It was an unremarkable place, with two unremarkable women working in front of two computers at the other end of the corridor.

The editor looked even more unremarkable in his rumpled, oversized suit and tie; he could be an apparatchik in some grey, concrete ministry building. All he wanted to know after I had introduced myself was when Zaq would be returning. When I told him Zaq was ill, he looked sceptical.

– Tell him to hurry up and get well, otherwise I'll stop his salary. 224 Wörter

From: Oil on Water, *2010.*

Annotations
1 **dump site** place where garbage is dumped
2 **bugle** *Signalhorn*
12 **rumple sth.** make a mess of sth.
13 **apparatchik** blindly devoted official

Info
In **direct characterization**, characters are presented directly through descriptions by the narrator or other characters. **Indirect characterization** means that characters are presented through their use of language, actions, attitudes, behaviour and by their relationships to other characters.

Looking at the *characterization

HA **8** a Make notes on the following aspects of the text above:
1 the surroundings
2 the description of the office
3 Beke Johnson's appearance
4 his behaviour
5 his reaction to Rufus's information

HA b Use your notes to write a short description of the impression Beke makes.

► Support (task 8b), p. 195

HA **9** *** Rewrite the excerpt from the novel using mainly *direct characterization.

Now read one more excerpt from the same novel.

DIF vorbereitend in PA Passagen markieren, die deutlich umgeschrieben werden müssen

The next village was almost a replica of the last: the same empty squat dwellings, the same ripe and flagrant stench, the barrenness, the oil slick, and the same indefinable sadness in the air, as if a community of ghosts were suspended above the punctured zinc roofs, unwilling to depart, yet powerless to return. In the village centre we found the communal well. Eager for a drink, I bent under the wet, mossy pivotal beam and peered into the well's blackness, but a rank smell wafted from its hot depths and slapped my face; I reeled away, my head aching from the encounter. Something organic, perhaps human, lay dead and decomposing down there, its stench mixed with that unmistakable smell of oil. At the other end of the village a little river trickled towards the big river where we had left our boat. The patch of grass growing by the water was suffocated by a film of oil, each blade covered with blotches like the liver spots on a smoker's hands. 171 Wörter

From: Oil on Water, *2010.*

Annotations
1 **replica** copy
2 **flagrant** (here) clearly perceptible
2 **stench** unpleasant smell
4 **punctured** containing holes
6 **pivotal** important
6 **rank** *(adj)* (here) smelling unpleasantly
6 **waft** float
7 **reel** *(v) taumeln*
12 **blotch** mark; spot

Achtung: Die detaillierten Beschreibungen von Tod und Verwesung können starke Reaktionen auslösen.

Looking at the *setting and *atmosphere

10 **a** Together with a partner, discuss your first reaction to the text above.
b Compare your expectations: What do you think will happen?

HA **11*** Examine the language of the excerpt, including examples of the following: DIF Bearbeitung in PA

*repetition • *enumeration • *connotation • *simile • *metaphor

Lernen App: Video on stylistic devices Overview of stylistic devices
► Getting started
► WOB: A9 Narrative prose, pp. 28–31

HA **12** Read the Info box on the right, take a look at the picture below and relate how this information helps you better understand Habila's description of the Niger Delta. DIGI/DIF *mini-presentation* zu Umweltproblemen durch Ölförderung im Niger-Delta erstellen

Info

The **Niger Delta** sits directly on the Gulf of Guinea on the Atlantic Ocean in Nigeria and covers about 70,000 km². Sometimes referred to as the Oil Rivers, the Niger Delta used to be an important producer of palm oil. Today, about 2 million barrels (that's 317,974,590 litres!) of another kind of oil – petroleum – are extracted there daily. The environmental degradation and the unequal distribution of the oil wealth continue to be the motivation for environmental movements and conflicts in the Niger Delta region. For the indigenous population, the standard of living has hardly improved, while their natural environment continues to be severely damaged.

HA **13*** After having read several excerpts from *Oil on Water* and learning more about the Niger Delta, are you interested in reading the novel? Why or why not?

Chapter 6
Science and Technology – an Everchanging Field

Einstiegsidee: ergänzend das Bild mit Michelangelos „Die Erschaffung Adams" vergleichen

▸ More info
Lernen App: The Creation of Adam

DIGI Ideen mit digitalem Tool sammeln

DIF aufgabenrelevante Kollokationen vorgeben, z. B. *the rising impact of sth., the prospects of technology, machine learning, to drastically change sth., to open up new perspectives*

Begriff *caption* erläutern und ein Beispiel geben

DIF Kriterien für das Finden einer gelungenen Bildunterschrift vorgeben

DIF zusätzliche inhaltliche Anregungen geben, z. B. *quality of life, health care, connectivity, privacy issues, security issues, governmental power*

CT **1** **a** **Think** Work on your own. Write down ideas and emotions that the picture evokes for you.

Language help

The picture depicts/makes me think of ... • It refers/alludes to ... • It suggests/symbolizes ... • It can be connected to the idea of ... • almost touching hands • artificial/robotic arm • artificial intelligence • give life to sb./sth. • reach out to sb./sth. • create life

CT **b** **Pair** Compare and discuss your ideas with a partner. Together agree on a suitable caption for the picture.

CT **c** **Share** Present your captions in class. Then discuss what questions the picture and captions raise about the role of science and technology today.

CT **2** **a** Will science and technology give us a better future? Write down a few ideas.

CT **b** Share your ideas with a partner. Then have a look at the Chapter map on the right and speculate about what you will learn in this chapter.

CT **c** Taking the keywords in the Chapter map into consideration, discuss with your partner what the future will most probably be like.

Alternative: stummes Schreibgespräch in PA

Alternative: Aufgabe als *Quick-write*-Schreibimpuls verwenden

DIF *Elevator pitch talk* vorbereiten und vortragen

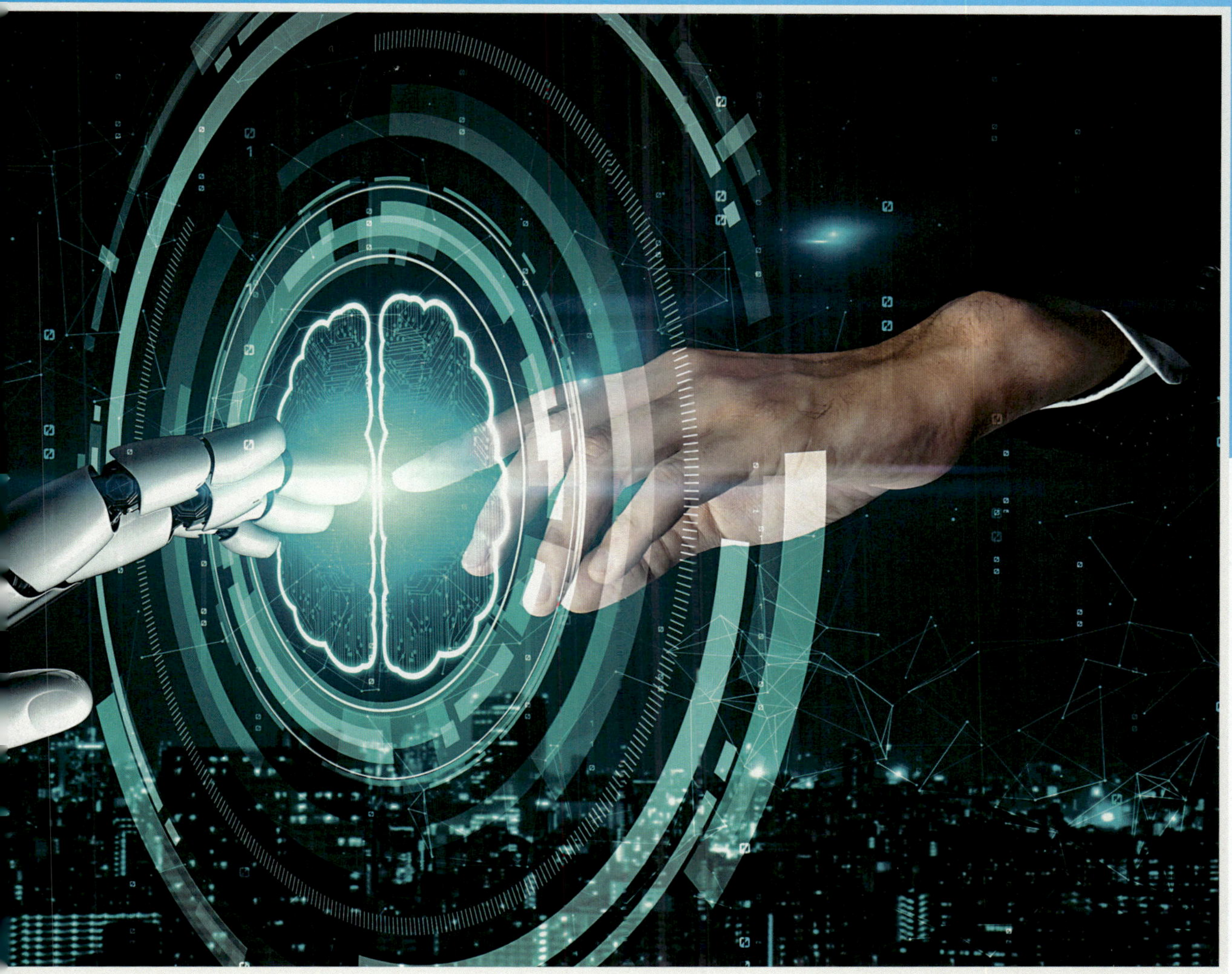

Chapter map

benefits
surveillance
progress
replacement
Chapter task: an argumentative text
Will science and technology give us a better future?
Argumentative writing
risks
sustainability
innovation
ethics

Lernen App: Useful vocabulary for the chapter

▶ More language

Lernen App: Science – motor of progress? (00:03:41)

Human life – shaped by science and technology

Science and technology: drivers of progress

Ground-breaking new developments in science and technology have fundamentally altered the ways people live, connect and communicate with each other – often with profound effects on society, politics, the economy and the environment. Scientific knowledge and technological advances have improved the quality of life and been key drivers of economic progress and global change – from the invention of the wheel to driverless cars. Modern technology has become an indispensable part of our lives by making information more accessible and thus empowering people. It has changed the way we get around as well. E-cars have long ceased to be a rarity, and e-buses are now charged by induction while driving. While innovations in areas such as computing, biotechnology and artificial intelligence are bound to transform our human experience in the years to come, innovative environmental technologies – for example to clean water or air or to generate electricity – could change the whole world in the near future.

Science and technology are everywhere

Both science and technology can be found in every conceivable area of our lives these days. They are always present. Nowadays, even the youngest children learn how to use tablets and smartphones. Technology helps them learn, inspires their ideas and lays the foundation for them to go on to develop future inventions. Science is now so advanced that it can save us from many illnesses. Technology records every step we take and monitors our vital functions on our wrist. Even our leisure time is affected: at a football match, no foul or offside on the pitch goes undetected, no one in the crowd in the stadium can avoid surveillance – because surveillance has many faces these days.

Challenges and dangers

There is no doubt that scientific and technological changes will pose complex challenges in the future. Innovations and discoveries are likely to raise new concerns and ethical questions. Some people object to their every move being recorded. Others are worried about the growing impact of artificial intelligence, which may render traditional jobs obsolete, maybe even social relationships. Others are concerned that, despite its potential for curing diseases, genetic engineering might have harmful effects on the health of future generations. Scientists and engineers worldwide will evidently need to proceed with great care and caution, continually reflecting on the ethical implications and social consequences of their inventions and innovations.

398 Wörter

1 Main ideas
Aufgaben 1a und b können in PA erledigt werden

▶ Check Lernen App: Answer key for task 1a

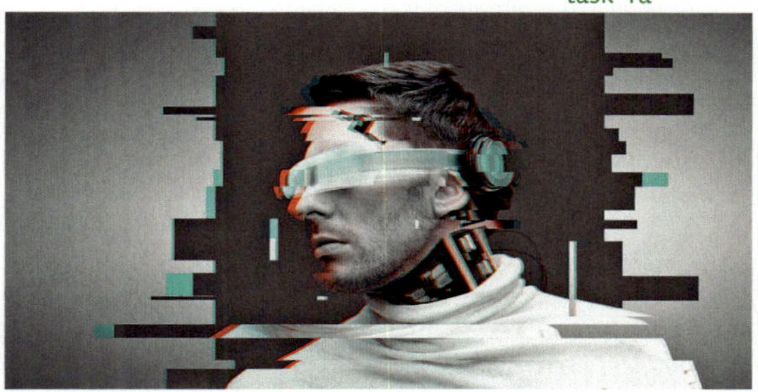

a Read the text and complete the sentences.
 1 Science and technology have been a positive force in that …
 2 Examples of the advancement of science and technology are …
 3 Humankind will have to be careful that …

b Compare your ideas with a partner.

2 Reflect
das Konzept *spidergram* vorbereitend wiederholen

a Read the text again and create a *spidergram about science and technology using the information in the text.

b Add words and phrases from the exercises on this page and keep adding to your spidergram throughout the chapter.

DIF Oberbegriffe vorgeben oder KV 17: Spidergram graphic organizer verwenden

DIGI *spidergram digital* erstellen

3 Singular and plural forms
Besonderheiten von *countable* und *non-countable nouns* wiederholen

Lernen App: Video on countable and uncountable nouns

▶ More language 

a Uncountable nouns are only used in their singular form, e. g. *happiness*. Find at least five uncountable nouns in the text.

b Now find nouns in the text that are used both in their singular and in their plural forms.

c Choose four of the words you collected and write a short paragraph about the topic 'What science and technology mean to me'.

Methode: *milling around* (SuS lesen einander ihre Texte vor, Zuhörer/innen achten auf korrekte Verwendung der Nomen)

▶ Check Lernen App: Answer key for tasks 3a and b

LÖS 3b
life/lives (ll. 5, 22) • technology/technologies (ll. 7, 16) • invention/inventions (ll. 6, 25)

4 Chunk it!

Lernen App: Video about chunks

▶ Getting started 

a Match the verbs on the left with the nouns on the right to form common collocations.

Verbs	Nouns
create	challenges
empower	ideas
gain	concerns
pose	opportunities
raise	people
solve	popularity
inspire	problems

b Check which collocations are used in the text.

▶ Check Lernen App: Answer key for tasks 4a and b

▶ WOB: B8 Collocations with prepositions, p. 56

DIGI Richtigkeit der Lösungen mit einem digitalen Kollokationslexikon selbst überprüfen

5 You choose Science and technology
Work on task **a** or **b**. Use as many words and phrases from your *spidergram and *collocations from task **4** as possible.

HA CT **a** Write a short report for your school magazine in which you introduce one of your hobbies and explain how science and technology are involved.

Beiträge in PA präsentieren, z. B. im *double circle*

DIF zusätzliches Sprachmaterial vorgeben

HA CT **b** Work with a partner. Write a dialogue about the importance and dangers of scientific and technological progress. In your dialogue use words from your spidergram and task **4**.

DIF *persuasive phrases* vorgeben, z. B. *absolutely important, totally convinced, there is no denying the fact that*

als Rollenspiel durchführen; mögliche Rollen: *politician, environmental activist, concerned parent, young businessman/woman*

▶ SF 33: Writing a report, p. 243

▶ SF 38: Creative writing, p. 249

Life-changing innovations

gallery walk mit Bildern bahnbrechender Erfindungen, z. B. *wheel, telephone, printing press, airplane, Internet, personal computer, telescope*

DIGI *gallery walk* als *web quest* mit Links zu Texten im Internet gestalten

1 a **Think** Make a list of technological innovations that have changed the world. You may use a German-English dictionary.
b **Pair** Compare your lists and give reasons for your choices.
c **Share** Discuss which innovation has had the greatest impacted on your lives.

The pictures below show 21st century innovations.

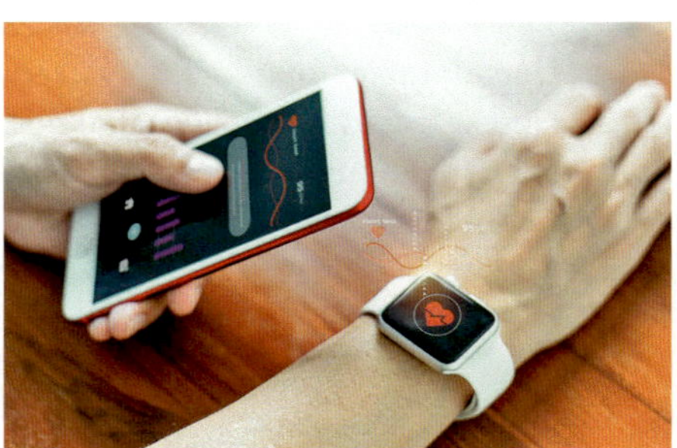

DIF zusätzliches Sprachmaterial vorgeben, z. B. *to fly autonomously, to activate sth., voice commands, wearable computer, to be immersed in sth., computer-generated environment, to connect to a smartphone*

Annotation
gadget small device or machine with a particular purpose

in PA Informationen über die vier *gadgets* in einer Tabelle zusammentragen → im Plenum ergänzen

Comprehension

2 a Identify the latest technological innovations in the pictures and briefly outline their functions.
b Brainstorm ideas on how useful these gadgets are and how they could help to make society more eco-friendly.

Language help

a smart/new/widely used invention/gadget/device • have a significant/major/minor influence/impact on sth. • make life easier / more complex • be easy/difficult to use • be cheap/expensive/cost-efficient • have a small/large environmental footprint/impact

Lernen App: Prefixes

► More language

► SF 8: Working with dictionaries, p. 209

DIGI Beispiele für Wörter mit den angeführten Präfixen und Adjektiven in einer Wortwolke sammeln

Language awareness

3 With the arrival of new technologies, new words have entered the English language. To describe the latest technological products or ideas, the prefixes *e-*, *i-*, *cyber-*, *info-*, *tech-*, *techno-* and *net-* or adjectives like *smart* and *virtual* are often added to existing words, thereby creating new words. Write a short text of between 50 and 100 words describing your everyday use of technology. Use at least five words with the listed prefixes or adjectives.

DIF einsprachiges Wörterbuch nutzen

Beyond the text

Lernen App: Video on giving a presentation
► Getting started (task 4 a)
► SF 13: Doing research, p. 214

4 You choose Work on either **a** or **b**.

HA **a** Speaking Research one of the technological innovations in the box. Then give a short presentation on its potential to change the world.

digital tattoos • brain chips • autonomous driving • face recognition • cow-free burger • holo learning • smart toaster

HA **b** Intercultural communication Choose a country from the box and research the technologies it has invented. Report back to the class.

Switzerland • Sweden • U.S.A. • Netherlands • UK • Finland • Denmark • Austria • Singapore • Germany • Israel • South Korea • India • China • Ireland • Nigeria • United Arab Emirates

► WOB: A4

DIGI SuS erstellen ein *explainer video* über eine technische Errungenschaft ihrer Wahl

Text 2

* Two teenage inventors

Zaria Gorvett

Lernen App: Video on modal auxiliaries
► More language

HA • ***Quick write:** How might teenagers make valuable contributions to the world of technology? Write a short paragraph using auxiliary verbs.

Aufgabe als HA vorbereiten → anhand der Ergebnisse im Unterricht Form und Funktion von *modal auxiliary verbs* an Beispielen wiederholen

Language help

be inspired • plan to do sth. • discover sth. • invent sth. • come up with sth. • have a passion for sth. • dedicate time to sth.
Use **modal auxiliaries** to talk about ...
ability: can / could / be able to obligation: should / ought to / be supposed to
necessity: have to / have got to / must
possibility: be likely to / will / may / might

Partner B: Go to page 195.
Partner A: Look at the picture. Speculate about the purpose of the gadget she is showing. Then read the text on p. 156, do the tasks **1** to **4** below and present your results to your partner.

Language help

With her invention people could ... / might be able to ... • The purpose of the gadget could/might be to ... • Users should / have to / are supposed to ... • The gadget is likely to / will/won't ...

You are going to read a text about a teenage inventor.

Many are too young to drink, drive, or even catch an Uber – but they're already filing patents. They're known for their mood swings, social media addiction and dubious fashion choices. But some teenagers break the mould. A new generation of precocious youths is solving the problems of today with ambitious, ground-breaking tech [...]

Hannah Herbst, 17, Florida

Herbst was inspired to invent at the age of 15 by her then-nine-year-old pen pal, who lives in Ethiopia and did not have access to lights. This is surprisingly common: there are 1.3 billion people alive today without electricity. So this student came up with the Beacon (Bringing Electricity Access to Countries through Ocean Energy), which captures energy directly from ocean waves.

Herbst's thinking was that populations tend to settle around bodies of water; about 40 % of the world's population lives within 100 km (62 miles) off the coast and only 10 % lives further than 10 km (6.2 miles) away from a source of freshwater that you don't have to dig for, such as a river or lake.

The technology consists of a hollow plastic tube, with a propeller at one end and a hydroelectric generator at the other. As tidal energy drives the propeller, it's converted into useable energy by the generator. After designing a prototype turbine as a computer model, Herbst 3D-printed a prototype which she tested in an intercoastal waterway.

If the design were to be scaled up, Herbst has calculated that Beacon could charge three car batteries simultaneously in an hour. She suggests that the energy generated could be used to power water purification technologies, or blood centrifuges at hospitals in the developing world.

The invention won the Discovery Education 3M Young Scientist Challenge in 2015, among numerous other awards, and Herbst is currently studying for a degree in computer engineering while she completes high school. [...]

314 Wörter

From: 'Four teenage inventors changing our world', bbc.com, *16 March 2018*

Annotations
- 2 **file a patent** officially record the right to make or sell an invention
- 3 **break the mould** be completely new and different
- 4 **precocious** a child being very mature or having above average mental or physical abilities for their age
- 16 **hollow** having a hole or empty space inside
- 17 **tidal** connected with the rise and fall of the sea
- 21 **scale up** increase the size, amount or importance of sth.
- 23 **purification** the act of removing harmful substances from sth.

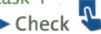

▶ More info
Lernen App: More about Hannah Herbst

Fehlerquelle: Aussprache von *turbine* [ˈtɜːbaɪn] (Z. 18)

Comprehension

Lernen App: Answer key for task 1
▶ Check

HA **1** Complete the sentences using information from the text:
1. Hannah Herbst invented ...
2. Hannah Herbst's invention was inspired by ...
3. Scaling the invention up could ...

DIF den Satzanfängen fertige Antworten zuordnen

HA **2** Were your ideas about the purpose of the invention correct? List the differences between your speculations and what it was originally intended for.

Analysis

HA **3** The *register of the text ranges between neutral and scientific. Find examples and examine the effect this has. Pay attention to language and structure.

Begriff *register* vorbereitend erläutern und an Beispielen illustrieren

▶ WOB: B14 Register, pp. 64–65

DIGI SuS informieren sich online über Form und Verwendung der *were to*-Struktur (Partner A) und des Hilfsverbs *would* für *habitual actions* (Partner B).

Language awareness

Lernen App: Video on conditional sentences

▶ More language

HA **4 a** Examine the choice of *were to be* in the following sentence: 'If the design were to be scaled up ...' (l. 21).

HA **b** Make similar sentences using *were to be*.

LÖS **4a**
Were to is used in a conditional clause to say that the condition (i.e. scaling up the design) is rather unlikely to happen.

Beyond the text

5 Describe the purpose of the invention you have read about to your partner and together decide which of them is more likely to change society for the better.

DIGI mithilfe einer App abstimmen und das Ergebnis im Plenum diskutieren

Lernen App: Audio (06:30 min.)

6 a Listening Listen to an article about young inventors read by AI. Summarize
HA the gist of the article in three sentences.

DIGI/DIF den Text online in passender Geschwindigkeit anhören

b Listening Listen again. Then name
HA
1 three old inventions that changed the way we live.
2 at least three fields in which contestants developed their innovations.
3 the two mentioned winning inventions.

c In small groups, discuss which of the inventions you find most useful.

▶ WOB: A5

▶ SF 40: Listening for gist/detail, p. 253

▶ WOB: A6 Listening, pp. 20–23

im Anschluss KV 18: Listening for language in context bearbeiten und thematisch relevante *chunks* heraushören

Text 3

Lernen App: A photo stimulus: Reducing your impact on the environment?

▶ Getting started

Towards a sustainable future? Peter Sänger

HA CT
- Name and discuss inventions or projects that are aimed at reducing humans' harmful impact on the environment in your neighbourhood or city.

The German start-up Green City Solutions attempts to tackle one of the modern problems we face: air pollution. Read the excerpt from their press release.

SuS recherchieren als HA Maßnahmen / Projekte in ihrer Heimatgemeinde und machen sich Notizen, die im Unterricht in einer *milling-around*-Übung besprochen werden.

Was treibt Euch bei Green City Solutions an?

Städte sind unzweifelhaft der Lebensraum der Zukunft. Bis 2030 werden voraussichtlich zwei Drittel aller Menschen in Städten leben. Damit also der Großteil der Menschheit ein gesundes und lebenswertes Wohn- und Arbeitsumfeld haben kann, muss in Städten einiges passieren. Städte sind zum einen der Haupttreiber der Erderwärmung – mehr als 70 Prozent aller CO2 – Emissionen entstehen in der Stadt. Gleichzeitig sind urbane Räume besonders anfällig für die Folgen des Klimawandels. Hier staut sich schlechte Luft und Hitze. Die überwiegende Versiegelung des Bodens macht es enorm schwer, mehr Grün [...] einzusetzen, um Emissionen schon am Entstehungsort zu binden. Doch nicht nur die Neupflanzung ist vielerorts schwer möglich. Auch die bestehenden Stadtbäume leiden enorm unter den Klimafolgen und gehen reihenweise ein. Wir wollen dort eine Alternative sein, wo klassisches Grün es schwer hat. Dort kann das sehr flächeneffiziente Moos in Verbindung mit unseren Biofiltern dafür sorgen, dass Luftverschmutzung in Wohn- und Arbeitsräumen gezielt verringert und der Schaden für Mensch und Klima begrenzt wird.

Moos in die Stadt? Wie soll denn das funktionieren?

Wir finden: Moos muss in die Stadt! Unser Kernprodukt ist ein Moosfilter. Er basiert auf der Idee, Natur mit digitaler Technologie zu kombinieren, um so die Luftqualität zu verbessern. In der natürlichen Pflanze Moos steckt so viel mehr, als man denkt! Moose binden Feinstaub, manche sind antiseptisch, antiviral und fungizid; echte Allrounder für Luftreinhaltung und Gesundheit. Mit dem Zusam-

Annotation
21 **fungizid** pilztötend

menspiel von Sensoren, intelligenter Ventilation, Bewässerung und Software können wir diese natürliche Reinigungsleistung steigern sowie nutz- und messbar machen. All unsere Produkte basieren auf der Idee, warme und verdreckte Stadtluft aktiv durch reinigende Moosmatten zu leiten und so zu kühlen und zu reinigen. Smarte Internet-of-Things-Technologie steuert die Wasserversorgung des Mooses und misst Umwelt- und Luftqualitätsdaten. Die Moose sind in der Lage Feinstaub zu binden und sogar zu verstoffwechseln, daher sind unsere Biofilter nachhaltig und kommen vollständig ohne Filtermüll aus. Bis 2030 wollen wir 100.000 Quadratmeter an Moos in die urbanen Räume der Welt gebracht haben und damit 500 Millionen Menschen vor Luftverschmutzung und Hitzestau schützen. Damit dieses sportliche Ziel erreicht werden kann, bauen wir verschiedene Wege in die Stadt. Angefangen mit dem CityTree. Der größte und leistungsstärkste unserer Biofilter ist gleichzeitig der, mit dem alles angefangen hat. Schon 2016 haben wir eine erste Version in ganz Europa aufgestellt, die in der Zwischenzeit jedoch enorm weiterentwickelt wurde. Die neueste Version des CityTrees ist mit seinem Vorgänger nicht mehr zu vergleichen – sowohl äußerlich als auch bezogen auf das, was drinsteckt. Der CityTree wälzt in der Stunde 5.000 Kubikmeter Luft um, das entspricht der Menge, die 10.000 Menschen in derselben Zeit atmen. Er wird an vielbefahrenen Straßen, auf Marktplätzen, Schulhöfen, aber auch in Industriehallen eingesetzt. In Verbindung mit der Sitzbank entsteht eine Begegnungszone in Waldluftatmosphäre. Die zweite Lösung ist der CityBreeze, ein Außenbildschirm mit Moosfilter im Rücken. [...] In Städten sind viele Orte bereits für digitale Stelen vorgesehen. In der Regel werden diese nach sieben Jahren ausgetauscht. Wir finden, dass dann ein Upgrade sinnvoll ist. Warum nicht den Bildschirm mit einem Mehrwert versehen? Das Tolle daran: Außenbildschirme werden dort eingesetzt, wo viele Menschen sich aufhalten. Genau da wollen wir auch die Luft reinigen. Die dritte Lösung ist unser Fassadenmodul namens Wall-Breeze. Ohne aufwendige Nachrüstung passt er an jede Wand und ist durch die Ventilation unabhängig von Windverhältnissen. Das macht ihn im Gegensatz zu Rankpflanzen, die zunehmend an Fassaden eingesetzt werden, leistungsfähiger und wirksamer. Wir können bis zu 48 Wall-Breeze verbinden und damit enorme Mengen an Dreck aus der Luft ziehen. Für alle drei Lösungen gelten dieselben Leistungsdaten: Bis zu 82 % des Feinstaubs wird vom Moos gereinigt, während die Umgebungsluft gleichzeitig um etwa 4 °C runtergekühlt wird.

Welche Lösungen hat Green City Solutions im Angebot? Woher kommt das Moos, das in den Moosfiltern genutzt wird, und wie lange hält es?

Es gibt etwa 20.000 Moosarten auf der ganzen Welt, von den Polarregionen bis in die Wüste kommen sie vor. Da wir die Moose natürlich nicht aus der Natur entnehmen wollen und wir konstant bestrebt sind, immer bessere Moosarten und -mixe für unsere Zwecke zu finden, haben wir in Bestensee nahe Berlin die weltweit erste vertikale Moosfarm aufgebaut. Hier wachsen auf gut 1.200 Quadratmeter Moose in Form von vertikalen Moosmatten. [...] Einmal in die Moosfilter eingesetzt, trägt unser spezieller Bio-Algorithmus dafür Sorge, dass die Moose bestens versorgt werden. Wir arbeiten mit natürlichen und nachhaltigen Filtern, die sich selbst regenerieren können. [...] Mit jedem Tag, an dem der Bio-Algorithmus dazulernt, verlängert sich die Ausdauer der Moose. Ein bis zwei Mal im Jahr überprüfen wir die Biofilter vor Ort, um einen reibungslosen Betrieb zu garantieren. Sind wir vor Ort, dann haben wir frisches Moos im Gepäck und geben dem eingesetzten Moos eine Verschnaufpause. [...] *782 words*

From: 'we grow fresh air', greencitysolutions.de, *2022*

Lernen App: Video on giving a presentation

Lernen App: Video on mediation

- ▶ Getting started
- ▶ SF 49: Mediating from German into English, p. 270
- ▶ SF 43: Giving a presentation, p. 259
- ▶ WOB: A7 Mediating, pp. 24–25

1 You choose | Mediating | Intercultural communication Do either task **a** or **b**.

HA CT **a** Writing You are part of an international student group that is preparing an online presentation on the topic 'How technology can help to make the world more eco-friendly'. Use the information given in the article to write an informative text for your presentation leaflet.

DIGI *presentation leaflet* mit Online-Tool gestalten

HA CT **b** Speaking As part of an international workshop for students you have to prepare a presentation on the topic: 'We can't breathe – the future of modern cities'. Present the advantages of the Green City Solutions' inventions mentioned in the text.

DIGI Präsentation aufzeichnen, auf digitaler Plattform hochladen und einander Feedback geben

Beyond the text

2 Research which technological tools are already being used to reduce air pollution in cities. Rechercheergebnisse in *infographic* festhalten und einander im *double circle* vorstellen
HA CT

Text 4

Lernen App: Kenan Malik

▶ More info 

Technology will never replace human judgement. Look at football ...

Kenan Malik

DIGI idiomatische deutsche Entsprechungen über Suchmaschine finden

- Make two groups: **A** football experts, **B** questioners. **B:** Ask **A** for the German equivalents of the football expressions in the box. **A:** Name the German terms and explain their meaning in the context of the game.

VAR referee • VAR check • on-field referee • to be offside • deem offside • Premier League • contentious incidents • a refereeing decision • refereeing errors • TV replays • fan fury • a forward • a striker • disallow a goal • stoppages • TV feeds

Now read an article by the British writer, lecturer and broadcaster Kenan Malik in which he discusses the use of VAR (video assistant referee) in football.

Even if you can't tell your offside from your elbow (in the face), you've probably heard of VAR. The video assistant referee has been introduced into top-level football to cut out errors by referees. At every Premier League game, a VAR referee watches TV feeds of the game to check potentially contentious decisions.

Moaning at referees has long been the staple of football fans. 'That was never a penalty!' 'Ref, do you need glasses? It was offside by a mile.'

VAR was supposed to resolve, or at least reduce, such disagreements. Instead, it has generated even more discord. So much so that the debate about VAR has

Annotations
4 **contentious** controversial
5 **staple** important part of sth.

spilled over from the sports pages into the news pages and discussions on the Today programme.

It's tempting to dismiss the controversy over VAR as a story of interest only to football fans. But it's also one that helps illuminate our broader relationship to technology, at a time when technology, especially AI, is beginning to shape many aspects of our lives, from the possibility of driverless cars to algorithms that can make decisions about medical treatment.

In many of these areas, we worry that human judgments may be flawed and expect technology to provide better, more objective solutions. That's exactly the argument for VAR, too. So, non-football fans, bear with me, while I talk football and VAR, for the debate about VAR should be of interest to all of us.

VAR aims to eliminate 'clear and obvious errors' by referees by using TV replays to allow officials to view contentious incidents from different camera angles and by reconstructing the movement of the ball or players to check whether a goal was actually scored and whether a player was offside.

The trouble is, what constitutes a 'clear and obvious error' is itself a judgment call. Much of the controversy has arisen from fans disagreeing with VAR overturning a refereeing decision that they think should have stood or not overturning a decision they think is flawed. Instead of fan fury being directed at the on-field referee, it's now directed at both the on-field and the VAR referee.

What are seen as 'objective' decisions are often problematic. Take the offside rule. The rule has become more complicated in recent years, but in essence it states that a player is offside if any part of his body is nearer to the opponents' goal line than both the ball and the second-last opponent. The rule is there primarily to stop a forward gaining an unfair advantage by ignoring the play and simply standing near the goal waiting for the ball.

VAR shows that we should be wary of imagining technology as necessarily providing more objective answers.

VAR ignores that context – the attempt to gain an unfair advantage. Instead, the technology can rule even the slightest hint of a supposed infringement "offside". Recently, the Liverpool striker Roberto Firmino had a goal disallowed because his armpit was deemed offside. That the Premier League could tweet that explanation for the decision in all seriousness shows much of what is wrong with VAR.

So, what can we learn from VAR about the broader use of technology? First, that human judgment is indispensable. Technology can help us make better decisions. But, in important issues, it can rarely replace human decision-making.

Second, VAR reminds us that context matters. Whether in football or in society, we don't start with the rules that have to be followed. We start with a vision of how we want the game, or society, to be and use rules, or laws, to achieve those ends. Mechanically enforcing rules or laws, irrespective of the context, makes little sense. Too often, we forget that what algorithms lack is precisely that understanding of context.

Third, there are trade-offs. In football, stoppages to check VAR kill the flow of the game and expunge the joy of celebrating a goal that may later be disallowed through a VAR check. Many fans would rather accept old-fashioned refereeing errors to

Annotations

11 **dismiss sth.** decide that sth. is not important; reject or dispute sth.
12 **illuminate sth.** make sth. easier to understand
16 **flawed** not perfect
18 **bear with sb./sth.** be patient with sb./sth.
24 **judgment call** a difficult decision because there is no correct or easy answer
25 **overturn sth.** change a decision
33 **forward** (*n*) offensive football player
38 **rule sth.** decide sth. officially
38 **infringement** action that breaks a rule
43 **indispensable** essential
49 **lack sth.** not have sth.
51 **expunge sth.** remove sth.

retain the old-fashioned thrill of the game. Similar trade-offs exist in our social lives, for instance, between the ease that technology provides and the loss of privacy it often entails. We need a proper acknowledgement of, and public debate about, such trade-offs.

Finally, VAR shows that we should be wary of imagining technology as necessarily providing more objective answers. A machine or an algorithm is only as good as the humans who created it and the data with which it's fed. That is why algorithms are often biased in their working. And why debates about refereeing don't end with the introduction of VAR. Technology may amplify rather than eliminate the flaws of human judgment.

Technology is a boon. We should, however, be wary of overestimating its ability to provide better answers and underestimating the significance of human judgment.

819 Wörter

From: guardian.com, *16 November 2019*

Annotations
53 **trade-off** situation in which you accept sth. bad to have sth. good/have to give up one thing to have sth. else
55 **entail sth.** involve sth.
60 **biased** not accurate; unfair; one-sided
61 **amplify sth.** increase the effect of sth.
63 **boon** sth. that is very helpful
63 **be wary of sth.** be careful/cautious about sth.

Comprehension

CT **1** List the pros and cons of VAR in football as mentioned in the text.

Pro- und Kontra-Argumente auf Textkopie/Tablet in verschiedenen Farben markieren → in einer Tabelle mit Zeilenangaben zusammentragen und im Plenum besprechen

Analysis

CT **2** **a** Identify the introduction, the main part and the conclusion of the text.

b CT Examine how the introduction of the text shows the significance of the topic, how Kenan Malik tries to create interest, and how he presents his personal opinion.

c CT In the main body of his text, Kenan Malik presents his arguments. Analyse whether the author's line of argumentation follows a logical order.

d Examine whether the conclusion is effective. Add quotes

LÖS 2a
- introduction (ll. 1–19): presents the topic
- main body (ll. 20–41): presents arguments for and against the use of VAR technology
- conclusion (ll. 42–64): presents the author's personal conclusion

Vorwissen aus dem Fach Deutsch über gängige Bauformen argumentativer Texte aktivieren, z. B. lineare Erörterung *(comment)*, dialektische Erörterung *(discussion)*, Sanduhrprinzip *(hourglass format)*, Reißverschlussprinzip

▶ SF 17: Reading and understanding non-fictional texts, p. 221

▶ WOB: A1 Reading for analysis, pp. 4–7

Language awareness

3 Work on either **a** or **b**.

HA CT **a** Find four sentences in which Kenan Malik uses 'we' and rewrite them without using 'we'. What effect does this have on the text as well as on the reader?

HA CT **b** Challenge Analyse and explain the effect which the repeated use of the pronoun 'we' has on the presentation of the author's arguments.

DIF Leistungsstärkere SuS übernehmen die Moderation der Diskussion, leistungsschwächere SuS nutzen SF 46 und die dort aufgelisteten sprachlichen Hilfsmittel

Beyond the text

4 Speaking Discuss if nowadays technology makes people enjoy sports more. Take notes first and then have your discussion. At the end of your discussion, evaluate which opinion is predominant.

▶ SF 46: Having a discussion, p. 264

▶ WOB: A5 Speaking – discussion, pp. 18–19

▶ Getting started Lernen App: Interviews

5 Imagine you have the opportunity to meet a famous personality (athlete, artist, etc.) and interview them about the role of technology in their field.

HA **a** Write down questions you would like to ask.

b Work in pairs and role-play the interview. Then swap roles.

DIF ohne note *cards* arbeiten

Lernen App: Video on argumentative writing

Schwerpunkt-Kompetenz Chapter 6: Argumentative Writing

► Getting started

► SF 27: Essentials: the stages of writing, p. 234

► WOB: A2

Reactivate

You have already written quite a few argumentative texts in your native language as well as in a foreign language. Take a minute to reflect on your own writing experiences.

1 Writing an argumentative text

a CT Read the recommendations for writing a good argumentative text in the box. For each tip, note down how much it could help you to improve your writing:
+: very helpful advice that I should definitely follow next time I write this kind of text.
o: nice reminder of what I already know
-: I don't need this tip, it's beside the point/not relevant

b CT Share your ideas in class, then collect more tips on what makes good argumentative writing. The information about the writing process in the diagram will help you.

SuS übertragen die für sie relevanten Tipps in eine Tabelle mit zwei Spalten (+, o), die sie in 1b ausbauen können.

A good argumentative text should ...
- have a central idea.
- have a clear structure.
- have paragraphs which support the central idea.
- be neutral/objective.
- create interest in its introduction.
- wrap up the main ideas in its conclusion.
- be written in correct English.

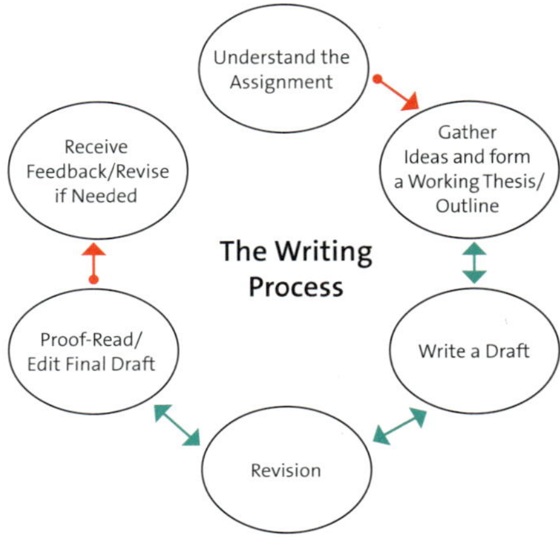

Lernen App: Video on writing

► Getting started

Step ahead

Writing an argumentative text, writers need time to generate ideas and plan their texts.

2 Planning your text

DIGI in Kleingruppen gemeinsam Ideen entwerfen, mit einem digitalen Tool festhalten → im Plenum sammeln und bündeln

DIF mithilfe der Suchbegriffe *scientific breakthrough / technological breakthrough* im Internet Beispiele für neueste wissenschaftliche und technische Entwicklungen suchen

CT **a** Your topic is: 'Has mankind reached a dangerous level of scientific and technological development?' To better understand what this topic is about, it is important to start by brainstorming ideas. Work in pairs. Focus on the key terms 'scientific development' and 'technological development' and add your own ideas to the two lists:

scientific development:
- genetic engineering: curing diseases, 'designing' babies ...
- biotechnology: vaccines, modified crops, drugs ...
- ...

technological development:
- artificial intelligence: voice assistants, smart homes, communication ...
- nano technology: micro robotics, water-repellent textiles, sunscreen ...
- ...

Schwerpunkt-Kompetenz Chapter 6: Argumentative Writing

CT **b** Work on your own. Identify some controversial points relating to the topic. Complete the sentences below in as many ways as you can:
- It is great that scientific progress makes it possible to ..., but this could also be a problem because ...
- On the one hand, it is great that we can ..., but on the other, this can also create problems if ...
- It may be true that when citizens use ..., they ..., but we must also consider that ...

► Support, p. 197
► WOB: A2

CT **c** Compare and discuss your ideas with a partner. Do you know enough about the topic to turn your ideas into convincing arguments? What other facts, data or examples do you need to research? *Methode: milling around activity*

HA CT **d** Do the additional research you think is necessary to have enough convincing arguments.

CT **e** Now you are ready to plan your text. Outline the structure of your text on whether scientific and technological development has reached a dangerous level.

A well-structured argumentative text usually has three parts: an introduction in which you create interest for your topic (one paragraph), a main body in which you present your arguments (three to five paragraphs), and a conclusion (one paragraph). There are two ways of structuring your text:

1 You start by presenting the counter-arguments, i. e. the arguments that are <u>not</u> in line with your own position (one to two paragraphs). Then you state <u>your</u> points (in two to three paragraphs).

counterargument 1
counterargument 2
your argument 1
your argument 2
your argument 3

If you choose this option, follow the hourglass format by presenting counterarguments from strong to weak and your own arguments from weak to strong. This will be an effective way of lending weight to your position.

2 You start out with a counter-argument and refute it right away, you then present another counter-argument and refute it as well, etc.

counterargument → your point
counterargument → your point
counterargument → your point
(one to two paragraphs each)

If you choose this option, make sure that the points supporting your own opinion are strong enough to refute the preceding counterarguments.

Aufbau eines überzeugenden Arguments wiederholen *(thesis – evidence – example)* und SuS bitten, bei der Recherche auf schlüssige Begründungen und interessante Beispiele zu achten

Pro-Argumente auf grünen *note cards* notieren, Kontra-Argumente auf roten

SuS besprechen die Informationen in der Box, entscheiden sich für eine der beiden Varianten, ordnen ihre Argumente auf den *note cards* sinnvoll an und stellen ihre Gliederungen im Plenum vor.

Practise

After brainstorming ideas, planning your text, and doing research, you are ready to turn your outline into a coherent text.

► Support, p. 197

LÖS 3
Pro (development has reached a dangerous level):
- Humankind is capable of destroying itself using technology (e.g. nuclear warfare).
- Genetically modified food may harm human health.
- Pesticides may destroy the environment.

Con (development has not reached a dangerous level):
- Science has enabled humankind to fight against diseases.
- Advantages of technology outweigh risks.
- As science progresses, we will find solutions for the problems mentioned.

3 Writing your argumentative text

HA CT

Write the first draft of your text about whether mankind has reached a dangerous level of scientific and technological development.

Take another look

Editing is a very important final step in writing. By carefully reading your text again another two or three times, you can make sure that your ideas are clear and to the point, and you can also spot language mistakes and correct them.

4 Editing your text

mithilfe der erarbeiteten Kriterien Rückmeldebogen für Mit-SuS erstellen

CT **a** Work with a partner. Swap your first drafts, read your texts and give each other feedback. Pay attention to the criteria for good texts you collected in task **1**.

CT **b** Using your partner's comments, edit your text and write your final draft.

5 Self-assessment

CT **a** Copy the *method card and decide for each step of the writing process whether you are already good at it or if it needs more practice.

Method card – writing	
What I am good at	What I need to practise
…	…

Methoden: *double circle* oder *milling around activity*

CT **b** Together with a partner discuss how you could enhance your writing skills. Take notes on your method card.

► WOB: A2 Writing, pp. 8–11

Artificial intelligence

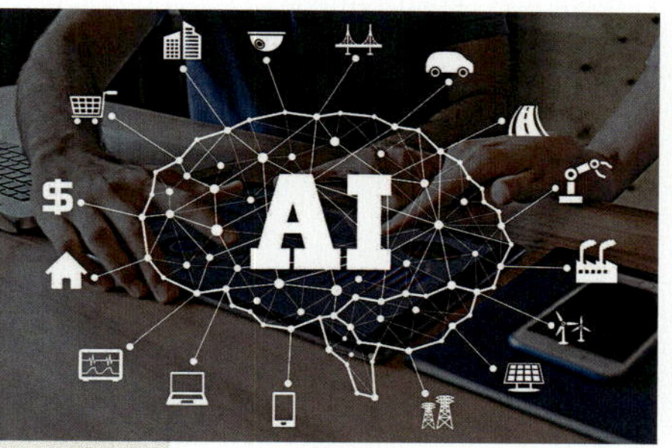

Info

AI – a driving force of technological change

Artificial intelligence (AI) has been rapidly evolving since the term was first coined in the 1950s. It is an interdisciplinary field that seeks to create intelligent machines that can think, learn, and act like humans. One of the earliest examples of AI is the Logic Theorist (1955), developed by Allen Newell and Herbert A. Simon. It was a computer program designed to prove mathematical theorems automatically using symbolic logic. Over the years, AI has developed from simple rule-based systems – a chatbot responding to specific questions for example – to advanced deep learning neural networks capable of processing vast amounts of data and making complex decisions. An example is self-driving cars that navigate through traffic based on sensor data and computer vision algorithms.
In the early years, AI research focused on creating machines that could reason, plan, and understand natural language. However, progress was slow, and the field was plagued by technical limitations, lack of funding, and limited access to data. In the 1990s, breakthroughs in machine learning and statistical modelling enabled the development of more advanced AI systems capable of recognizing patterns in data and making predictions.
In the 2000s, with the beginning of big data and cloud computing, AI development accelerated rapidly. Companies like Google, Facebook, and Amazon invested heavily in AI research, and the availability of massive amounts of data enabled the development of deep learning neural networks that could recognize complex patterns in images, speech, and text.
In recent years, AI has become more accessible to businesses and individuals due to the development of cloud-based AI platforms and open-source libraries. Easy-to-use tools, like the chatbot ChatGPT (Generative Pre-Trained Transformer), make it possible for both individuals and organizations of all sizes to use the power of AI.
As AI continues to evolve, there are concerns about the ethical and societal implications of intelligent machines. The development of AI must be guided by principles to ensure that it benefits humanity rather than harming it. One of the most significant initiatives in this area is the AI Ethics Guidelines developed by the European Commission's High-Level Expert Group on Artificial Intelligence. These guidelines provide a framework for the ethical development and deployment of AI and include principles such as transparency, accountability, and human-centricity. Another example is the IEEE (Institute of Electrical and Electronics Engineers) Global Initiative on Ethics of Autonomous and Intelligent Systems, which has drawn up a set of principles for the ethical design and development of autonomous and intelligent systems, including transparency, privacy, and responsibility.
The development of AI has been a long and complex journey, driven by advances in computing, data, and algorithms. While AI is still in its early stages, it has the potential to revolutionize many aspects of our lives and transform industries. However, it is essential to ensure that its development is guided by ethical principles in order to fully harness its potential.

► Skills Lab: Digital media and AI in language learning, p. 84

Quick write zum Titel der Infobox möglich. Anschließend tauschen die SuS sich aus und halten Argumente in einer Tabelle fest *(yes / no)*.

DIGI Antworten mithilfe eines digitalen Tools clustern

Fehlerquelle: Aussprache von *privacy* [ˈprɪvəsi] (BE) / [ˈpraɪvəsi] (AE) (Z. 37)

HA CT **1** Write a short timeline tracing the evolution of AI and its capabilities.

HA CT **2** List the different guidelines for the use of AI mentioned in the text and explain why they should be important. Write down some examples of different uses of AI.

485 Wörter

Einstiegsidee: Brainstorming oder Kurzreferate zu früheren technischen Innovationen, die Skepsis begegneten (Eisenbahn, Fotografie, Internet, E-Books …)

People are always sceptical at first when new technologies are introduced. It seems to be no different with AI, which has already become part of our everyday lives and is increasingly used in many different areas. Have a look at the diagrams showing how people in the US feel about the use of AI. ***Partner B****, go to page 198.* ***Partner A****, do the tasks below.*

vor der Bearbeitung von Aufgabe 1 mithilfe von SF 22 Redemittel zur Beschreibung und Analyse statistischer Daten rekapitulieren

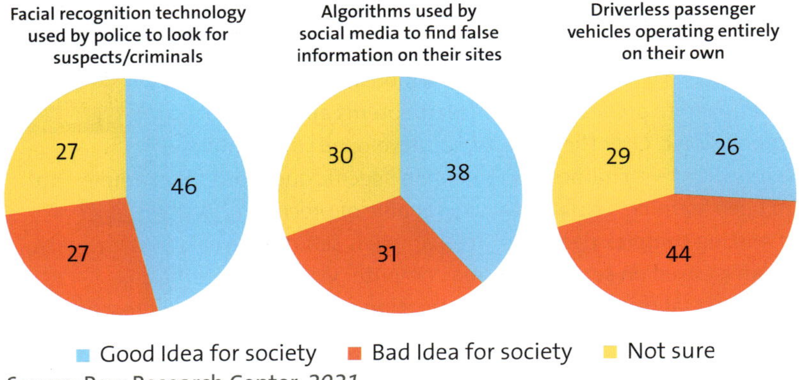

Source: Pew Research Center, *2021*

Lernen App: Video on analysing diagrams

▶ Getting started

▶ SF 22: Analysing diagrams, p. 227

▶ WOB: A1 Reading for analysis, pp. 4–7

Comprehension

1 Describe the data published by the Pew Research Center in 2021 to **Partner B**.

2 Summarize the conclusions that can be drawn in one or two sentences.

Beyond the text

3 What are your views on the implementation of the three AI applications mentioned in the diagrams?

a Do a class survey. Use a digital tool and visualize the results, e.g. by using bar charts, pie charts or graphs.

DIGI Fragebogen digital erstellen und bearbeiten

CT **b** In a double-circle activity, discuss what conclusions you draw from your survey results. Reconsider the guiding question: Do you think using the three above mentioned technologies would give us a better or a worse future?

▶ SF 46: Having a discussion, p. 264

Alternative: *Find someone who*-Übung unter Verwendung von KV 19: Artificial intelligence

Text 6

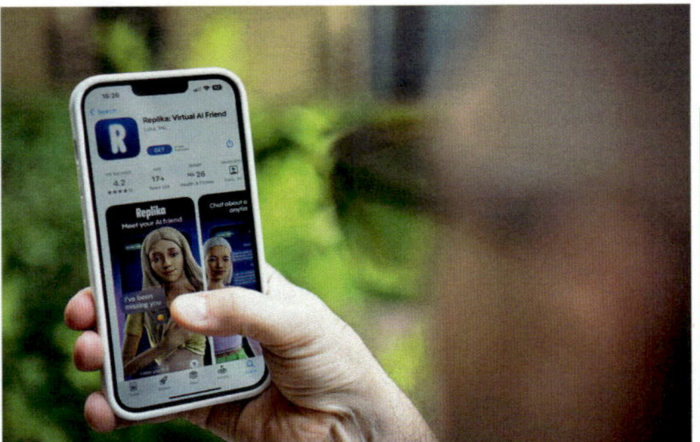

Communicating in a tech world

• Brainstorm situations in which human beings talk to machines today. Then discuss why people do this, what 'talking' to a machine feels like and whether you could ever imagine becoming 'friends' with a machine one day.

In addition to the mostly scientific and technical services, AI can also perform social functions. In the following video, the use of a special AI tool for communication is presented.

DIGI digitale Plattform nutzen, um Ideen zu sammeln und zu ordnen

LÖS **Pre-reading**
- situations: using chat bots, smart speakers, car navigation systems, auto attendants
- reasons: searching for information, getting help

Lernen App: Video on chatbots (10:35 min.)

Comprehension

1 a Viewing Watch the first part of the clip and take notes on
- the purpose of the Replika chatbot
- what it can do
- users' reactions to Replika.

DIF Ausschnitt einmal oder zweimal zeigen

b Viewing Watch the next part of the clip and find answers to the questions:
- Why did Genia Kuyda start to develop a new chatbot?
- How did she manage to make her chatbot talk like Roman?
- What did Genia notice when she made her 'Roman chatbot' available to the public?

c Viewing Watch the last part of the clip and complete the sentences:
- The conversations that Replika can recreate are ...
- Users talk to Replika about ...
- Unlike other social networking sites, Replika ...

d Which ideas presented in the clip do you find most thought-provoking?

Alternative: 3-2-1-Format: drei interessante, 2 problematische Aspekte und eine Frage notieren

► SF 40: Listening/Viewing for gist and detail, p. 253

Lernen App: Answer key for task 1c
► Check

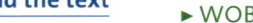

► WOB: A8 Viewing, pp. 26–27

Analysis

2 Viewing Watch the first part of the clip again and analyse how it tries to make the Replika chatbot appear human. Consider visual elements, colour, sound and language.

arbeitsteilig in Dreiergruppen bearbeiten: *visual elements / colour – sound – language*

Lernen App: Video on viewing skills
► Getting started

► SF 41: Analysing films, series and videos, p. 253

Language awareness

3 English has several adverbs that can be used before other adjectives or adverbs to express strong emotions. They are called intensifiers.

a Listening Listen carefully again to the first part of the clip and fill in the gaps:
1 This was the first ... emotional experience that I've seen people have with a bot.
2 I found myself ... missing my Replika.
3 It's a ... new kind of social media.

b Describe how the adverbs you added in **a** changed the statements.

HA **c** Imagine you have tried out the Replika chatbot yourself. Write a short message to a friend using intensifiers from the box.

fairly • pretty • somewhat • very • quite • so • absolutely • rather • incredibly

► WOB: B5 Adjectives and adverbs, p. 51

► Check

Lernen App: Answer key for task 3a

LÖS **3a**
1 really **2** deeply **3** totally

LÖS **3b**
1 intensify the meaning of the expressions following them
2 highlight the speaker's emotions
3 make the statements sound very informal

Beyond the text

4 HA CT Writing Think back to the guiding question of this chapter. Do you think the above mentioned kind of social AI technology represents a gain for society and its future? Write a *comment.

vorbereitend den Unterschied zwischen linearer Erörterung *(comment)* und dialektischer Erörterung *(discussion)* wiederholen

► WOB: A2

► SF 28: Argumentative writing, p. 236

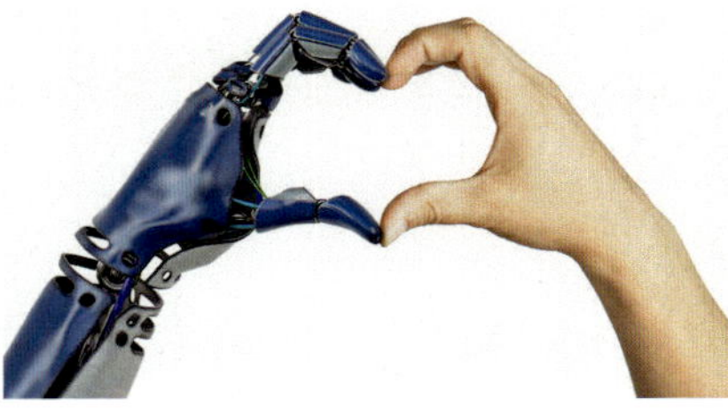

Schwerpunkt-Kompetenz Chapter 6: Argumentative Writing

Lernen App: Video on will-future and going-to-future

► SF 6: Essentials: language and study skills, p. 208

► More language

► Check

Lernen App: Answer key for task 1a

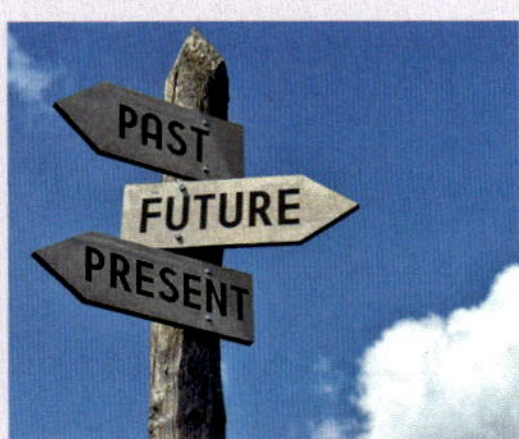

Reactivate

1 Different future forms

Do you remember how to use the different future forms?

HA **a** Choose a, b or c to fill the gaps. Give reasons for your choice:

1 Soon robots ...
   a) are taking over our jobs.
   b) will take over our jobs.
   c) take over our jobs.

2 In 150 years, digital media ... television.
   a) will replace
   b) will be replacing
   c) will have replaced

3 The spaceship ... at 5 p.m.
   a) departs
   b) will depart
   c) is departing

4 We ... a Star Wars party this weekend – come and join us!
   a) will have
   b) have
   c) are having

5 I ... chess with Yoda tonight – I can't wait!
   a) am going to play
   b) play
   c) will be playing

► WOB: B1

LÖS 1a
1b 2c 3a 4c 5a

Lernen App: Answer key for task 1b
► Check

HA **b** Which future form to choose often depends on how confident a speaker is that something will happen. Read the following sentences carefully and identify the forms used to talk about the future (A–F) and their respective functions (a–h). Note that each form may have different functions.

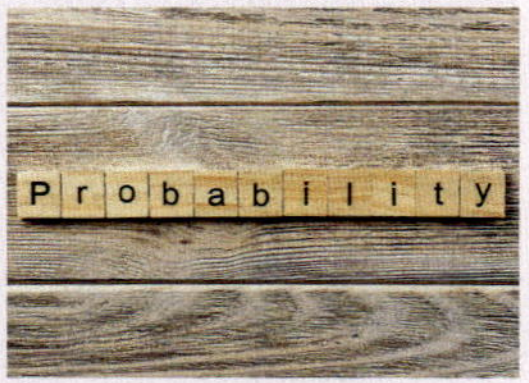

LÖS 1b
1Fa 2Cb 3Dg 4Dc 5Cb
6Ef 7Bd 8Cb 9Ee 10Ah
11Dc 12Fa

1 By the end of the century, many traditional jobs will have disappeared.	A simple present
2 Hold on. I'll help you with your work.	B present progressive
3 How long will you be using this computer for?	C will-future
4 I'll be spending this weekend at a science fair in London.	D future progressive
5 I'll come round and see you tonight, I promise.	E going to-future
6 I'm going to be an engineer.	F future perfect
7 I'm spending this weekend at home doing more research.	a imagining yourself in the future looking back
8 I won't be able to attend the conference opening tonight. I'm still at the hotel.	b expressing a belief or make a promise/offer
9 Look at the clouds – it's going to snow tonight!	c talking about an action at a moment in the future
10 The bus back to the airport departs at 9.30 a.m. tomorrow morning.	d talking about your own plans or intentions
11 We'll be having a staff meeting on Wednesday evening. Want to join us?	e making a prediction based on clear evidence
12 By the time we arrive on Mars, our Martian friends will have gone to sleep.	f talking about fixed plans and arrangements
	g asking others politely about their plans
	h talking about something that has been scheduled

Schwerpunkt-Kompetenz Chapter 6: Argumentative Writing

2 Language awareness

► WOB: B1

HA **a** German often uses the present tense to talk about the future. Translate these sentences into English.

1 Wir schicken heute Abend sechs Astronautinnen ins All.
2 Es kommen über 500 Journalistinnen und Journalisten, um über den Start zu berichten.
3 Wir hoffen, dass es keine technischen Probleme gibt.
4 Es ist sehr wahrscheinlich, dass unser Raumschiff nach 15 Monaten den Mars erreicht.
5 Im nächsten Jahr startet mein Training; ich bin schon angemeldet.
6 In sechs Jahren fliege ich auch zum Mars.

HA **b** Imagine you are a journalist interviewing a trainee astronaut who hopes to land on Mars in the near future. Write the interview using the translated sentences from **a**.

3 Work with words

Lernen App: Answer key for task 3a
► Check
► WOB: B1

HA **a** There are different expressions in English to say how sure you are about what will happen in the future. Order the sentences according to the degrees of certainty they express (from 'very sure' to 'not sure').

1 We're likely to destroy the world we live in.
2 Science may find solutions to our current problems.
3 Humankind is certain to settle on Mars one day.
4 Humans might die out in the future.
5 I expect global warming to get worse.

HA **b** Imagine that the sentences above are answers given by an environmental scientist during a press conference. Write down the questions she was asked first, then translate questions and answers into German.

4 Practise

a Work in pairs and talk about life in 2100. Take turns to create scenarios based on the key words below.

SuS darauf hinweisen, möglichst flüssig zu sprechen und *discourse markers* zu verwenden *(you know, I think, well …)*

cargo liners • float down from space • move your furniture • smart robots • unnecessary • people • work• buildings • global green cities • AI • develop • compete with • humans • jobs

b Contradict the statements in the text below by making them negative and give a short, emotional talk using the *will*-future and the *going to*-future.

► Support, p. 199

Computers will ultimately improve the quality of human decisions. We'll all be using chatty cyber-assistants that will warn us when we are about to make a wrong decision and advise us on the best course of action. We'll be able to buy a wide variety of personalities for our little cyber-buddies based on cartoon characters, movie stars or historical figures. Computers will eventually become smarter than we are.

► WOB: B1 Tense and aspect, pp. 44–47

in Kleingruppen Texte einander mit passender Betonung vorlesen

Lernen App: App: George Orwell and "Nineteen Eighty-Four"

George Orwell

▶ More info 

Annotations

3 **nuzzle** press
3 **vile** extremely unpleasant
6 **rag mat** small carpet made from scraps of fabric
9 **rugged** (here) attractive in a strong, masculine way
12 **economy drive** planned effort to spend as little as possible
12 **flight (of stairs)** set of stairs between two floors
13 **varicose ulcer** skin disease caused by a swollen vein, usually in the leg
16 **contrived** artificial and unrealistic
19 **pig-iron** form of iron that is not pure
19 **oblong** rectangular
24 **frail** weak
24 **meagreness** state of being lean or thin
26 **sanguine** red
29 **eddy** wind, air or water moving in a circle
36 **INGSOC** English Socialism (in the fictional language Newspeak)
37 **bluebottle** big fly
38 **snoop into sth.** look around secretly to find information about sth.

DIGI innovative Technologien und ihre möglichen negativen Auswirkungen mit einem digitalen Tool in einer *T-chart* auflisten

*** Big brother is watching you George Orwell

HA CT • Work in pairs. Think about the different technologies you have read about in this chapter and their uses. Brainstorm how those technologies as well as others could have a negative impact on society.

Now read an excerpt from George Orwell's dystopian novel Nineteen Eighty-Four *in which he paints a dark picture of a technologically advanced future.*

Part One

It was a bright cold day in April, and the clocks were striking thirteen. Winston Smith, his chin nuzzled into his breast in an effort to escape the vile wind, slipped quickly through the glass doors of Victory Mansions, though not quickly enough to prevent a swirl of gritty dust from entering along with him.

The hallway smelt of boiled cabbage and old rag mats. At one end of it a coloured poster, too large for indoor display, had been tacked to the wall. It depicted simply an enormous face, more than a metre wide: the face of a man of about forty-five, with a heavy black moustache and ruggedly handsome features. Winston made for the stairs. It was no use trying the lift. Even at the best of times it was seldom working, and at present the electric current was cut off during daylight hours. It was part of the economy drive in preparation for Hate Week. The flat was seven flights up, and Winston, who was thirty-nine and had a varicose ulcer above his right ankle, went slowly, resting several times on the way. On each landing, opposite the lift-shaft, the poster with the enormous face gazed from the wall. It was one of those pictures which are so contrived that the eyes follow you about when you move. BIG BROTHER IS WATCHING YOU, the caption beneath it ran.

Inside the flat a fruity voice was reading out a list of figures which had something to do with the production of pig-iron. The voice came from an oblong metal plaque like a dulled mirror which formed part of the surface of the right-hand wall. Winston turned a switch and the voice sank somewhat, though the words were still distinguishable. The instrument (the telescreen, it was called) could be dimmed, but there was no way of shutting it off completely. He moved over to the window: a smallish, frail figure, the meagreness of his body merely emphasized by the blue overalls which were the uniform of the party. His hair was very fair, his face naturally sanguine, his skin roughened by coarse soap and blunt razor blades and the cold of the winter that had just ended.

Outside, even through the shut window-pane, the world looked cold. Down in the street little eddies of wind were whirling dust and torn paper into spirals, and though the sun was shining and the sky a harsh blue, there seemed to be no colour in anything, except the posters that were plastered everywhere. The black moustachio'd face gazed down from every commanding corner. There was one on the house-front immediately opposite. BIG BROTHER IS WATCHING YOU, the caption said, while the dark eyes looked deep into Winston's own. Down at street level another poster, torn at one corner, flapped fitfully in the wind, alternately covering and uncovering the single word INGSOC. In the far distance a helicopter skimmed down between the roofs, hovered for an instant like a bluebottle, and darted away again with a curving flight. It was the police patrol, snooping into people's windows. The patrols did not matter, however. Only the Thought Police mattered.

Behind Winston's back the voice from the telescreen was still babbling away about pig-iron and the overfulfilment of the Ninth Three-Year Plan. The telescreen received and transmitted simultaneously. Any sound that Winston made, above the level of a very low whisper, would be picked up by it, moreover, so long as he remained within the field of vision which the metal plaque commanded, he could be seen as well as heard. There was of course no way of knowing whether you were being watched at any given moment. How often, or on what system, the Thought Police plugged in on any individual wire was guesswork. It was even conceivable that they watched everybody all the time. But at any rate they could plug in your wire whenever they wanted to. You had to live – did live, from habit that became instinct – in the assumption that every sound you made was overheard, and, except in darkness, every movement scrutinized.

Winston kept his back turned to the telescreen. It was safer, though, as he well knew, even a back can be revealing. A kilometre away the Ministry of Truth, his place of work, towered vast and white above the grimy landscape. This, he thought with a sort of vague distaste – this was London, chief city of Airstrip One, itself the third most populous of the provinces of Oceania. He tried to squeeze out some childhood memory that should tell him whether London had always been quite like this. Were there always these vistas of rotting nineteenth-century houses, their sides shored up with baulks of timber, their windows patched with cardboard and their roofs with corrugated iron, their crazy garden walls sagging in all directions? And the bombed sites where the plaster dust swirled in the air and the willow-herb straggled over the heaps of rubble; and the places where the bombs had cleared a larger patch and there had sprung up sordid colonies of wooden dwellings like chicken-houses? But it was no use, he could not remember: nothing remained of his childhood except a series of bright-lit tableaux occurring against no background and mostly unintelligible.

The Ministry of Truth – Minitrue, in Newspeak – was startlingly different from any other object in sight. It was an enormous pyramidal structure of glittering white concrete, soaring up, terrace after terrace, 300 metres into the air. From where Winston stood it was just possible to read, picked out on its white face in elegant lettering, the three slogans of the Party:

WAR IS PEACE

FREEDOM IS SLAVERY

IGNORANCE IS STRENGTH

955 Wörter

From: 1984, *1949*

Annotations

47 conceivable possible to imagine or believe
49 habit what you do frequently without even thinking about it
51 scrutinize sb/.sth. examine sb./sth. closely
53 revealing giving information; showing sth. not previously seen or known
58 vista view
59 baulk *Balken*
59 corrugated iron *Wellblech*
60 sag sink in the middle
61 plaster dust Gipsstaub
61 willow-herb *Weidenröschen*
61 straggle (here) grow in an untidy way
61 heap pile
62 rubble broken stones and bricks
63 sordid dirty
63 dwelling place of residence
65 tableau (*pl* tableaux) scene
65 unintelligible impossible to understand
67 startlingly surprisingly

Alternative: arbeitsteilig in Vierergruppen bearbeiten, Verständnisfragen im Plenum klären

Comprehension

HA CT **1 a** Collect essential information by answering the *wh*-questions *who, what, where* and *when*.

HA CT **b** Compare your results with a partner.

HA CT **2** With your partner, take turns explaining the significance of the details in the box. What do they tell you about life in this society? What role does technology play there?

electric current cut off during daytime • Hate Week • BIG BROTHER posters • telescreen • blue overalls • the party • coarse soap • blunt razor blades • no colour • Victory Mansions • police patrol • Thought Police • Ministry of Truth • Oceania • bombed sites • Newspeak • party slogans vorbereitend den Begriff *atmosphere* wiederholen

Analysis

▶ SF 19: Reading and understanding narrative texts, p. 223
▶ WOB: A9 Narrative prose, pp. 28–31

HA CT **3** Analyse the atmosphere George Orwell created in this extract. Pay attention to language and give examples.

DIF arbeitsteilig bearbeiten (Darstellung der Natur, von Winstons Wohnung, der Gesellschaft, Londons)

Language awareness

phrasal verbs anhand von Beispielen wiederholen

4 Many verbs in English can be combined with prepositions or adverbs to form phrases with new meanings, the so-called *phrasal verbs*.

HA CT **a** The three phrasal verbs in the box are used in the text above. Find them and match them to the meanings on the right.

1	to make for	A	to appear suddenly
2	to shore up	B	to keep from falling
3	to spring up	C	to go towards

LÖS **4a**
1C 2B 3A

▶ SF 8: Working with dictionaries, p. 209

DIGI elektronisches Wörterbuch oder Textkorpus nutzen

HA CT **b** Make sentences about Winston's thoughts using the phrasal verbs below. Consult a dictionary if necessary.

think about • think of • think on • think back to • think ahead

Beyond the text

▶ SF 28: Argumentative writing, p. 236
▶ WOB: A2 Writing, pp. 8–11

5 You choose Do either task **a** or **b**.

HA CT **a** Speculate about a major conflict that might be depicted in this novel and present your ideas to the class.

Idee für den weiteren Verlauf des Romans in Analogie zu einer *Movie in five seconds*-Grafik präsentieren

HA CT **b** Writing Are we on our way to an Orwellian future? Write a *comment.

LÖS **5a**
violation of personal freedom, conflict between individual and state, London citizens revolt against the state, personal tragedy caused by surveillance …

⁂ The burden of responsibility
Yuval Harari

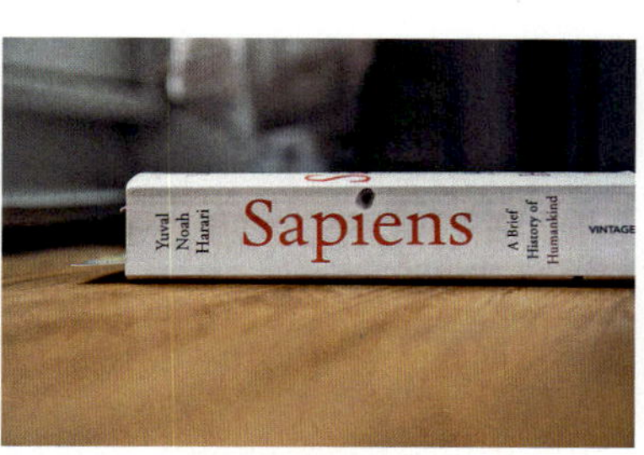

- Considering what you have learned in this chapter, complete the following sentence: Using science and technology responsibly means ...

The following extract is taken from a non-fiction book that traces and discusses human history from its beginnings to today's political and technological revolutions.

[D]espite the astonishing things that humans are capable of doing, we remain unsure of our goals and we seem to be as discontented as ever. We have advanced from canoes to galleys to steamships to space shuttles – but nobody knows where we're going. We are more powerful than ever before, but have very little idea what to do with all that power. Worse still, humans seem to be more irresponsible than ever. Self-made gods with only the laws of physics to keep us company, we are accountable to no one. We are consequently wreaking havoc on our fellow animals and on the surrounding ecosystem, seeking little more than our own comfort and amusement, yet never finding satisfaction.

Is there anything more dangerous than dissatisfied and irresponsible gods who don't know what they want?

137 Wörter

From: Sapiens: A Brief History of Humankind, 2020

Annotations
1 **astonishing** extremely surprising
2 **discontented** unhappy
3 **galley** long ship with one or more sails
6 **accountable** responsible
7 **wreak havoc on sth.** cause damage to sth.

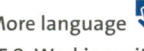

► More info
Lernen App: Yuval Harari

Comprehension

1 You choose Do either task **a** or **b**.

CT **a** Summarize Yuval Harari's view of humankind in two sentences.

HA CT **b** Summarize Yuval Harari's view of humankind in the form of an acrostic (cf. Info box on the right).

DIGI *acrostics* mithilfe eines digitalen Tools gestalten

Info

An **acrostic** is a poem or word composition in which a particular set of letters — usually the first letter of each line, word, or paragraph — spells out a word or phrase, typically with special significance to the text.

An acrostic
Can
Reach
Others'
Senses
Thanks to
Its
Composition

Analysis

HA CT **2** Yuval Harari twice refers to human beings metaphorically as 'gods' (l. 6, l. 10). Explain this metaphor.

in einer *brainstorming activity* Assoziationen zum Begriff *god* in einer *mind map* sammeln, die Begriffe *self-made gods* und *irresponsible gods* hinzufügen und erläutern

Language awareness

HA **3** In English, many adjectives can be turned into their opposites by adding a prefix which reverses the meaning of the word, as in 'illegal' or 'unfair'.

CT **a** Find negative adjectives formed by adding a prefix in the text.

HA CT **b** Make the positive adjectives in the box negative. You may use a dictionary for help.

moral • happy • prepared • perfect • logical

LÖS **3b** immoral • unhappy • unprepared • imperfect • illogical

HA CT **c** Use the adjectives you formed in **b** to write a short statement about how to use science and technology more responsibly in the future.

► More language 
► SF 8: Working with dictionaries, p. 209
Lernen App: Video about negative prefixes

Beyond the text

► SF 28: Argumentative writing, p. 236
► WOB: A2 Writing, pp. 8–11

4 You choose Do either task **a** or **b**.

a Writing Discuss the rights and the social responsibilities of scientists.

b *** Make a (digital) collage in which you present your own artistic vision of what it means to be a responsible human at a time of fundamental scientific and technological change. Write a short artist's statement, then display your artwork and your statement in class.

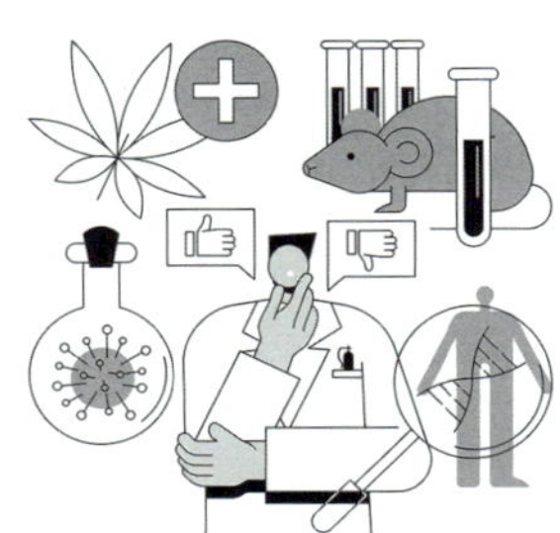

Chapter task

► SF 28: Argumentative writing, p. 236
► WOB: A2 Writing, pp. 8–11

1 Put your argumentation and writing skills to the test and show what you have learned about science and technology by taking part in a writing contest.
A teen science magazine launches a 300-word writing competition for high school students aged 14–18:

We want to feature the voices and ideas of the younger generation.
The topic of this year's competition is:

Science and technology are needed to make the world a better place for future generations.

We are looking for texts that are well reasoned, well researched, well written and forward-looking. The texts must be supported by science, and incorporate personal perspectives and anecdotes. You should also point out the relevance of your topic to young people in years to come.

▸ WOB: A10

A good story

1 Discuss what makes a 'good' story. List as many criteria as possible.
2 With a partner, rank the criteria in **1** according to importance.

DIGI Antworten mit einem digitalen Tool sammeln, strukturieren und in eine Rangfolge bringen

Approaching the story

3 Read the story 'August 2026: There will come soft rains' by Ray Bradbury.
Note down your first reactions to it by naming:
- one thing that surprised you
- one quote that you found especially relevant
- one significant detail
- something you want to know more about.

Compare your results with a partner.

vor der Lektüre über den Titel spekulieren *(kind of story, possible plot)*

August 2026: There will come soft rains Ray Bradbury

In the living room the voice-clock sang, Tick-tock, *seven o'clock, time to get up, time to get up, seven o'clock!* as if it were afraid that nobody would. The morning house lay empty. The clock ticked on, repeating and repeating its sounds into the emptiness. *Seven-nine, breakfast time, seven-nine!*

In the kitchen the breakfast stove gave a hissing sigh and ejected from its warm interior eight pieces of perfectly browned toast, eight eggs sunny side up, sixteen slices of bacon, two coffees, and two cool glasses of milk.

'Today is August 4, 2026,' said a second voice from the kitchen ceiling, 'in the city of Allendale, California.' It repeated the date three times for memory's sake. 'Today is Mr. Featherstone's birthday. Today is the anniversary of Tilita's marriage. Insurance is payable, as are the water, gas, and light bills.'

Somewhere in the walls, relays clicked, memory tapes glided under electric eyes.

Eight-one, tick-tock, eight-one o'clock, off to school, off to work, run, run, eight-one! But no doors slammed, no carpets took the soft tread of rubber heels. It was raining outside. The weather box on the front door sang quietly: 'Rain, rain, go away; umbrellas, raincoats for today.' And the rain tapped on the empty house, echoing.

Outside, the garage chimed and lifted its door to reveal the waiting car. After a long wait the door swung down again.

▸ SF 16: Essentials: reading strategies and text types, p. 219

Info

Ray Bradbury
(1920–2012) was an American author of science fiction and fantasy stories and novels. His best-known novel is *Fahrenheit 451*, published in 1953, a dystopian description of a future American society. He won many awards, including a Pulitzer Prize in 2007. His short story 'August 2026: There will come soft rains' was published in 1950 as part of his story collection *The Martian Chronicles*. It includes a 12-line poem with the same title by Sara Teasdale, which was published in 1918.

Annotations
- 5 **eject sth.** throw sth. out
- 6 **sunny side up** fried on one side only
- 10 **anniversary** recurrence of an important date, e.g. sb.'s wedding day
- 17 **chime** make a bell-like sound

Annotations

19 shrivelled dry and wrinkled
20 wedge *Keil*
25 twinkle sparkle; shine
27 warren labyrinth; tunnels in which rabbits live
27 dart move suddenly
29 rug nap *Teppichflor*
33 rubble broken fragments of brick and stone from ruined buildings
36 pelt sth. strike sth. regularly
37 charred burned
40 titanic forceful
44 charcoaled burned
48 draw shades *Rollläden schließen*
50 quiver shake slightly
57 sore *(n)* painful, red wound or infection

Fehlerquelle: Aussprache von *silhouette* [ˌsɪluˈet] (Z. 39)

At eight-thirty the eggs were shrivelled and the toast was like stone. An aluminium wedge scraped them into the sink, where hot water whirled them down a metal throat which digested and flushed them away to the distant sea. The dirty dishes were dropped into a hot washer and emerged twinkling dry.

Nine-fifteen, sang the clock, *time to clean.*

Out of warrens in the wall, tiny robot mice darted. The rooms were a crawl with the small cleaning animals, all rubber and metal. They thudded against chairs, whirling their moustached runners, kneading the rug nap, sucking gently at hidden dust. Then, like mysterious invaders, they popped into their burrows. Their pink electric eyes faded. The house was clean.

Ten o'clock. The sun came out from behind the rain. The house stood alone in a city of rubble and ashes. This was the one house left standing. At night the ruined city gave off a radioactive glow which could be seen for miles.

Ten-fifteen. The garden sprinklers whirled up in golden founts, filling the soft morning air with scatterings of brightness. The water pelted window panes, running down the charred west side where the house had been burned, evenly free of its white paint. The entire west face of the house was black, save for five places. Here the silhouette in paint of a man mowing a lawn. Here, as in a photograph, a woman bent to pick flowers. Still farther over, their images burned on wood in one titanic instant, a small boy, hands flung into the air; higher up, the image of a thrown ball, and opposite him a girl, hands raised to catch a ball which never came down.

The five spots of paint – the man, the woman, the children, the ball – remained. The rest was a thin charcoaled layer.

The gentle sprinkler rain filled the garden with falling light.

Until this day, how well the house had kept its peace. How carefully it had inquired, 'Who goes there? What's the password?' and, getting no answer from lonely foxes and whining cats, it had shut up its windows and drawn shades in an old-maidenly preoccupation with self-protection which bordered on a mechanical paranoia.

It quivered at each sound, the house did. If a sparrow brushed a window, the shade snapped up. The bird, startled, flew off! No, not even a bird must touch the house!

Twelve noon.

A dog whined, shivering, on the front porch.

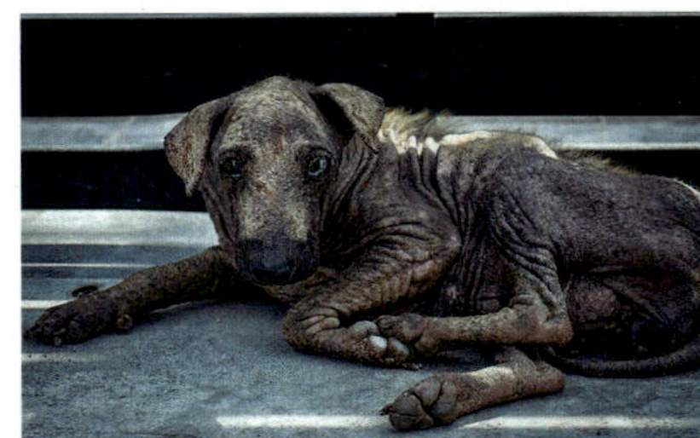

The front door recognized the dog voice and opened. The dog, once huge and fleshy, but now gone to bone and covered with sores, moved in and through the house, tracking mud. Behind it whirred angry mice, angry at having to pick up mud, angry at inconvenience.

For not a leaf fragment blew under the door but what the wall panels flipped open and the copper scrap rats flashed swiftly out. The offending dust, hair, or paper, seized in miniature steel jaws, was raced back to the burrows. There, down tubes which fed into the cellar, it was dropped into the sighing vent of an incinerator which sat like evil Baal in a dark corner.

The dog ran upstairs, hysterically yelping to each door, at last realizing, as the house realized, that only silence was here.

It sniffed the air and scratched the kitchen door. Behind the door, the stove was making pancakes which filled the house with a rich baked odour and the scent of maple syrup.

The dog frothed at the mouth, lying at the door, sniffing, its eyes turned to fire. It ran wildly in circles, biting at its tail, spun in a frenzy, and died. It lay in the parlor for an hour.

Two o'clock, sang a voice.

Delicately sensing decay at last, the regiments of mice hummed out as softly as blown gray leaves in an electrical wind.

Two-fifteen.

The dog was gone.

In the cellar, the incinerator glowed suddenly and a whirl of sparks leaped up the chimney.

Two thirty-five.

Bridge tables sprouted from patio walls. Playing cards fluttered onto pads in a shower of pips. Martinis manifested on an oaken bench with egg-salad sandwiches. Music played.

But the tables were silent and the cards untouched.

At four o'clock the tables folded like great butterflies back through the paneled walls.

Four-thirty.

The nursery walls glowed.

Animals took shape: yellow giraffes, blue lions, pink antelopes, lilac panthers cavorting in crystal substance. The walls were glass. They looked out upon color and fantasy. Hidden films clocked through well-oiled sprockets, and the walls lived. The nursery floor was woven to resemble a crisp, cereal meadow. Over this ran aluminum roaches and iron crickets, and in the hot still air butterflies of delicate red tissue wavered among the sharp aroma of animal spoors! There was the sound like a great matted yellow hive of bees within a dark bellows, the lazy bumble of a purring lion. And there was the patter of okapi feet and the murmur of a fresh jungle rain, like other hoofs, falling upon the summer-starched

Annotations

62 scrap leftover food
63 seize sth. capture sth.; take sth. using force
63 jaw *Kiefer*
64 vent opening
64 incinerator machine that burns sth.
65 Baal demon
71 froth *(v)* foam
75 decay the process of rotting
83 pip a short, high sound, especially one of a series
89 nursery *(old-fashioned)* baby's room or playroom
92 cavort leap about playfully
95 sprocket toothed wheel
96 cereal meadow field where corn, wheat, etc. is grown
97 roach *Schabe*
97 cricket *Grille*
98 waver move around
98 spoor track or smell of an animal
99 matted tangled; forming a thick mass
99 bellows *Blasebalg*
100 purr *brummen*
101 starched dry and without color

Annotations
102 dissolve disappear
102 parched dry
103 thorn brake a type of shrub
107 hearth area in front of a fireplace
109 circuit electrical line
117 swallow *Schwalbe*
119 tremulous slightly trembling; shaking
121 whim sudden idea; impulse
125 perish die; be destroyed
125 utterly totally; completely
132 bough large branch
133 solvent *Lösungsmittel*
140 scurry move fast

grass. Now the walls dissolved into distances of parched grass, mile on mile, and warm endless sky. The animals drew away into thorn brakes and water holes. It was the children's hour.

Five o'clock. The bath filled with clear hot water.

Six, seven, eight o'clock. The dinner dishes manipulated like magic tricks, and in the study a click. In the metal stand opposite the hearth where a fire now blazed up warmly, a cigar popped out, half an inch of soft gray ash on it, smoking, waiting.

Nine o'clock. The beds warmed their hidden circuits, for nights were cool here.

Nine-five. A voice spoke from the study ceiling: 'Mrs. McClellan, which poem would you like this evening?'

The house was silent.

The voice said at last, 'Since you express no preference, I shall select a poem at random.' Quiet music rose to back the voice. 'Sara Teasdale. As I recall, your favourite ...

There will come soft rains and the smell of the ground,
And swallows circling with their shimmering sound;

And frogs in the pools singing at night,
And wild plum trees in tremulous white;

Robins will wear their feathery fire,
Whistling their whims on a low fence-wire;

And not one will know of the war, not one
Will care at last when it is done.

Not one would mind, neither bird nor tree,
If mankind perished utterly;

And Spring herself, when she woke at dawn
Would scarcely know that we were gone.'

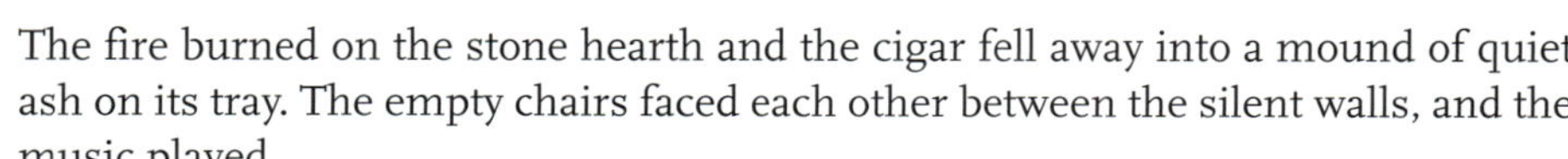

The fire burned on the stone hearth and the cigar fell away into a mound of quiet ash on its tray. The empty chairs faced each other between the silent walls, and the music played.

At ten o'clock the house began to die.

The wind blew. A falling tree bough crashed through the kitchen window. Cleaning solvent, bottled, shattered over the stove. The room was ablaze in an instant!

'Fire!' screamed a voice. The house lights flashed, water pumps shot water from the ceilings. But the solvent spread on the linoleum, licking, eating, under the kitchen door, while the voices took it up in chorus: 'Fire, fire, fire!'

The house tried to save itself. Doors sprang tightly shut, but the windows were broken by the heat and the wind blew and sucked upon the fire.

The house gave ground as the fire in ten billion angry sparks moved with flaming ease from room to room and then up the stairs. While scurrying water rats squeaked from the walls, pistolled their water, and ran for more. And the wall sprays let down showers of mechanical rain.

But too late. Somewhere, sighing, a pump shrugged to a stop. The quenching rain ceased. The reserve water supply which had filled baths and washed dishes for many quiet days was gone.

The fire crackled up the stairs. It fed upon Picassos and Matisses in the upper halls, like delicacies, baking off the oily flesh, tenderly crisping the canvases into black shavings.

Now the fire lay in beds, stood in windows, changed the colors of drapes!

And then, reinforcements.

From attic trapdoors, blind robot faces peered down with faucet mouths gushing green chemical.

The fire backed off, as even an elephant must at the sight of a dead snake. Now there were twenty snakes whipping over the floor, killing the fire with a clear cold venom of green froth.

But the fire was clever. It had sent flame outside the house, up through the attic to the pumps there. An explosion! The attic brain which directed the pumps was shattered into bronze shrapnel on the beams.

The fire rushed back into every closet and felt of the clothes hung there.

The house shuddered, oak bone on bone, its bared skeleton cringing from the heat, its wire, its nerves revealed as if a surgeon had torn the skin off to let the red veins and capillaries quiver in the scalded air. Help, help! Fire! Run, run! Heat snapped mirrors like the first brittle winter ice. And the voices wailed. Fire, fire, run, run, like a tragic nursery rhyme, a dozen voices, high, low like children dying in a forest, alone, alone. And the voices fading as the wires popped their sheathings like hot chestnuts. One, two, three, four, five voices died.

In the nursery the jungle burned. Blue lions roared, purple giraffes bounded off. The panthers ran in circles, changing color, and ten million animals, running before the fire, vanished off toward a distant steaming river ...

Ten more voices died. In the last instant under the fire avalanche, other choruses, oblivious, could be heard announcing the time, cutting the lawn by remote-control mower, or setting an umbrella frantically out and in, the slamming and opening front door, a thousand things happening, like a clock shop when each clock strikes the hour insanely before or after the other, a scene of maniac confusion, yet unity; singing, screaming, a few last cleaning mice darting bravely out to carry the horrid ashes away! And one voice, with sublime disregard for the situation, read poetry aloud in the fiery study, until all the film spools burned, until all the wires withered and the circuits cracked.

The fire burst the house and let it slam flat down, puffing out skirts of spark and smoke.

In the kitchen, an instant before the rain of fire and timber, the stove could be seen making breakfasts at a psychopathic rate, ten dozen eggs, six loaves of toast, twen-

Annotations

- 143 **shrug** (here) slow down abruptly
- 143 **quenching** (here) putting out fire
- 150 **reinforcement** soldiers sent to join an army to make it stronger
- 151 **attic** room below the roof
- 151 **faucet** *Wasserhahn*
- 155 **venom** poison
- 158 **shrapnel** pieces of metal thrown out of a bomb
- 158 **beam** long piece of wood that supports the roof's weight
- 160 **cringe** (here) shrink
- 162 **scalded** very hot
- 165 **sheathing** *Ummantelung*
- 169 **vanish** disappear
- 170 **avalanche** *Lawine*
- 171 **oblivious** ignorant of; unconscious of
- 172 **frantic** almost out of control
- 174 **maniac** mad
- 176 **sublime** grand; very great

Annotations
185 parlour (*old-fashioned*) room used for entertaining guests
189 faintly weakly

ty dozen bacon strips, which, eaten by fire, started the stove working again, hysterically hissing!

The crash. The attic smashing into kitchen and parlour. The parlour into cellar, cellar into sub-cellar. Deep freeze, armchair, film tapes, circuits, beds, and all like skeletons thrown in a cluttered mound deep under.

Smoke and silence. A great quantity of smoke.

Dawn showed faintly in the east. Among the ruins, one wall stood alone. Within the wall, a last voice said, over and over again and again, even as the sun rose to shine upon the heaped rubble and steam: 'Today is August 5, 2026, today is August 5, 2026, today is ...'

From: The Martian Chronicles, *1950*

► WOB: A10

In Dreiergruppen bearbeiten die SuS arbeitsteilig je zwei Fragen und tauschen ihre Antworten aus. Gemeinsam erstellen sie eine *story map* basierend auf den *wh*-Fragen.

Understanding the story

4 Answer the following wh-questions with one short sentence each.
1 Where and when does the story take place?
2 What happened there?
3 Who lived in the house?
4 Why is the house empty now?
5 What makes the house special?
6 How does the story end?

Analysing the story

To be able to understand the story even better, you need to read between the lines.

Info
Inferring meaning from clues in a text, i.e. reading 'between the lines', is an important part of interpreting any piece of literature. When making inferences, readers draw conclusions about characters, setting, and plot from textual details, for example single words or images.

► More info
Lernen App: Sara Teasdale

5 In the story it is not stated directly what happened to the family and their dog or why there is a fire. Find clues in the text that help you to answer these questions.

6 One striking feature of the short story is the inclusion of the poem 'There will come soft rains' (ll. 116–127) by Sara Teasdale (1918).
a Examine the poem and find more clues about what might have happened to the family and the house. ► WOB: A12
b Contrast the depiction of nature in the poem to the depiction of nature in the short story. Illustrate your findings in a table. ► WOB: A10, A12

7 Explain the title of the story and point out what the use of the poem 'There will come soft rains' suggests about the message of the story.
SuS notieren Ideen zum Titel und tauschen sich mit verschiedenen Partner/innen darüber aus. Mit dem/der letzten Partner/in formulieren sie die *message* der Geschichte.

Characteristics of a short story

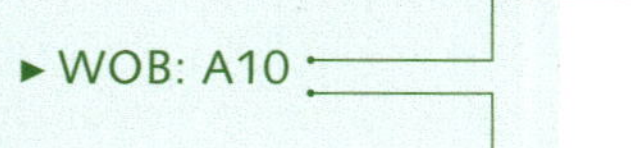

► WOB: A10

8 Discuss whether the criteria for good stories you compiled in tasks **1** and **2** apply to 'August 2026: There will come soft rains' by Ray Bradbury. Give reasons.

9 **a** Although there are many different types of short stories, e. g. love stories, ghost stories or science fiction stories, there are certain elements found in all of them. Complete each sentence using a term from the box on the next page.

LÖS 9a

1 A short story often begins 'in medias res', which means that there is ..., the story begins abruptly. no introduction
2 A short story usually has a limited number of central ..., which are normally human, but not always. characters
3 A short story usually revolves around a short sequence of events, which is called ... plot
4 A short story usually has a confined ..., which tells us where and when the action takes place. setting
5 In a short story, there is usually one surprising ... or ... , i.e. a moment at which an important change occurs. turning point, climax
6 A short story is usually told from a specific ..., which refers to the storyteller and his/her angle from which the story is told. point of view
7 The central idea of a story is called its ... theme
8 Many short stories have an ... because it leaves room for imagination. open ending

Lernen App: Answer key for task 9a
► Check

characters • climax • plot • open ending • point of view • setting • theme • turning point • no introduction

b Now use the nine terms from the box to write a short informative text about the story for a literary *blog.

Lernen App:
Video on stylistic devices
Overview of stylistic devices
► Getting started 
► Check
Lernen App: Answer key for task 10a

10 A short story normally makes use of *stylistic devices providing important details for a full understanding of what happens and why.

a Match the literary terms on the left to the definitions on the right.

1 onomatopoeia	A concrete things standing for abstract ideas
2 symbol	B direct comparison using 'like' or 'as'
3 alliteration	C giving a thing human qualities
4 metaphor	D indirect comparison
5 simile	E using the same sound at the beginning of words
6 personification	F visually descriptive language
7 imagery	G words sounding similar to real sounds

LÖS 10a
1D 2B 3C 4F 5E 6A 7G

b Scan the story and look for examples of stylistic devices. Record your findings in a chart like this:

Example from the story	Type of stylistic device	Function
...	...	...

c Work with a partner. Choose one example that you find particularly appealing and tell your partner why you chose it and in what way(s) it enhances the meaning of the story.

Technology and the story

11 Ray Bradbury wrote this story in 1950, five years after the end of World War II. Discuss to what extent it can be interpreted as a response to this aftershock.

► SF 46: Having a discussion, p. 264

12 Discuss the message of the story concerning human nature and the use of science and technology. ► WOB: A2

► Support, p. 199
► WOB: A10 Short story, pp. 32–35

Chapter 1 Text 3

▶ p. 22

Social mobility – real opportunity or only a dream?

Partner B

Watch the video about social mobility and do the task below.

(08:47 min.)

▶ WOB: A8

1 a Viewing While watching the video for the first time, make notes on the following topics. Don't write complete sentences.

1 three pieces of information about Sophie Pender
2 three pieces of information about social mobility in the past
3 three pieces of information about head teacher Mouhssin Ismail

*Now go back to task **1 b**.*

▶ p. 23

3 a Support

The following films, books and songs might serve as a starting point.

Films:	Books:	Songs:
– *Slumdog Millionaire* – *The Hunger Games* film series – *The Blind Side*	– *Oliver Twist*, Charles Dickens – *The Hate you Give*, Angie Thomas	– *Nowhere Generation*, Rise Against

Text 4

Living through social media

▶ p. 26

4 a Support

Some of the filler words that are used in this excerpt are 'like' (l. 40) and 'oh' (l. 45.)

b

The use of filler words could have the following effect:

1 The dialogue sounds authentic and, therefore, believable.

...

What's on a teenager's mind?

► p. 31

The following poem by Jon Loomis was first published in 2001.

Deer Hit Jon Loomis

You're seventeen and tunnel-vision drunk,
swerving your father's Fairlane wagon home

at 3:00 a.m. Two-lane road, all curves
and dips – dark woods, a stream, a patchy acre

of teazle and grass. You don't see the deer
till they turn their heads – road full of eyeballs,

small moons glowing. You crank the wheel,
stamp both feet on the brake, skid and jolt

into the ditch. Glitter and crunch of broken glass
in your lap, deer hair drifting like dust. Your chin

and shirt are soaked – one eye half-obscured
by the cocked bridge of your nose. The car

still running, its lights angled up at the trees.
You get out. The deer lies on its side.

A doe, spinning itself around
in a frantic circle, front legs scrambling,

back legs paralyzed, dead. Making a sound –
again and again this terrible bleat.

You watch for a while. It tires, lies still.
And here's what you do: pick the deer up

like a bride. Wrestle it into the back of the car –
the seat folded down. Somehow, you steer

the wagon out of the ditch and head home,
night rushing in through the broken window,

headlight dangling, side-mirror gone.
Your nose throbs, something stabs

in your side. The deer breathing behind you,
shallow and fast. A stoplight, you're almost home

and the deer scrambles to life, its long head
appears like a ghost in the rearview mirror

and bites you, its teeth clamp down on your shoulder
and maybe you scream, you struggle and flail

till the deer, exhausted, lets go and lies down.

2
Your father's waiting up, watching tv.
He's had a few drinks and he's angry.

Christ, he says, when you let yourself in.
It's Night of the Living Dead. You tell him

some of what happened: the dark road,
the deer you couldn't avoid. Outside, he circles

the car. Jesus, he says. A long silence.
Son of a bitch, looking in. He opens the tailgate,

drags the quivering deer out by a leg.
What can you tell him – you weren't thinking,

you'd injured your head? You wanted to fix
what you'd broken – restore the beautiful body,

color of wet straw, color of oak leaves in winter?
The deer shudders and bleats in the driveway.

Your father walks to the toolshed,
comes back lugging a concrete block.

Some things stay with you. Dumping the body
deep in the woods, like a gangster. The dent

in your nose. All your life, the trail of ruin you leave.

417 Wörter

From: The Pleasure Principle, *2001*

Annotations

- 1 **tunnel vision** *Tunnelblick*
- 2 **swerve** change direction surprisingly
- 5 **deer** animal with long legs that lives mainly in the forest, male has antlers
- 15 **doe** [dəʊ] female deer
- 18 **bleat** *Geblöke*
- 52 **dent** *Beule; Delle*

Comprehension

► WOB: A12

1 Read the poem and sum it up in not more than three sentences.

2 Outline the central conflict and the emotions depicted in the poem.

Analysis

3 Examine the perspective taken over in the poem and how the reader is addressed.

rhetorische Mittel vorbereitend wiederholen

*** 4 Analyse elements of language and structure that underline the message of the poem.

Language awareness

LÖS 5
'swerving' (v. 2), 'glowing' (v. 7), 'drifting' (v. 10), 'running' (v. 13), 'spinning' (v. 15), 'scrambling' (v. 15) … → present progressive forms show the immediacy of the action, they are happening right now

*** 5 Examine the use of *ing*-forms in the poem.

*Now go back to task **6**.*

Language Lab

► p. 33

8 Support

The following tips might help you to handle stress:

1 Taking a relaxing walk.
2 Listening to calming music.
3 Meditating.
4 Painting a picture.
5 Doing sports.

Text 9

► p. 35

Forced to grow up

3 a Support

Take a look at ll. 32–34 on p. 34 and identify the structure Noelle uses to talk about her regrets.

Text 10

Defining a generation

► p. 37

4 Support

Take a look at the personal pronouns used in Grace's speech. The following pronouns might be a good starting point: *I, me, you, us, we, they*.

Making a difference

► p. 54

Partner A

Look at the infographic below. Examine the UK parliamentary system by looking at the separation of powers, how laws are passed, and what the roles of the head of state and the electorate are. Explain your infographic to your partner.

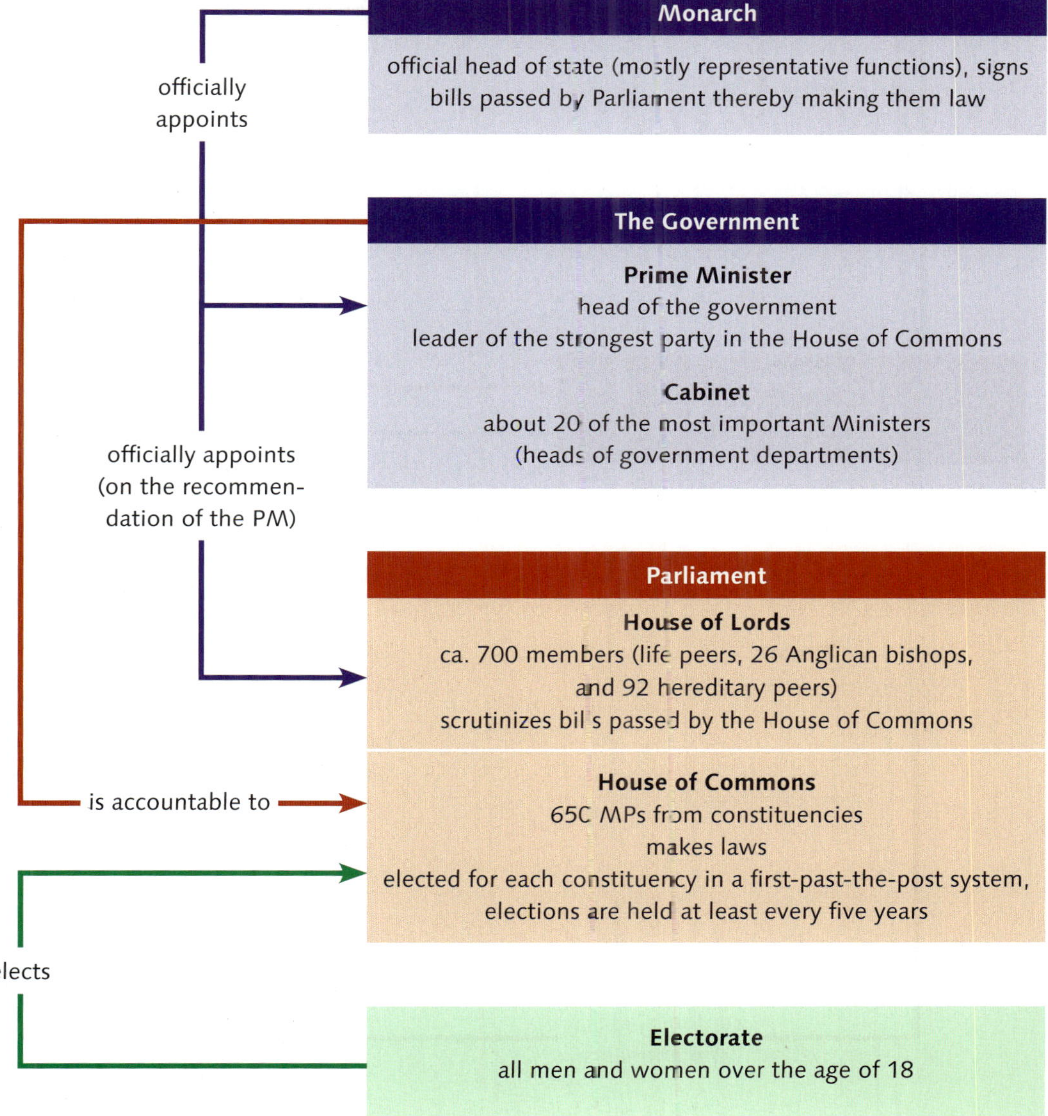

Monarch
official head of state (mostly representative functions), signs bills passed by Parliament thereby making them law
officially appoints
The Government
Prime Minister
head of the government
leader of the strongest party in the House of Commons
Cabinet
about 20 of the most important Ministers
(heads of government departments)
officially appoints (on the recommendation of the PM)
Parliament
House of Lords
ca. 700 members (life peers, 26 Anglican bishops, and 92 hereditary peers)
scrutinizes bills passed by the House of Commons
is accountable to
House of Commons
650 MPs from constituencies
makes laws
elected for each constituency in a first-past-the-post system, elections are held at least every five years
elects
Electorate
all men and women over the age of 18

*Now go back to task **2 b**.*

► p. 54

Partner B

Look at the infographic below. Examine the U.S. system of government by looking at the separation of powers, how laws are passed, and what the roles of the head of state and the electorate are. Explain your infographic to your partner.

System of Checks and Balances

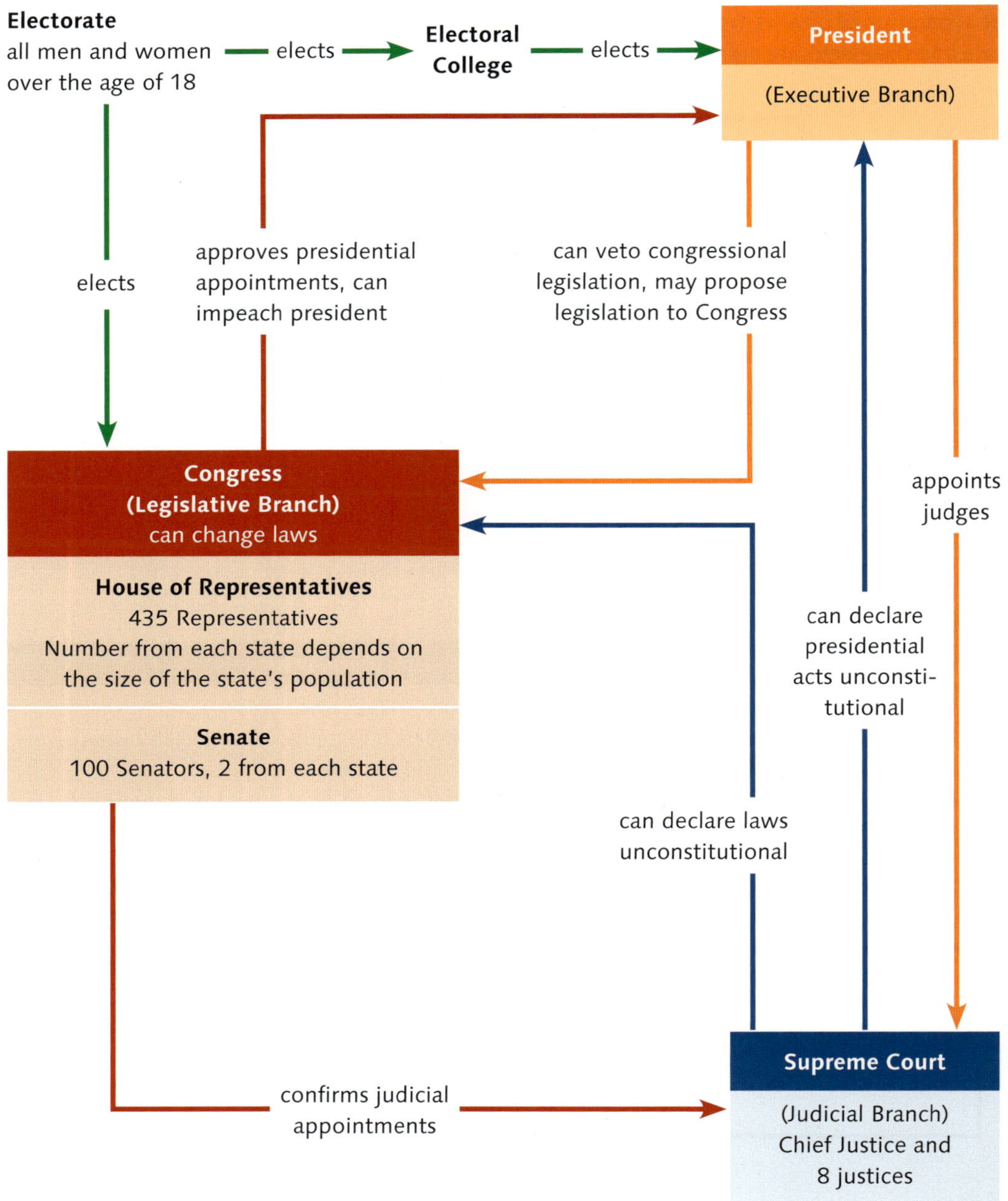

Now go back to task ***2 b****.*

Text 2

Fighting for girls' education

► p. 50

3 Support

Look for examples of the following:

1 *Repetition in her fourth answer
2 *Imagery in her fourth answer
3 *Enumeration (especially enumerating three things) in her final answer
4 *Rhetorical questions in her final answer

Text 5

The move to gender-neutral toys

► p. 62

3 b Support

It is important to note who has long passages of direct speech and why. Then consider why the organizations mentioned are cited in indirect speech.

Language Lab

► p. 66

1 b Support

The following example sentences of adverbial clauses might help you:

Adverbial clause of time	*Ezra joined a political party **as soon as** he was old enough to do it.*
Adverbial clause of place	*During my studies abroad I was warmly welcomed **wherever** I went.*
Adverbial clause of reason	***As** Emily was ill, I decided to help her with her homework.*
Adverbial clause of purpose	*She wants to study in England **so that** she will become fluent in English.*
Adverbial clause of contrast	***Although** the sun is out, it's really chilly.*
Adverbial clause of comparison	*Billy delivered his speech **as if** his life depended on it.*
Adverbial clause of condition	*Lexie won't make the deadline **unless** she starts writing right now.*

Text 8

► p. 69

World geography and the rainbow alliance

5 Support

In English, the if-clause is used more often than the conditional with 'should'. Replace the questions with 'should' in stanza two with if-clauses. Read both versions aloud and compare the difference(s) in sound.

Chapter 3 Text 1

► p. 81

Tech no language

3 Support

The following words and phrases may help you to analyse how body language and silence are used to contribute to the rising tension and the climax.

Language help

The use of non-verbal communication in the play
helps/fails to ...
... increases/decreases clarity.
... is intended to generate tension/confusion/meaning.
... has the effect of reinforcing/underlining/weakening a message.
... visualizes an emotion by ...

► p. 81

5 Support

Following these steps may help you:

1 Discuss what the main message of the play is and how to get it across to the audience.
2 Plan your performance and consider the following questions: What should the stage look like? Do you need any props or costumes? Do you want to use sound?
3 Rehearse your performance several times. Don't forget to set your alarm for one minute.
4 Give your one-minute performance.

Text 2

► p. 82

How advertising haunts us

Pre-reading Support

The following phrases may be helpful in your discussion about your personal digital footprint and the risks and dangers it may imply.

Language help

find information about yourself and others easily • create a digital portrait of yourself • help companies/advertisers track your movements • pass on personal data • endanger one's privacy • marketing purposes • surveillance • retargeting

Skills Lab

1 Support

► p. 84

You might have used the help of AI or digital media to tackle one of the following challenges:

- finding the right vocabulary
- pronouncing an unknown word
- evaluating your knowledge about a topic
- being insecure about how to start a text

Text 3

The hardships of an orphan

► p. 86

Pre-reading Partner B

Partner B: Read the Info box below and do the tasks.

Info

Who was Charlotte Brontë?

Charlotte Brontë, who was born on 21 April, 1816, in Yorkshire, Northern England, was a famous novelist and poet. Charlotte was the third of six children, and her sisters Emily and Anne also became famous authors. The sisters published their works under the male pseudonyms of Currer, Ellis and Acton Bell because the societal norms and gender biases of the time made them fear they would be overlooked and not taken seriously as writers. Charlotte grew up in Haworth, where her father was the clergyman. Her mother died when she was young. Charlotte married in 1854 but died a year later aged 38. Her most famous novel *Jane Eyre* was published in 1847 and immediately became a success. A classic of English literature, it is a coming-of-age story with a strong female protagonist, Jane Eyre, an unwanted and mistreated orphan who becomes a governess. In her struggles for independence and love with the mysterious Mr Rochester, Jane confronts the limitations and traditional gender roles of women in Victorian society and is determined to seek self-fulfilment.

179 Wörter

1 Select a total of ten words from the Info box to use as prompts which you can use to retell the content of the box.
2 Listen to **Partner A**. Then use your prompts to retell the information from the Info box above to your partner in your own words.

zusammenhängende Begriffe wie *gender biases* als ein Wort zählen

Now go back to p. 86 and read the text.

► p. 88

2 Support

There are two types of *characterization: direct and indirect. Both are used in the excerpt to describe Jane and John. The following words and phrases may help you with your analysis of these characterizations.

Language help

Direct characterization: through explicit details, the author shows ... • with specific statements ... • descriptions of ... appeareance • the narrator commentary ...
Indirect characterization: ... is revealed through actions/thoughts/dialogue/interactions • mannerisms • the reader must make inferences • one has to interpret ... • you can draw conclusions from ...

Text 4

Looking back on childhood

► p. 90

2 b Support

The following words and phrases may help you to describe both how Craig feels in the presence of his parents, and the quality of their relationship.

Language help

feel awkward/restless/anxious/tense/uneasy/strained • be on edge • traumatized • be reminded of sb./sth. • revisiting moments of ... • be transported back to childhood ... • reminiscent of sb./sth.

Chapter 4 Text 1

► p. 97

2 Support

2 Look closer at the following lines.
- 'There's ... world is' (ll. 4f.)
- 'Along ... even scared' (ll. 12f.)
- 'the power ... life' (l. 19)
- 'what starts ... vocation' (l. 27)
- 'But ...your life' (ll. 40f.)
- 'The intangibles ... life (l. 45)

Text 3

Partner B

2 Summarize what advice the article gives about presenting your gap year experience in job applications after you have returned home. Take notes and prepare a short oral presentation on the relevant facts to your partner. ► p. 104

► WOB: A1

*Now go back to task **3**.*

5 Support ► p. 105

The following aspects might be worthwhile to mention during the interviews:

1 language skills
2 understanding of cultural differences
3 adapting to a new and different environment
4 facing challenges

Text 4

3 Support ► p. 106

Take a closer look at the following lines:

– l. 11: 'plus Big Red'
– l. 16: 'engorged red opponent'
– l. 18: 'girth'
– l. 18 'precarious balance ... girl'
– l. 21: 'leaving enough ... wallet'

Language Lab

2 Support ► p. 107

The following keywords can be helpful.

1 colonial past
2 Hollywood
3 computer industry
4 globalization

Text 6

Partner B ► p. 111

Read the text on the next page; then do the tasks on p. 193.

'Voluntourists' can make a difference

Sam Blackledge

Annotations

- 1 **rear its head** appear
- 4 **ensue** follow
- 7 **assuage** make unpleasant feelings less strong
- 9 **merit** *(n)* worth
- 15 **enlist sb.** secure the support and aid of sb.
- 16 **self-sufficient** able to provide everything you need without outside help
- 20 **genuine** real; honest; sincere
- 27 **gateway to sth.** possibility to achieve sth.
- 28 **prompt** *(v)* make sth. happen
- 30 **reconciliation** the process in which people find a way to make opposing beliefs or situations agree or coexist
- 32 **quick-fix** *(adj)* seemingly fast and easy solution but in fact not long-lasting or very good

The debate about 'voluntourism' – that unsightly word – has reared its cynical head yet again. Every so often the spotlight is turned on western students using their free time to help those less fortunate in developing countries, and much head-scratching and soul-searching ensues.

Recently the Guardian published a piece by Somalian blogger Ossob Mohamud, with the headline 'Beware the 'voluntourists' doing good'. She argues that the west is turning the developing world into 'a playground' for the rich to 'assuage the guilt of their privilege'. [...]

There is a discussion to be had about the merits or otherwise of overseas volunteering schemes which attract crowds of well-meaning westerners to build schools and playgrounds, teach English or care for orphans. But Mohamud's insistence on drawing a wider social message from her own unsatisfactory trip is unfair and potentially damaging.

Last summer I visited Uganda to report on the work of East African Playgrounds. The charity enlists British students to build play facilities and run sporting projects for primary school children. In just a few years it has grown to be self-sufficient, employing a team of young Ugandans as builders, to the point where the charity's British founders will soon be able to step back and let it run itself.

I witnessed the volunteers – students and recent graduates from UK universities – forming genuine friendships with the locals, developing emotional attachments to the children and becoming truly invested in their future. Cynics might that say when they return to Britain they leave it all behind and life moves on. But for many, volunteering can be life changing. Mark Deeks, 28, was deeply affected by the experience, and is still shaken by the country's poverty, healthcare and corrupt political system. When he returned to university he wrote his masters dissertation on gay rights in Uganda.

He says: 'It was the gateway to everything I do today and everything I will go on to do. I was alerted to a whole different world, one so different that it prompted greater evaluation. That prompted within me the desire to study these differences. And that study will lead me to work towards necessary reconciliation of the two. Assuaging guilt never entered into it – I have no guilt. Only pride.'

East African Playgrounds founder Tom Gill admits frustration that many quick-fix 'gap year' companies are 'built to maximise profits and reduce costs wherever they can' without investing in communities. But, he says, many charities are working hard to counter this.

'Charity in its essence is a chance for those who have more than enough to help those who don't have enough,' he says. 'If privileged people stopped volunteering and making donations then what would happen to the work of thousands of charities worldwide?

'Volunteers play a vital role in the model of charities that are looking to become financially independent and self-sufficient. Charities that rely heavily on grants and trusts have almost all suffered reductions in donations, which has a huge impact on the ground with funding having to be pulled from grassroots projects.

'No approach is without its flaws, but it is vital that people do not group charities doing this well with companies who are putting very little into the developing world.'

Undergraduates face a stark choice about how to spend their time before entering employment, particularly now that money is tight and jobs are scarce. Charities that invest in the developing world need keen, energetic, ambitious people to help them along. 'Voluntourists' they may be – but their work can have a huge impact on their own lives and the lives of those they help. It would be an awful shame if they were put off.

614 Wörter

From: 'In defence of 'voluntourists'', theguardian.com, *25 February 2013*

Comprehension

1 Summarize Sam Blackledge's defence of voluntourists for your partner. Take notes only.

► WOB: A1

Analysis

2 Examine the effect the extensive quotations from Tom Gill (ll. 32–46) in Blackledge's article have.

LÖS 2
- introduction of Gill as an expert who supports Blackledge's view gives credibility to his argument
- he clearly has a deeper knowledge of the business and can distinguish useful charities from the merely profit-oriented organisations

► WOB: A1

Language Awareness

3 In his article the author uses quite a few judgmental terms and phrases (e.g. 'unfair' (l. 12), 'genuine' (l. 20). Find more examples and think about the effect they might have in the context here.

► Support below
► WOB: A1

*Now go back to task **4** on p. 113.*

3 Support Partner B

► p. 193

Judgmental terms have either a positive or a negative connotation. Decide which connotation the examples you collected have. Have a closer look at what exactly is described or judged with the terms you chose.

3 Support Partner A

► p. 113

Sophisticated terms often have Latin roots. Look out for words that you think have Latin roots. Quite often those expressions have 'easier' sounding synonyms. For example, 'condescending' has the synonym 'snobbish'. Why would an author opt for the more complicated sounding expression?.

Text 8

2 Support

► p. 116

The following aspects might help you:
- The last *stanza is different from the others. Think about possible reasons by looking at what is actually said in the last stanza.

- Think about the function of the quotations in the first part of the poem by relating them to the second part.
- Take a look at the use of personal pronouns and think about their function.
- Look out for *images to describe the life of the natives. What is their life compared with and which connotations does this have?

Chapter 5 Text 1

▶ p. 126

Globalization: How does it work?

Partner B

HA • Read the Info box below and take notes.

Info

The giant awakens

During the three centuries following the founding of the first British colonies in North America, colonists and their descendants were busy with the task of exploring and settling the continent, often at the expense of Native American tribes whose lands were seized and whose population was decimated throughout the process. It wasn't until 1890 that the 'frontier' was officially declared closed. The Civil War (1861–65) and its consequences remained a source of permanent social and political unrest. At the same time, the young USA was rising slowly but surely to the status of a leading centre of manufacturing. Under these circumstances, US politicians were more than willing to heed George Washington's famous advice to steer clear of Europe and its quarrels. While US troops fought briefly on the British side in World War I, it wasn't until the Japanese attack on Pearl Harbor in 1941 that the USA became deeply involved in world affairs, ultimately deciding the course of World War II both in Europe and in Asia. In the post-war era, the USA played the decisive role of the defender of the balance of power vis-à-vis the Soviet Union. While there is no other Western nation that can compete with the global influence of the USA, its self-perception as the protector of Western principles has often led to the country being criticized for its heavy-handed involvement in regional conflicts (Korea, Vietnam, Iraq, Afghanistan). Moreover, the bipolar world of the Cold War has yielded to a more multipolar concept in which emerging nations such as China and India play a greater role in world affairs in recent decades. 272 Wörter

Now go back to the second Pre-reading task.

3 Support

▶ p. 128

The following examples might help you to analyse the author's attitude:
- 'many benefits' (l. 6)
- 'not to everyone' (l. 6)
- 'disaster struck' (l. 17)
- 'not helping ... nations' (l. 60)

Text 4

3 Support

► p. 135

The following visual means might serve as a starting point for your analysis:

- teenage presenters
- animations
- text inserts
- ...

Text 8

Things we carry on the sea

5 Support

► p. 143

More common alternatives for the terms used could be e.g. *back* instead of *spine* and *heart* instead of *chest*.

Text 9

Young climate activists

5 Partner B

Lernen App: Podcast (03:55 min.)

► p. 145

Listen to the second part of the podcast. Then tell your partner in English what Luisa Neubauer says about working with politicians and about differences between countries.

Now go back to task **6**.

Literature Lab

8 b Support

► p. 148

The following words might help you to describe the impression Beke Johnson makes: arrogant • indifferent • self-centred • uncooperative • impolite • insensitive • bossy • selfish.

Chapter 6 Text 2

Two teenage inventors

2 Partner B

► p. 155

Look at the picture on p. 196. Speculate about the purpose of the gadget. Then read the text on p. 196 and do the following tasks. Present your results to your partner.

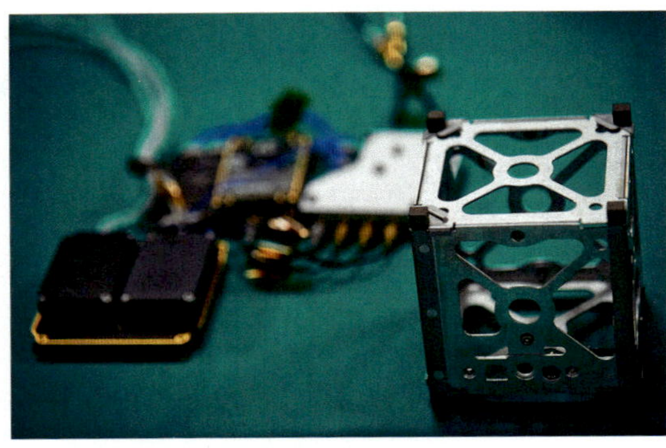

Language help

With the invention people could .../might be able to ... • The purpose of the gadget could/might be to ... • Users should/have to/are supposed to ... • The gadget is likely to / will/won't ...

You are going to read a text about a young inventor.

Annotations
- 11 **nurture** help sb./sth. to develop and be successful
- 18 **carbon fibre** very strong synthetic thread
- 20 **altitude** height above sea level
- 20 **strain** force that pulls or stretches something to a damaging degree
- 23 **reinforce sth.** strengthen or support sth.
- 24 **gravity** force that attracts sb./sth. towards the centre of the earth

► More info
Lernen App: More about Rifath

Many are too young to drink, drive, or even catch an Uber – but they're already filing patents. They're known for their mood swings, social media addiction and dubious fashion choices. But some teenagers break the mould. A new generation of precocious youths is solving the problems of today with ambitious, ground-breaking tech [...]

Rifath Shaarook, 18, India

When Shaarook was a child, he'd spend hours staring through the lens of a telescope with his dad. Sadly Mohamed Farook, a local professor and scientist, passed away when his son was in primary school.

But Shaarook's passion for space lived on. As a young teenager he joined Space Kidz India, an organisation dedicated to nurturing young people with a passion for technology. He formed a six-person team and dedicated the next four years to making a satellite, under the guidance of the organisation's founder and director.

Every night, the teenagers would discuss their plans on video calls, often until 4:30 in the morning. Eventually they invented KalamSat: the lightest satellite in the world.

At just 64g, it weighs about as much as a large battery. It's essentially a 3.8cm-wide cube made from 3D-printed plastic, reinforced with carbon fibres. It contains several different kinds of sensor, including those to measure temperature, magnetism, altitude and any strains on the structure as it hurtles through space. It also has its own power source and a small computer, to turn on all the sensors at the right moment and store their data.

The plan was to get KalamSat into sub-orbit, to test the performance of reinforced plastic in micro gravity. Lightweight materials that can withstand the stresses of space travel are extremely useful, since it costs around $10,000 (£7,191) to launch a pound (450g) of any substance into space. After reaching its destination, it would spend just 12 minutes collecting data, before falling back down to Earth and landing in the sea.

On 22 June 2017, the device was successfully launched at Nasa's Wallops Island facility in Virginia – the very same spot that its namesake, famous rocket scientist and former president APJ Abdul Kalam, once visited over half a century earlier.

358 Wörter

From: Four Teenage Inventors Changing Our World, www.bbc.com, *March 16, 2018*

Annotation

29 **launch sth.** introduce sth. new

Comprehension

HA **1** Complete the sentences using information from the text:
1. Rifath Shaarook invented ...
2. He invented it because ...
3. His invention was ...

► Check
Lernen App: Answer key for task 1

HA **2** Were your ideas about the purpose of the invention correct? List the differences between your speculations and what it was originally intended for.

Analysis

HA **3** The *register of the text ranges between neutral and scientific. Find examples and examine the effect this has. Pay attention to language and structure.

Language awareness

HA **4** **a** Examine the choice of *would* in the following sentence: 'Every night, ... morning.' (l. 14 f.) You may consult a grammar book.

b Make similar sentences using *would*.

Now go back to page 157 and do task **5***.*

► WOB: A4

LÖS **4a**
Would + infinitive is used to talk about what Rifath used to do repeatedly in the past but doesn't do any more today.

Skills Lab

2 b Support

► p. 163

Some controversial points that may help you identify others are:
- Genetic engineering: can help to cure hereditary diseases but also to get rid of unwanted hereditary bodily features.
- Artificial intelligence: can write highly intelligent texts but, due to lack of emotions, can make highly questionable decisions. ...

3 Support

► p. 164

You are now ready to write a first draft of your argumentative text. As an example of an introduction, look at Kenan Malik's article on page 159.

The following phrases may help you to write your argumentative text.

Language help

Introduction:
- Some people claim that ... To them ...
- But there are other people who believe that ... They feel that ...
- Thus, the question arises whether ...
- In the following, I will discuss whether ...

Main body:
- The main reason people often give to support their opinion that ... is ...
- Many say that ...
- On the one hand, ...
- On the other hand, ...
- Another reason why ... is that ...

Conclusion:
- Weighing the arguments, I come to the conclusion that ...
- It is clear that ...
- In my view, ...
- I strongly believe that ...
- In sum ...

Text 5

► p. 166

Artificial Intelligence

Partner B

What U.S. citizens think about the impact of AI (% of U.S. adults)

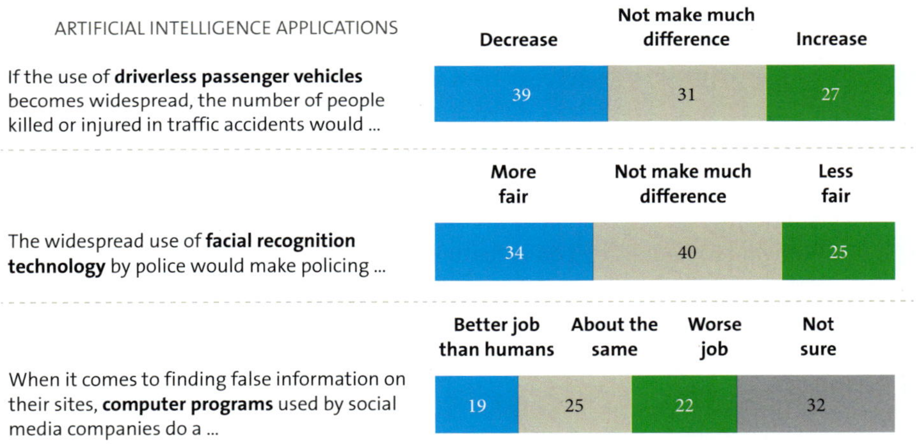

ARTIFICIAL INTELLIGENCE APPLICATIONS	Decrease	Not make much difference	Increase
If the use of **driverless passenger vehicles** becomes widespread, the number of people killed or injured in traffic accidents would ...	39	31	27

	More fair	Not make much difference	Less fair
The widespread use of **facial recognition technology** by police would make policing ...	34	40	25

	Better job than humans	About the same	Worse job	Not sure
When it comes to finding false information on their sites, **computer programs** used by social media companies do a ...	19	25	22	32

From: Pew Research Center, *2021*

Lernen App: Video on analysing diagrams

► Getting started

► SF 22: Analysing diagrams, p. 227

Comprehension

1 Describe the data published by the Pew Research Center in 2021 to **Partner A**.

2 Summarize the conclusions that can be drawn in one or two sentences.

Now go back and do task ***3****.*

Language Lab

4 b Support

► p. 169

Start like this: 'I really don't think computers will ever improve the quality of human decisions. This won't happen in the next hundred years. I'm absolutely sure we're going to ...'

Literature Lab

Technology and the story

► p. 181

12 Support

Now that you have read the short story, discuss its message concerning human nature and the use of science and technology. The following words and phrases may help you with your discussion.

Language help

the role of nature • scientific/technological advances • consequences of science/technology/human actions • ethical implications of sth. • irresponsible use of sth. • boost/threaten the development of sth. • change our lifestyles • lead to humankind's downfall • outlast humans

General exam skills

Language and study skills

Reading, text and media skills

Writing skills

Listening and viewing skills

Speaking skills

Mediating skills

General exam skills

SF 1 Essentials: exams

You will encounter many different English tests and exams at and after school. Before any exam, you should familiarize yourself with its specific format. However, there are some general tips that will help you to be successful. Most important: start early and organize your work.

Preparing for the exam

Step 1 Collecting information

- Find out where the exam will take place, how long it is and, especially for speaking exams, if you will be given preparation time.
- Look at past exam papers to see what they require.
- Make sure you understand what the different tasks require you to do.
- To get the maximum number of points in your exam, find out about the evaluation criteria to help you to focus on the relevant aspects.
- Make sure you know how to use aids that are allowed in the exam, e.g. dictionaries.

Step 2 Practising

- Go over past exam or homework tasks to identify any problem areas and learn from your mistakes.
- Focus on your weak areas. Don't practise what you already know.
- Practise the specific type of exam you will be doing.

Doing the exam

- Read the instructions carefully. They provide crucial information. Make sure you understand what you are supposed to do – it may help to highlight the exam tasks ('Operatoren') and content keywords.
- If you have to choose between tasks, read all the alternatives before deciding which one to do.
- If you notice that you are becoming nervous, take a quick break before continuing.
- Use your time efficiently and leave enough time to check your work.

SF 2 Working with closed test formats

During lessons and in written exams, you will come across test formats that do not require you to write complete texts or answers to questions. In **half-open** formats, you write keywords only, e.g. note-taking, completing tables or finishing sentences. In **closed** test formats, you only indicate which of the given solutions is correct or which items go together. The most common closed test formats are:

- **multiple-choice task** (choosing the correct answer from several options)
- **true/false statement** (classifying each statement as 'true' or 'false')
- **matching task** (matching items from two lists, e.g. paragraphs with headings)
- **gapped text** (identifying sentences or passages that have been omitted)

Closed test formats occur mostly in listening and reading comprehension tasks. In exams such as TOEFL, Cambridge Certificate and TELC, they may also be used for grammar or vocabulary.
The following strategies will help you deal with closed test formats.

Step 1 Reading the instructions

- Read the instructions carefully, work out which information is important, and underline keywords.
- Make predictions about the listening/reading text and the answers to the questions.

Step 2 Doing the closed test

- Focus on the information that is necessary to complete the task. Take notes.
- Read all the answers even if you are sure that you have found the correct one. The differences between the right and the wrong answers are often subtle or tricky.
- Fill in answers to questions that you are sure about straight away. If you are unsure, leave the question and come back to it later.
- Do not skip questions you cannot answer. Make educated guesses – for a multiple-choice question with four options, you have a 25% chance of success!
- Keep an eye on the time. Tasks that require you to read for gist only allow you a short time to skim the texts.
- In listening tasks, complete as much as possible during the first listening. Use the second listening to add any missing information or to correct your answers.

Tips

Working with closed test formats

Multiple-choice task

- Read the options carefully – they may contain traps. They may use keywords from the text, but say the exact opposite of what is said in the text.
- If you are unsure which of the options is correct, go through them one by one and ask yourself if you can exclude any answers.

True/False statements

- With false statements, you will often find the opposite information in the text.
- In a half-open version of this format, you may be asked to give evidence as to why you think an answer is right or wrong or to correct it.

Matching task

- Do not match items just because they contain words or phrases that are similar. Instead, paraphrase the items and match those with a similar meaning.

Gapped text

- Watch out for words that link sentences/ideas such as connectors (e.g. *therefore, moreover*), pronouns and adverbs (e.g. *she, this, there*) or connected vocabulary (e.g. *bird – eagle, sparrow*) and pay attention to the sequence of time in the text. They may all provide useful hints.
- After completing the text, make sure that the grammar is correct and the line of thought logical (e.g. cause and effect).

SF 3 Understanding text-based tasks ('Operatoren')

In general, when dealing with a text, you will be asked to consider the following three aspects:

'Anforderungsbereich I'	'Anforderungsbereich II'	'Anforderungsbereich III'
comprehension (focus on content)	analysis/interpretation (focus on form and function)	composition (focus on evaluation and re-creation)

In an exam (as well as for homework), you may be given tasks that clearly relate to one of these three aspects, or there might be complex tasks that combine two or all three of them.

Comprehension (understanding) ['Anforderungsbereich I']

This type of task focuses on the content of a text and is intended to check whether you have understood it. Comprehension tasks can be quite open, i.e. they require you to write a free text, as in summary writing ► SF 34: Writing a summary or an outline, p. 242, or answer comprehension questions. They can also occur in the form of closed test formats, e.g. multiple choice or true/false exercises.

Below are some instructions that are frequently used for comprehension tasks. For the complete list of instructions, see ► pp. 287–288 ('Verbs for tasks').

Instruction ('Operator')	What you are expected to do	Example	Tips
outline [ˈaʊtlaɪn] *umreißen, skizzieren*	Give the main features, structure or general principles of a topic, omitting minor details.	Outline the writer's views on genetic engineering.	Structure your answer using main and subordinate points.
state *darlegen*	Specify something clearly.	State the *author's opinion on the main character's decision.	Be precise and brief.
summarize (also: **give/write a summary of; sum up**) *zusammenfassen*	Give a concise account of the main points of something.	Summarize the incident in the church in no more than four sentences.	Be concise; leave out details and examples.

You may also get (half-)closed tasks to test your understanding.

complete *vervollständigen, ausfüllen*	Finish the sentence with a few words from the text.	Complete the sentences with words from the text.
tick *ankreuzen, abhaken*	Put a tick (✓) next to the right answer.	Tick which adjectives characterize the girl most appropriately.

Analysis/Interpretation ['Anforderungsbereich II']
This type of task requires you to 'read between the lines' of a text. You might have to examine why an author gives the text a certain form, why he/she characterizes the characters in a certain way, etc.

Below are some instructions that are frequently used for analysis tasks.

Instruction ('Operator')	What you are expected to do	Example	Tips
analyse *(BE)*, **analyze** *(AE)* ['ænəlaɪz] / **examine** [ɪg'zæmɪn] *analysieren, untersuchen*	Describe and explain certain aspects and/or features of the text in detail.	Analyse the main elements of the poster. Examine the writer's attitude towards the *protagonist.	Do not just list the *stylistic devices the author uses, but explain the effect they create.
explain *erklären*	Describe and define in detail.	Explain the main character's reaction to her mother in the first *scene.	Do not just describe something, but give reasons as to why it is the way it is.

Beyond the text (evaluation: comment and/or text production) ['Anforderungsbereich III']
This type of task goes beyond the text and requires you to give your opinion and/or evaluate a question or problem arising from the topic of the text or visuals. You may also be asked to be creative. The task may be called **comment, composition, re-creation of text, creative writing* or simply *writing*. Sometimes you will be asked to write a certain *text type, e.g. a *letter to the editor or an *interior monologue. The task may also give you aspects that need to or may be taken into consideration. If the text type is not specified, you may find one of the instructions listed below.

Instruction ('Operator')	What you are expected to do	Example	Tips
comment on ['kɒment] *kommentieren, Stellung nehmen zu*	State clearly your opinions on the topic in question and support your views with evidence.	Comment on the *speaker's belief that ...	Say exactly what you think and why.
discuss *diskutieren, erörtern*	Investigate or examine an issue; give reasons for and against your position.	Discuss how education influences attitudes towards immigration.	Structure your ideas clearly. Weigh up both sides of an issue and support your final position with arguments.
justify *begründen, rechtfertigen*	Show adequate grounds for decisions or conclusions.	Justify your answer.	If possible and appropriate, use statistics or research results as support.

SF 4 Writing a text analysis

Text analysis (of *fictional or *non-fictional texts) is an essential part of most written exams including the *Abitur.* The aspects you analyse will differ depending on the text type ► SF 16–24, p. 217, but the process of analysing is usually the same.

Preparing the text analysis

Step 1 **Reading the task carefully**
Make sure you know exactly what you are asked to do. ► SF 3: Understanding text-based tasks, p. 201
You may be given a specific aspect to analyse, or will be free to select aspects yourself.

Step 2 **Reading the text**
Make sure you understand the text properly. Use a dictionary where necessary. Here are some suggestions for questions you might ask yourself.

- Which stylistic devices and/or communicative strategies are used? To what effect?
- Which noteworthy words and phrases are used? To what effect?
- How does the structure of the text add to its general meaning / line of argument?
- How is the reader influenced by the text? To what effect?
- What information is being withheld? Why / To what effect?
- In what way does this text differ from other texts of the same type?

Step 3 **Making notes**
Make notes on features or aspects of the text that seem relevant for your analysis. Remember to note down references from the text that support your analysis.

Step 4 **Structuring your ideas**
Do not follow the text chronologically but structure your ideas according to the different aspects you are analysing.

Writing the text analysis

A text analysis is usually written in the present tense.

Step 1 **Introduction**
Write a short introductory paragraph that contains the following:

- the title, the author, the year of publication and the text type
- a first general idea (interpretive hypothesis) of the central message of the text.

Step 2 **Main part (body)**
Write the main part of your text.

- Present your findings to support the central message stated in the introduction.
- Use different paragraphs for different ideas and introduce each paragraph with a topic sentence to guide the reader. Structure your paragraphs coherently.
- Use linking words.
- Remember to provide evidence from the text, i.e. to use quotations with line references.
► SF 14: Quoting from texts, p. 213

Step 3 **Conclusion**

Write a short conclusion.

- Refer back to your introduction and restate your first general idea in different words and based on your findings. Summarize the main points you have made.
- Do not add new aspects at this point.
- Do not give your personal opinion or an evaluation.

Step 4 **Proofreading**

Check your text for any spelling and or grammatical mistakes. Make sure that quotations from the text have been copied correctly.

SF 5 Doing a speaking exam

Many exams include a part in which you have to prove your speaking skills. ► SF 42–47, p. 256 Preparing for and successfully passing a speaking exam is different from a written exam because of the different skills and strategies required. Speaking exams usually consist of two parts which are thematically linked, a *monologue and a *dialogue.

Monologue	Dialogue
In this part, you are asked to give a presentation based on, for example, a diagram, statistics, a picture, *cartoon, quote or short text.	In the second part, you are asked to interact with a partner or a group of students in a role-play or a discussion. It may be based on the material you have worked on for the monologue. Your fellow students have probably dealt with similar material.

Preparing for the speaking exam

Step 1 **Finding out the conditions of the examination**

Ask your teacher about the specific conditions of your exam, e.g.:

- What kind of prompts can you expect (i.e. cartoons, pictures, quotes, etc.)?
- Will you be given time to prepare only the monologue or both parts?
- If there is preparation time for the dialogue, will it be at the very beginning or shortly before the dialogue?
- How long will the preparation time be?
- How long will both parts of the exam be?
- How many people will take part in the dialogue?
- Will the participants in the dialogue be other students or teachers?

Step 2 **Finding out the assessment criteria**

To get the maximum number of points in your exam, find out which criteria your teacher will apply when assessing your exam:

- communicative strategies (structure, eye contact, interaction with partners, etc.)
- pronunciation (clarity, fluency, *intonation, accuracy)
- powers of expression (choice of words, ability to deal with unknown words / technical terms, flexibility, etc.)
- grammar: amount and types of mistakes
- content: quality and meaningfulness of statements/arguments, etc.

Step 3 Practising

- Practise monologues, e.g. by describing and explaining to a fellow student a picture or text that might appear in the exam.
- Practise dialogues, e.g. by discussing with a fellow student a picture or text that might appear in the exam.

Doing the speaking exam

- If there is preparation time, arrange your material so that you can use it effectively. Structure your ideas clearly. Use clear handwriting. Use abbreviations, keywords, etc.
- You may have to adopt a role or defend a position which you do not like. Try to disregard your personal opinion, stick to the facts and give evidence if possible.
- In the dialogue part, take your time to react but do not hesitate too long.
- Ask for clarification of crucial points. Be provocative and polite at the same time; avoid attacks or insults.
- Do not be too emotional.
- Use appropriate body language and facial expressions.
- Choose the right moment to sum up your points and introduce a new aspect.

Tips

Preparing for a speaking exam

- Learn phrases which you can use during presentations ► SF 43, p. 257, *speeches ► SF 44, p. 260 or discussions. ► SF 46, p. 262
- Study your classroom material and look for controversial issues which could be discussed, then collect arguments for and against them.
- Watch (current) political debates online to get an idea of the culture of reflection and debate.

Language and study skills

SF 6 Essentials: language and study skills

You already use some of the skills and strategies presented in this Skills File. In the future, you will need to adapt them to support your language learning at school and beyond, for English or any other foreign language. There are three important questions you should ask yourself – and be honest with your answers!

Step 1 **Where am I?**
Take stock and review your language skills and learning strategies.

- Look at your results and achievements in English.
- Consider the results of self-assessment and peer assessment.
  ► SF 15: Assessing yourself and giving feedback, p. 215
- Ask your teacher where you stand with learning English.
- Do you know how to actively learn more English to improve your results?

Step 2 **Where would I like to be?**
Set yourself achievable goals.

- Do you simply want to avoid some of your most frequent mistakes, or would you like to speak and write better English?
- Do you wish to be well prepared for your next exam?
- Do you need to write an application for a job, scholarship or an exchange year?

Step 3 **What are the next steps?**
Now you know where you are and what your aims are, you have to consider which methods and strategies you can use to achieve these goals.

- If your main aim is to expand your vocabulary, how can you best do this, for example by reading and writing more texts or by using a vocabulary app?
- If you have problems with mediation, is it because you have difficulties mediating ideas, concepts or arguments expressed in German into English? Should you practise explaining things in English?
- If you are not very good at giving presentations in English, do you need to improve your oral skills, or are you unsure about what to present? Should you practise how to identify relevant content or how to get your message across in front of an audience?

SF 7 Dealing with unknown words in a text

When you read or listen to texts, you don't usually understand every single word. Luckily, in many cases, you don't need to because you can understand texts without knowing each individual word. However, if the meaning of a word is essential to a sentence, there are some techniques that can help you work it out.

Look at the highlighted words in the text on the left, then at the strategies on the right to work out their meaning.

In order to remain competitive, industrial nations have to raise their productivity, encourage innovation and lower their production costs.
To reduce costs and to maximize profits, multinational companies often relocate facilities to other countries (= outsourcing) to profit from the lower wages they pay their workers and from less restrictive laws. The problem is that it diminishes work prospects for workers here.

- *competitive* Think of words from the same *word family that you know: *competition / (to) compete / competitor.*
- *encourage* Identify parts of the word that you know: *courage → give sb. courage.*
- *maximize* Think of similar words in other languages: German 'maximieren'.
- *multinational* Identify prefixes or suffixes, e.g. *multi* (= *many*): *multinational = belonging to many nations.*
- *wages* Use the context of the word: *they pay their workers.*
- *prospects* Watch out for false friends: *prospects* = 'Aussichten', not: 'Prospekte'.

Tips

Help with understanding new words

- Illustrations in the text (photos, charts, etc.) can help you to understand unfamiliar words.
- Sometimes there are annotations explaining the meaning of certain words.
- An e-book version of your text often gives you direct access to a dictionary.

SF 8 Working with dictionaries (print and online)

If you do not know the meaning or translation of a word, you can look it up in a bilingual or in a monolingual dictionary. The two types of dictionaries are useful in different situations. Practise using them before the exams.

Using a bilingual dictionary

A bilingual (English-German, German-English) dictionary is useful for finding translations and checking the meaning of individual words, e.g. the English word for 'Ruf' or the German translation of *reputation*. Familiarize yourself with the form of the entries in your dictionary.

- The running heads at the top of each page help you find the right page quickly (top left-hand corner: first entry on page, top right-hand corner: last entry at bottom of page).
- In the example on the right, 'Ruf' is the headword: the different translations are listed; numbers or letters in boxes indicate the different meanings.
- The notes in *italics* (e.g. *'auch übertragen'*) help you to find the particular meaning you are looking for.
- Examples and *collocations *('der **Ruf nach** ...')* are found below the headword.

Ruf
1 *auch übertragen* call /kɔːl/; *lauter* shout /ʃaʊt/: **der Ruf nach *schärferen Gesetzen*** the **call for** tougher laws
2 ≈ *Ansehen* reputation /ˌrepjuˈteɪʃn/

From: *Schulwörterbuch English G 21*

If you are writing on a laptop or PC, it is convenient to use an online dictionary. *Linguee*, for example, is a useful and reliable website (and dictionary app) for translating individual words. Here too you can hear the correct pronunciation. Under each main entry, you will find example sentences from various sources on the internet, together with the corresponding translations. But be careful: the translations are marked as 'not reviewed', i.e. there is no guarantee that the text on the left has been translated correctly.

Using a monolingual dictionary

If you know the English word you need, but are not sure how to use it, then a monolingual dictionary is the right choice. It contains definitions and example sentences that help you to find the words that express exactly what you want to say. In order to choose the right meaning, always read the whole entry.

> **grim** /grɪm/ *adj.* (**grim•mer**, **grim•mest**) **1** looking or sounding very serious: a ***grim face/look/smile*** ◊ *She looked grim.* ◊ *with a look of **grim determination** on his face* ◊ ***grim-faced** policemen* **2** unpleasant and depressing: *grim news* ◊ *We face the grim prospect of still higher unemployment.* ◊ *The outlook is pretty grim.* ◊ *Things are **looking grim** for workers in the building industry.* **3** (of a place or building) not attractive; depressing: *The house looked grim and dreary in the rain.* ◊ *the grim walls of the prison* **4** [not before noun] *(BrE, informal)* ill/sick: *I feel grim this morning.* **5** [not usually before noun] *(BrE, informal)* of very low quality: *Their performance was fairly grim, I'm afraid!* ► **grim•ly** *adv.*: *'It won't be easy,' he said grimly.* ◊ *grimly determined* **grim•ness** *noun* [U]
>
> From: *Oxford Advanced Learner's Dictionary*

Monolingual dictionaries contain useful supplementary information:
- information on spelling and grammar
- examples of common collocations and idioms
- information on usage and *style
- typical sources of error.

Monolingual dictionaries such as the *Oxford Advanced Learner's Dictionary* are usually also (easily) accessible online. The online versions provide the same (often more clearly arranged) information as the printed versions and sometimes even more. Usually, you can hear the words spoken (BE and AE). Most online dictionaries are regularly updated and supplemented.

grim *adjective*
/grɪm/
/grɪm/
(comparative **grimmer**, superlative **grimmest**)

Idioms

1 ★ looking or sounding very serious
- *a **grim face/look/smile***
- *She looked grim.*
- *with a look of **grim determination** on his face*
- *He set about the task with grim concentration.*
- ***grim-faced** policemen*

From: *www.oxfordlearnersdictionaries.com*

SF 9 Learning new words

Learning vocabulary is a lifelong activity – even in your own language. There are different methods for expanding your vocabulary. Try out various ways until you find the one that works best for you.

Step 1 **Identifying useful words**

Identify words that could be useful to you. These might be:

- words that are related to the topic you are dealing with (e.g. Shakespeare's plays)
- words that help you talk or write about texts or topics in class
- words that go together with other words (collocations) or that belong to a word family that you already know
- words that belong to a *neutral register (very formal or very informal words can only be used in limited situations).

Step 2 **Arranging the words**

Arrange your words in a suitable form. This could be on index cards, using a list or any form of *clustering as in mind maps, topic webs and flow charts.Indicate the meaning of your words by

- giving *synonyms (e.g. *dogma = belief/principle*) or antonyms (e.g. *upheaval ≠ stability*)
- establishing word families
- making sketches/drawings
- giving examples (e.g. *the arts = art, music, literature, etc.*)
- giving the German equivalent (e.g. *achievement* = 'Errungenschaft', 'Leistung').

If possible, write down words in contexts or collocations. This will help you to use them in a sentence (e.g. *be torn between, remember sth. as sth.*).

The Elizabethan Age is often remembered as a Golden Age for its many achievements in the arts. However, England was struggling for peace and stability at home – religious, social, political and economic developments challenged society. People were torn between a traditional world view and a more modern one; they generally accepted the Earth as the centre of the cosmos and the Church as the centre of life on Earth, but were keen to discover new truths beyond the old dogmas. Shakespeare's drama reflects this upheaval.

Step 3 **Using new vocabulary**

Use new vocabulary as often as possible: include it in a short text, study your index cards, etc.

Step 4 **Revision**

Revise your vocabulary regularly; first in short intervals, then in longer ones.

Tips

Being active when learning new words

- Do not just write new words down, say them out loud as well
- Walking around while learning new words can be helpful.
- Giving new words a *rhythm or tune can be helpful.

SF 10 Learning languages through digital media

Here are some suggestions on how to use digital media to help you improve your English.

Help with your writing skills

Electronic (rather than handwritten) versions of texts are easier to change and correct. Rewriting and editing longer texts will help improve them – and your English! Giving a text a clear *layout helps the reader to follow your line of thought.

Help with your reading skills

Online dictionaries are a quick way to check the meaning of a word – if you are careful to check a word in its context. You can also listen to the pronunciation. ► SF 8: Working with dictionaries, p. 207

Help with your listening and viewing skills

Watching films and videos in English is a good way to internalize sounds and speech patterns. Try to get as much language input as you can, whenever you can.

Help with your speaking and presentation skills

- Digital presentations are the best way to combine text, images and sound. There are lots of fun things that you can do with digital media to make your presentation more interesting. But remember: your message is the most important thing – and YOU are the most important medium!
- Record yourself to check how your ideas come across. Ask others for feedback.

Help with your language and study skills

- Both vocabulary apps and grammar apps help you to keep track of what you want or need to learn. They also keep track of your progress. Use them as your personal coach.
- It is becoming more and more important to work in a team even when you cannot meet in person. Video conference tools make it easy to work together online. Chats and shared documents saved in the cloud allow all the team members to make their own contributions at any time – no matter where they are.

Tips

Blended learning – the best of both worlds

- Your English book has gone digital too. Make sure you are familiar with the digital extensions your book or e-book offers. Use them when you need language help or online practice, background information or a kickstart with an assignment.
- Books are not everything – neither are digital media. Learning and working in a hybrid world means that you decide what is best for you and your language learning in any given situation.

SF 11 Building language awareness

To improve your language skills, it is not enough to write and speak English fluently. You also need to be aware of the following aspects of language and language use:

- How is language structured as a system?
- How does it work in different contexts?
- How can it have a certain effect on other people?

For different usages of English, you must therefore develop a sensitivity to language (called language awareness) that goes beyond the rules of grammar and how verbal communication works. The following steps will help you to develop/improve your language awareness.

Step 1 **Focusing on a language phenomenon**

When reading, writing, listening to or speaking English, you may encounter and should focus on linguistic phenomena or obstacles such as the following:

- a special accent
- a grammatical form that is different from your mother tongue, e.g. the progressive forms in English

- the fact that in English commands are often given in the form of a polite question
- a communication problem that involves explaining something in a different way, using different words and structures so that another person can understand it
- so-called false friends (e.g. English *sensible* and German 'sensibel')
- different stylistic levels that English speakers use when communicating with different audiences
- how the use of certain words with specific *connotations affects the reading or understanding of a text.

Step 2 **Analysing form**

Analyse the linguistic form of specific uses of English very carefully to understand how they work or why they did not work in case of misunderstanding.

- Try to identify the structure or phenomenon.
- Consider what (grammar) rules might apply.
- Consider how you can explain this specific form of English or why there was a misunderstanding.

Step 3 **Analysing function and meaning**

To be fluent in English, you need to know and understand not only the form of such (specific) language uses, but also what they express, i.e. when and with what intention they are used.

- Find out the function and meaning of the uses of language.
- Find out how they influence communication. For example, if somebody uses very formal English in communication, this might be due to the fact that there is a difference in authority between the communication partners. The speaker either wants to demonstrate power or, by adding politeness to formal English, addresses the other person in a way that achieves a certain goal, such as in a job interview.

Step 4 **Building language awareness and making use of it**

Once you have analysed a language phenomenon and recognized its form, function and meaning, you will be able to:

- use it in your own communication
- analyse the language use of others
- address different target audiences and use the appropriate language for the situation
- convince other people of your ideas because you are aware of how to use language correctly, appropriately and understandably.

SF 12 Communicating across cultures

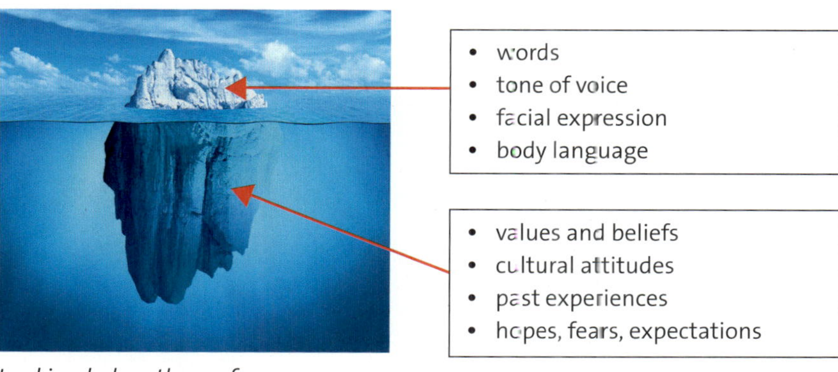

Looking below the surface

When we communicate with other people, what we see and hear is only part of the story – sometimes the smaller part, as illustrated in the photo above. The image of the iceberg shows that most of the meaning of language is determined by factors beyond words written, read and heard. This is especially true when communicating with people from a different culture. Not only language itself, but also the way we use it can vary. It is important to be aware that each culture may have different social conventions, e.g. regarding directness or sincerity.

- In some societies, you must say what you want directly if you wish to be taken seriously, e.g. *I want to speak to the manager – now.* In other parts of the world, it is good manners to express yourself as indirectly as possible, e.g. *I was wondering if it might be possible to speak to the manager.*
- People in the UK are generally far more indirect in their speech than US-Americans or Germans.
- In some cultures, it is considered impolite to express your opinion openly, especially if it is negative. The use of adjectives that are not very meaningful, such as *interesting* or *remarkable* is a polite way of expressing disapproval. In other cultures (e.g. US-American), people are extremely generous with praise and with vague, non-committal promises that are not necessarily to be taken literally, e.g. *You must come for dinner some time.*

Tips

Getting by in an unfamiliar culture

- Observe other people and behave accordingly, for example if they all queue up, then get in line too; if they all rush to the front, then do the same.
- Never take for granted that the person you are talking to understands what you mean just because they smile, nod or say *yes.*
- Be as polite as possible.
- If you do become involved in a misunderstanding, it is often best to apologize, even if you are convinced you are right. An unexpected apology will generally defuse the situation and motivate the other side to seek an agreement.

Language help

Being polite

Asking for confirmation

- So, you mean/think/believe that ...?
- Let me see if I've understood you correctly. You ...

Expressing wishes as questions

- Do you think it would be possible to ...?
- Would anyone mind if I ...?

Avoiding imperatives

- Would you mind taking your bags off my seat?
- Could I ask you to take your bags off my seat?

Apologizing

- I'm very sorry – it was probably my mistake.

SF 13 Doing research

For projects, presentations or other schoolwork, you usually have to research for specific information. To do so, you can use the internet or other sources of information. Here are some ways to make your research more effective.

Step 1 **Clarifying the topic**

- Make sure you understand exactly what the topic is, then brainstorm it. Decide what information you need so that you can structure your research accordingly.
- Make a list of keywords that you want to check.

Step 2 **Choosing sources**

- Decide which sources will be most helpful for your research: the internet, textbooks, encyclopaedias, newspapers or magazines, experts or contemporary witnesses.
- Concentrate on English language sources. Using information in German and translating it into English will take a long time and often leads to unidiomatic English.

Step 3 **Checking source quality and reliability**

- Older publications may contain outdated information – make sure you have the most up-to-date facts.
- Information published by individuals, interest groups or companies may be biased (i.e. in favour of this group or company). Check and do not rely on just one source.

Step 4 **Making notes on the information found**

- Use index cards to make it easier to organize your information later.
- Copy the exact wording and note down the source, as it normally needs to be given in a bibliography (an alphabetical list of sources used) at the end of your project work. If you use a URL, include the last date of access.

Tips

Finding the most useful information on the internet

Determine whether a website provides reliable information.

- Domain names ending with *.gov* or *.edu* indicate that the information is likely to be accurate, as it is usually an official website. Sites of scientific institutions are also usually reliable.
- Personal *blogs or home pages often just give statements by individuals – they tend to be biased.

Limit the number of hits so that you will find useful information more quickly.

- Brainstorm which keywords will most likely appear in an *article which answers your search question.
- Combine them to get the most exact results. Typing in five or six keywords is better than just two or three.
- The more specific the words, the better.

Find the original source of a quote.

- Enter the full quote or parts of it, using quotation marks to find websites with this exact quote and thus normally the original source of the quote.

SF 14 Quoting from texts

Quoting is used when you want to support your own statements (e.g. in an analysis) by giving evidence from other texts or the text you are working on. You can either use a **direct quote** (i.e. use the exact words of the text) or **paraphrase / quote indirectly** (i.e. use your own words to express ideas from a text).

► SF 50: Paraphrasing, p. 268

Here are some rules for quoting properly:

- Always give the exact **source** of your quotation: *line or *verse numbers and – when dealing with longer texts – page numbers. If you are quoting from more than one text, indicate the *author and year of publication.

- Remember these **abbreviations:**
  - *p./l.* is used for one page/line, e.g. *p. 4*
  - *pp./ll.* is used for more than one page/line, e.g. *pp. 11–14*
  - *f./ff.* is used after the number of a page/line and means 'and the following page(s)/line(s)', e.g. *p. 4ff.*
- When working on projects, you may have to quote from more than one source. In this case, you need to indicate in a **bibliography** which texts you have used. For each text, provide the author, title, place and date of publication, publisher or URL.

Indirect quotes

- If you use an indirect quote, you do not use quotation marks.
- Indirect quotes are often, but not always, preceded by *that* or *if.*
- Indicate that you are referring to somebody else's ideas by using *cf.* (German 'vgl.') and the page number and/or line.

Example
Franklin D. Roosevelt suggests in his speech that people who are threatened by poverty are easy prey for dictators (cf. p. 212, ll. 2f.).

Direct quotes

- In a direct quote, repeat exactly what the author wrote – this also applies to spelling, punctuation, etc.
- Use quotation marks to show where the direct quote begins and ends. A direct quote must be clearly indicated as someone else's thoughts to avoid plagiarism. Remember that in English, quotation marks start and end above the line ('...' or "...").
- When quoting complete sentences, make sure that you explain them, refer to or comment on them to avoid disconnected quotations.
- If you want to refer to individual words or phrases from the text (e.g. in an analysis), you can 'build' them into your own sentence. Be careful: work the quotations into your sentences as smoothly as possible so that they fit syntactically.

Example
'We must act now to save our planet and our future', writes a young climate activist in a letter to the editor of the *Guardian.*

Quoting poems or plays in verse

With texts written in verse, indicate the end of lines with a slash (/). When quoting from *plays, provide the *act, *scene and verse, e.g. *II/2/6 = act II, scene 2, verse 6.*

Example
The first two lines of the poem 'The Road Not Taken' by Robert Frost introduce the dilemma of choice that every human faces: 'Two roads diverged in a yellow wood, / And sorry I could not travel both' (ll. 1–2).

Deleting from or adding to a direct quote

- If you want to leave out part of a quote, indicate this by using square brackets [...].
- If you need to add to a quote, e.g. to make it fit into your sentence syntactically or logically, indicate this by adding words in square brackets too. Make sure that you don't change the meaning of the quote and that it is still syntactically correct.

Example
The author says that '[l]ove has made [her] a new [...] person'.
Cf. the original:
Love has made me a new, much more optimistic and likeable person.

Quoting texts containing quotation marks

When quoting a passage that includes quotation marks (e.g. in direct speech), use two different kinds of quotation marks, i.e. '...' and "...".

Example

In Genesis, the first book of the Bible, it says:
'And God said, "Let there be light" and there was light' (Genesis 1.6).
OR
"And God said, 'Let there be light' and there was light" (Genesis 1.6).

Tip

When not to use quotes

Check the assignment carefully before using quotes. For example, in comprehension tasks you are asked to express ideas from the text in your own words and are therefore not supposed to quote.

► SF 3: Understanding text-based tasks, p. 201

Language help

Quoting

Indirect quotes

- The author says/claims/states/argues/believes that .. (cf. ll. 00–00).
- He/She draws attention to the fact that ... (ll. 00f.) and asks if ... (l. 00).
- Franklin D. Roosevelt suggests in his *speech that ... (cf. p. 00, l. 00f.).
- The work of ... shows/indicates that ...
- According to Albert Einstein, ...

Direct quotes

- Biden is convinced that immigration has benefitted the USA: '...' (p. 00. ll. 00–00).
- In her *essay ..., the author says, 'The world needs to wake up' (p. 00, l. 00).
- According to the author, 'British girls are among the most stressed at school' (p. 00, l. 00).
- The article goes on to say that more and more boys 'were also found to be ...' (p. 00, l. 00).
- 'It is disappointing', a teacher is quoted as saying, 'that you haven't learned from your mistakes' (p. 00, l. 00).
- In the *prologue to *Romeo and Juliet*, the unhappy ending of the play is already *foreshadowed by the phrase 'starcrossed lovers' (Prologue, v. 6).

SF 15 Assessing yourself and giving feedback

Self-assessment

Assessing yourself is an important part of learning. It helps you to learn by making you aware of your strengths and weaknesses. However, to assess your own performance, you must find and apply an objective benchmark.

- Try and compare your results, texts, presentations, etc with a set of rules, a good example text or another model or pattern that helps you to identify your strengths, but also your weaknesses or mistakes.

- Ask your teacher for self-assessment sheets with criteria to help you analyse and evaluate your own performance. The Common European Framework of Reference for Languages or the marking schemes your teacher uses may also be helpful.
- Make a list of your 'favourite' mistakes. Or decide on a particular aspect of the task in question that you want to review and improve on.

Peer assessment: giving and receiving feedback

Giving others feedback not only improves your evaluation skills – something that you will find useful in other fields of life too – but also teaches you alternative ways of dealing with and solving a task.

- Before you give feedback, ask if there are any aspects you should pay particular attention to.
- Do not just point out mistakes, also highlight positive aspects.
- Always start with the positive feedback.
- Do not only criticize, but also suggest how to correct a mistake or improve a weakness.
- Focus on the work and performance, not on the person.

It is always easier to assess somebody else's work than your own. But getting feedback from others helps you to evaluate your own skills and products more objectively.

Tips

Giving and receiving feedback

- Make your feedback as specific as possible and refer to aspects such as:
  - the given topic
  - the quality and meaningfulness of content
  - language (correct structures and vocabulary)
  - pronunciation (e.g. in presentations)
  - clarity and readability
  - the needs of the target audience
  - the use of effective strategies for written, oral or visual communication
- A feedback sheet or checklist is helpful when giving and receiving feedback.
- Note down useful strategies and methods to help you with specific activities and for self-assessment (= to be aware of your frequent mistakes and/or see how things have improved).
- Do not feel attacked by critical feedback. Peer assessment is about supporting each other.

Language help

Giving feedback

- You did a good / an excellent job. What I really like about your work/text is ...
- Your text contains quite a few / a lot of good elements; however, ...
- Your text meets many of the relevant criteria such as ...
- You might want to focus more on ...
- Why not try to ... instead of ...?
- If you changed/rewrote the beginning/conclusion / the passage where you ..., your text would sound even more convincing/professional/emotional/...
- I think it would be a good idea to ... Maybe you could ... in order to ...

Reading, text and media skills

SF 16 Essentials: reading strategies and text types

When working with longer texts, there are different ways of reading. Which strategy you apply depends on what you want to do with your text: look for the main ideas or specific information, read for pleasure or analyse it. You also need a strategy to deal with unknown words.

► SF 7: Dealing with unknown words in a text, p. 206

Skimming

Skimming (or reading for gist) means going through a text or material quickly to identify the main ideas. This technique is helpful when you are researching a certain topic and have to find relevant texts quickly.

Step 1 **Getting the gist**
Look at the title, (sub)headings, pictures, diagrams or keywords to get an idea of the content.

Step 2 **Going through the text quickly**
- Don't read every sentence.
- Read the beginning and end of each paragraph – the first sentence usually states the main idea and the last often contains a summary of the paragraph.

Step 3 **Summarizing**
Summarize the text. If you are able to do this, your skimming was probably successful.

Scanning

Scanning means looking out for specific information. This technique is helpful when you want to find answers to a particular question or to compare particular aspects in different texts.

Step 1 **Looking for particular keywords or details**
Think of useful keywords or phrases before looking for the information you need.

Step 2 **Reading the information around the keywords**
Move your eyes quickly down the page. Stop when you find a keyword or phrase and read the part where you found it. Then continue scanning the text.

Extensive reading

This means reading as much as possible, usually for pleasure, e.g. reading a *novel. You read at your own speed and concentrate on what is happening without looking up unknown words.

Close reading

Close reading is necessary when analysing a text in detail. ► SF 17–20, p. 219 To do so, you will have to read the text more than once and make sure you understand every word. You will also have to **read between the lines** to understand what is implied rather than stated explicitly.

Tips

Reading strategies

Before you read

- Activate your **prior knowledge** by making a list of what you already know about the topic.
- Make **predictions**. Use the title, (sub)headings, pictures and diagrams as well as your own experience to speculate about the topic and the central message of the text.

While you read

- Ask and answer **questions** to clarify that you really understand the text.
- Think of **headings** for the paragraphs as a way of understanding the main message of each.
- Analyse the text **structure** (e.g. introduction/main part/conclusion, paragraphs).

Text types

Texts can be classified into two main categories.

Non-fictional texts ► SF 17, p. 219	Fictional texts ► SF 18–20, p. 220
• A *non-fictional text deals with factual events, people and places which are described precisely and are thus verifiable. • It was written to convey information, convince the reader, criticize something or to entertain (while informing about factual events or information). • Non-fictional texts come in many types, e.g. *newspaper/magazine article, *essay, feature article, information leaflet, *advertisement, questionnaire, *letter, review, *biography, political *speech, travel writing.	• A *fictional text describes a world created by its *narrator. It is based on imagination. • The *setting, *characters and events are invented by the *author. • The main types of fiction are: – ***narrative prose**, e.g. novel, *short story – ***poetry**, e.g. ballad, *sonnet – ***drama**, e.g. *comedy, *tragedy • Fictional texts tend to use *stylistic devices. • Within each type of fiction, there are different *genres, e.g. science fiction (or sci-fi), historical fiction, romance fiction.

Tips

Non-fiction and fiction

- Sometimes it is difficult to distinguish between non-fiction and fiction, as the boundaries between these two genres can be blurred, e.g. in the case of diaries, *autobiographies or historical novels.
- Writers of non-fiction often use the techniques of fiction as well as stylistic devices to make their texts more appealing.

SF 17 Reading and understanding non-fictional texts

When analysing a non-fictional text, you have to say more than just what it is about. You have to find out what type of text it is, e.g. a *feature story, an *editorial or a *comment. By looking at how the content, structure and language of the text interact, you can find out what its function and message might be. Follow the steps below.

Step 1 Skimming the text

- Try to get a general idea of the topic and main arguments of the text.
- Sum up briefly what the text is about.
- If possible, find out when and where it was published (newspaper, book, journal, internet).

Step 2 Identifying the text type

Knowing the text type and its characteristic features will help you to anticipate what kind of information might be given and how it might be presented. The info box lists some of the most common text types you will encounter.

Info

Text types

Expository texts (e.g. feature story, *news story, scientific paper)
- contain comprehensive and detailed information
- are intended to be objective and factual
- give no personal opinion
- describe a situation, scientific findings, historic events

Descriptive texts (e.g. travel book, biography)
- describe actual places, objects, events or people based on the author's observations
- are intended to create a vivid picture in the reader's mind
- tend to give a lot of detail

Argumentative texts (e.g. [written] discussion, comment, editorial, *column, *letter to the editor, review, speech)
- discuss problems and controversial ideas
- evaluate a topic by giving reasons and stating the pros and cons of an issue
- arrange arguments in a clear and logical order
- tend to use expert opinions, statistics, quotations and technical/scientific language
- aim to convince the reader/listener
- often use stylistic devices

Persuasive texts (e.g. speech, advertisement)
- often use imperatives as an appeal to take specific action
- try to persuade or convince the reader/listener
- use stylistic devices

Instructive texts (e.g. manual, brochure, recipe)
- tell the reader what to do and how to do it
- use imperatives and passive constructions

Step 3 **Examining the text more closely**
- Focus on the content and purpose of the text: is it meant to inform, persuade, entertain, ...?
- Look at the structure of the text (heading or headline, introduction, main part, conclusion, argumentation / line of argument)
- Analyse the language, *style, *tone and *register of the text: is it *formal/*informal, simple/ complex, objective/*neutral/biased, *emotive, ...?
- Establish the author's reason for writing and what the reader is expected to do with the text.

Step 4 **Answering questions on the text**
- Always read the questions very carefully so that you know what to do or look for.
- Read the text or parts of it again before you answer.
- You may quote key words or (parts of) individual sentences to support your answer.

Language help

Analysing non-fictional texts
- The author uses vivid/informal/objective/emotive language.
- The sentences are long-winded/complex/simple.
- The author's tone is friendly/humorous/critical/optimistic/sarcastic.
- The author's choice of words underlines ...
- The stylistic devices used support/emphasize/underline ...
- The reader can easily picture the situation / follow the author's train of thought / line of argument.

SF 18 Analysing speeches

A speech is as much an argumentative text as it is a persuasive text, as it often tries to convince the audience of a certain point of view by giving a line of arguments. Despite being identified as non-fiction it makes use of many stylistic devices and techniques that are common in fiction.

Step 1 **Listening to or reading the speech**
Read or listen to the speech at least once. If there is a video of the speech, watch the speech itself, but also focus on the speaker as well as the audience and their reactions.

Step 2 **Examining the context**
Analyse the speech to identify the speaker, the audience and the general topic and purpose of the speech. The following questions may help you:
- Who is the speaker?
- When and where was the speech delivered?
- What was/is the occasion?
- Who is the (target) audience?
- Was it presented live and/or covered by any forms of media?

Step 3 **Finding out about the objectives of the speech**
Find out why the speaker delivers their speech. The following questions may help you:
- What is the speaker's goal? Is it to persuade, appeal, motivate, educate, commemorate or entertain?
- What is the primary message of the speech?
- Was the objective achieved? Why or why not?

Step 4 **Analysing structure and argumentation**
To be convincing every speech uses a special structure. It is often divided into three parts:
- opening/introduction: trying to grab the audience's attention

- main body: giving the line of arguments towards the general objectives of the speech
- conclusion: a concise and memorable summing up, often with a call-to-action

Step 5 **Examining language and style**

A speaker uses rhetorical devices and elements of style to underline their position. The following are common:

- *rhetorical questions
- *repetitions, (e.g. slogans), *anaphoras, *parallelisms
- use of imagery, e.g. *similes, *metaphors, *symbols
- *connotations to support one's argument
- pronouns like 'you/we/our/us' to address the audience directly

Step 6 **Giving an overall assessment**

In the end you can give feedback on the speech. The following questions may help you:

- How did the speech make you feel?
- Were you convinced?
- Did the speaker's voice, presence, gestures and eye contact add to their performance?

SF 19 Reading and understanding narrative texts

When you have to analyse a short story, a novel or any other narrative text, you are usually asked to pay attention to one or two specific aspects. The most common aspects are:

Characters, character constellations and character relationships

► SF 31: Writing a character profile, p. 239

Which characters in the story are the most relevant?

- How do the narrator and/or other characters characterize them, directly or indirectly?
- What relationships do the characters have to each other? Are they dependent on each other or equals, etc.? Do they like or dislike each other?
- Do they belong to similar/different groups (social/ethnic, etc.)?
- Do they serve as foils for each other, i.e. do they contrast with another character to highlight particular qualities of that character?
- How do the characters develop? Are they *'round characters' (complex and undergoing development) or *'flat characters' (not very complex and not changing over the course of the *plot)?

Narrator and narrative perspective

- From which *point of view (perspective) is the story told?
  - Is the narrator a *first-person or a *third-person narrator?
- How much does the narrator know or not know? What are the limiting factors?
  - Does the narrator have a *limited point of view – a limited third-person narrator?
  - Does the narrator have an *unlimited point of view – an *omniscient third-person narrator?
  - Does the narrator slip into one character and tell the story from that person's perspective (but still in the third person)? Is it the point of view of one character in the story? In this 'figural narrative situation', the narrator sees the world only through the eyes of the chosen character.
- What effect does the *narrative perspective have on the reader and the reading process?

Tip

The narrative perspective can change in the course of a story.

Plot

- How are the events connected by cause and effect to form a plot?
- How does the narrator attract or keep the reader's attention by creating *tension or *suspense?
- Is there a *climax and/or a *turning point? If so, what effect does it have?
- Does the story have an ending or a conclusion? Or is there an *open ending / a *denouement? What is the effect/consequence of the type of ending?

Setting and atmosphere

- Where and when does the *action take place?
- How do the characters react to the setting?
- How are the *atmosphere and mood created? The four most common ways of establishing atmosphere are setting, tone, the choice of words or the *theme (subject matter) the narrator uses, e.g. sunny spring days usually create an optimistic atmosphere, a crowded place may create a tense or an exciting atmosphere, etc.
- Is the atmosphere described directly, or does the reader have to draw conclusions?

Language help

Analysing narrative texts

- The relationship between the characters is strongly influenced by ...
- The power struggle between the characters reveals itself when ...
- The characters' lack of communication shows ...
- X's behaviour when ... reveals that ...
- The description underlines/emphasizes ... / conveys the impression that ...
- The *image suggests ...
- By using words like ..., the narrator stresses ...
- The overall effect is / can be portrayed as ...
- The perspective is biased/one-sided ...
- As the first-person narrator has a limited perspective, the reader must ...
- The author has chosen an omniscient narrator because ...
- The story has an open ending, so ...
- In the end, the *conflict is solved when ...

SF 20 Reading and understanding poetry

When you analyse a *poem, you should look at its poetic features (e.g. *rhythm or language) as well as at the content, and then link this to the structure and form of the poem. Only then will you be able to fully understand the message the poem is trying to convey.

Step 1 **Reading the poem**

Read the poem two or three times, then summarize it as briefly as possible. Consider:

- the title, setting and theme
- the *'speaker' and the addressee
- the link between the title and the content of the poem.

Step 2 **Analysing structure and form**

Look at the structure and form of the poem (*stanzas, *rhyme scheme, rhythm and *metre). It may help to read the poem out loud to get a feeling for the way it sounds.

- Is the rhythm or rhyme scheme regular or not? Are there interruptions?
- Is there a *refrain?
- How do structure and form contribute to the understanding/meaning of the poem?
- What type of poem is it? (e.g. sonnet, acrostic, limerick, ballad, *free verse)

Step 3 Analysing the language

Examine the language of the poem more closely. Look for:

- the poet's choice of words: how do they contribute to the meaning of the poem?
- *imagery, e.g. *simile, *metaphor, *analogy, *personification
- sound effects, e.g. *alliteration, *assonance, *onomatopoeia
- *contrasts, *repetitions and specific sentence structures (simple/complex sentences, *enjambement)
- mythological/literary/social/historical references
- *symbols and their meaning or function.

Step 4 Understanding the message

- Try to figure out the meaning of the poem. Ask yourself what the poet is trying to say.
- Connect your findings on the form, structure and language of the poem to its content. Describe how they link to the meaning and effects of the poem.

Language help

Analysing poems

- The poem '...' by ... deals with / is about ...
- In the poem, ... describes / reflects on ...
- The poet or speaker addresses ...
- The title reminds the reader of ... / refers to ...
- The poem is made up of ... / consists of ... verses/ stanzas.
- The rhyme scheme is ... / There is no consistent rhyme scheme. / The word ... rhymes with ... / The use of ... creates rhythm.
- Line ... runs into *line ..., which emphasizes ...
- The poet employs specific images, such as metaphors or similes, in order to ...
- The *diction/register is simple/*colloquial/formal, which intensifies the feeling of ...
- The most prominent stylistic device used in the poem is ..., which serves to ...
- All in all, ... / The overall effect is ... / The overall message of the poem is ...
- The poem aims to show/illustrate/convey/express the idea that ...

SF 21 Reading, watching and understanding drama

A drama or *play is a *script in which a *playwright presents what characters say and do. Usually, a drama is written to be performed on stage. When analysing drama, the following aspects should be considered.

Dramatic structure

- Is the structure of the play linear, with events occurring chronologically? This could include *exposition, *rising action, *climax, *falling action, *resolution.
- Is the structure of the play non-linear, with the action of the play moving backwards or forwards in time?
- Does the play include subplots? What is their function?
- Is the play divided up into *acts and *scenes, or is there a different structure?
- What function do these divisions have in the play?
- Do they correspond to action, time, place?
- To what extent do they correspond to the line/arc of suspense?

The construction of action

- How does the action unfold through the *dialogues?
- Are there *monologues? What function do they have?
- What kind of language is used?

Setting
- Do we know when (year, season, time of day) and where (location) the play takes place?
- What sights, sounds, smells and tastes are described?
- Does the script contain *stage directions? If so, what information do they provide?

Characters, character constellations and character relationships ► SF 31: Writing a character profile, p. 239
- Which characters in the play are the most relevant?
- Is one of the characters the *protagonist / the main character / the hero or heroine who fights against another character who is his/her *antagonist? Or are there only anti-heroes/anti-heroines?
- What relationships do the characters have to each other? Are they dependent on each other or equals, etc.? Do they like or dislike each other?
- Do they belong to similar/different groups (social/ethnic, etc.)?
- What issues do they have to deal with in the play?
- How do the characters develop? Are they 'round characters' (complex and undergoing development) or 'flat characters' (not very complex and not changing over the course of the plot)?
- Where do we get the information about the characters from (the stage directions, the characters themselves, other characters)?

Audience
- Does the audience know/see something that the characters do not know/see (*dramatic irony)?
- What is left to the audience's imagination?

Tips

Analysing plays
- Analysing a play is similar to analysing narrative fiction. The basic elements are the same: characters, a plot and a theme.
- When you read a play, imagine how it would look and sound on stage. This way you will understand it better and enjoy it more.

Language help

Analysing plays
- The play is divided into ... acts and ... scenes.
- The overall theme of the play is ...
- In the play, conflicts develop between ...
- The audience is drawn into the plot by ... / The action is supposed to please/shock/enrage/fascinate the audience.
- The ... act ends in a *cliffhanger, which causes the audience to ...
- At the end, the conflict is solved by ...
- The stage directions draw a concise picture of the scenery. / There are almost no stage directions, so ...
- The play works with almost no *props / a bare stage ...
- Even though X appears as a friendly character at first, later he/she demonstrates / stands for / represents ...
- The social differences between the characters can be seen in the language they use ...
- The characters speak in blank verse, which suggests ...

SF 22 Analysing diagrams

Charts and graphs present complex information visually. There are different types:

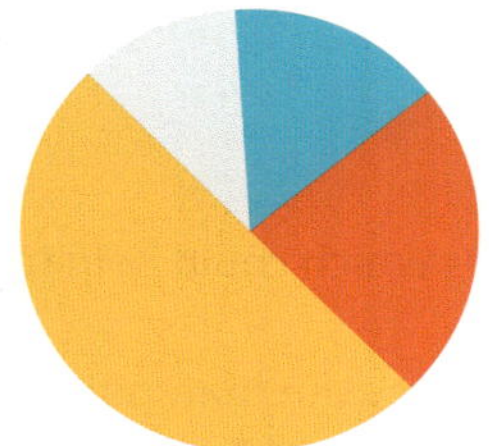

pie chart ('Tortendiagramm', 'Kreisdiagramm')

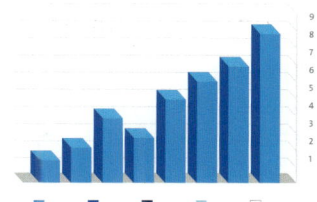

bar chart ('Balkendiagramm', 'Säulendiagramm')

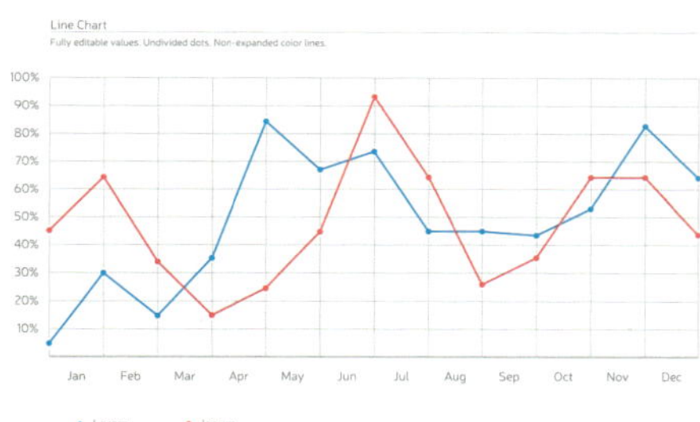

line graph / line chart ('Liniendiagramm', 'Kurvendiagramm')

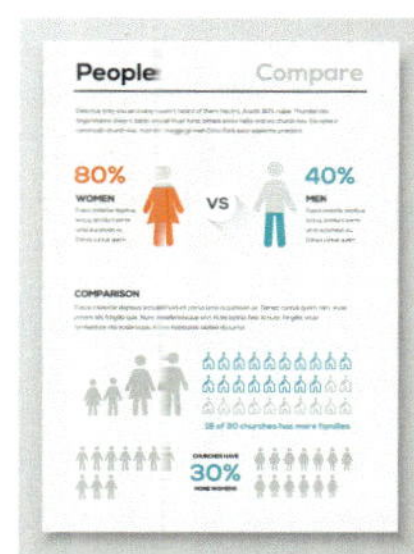

infographic ('Infografik', 'Piktogramm')

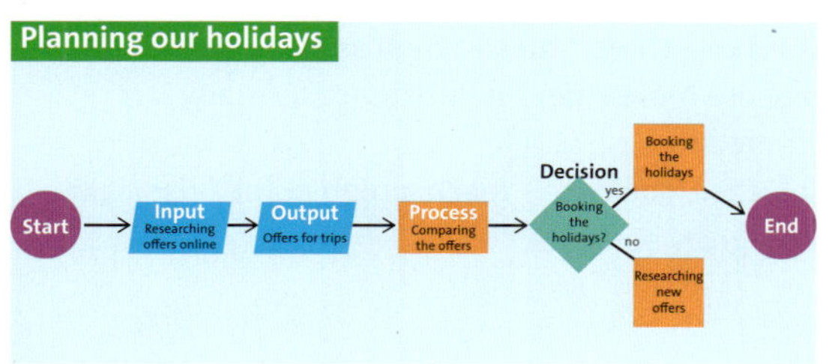

flow chart ('Flussdiagramm', 'Ablaufdiagramm')

Venn diagram ('Venndiagramm', 'Mengendiagramm')

Plans of graduate students after finishing school

	Percentage of students (in one class)
Gap year	20 %
Apprenticeship	15 %
Enroll *(study)* **at university**	40 %
Internship	15 %
Voluntary work	5 %
Other	5 %

chart/table ('Tabelle')

When analysing diagrams, follow these three steps:

Step 1 Identifying the type of diagram

- Identify the type of chart or graph you are dealing with.
- Try to determine whether the source is reliable. ► SF 13: Doing research, p. 212
- Check if the data is up to date.

Step 2 Describing the diagram

- What is it about and what information does it give?
- What period of time is covered?

- Does it show a development, or does it compare different items at one point in time?
- Does it use absolute figures or percentages?
- Which developments can be observed (e.g. where are peaks and low points)?
- Can the diagram be divided into periods which show contrasting or similar developments?

Step 3 **Analysing the diagram**

- What conclusions can you draw from the chart/graph?
- Can you think of historical, social, political, economic developments which could help to explain the chart?
- Is the chart designed to give a brief factual overview or to influence or even manipulate the reader, e.g. by using differing intervals on the x-axis from those on the y-axis?

Language help

Analysing diagrams

- The bar chart / pie chart / line graph / table ... shows the different ...
- It compares the size/number of ... / deals with / is about ... / contrasts ... with ...
- It shows ... in contrast to ...
- It is taken from / It contains data from ... / It was published in ...

Pie chart

- The chart is divided into ... segments which show/represent ...
- The smallest/biggest segment represents ...
- The segments representing ... and ... constitute the majority ...
- A huge majority/minority is ...

Bar chart

- The bars are arranged horizontally/vertically.
- There are big/vast/surprising differences between ...
- At the top/bottom of the ranking comes ...
- ... is first/last in rank.
- ... has the largest / second largest ...

Line graph

- The graph shows the relationship between ... and ...
- ... is twice / three times as high as ...
- There are more than / nearly twice as many ... as there are ...
- ... increase/decrease / reach a high point / rise/fall/ drop / grow steadily.

SF 23 Analysing visuals

There are different types of visuals: photos, posters, paintings, drawings or sketches. Often they are combined with a written text, either as a title or a caption.

Step 1 **Basic information / Introduction**

- What is your first impression of the visual?
- Read the title or caption. What is the general topic?
- When and where was the visual created or published?

Step 2 **Description**

Choose one of these approaches.

- Start with the main subject, i.e. a dominant object, describe it in detail, then describe the background (useful for a visual with one dominant image).

  or
- Start at the left of the visual and work across to the right or vice versa (useful for pictures with a lot of activity).

  or
- Start at the top of the visual and work down to the bottom or vice versa (useful for visuals where the interest tails off towards the top or bottom).

Step 3 **Analysis / Interpretation**

Draw conclusions about what the visual is meant to convey and how it achieves its effect. You might consider:

- the technique, colours
- the effect on the viewer
- who is addressed and why
- the artist's/photographer's message.

Step 4 **Evaluation**

Evaluate the image by thinking about the following questions:

- How effective is the image as a visual message?
- Can the visual be looked at in different ways?
- How does it compare/contrast to other examples that you know?
- If the image illustrates a text, to what extent does the image support, complement or contradict the text?
- If you are asked, say whether you like the image or not and why.

Language help

Analysing visuals

Basic information / introduction

- This picture/painting/photo/poster/drawing/sketch was created by ...
- It was published in ...
- It shows/depicts/portrays/illustrates ...
- It provides proof of / gives information on / introduces the topic of / conveys the impression that / is about ...
- In the picture, you/we can see ... / In the picture, ... can be seen.

Description

Analysis and interpretation

- The artist's/photographer's use of ... creates ... / conveys the impression of ...
- The dominance of ... / The way the light/shadow ... directs the viewer's attention to ...
- As the foreground/ background is ..., the impression given is that ...
- ... is a symbol of ...
- ... helps to create an atmosphere of / which ...
- This has the effect that ...

SF 24 Working with multimodal texts

What is a text? According to dictionaries, a 'text' is any form of written material. Traditionally, texts were seen primarily as collections of words. But all texts are 'multimodal' because they use not only words but also other forms ('modes') of communication (e.g. *layout, images or sounds) to convey meaning.

Step 1 Identifying the type of multimodal text

Multimodal texts can be print, digital or 'live'.

- **Print** ('paper-based') multimodal texts include textbooks, *graphic novels, *cartoons, posters and *comics.
- **Digital** multimodal texts include films, podcasts, social media or computer games.
- **Live** multimodal texts include dance, theatre performance and oral storytelling.

Step 2 Identifying the modes of communication used in the text

When dealing with (multimodal) texts, it is useful to look at **all** the modes involved. This will deepen your understanding of the text and help you analyse it. In general, five different modes can be distinguished:

- the **linguistic** [lɪŋ'gwɪstɪk] mode (spoken or written words)
- the **visual** ['vɪʒuəl] mode (visuals such as photos, but also typography)
- the **spatial** ['speɪʃl] mode (arrangement of objects in space, layout)
- the **gestural** ['dʒestʃərəl] mode (body language)
- the **auditory** (BE: ['ɔːdətri], AE: ['ɔːdətɔːri]) mode (sounds).

Step 3 Exploring the functions of multimodality

- Analyse how each mode contributes to the overall meaning of the text.
- Analyse how the different modes interact with each other to convey the message of the text.

Example:

The poster on the right uses four different modes of communication:

- linguistic mode: caption
- visual mode: picture of Uncle Sam, colours, capital letters
- spatial mode: layout (Uncle Sam in the centre, caption overlaps with the picture)
- gestural mode: fixed eyes, finger pointing.

A US Army recruiting poster (ca. 1917)

The combination of the four modes strongly communicates the recruitment efforts of the US military during World War I.

- The man in the centre immediately draws viewers in. Dressed in red, white and blue, he can be identified as Uncle Sam, a traditional personification of the US government or the nation in general. By looking the viewer straight in the eye and pointing at him/her, the impression of immediacy is created, as if Uncle Sam were addressing the viewer directly.
- The fact that the caption partly overlaps with the image suggests that the caption echoes Uncle Sam's own words. The use of capital letters in the caption adds emphasis and determination to the message. Significantly, the pronoun *YOU*, which is slightly bigger than the rest of the caption, has been highlighted in red to attract the viewer's special attention.

The message is very clear. Anyone who sees and reads this poster should immediately join the army.

SF 25 Analysing cartoons

The following steps will help you to systematically describe and analyse a *cartoon as a multimodal text.

Step 1 **Basic information / Introduction**
- What is your first impression of the cartoon?
- What is the cartoon about? What is its topic / central idea?
- Is the cartoon black and white or in colour?
- What is the name of the cartoonist?
- Where and when was the cartoon published?

Step 2 **Description**
- Describe the cartoon systematically.
- Describe the choice of colours and the drawing style.
- Name any labels, speech bubbles or captions.
- What people, events or trends does the cartoon refer to?

Step 3 **Analysis**
The following questions will help you when analysing a cartoon:
- Are the figures or issues presented in a positive or negative light? How is this achieved?
- What techniques are used to convey the message (symbols, *irony, exaggeration, caricature)? What is the effect?
- How do the drawing style and colour scheme contribute to the overall image of the cartoon?
- Does the cartoon express criticism of certain people, current events or trends? If so, what is criticized and how is this conveyed?
- What point is the cartoonist trying to make? What means are used to get the message across?

Step 4 **Evaluation**
The following questions will help you when commenting on a cartoon:
- How effective is the cartoon as a visual message? Give reasons, using your background knowledge of the topic.
- Do you agree or disagree with the message of the cartoon? Why / Why not?
- Do you find the cartoon convincing? Why / Why not?
- (if asked to compare the message of a text and a cartoon:) To what extent does the cartoon support, complement or contradict the text?

Info

Cartoon – caricature
A **cartoon** is an amusing drawing in a newspaper or magazine that deals with human nature or a current political or social issue. Complex issues are reduced to memorable pictures. Cartoons often include captions or speech bubbles. Techniques employed by cartoonists include ***caricature,** *exaggeration, *wordplay and the use of symbols.

Language help

Analysing cartoons

Description
- The cartoon is (in) black and white / coloured / in colour.
- The cartoonist uses thick outlines, geometric shapes and colourful colours.
- In the centre/foreground/background, ...
- At the top/bottom, ...
- On the left/right-hand side of the cartoon, ...
- There is a caption underneath. It says ...

Analysis
- The characteristics of the illustrated person are simplified/exaggerated through sketching / pencil strokes / artistic drawings.
- The cartoon may be meant to show ...
- The cartoon is very eye-catching because of its use of ...
- The cartoon speaks to the viewer directly by ...
- The layout / use of colour / ... criticizes / makes fun of ...
- The cartoon conveys its message through ...
- The cartoon gets its message across by ...

SF 26 Analysing graphic novels

*Graphic novels are texts that need to be perceived and read using not only textual literacy but also visual literacy skills. Thus they are one example of so-called multimodal texts (▸ SF 24). This means that you have to analyse the relationship of text and imagery, looking at both content and form. The arrangement of elements in the space of a page (page layout/mise-en-page) controls the direction and speed of the reader's gaze. The reader has to assume things that happen between the depicted moments to connect the panels into a story. Therefore, based on effects that you can find in a *cartoon in one frame, a *graphic novel or *comic can be described as an extended intricate form of a cartoon in which the design is inseparable from the narrative.

Step 1 basic information / Introduction
- What is your first impression of the graphic novel?
- Who is the author and who the illustrator?
- Name the full title.
- What is the main topic? What is it about?
- When and where was the graphic novel created and published?
- This information can be summarized in one sentence: title, author, topic, text type.

Step 2 Description

Choose one of these approaches:
- Start by describing the textual elements of the story (including a short summary of the story) and then move on to the visual elements.
  or
- Describe the visual elements and then move on to the textual elements.

In both cases, state clearly if you are referring to the whole of the text or if you are choosing a single page or panel as an example to describe what you think is typical of this graphic novel.

Step 3 Analysis / Interpretation

Explain how the overall effect is achieved and how the artist(s) bring(s) the message across. Consider how form and context work together to analyse the artistic choices made by the creator(s), especially regarding:
- the way the textual elements are used and the balance between textual and visual elements
- drawing technique, page layout, symbols, colours etc.
- aspects that are left out
- any intertextual references (to other texts or visuals)
- the way the characters/topics are presented
- the effect on the reader
- who is addressed by the text and how
- the message conveyed.

Step 4 Evaluation

Evaluate the *graphic novel by thinking about the following questions:
- How effective is the graphic novel in getting the story and its message across? Do you think the format worked well?
- How does it compare with other examples of graphic novels or *novels you know that are dealing with the same topic?
- Did you enjoy reading it? Say why or why not.

Language help

Analysing graphic novels

Basic information/introduction

- The graphic novel was written/created/ illustrated by ...
- It was published in ...
- The graphic novel deals with/is about/ reflects on ...

- The graphic novel was written/created/ illustrated by ...
- It was published in ...
- The graphic novel deals with/is about/ reflects on ...

Analysis and interpretation

- The story is told in a linear/non-linear way.
- The panels are ordered in a sequential style / conventional order (left-to-right + top-to-bottom) / more configurational style.
- Some panels bleed into each other/bleed off the page/overlap each other.
- The gutters are white/black/of different sizes ... and contribute to the effect ....
- The illustrator uses thought/speech bubbles/balloons, narrative boxes/caption boxes/voice-overs...
- The (most prominent) colours/symbols/stylistic elements used are ....
- The graphic novel (partly) is in black and white/ coloured/in colour/drawn like a sketch/in an elaborate style/very detailed ...
- The icons/symbols/colours used evoke associations of ...
- The atmosphere created is dark/tense/funny ...
- The text in this panel in general is redundant/ contrasting/complementary/unrelated to the image. The (overall) effect created by this is ... startling/ confusing/focusing on ...
- Time represented in the narrative is slowed down/fast forwarded/stopped.
- The perspective/'camera' angle used is a close up/ extreme close-up/long shot/shot-reverse shot ...
- Some panels are exaggerated in size/height/colour to emphasize ...
- The creators use irony/exaggeration/symbols ... to point out/criticize/stress ...
- To claim a reader's attention ... / to steer eyes from one point to another
- The imagery/story/symbols refer to ... / evoke associations of ...

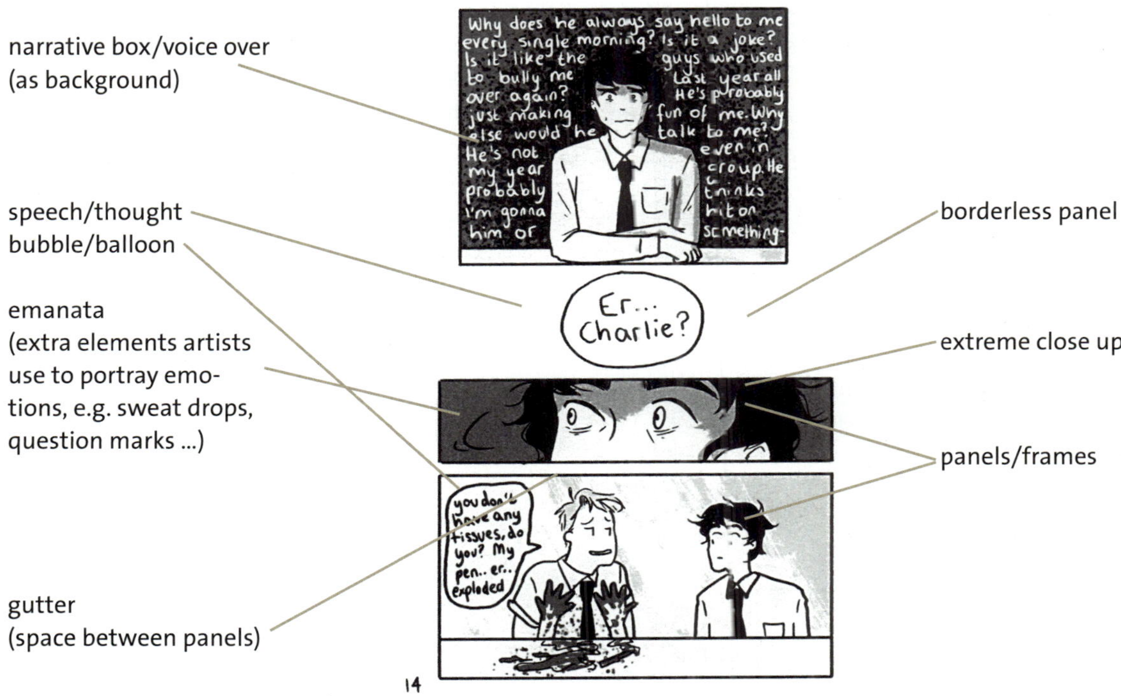

From: Heartstopper, *Alice Osemann, 2018*

Writing skills

SF 27 Essentials: the stages of writing

A well-structured text makes it easy for your reader to follow your line of thought and to understand your text. The structure you use will depend on the kind of text you are writing. There are some rules which apply to all kinds of texts.

Planning stage

Step 1 Collecting information and ideas

- Look at the task and make sure the topic you have to write about is clear.
- Collect ideas by brainstorming and going through class work you have done on the topic.

Step 2 Deciding on the structure of your text

- Most texts you produce will follow this general structure:
  1. Introduction – 2. Main part (body) – 3. Conclusion.
- Decide on the order in which to present your ideas in the main part. Often the text type you have to produce will require a specific structure. For example, if you are asked to discuss a statement, you will probably divide up your ideas into pro and con arguments. ► SF 28: Argumentative writing, p. 234 Other possibilities are a chronological order or *problem → cause → solution*. A flow chart may be helpful at this stage.

Step 3 Outlining your text / Structuring your ideas

- Make an outline of your text (cf. the box on the right). All the 'main ideas' are of equal importance, as are the 'important facts', etc.
- Add the ideas you have collected to your outline. Use keywords.
- Before you start writing notes or the final text, review your outline. Make sure that your main part follows a logical structure.

OUTLINE

1. Introduction

2. Main part (body)

I. Main idea 1
  A. Important fact
    1. Supporting fact
    2. Supporting fact
      a. Example or detail
      b. Example or detail
  B. Important fact

...

II. Main idea 2

...

3. Conclusion

Info

Outline

The term *outline* is used in two slightly different senses. Here it refers to the structure of a piece of writing in which each new thought or fact is separately written down (German: 'Gliederung', 'Entwurf', 'Konzept'). But it can also be used to mean a kind of summary of the main ideas or facts, without the details (German: 'Kurzfassung', 'Zusammenfassung').

Writing stage

Write out your text.

- Begin a new paragraph for each new event, point, argument or idea.
- Structure your text visually, for example by leaving spaces between your paragraphs.
- Each paragraph should start with a topic sentence stating what the paragraph will be about.
- Use linking words to make the connections between individual ideas clear.

Revision and proofreading stage

Step 1 Checking structure

- Have you included an introduction and a conclusion?
- Have you followed all the rules for a clear text structure? Do the ideas in your text develop from paragraph to paragraph?
- Are your paragraphs organized coherently? Do they include more than one sentence but still focus on one basic thought, argument or idea?

Step 2 Checking style

- Consider whether the sentence structure is clear and simple. If your text consists of a lot of unconnected main clauses only, make it more readable by adding linking words to express logical connections between your ideas.
- Decide if you can cut out any wordiness.
- Make sure you used the right *collocations. If in doubt, look them up in a dictionary.
  ► SF 8: Working with dictionaries, p. 207
- Check for *repetitions. Substitute words you have used repeatedly with *synonyms. Again, check your dictionary for help.

Step 3 Checking correctness

- Check the content.
- Check the grammar. Use a grammar book if possible.
- Check spelling and punctuation. If you type your text on a computer, you can use the spellchecker. But always double-check its suggestions (with the help of a dictionary) rather than accepting them blindly.
- If you have inserted quotations from other texts, check you have followed the citation rules and quoted correctly. ► SF 14: Quoting from texts, p. 213

Step 4 Rewriting your text

- If possible, give your text to a classmate to check for mistakes ('peer assessment'). Also ask them to tell you if your ideas are organized and presented well.
  ► SF 15: Assessing yourself and giving feedback, p. 215
- Based on the Steps 1–3, rewrite your text. Make a clean copy of your work.

Tip

When checking correctness, make sure you check your 'favourite' mistakes first.

Language help

Linking words

Enumeration/Structure

first(ly)/second(ly)/third(ly) • to begin with • to start with • in the first place • next • then • finally • last (but not least) • lastly • to conclude

Addition

furthermore • moreover • in addition (to that) • above all • what is more

Comparison

equally • likewise • similarly • in the same way

Summary/Conclusion

then • all in all • to conclude • to sum up • in summary • in conclusion

Exemplification

namely • for example (e.g.) • for instance • that is to say (i.e.)

Reasoning

that is why • because • one reason for this is that ...

Result

consequently • as a consequence • therefore • thus • after all • as a result • this leads to ... • this results in ...

Reformulation

or rather • to put it another way • in other words

Alternatively

on the one hand, ... on the other hand, ... • either ... or ... • neither ... nor ...

Contrast

on the contrary • in contrast to ... • unlike ...

Concession

however • nevertheless • still • though • in spite of that • despite that

SF 28 Argumentative writing: discussion and comment

The main purpose of an *argumentative text is to get a certain perspective of an issue across, i.e. the writer tries to convince the reader of his or her opinion on a topic with the help of arguments. He or she uses quotations from experts as well as figures and statistics to support his or her view. Usually argumentative texts are divided into three parts: an introduction, the middle part with the development of the writer's arguments and a conclusion which again states the central arguments for the writer's opinion.

When writing an argumentative text, you need to structure your text clearly and argue logically to get your message across. The starting point for an argumentative text can be a statement, a text you have read or a *thesis you have been given.

- In a written **discussion** ('Operator': *discuss*), you give arguments for and against something, weigh them up and come to a well-argued conclusion.
- In a *__comment__ ('Operator': *comment on / write a comment*), you want to convince the reader of your own opinion on an issue. You have to give arguments to support it and may even introduce counterarguments which you refute to make your own arguments even stronger.

Planning stage

Step 1 Understanding the task and brainstorming

- Make sure you understand the task.
- Are you supposed to
  - weigh up arguments (i.e. write a discussion)?
  - defend your own position (i.e. write a comment)?
- Brainstorm your topic and take notes of your first ideas.

Step 2 Collecting arguments

- [For a written discussion:] Collect arguments both in favour and against the thesis and note them down. Consider: What is your position on the topic/thesis?
- [For a comment:] Collect arguments in favour of your position and counterarguments you want to refute.

Step 3 Deciding on your line of argument and arranging arguments

- Decide if you are in favour of the thesis or against it.
- Then arrange your arguments in a way that will support your point of view. It is useful to follow one of these two patterns:

Pattern A	Pattern B
Present the arguments for and against in separate paragraphs: 1 Introduction 2 Arguments pro 3 Arguments con 4 Conclusion	Answer each argument immediately with its counterargument: 1 Introduction 2 Argument 1 > counterargument 1 3 Argument 2 > counterargument 2 4 Argument 3 > counterargument 3 5 Conclusion

Writing stage

Step 1 Introduction

- Write your introduction.
- Refer to the topic or thesis given. Introduce the topic in general and then narrow it down to the thesis to be discussed or commented on.
- Do **not** write 'In the following I am going to comment on ...'.

Step 2 Main part (arguments)

- Present your line of argument, following either pattern A or B (see above).
- Present your arguments in separate paragraphs (one argument = one paragraph).
- Structure your paragraphs clearly to guide the reader through your text.
- Connect the arguments coherently with linking words.

Step 3 **Conclusion**

- Round off your text with a conclusion in which you state your thesis once again.
- Do not give new information, and do not use the same phrases as in the introduction.
- If appropriate, outline consequences or future outlooks concerning the topic.

Tips

Arranging arguments

- It is usually a good idea to finish with the argument that supports your position most strongly because this is the one the reader will remember most.
- Sometimes, however, it may be helpful not to postpone your strongest argument until the very end, because you want to catch the reader's attention immediately.

Making your arguments more convincing

- Quote authorities, experts or statistics.
- Present facts.
- Refer to your personal experience whenever possible.

Language help

Argumentative writing

Presenting arguments

- One of the main reasons why ...
- It is often said that ...
- Some people think ...
- In addition to these points, ...

Ordering arguments

- To start with, ...
- First of all, ...
- Firstly/Secondly/Thirdly, ...
- Finally, ...

Contrasting arguments

- On the one hand, ... on the other hand, ...
- Contrary to what most people believe, ...
- ... while/although ...
- However, ...
- But it cannot be overlooked that ...

Giving examples

- This becomes clear when you look at ...
- For example, / For instance, ...
- ... can serve as an example ... / ... is an example of ...
- A good example to illustrate/prove this is ...

Summing up arguments:

- In conclusion, ...
- All in all, ...
- To sum up, ...
- Looking at the given arguments, ...

Explaining your conclusion

- [comment:] After looking into the matter in detail, ...
- [discussion:] After looking at both sides of the matter, ...
- Personally, I believe that ...
- It has been shown that ...

SF 29 Writing a blog post

Writing or mediation tasks often ask you to write a blog post, or blog entry. This is an online diary or informational website to showcase aspects of the blogger's life and/or attitudes.

Blog posts have a range of formats and may resemble an *article ► SF 32, p. 240, a review ► SF 30, p. 238 or a short, direct and conversational response to a point of view or an event. ► SF 37, p. 246 They are always written with a specific audience in mind, normally in an *informal style unless the expected readership is more intellectual. Even if the post is informal, it must not contain *slang, offensive terms or incorrect information.

A typical blog post consists of:
- a catchy headline
- an introduction ('lead') which captivates the reader and explains why he/she should read on
- a main part divided into short paragraphs, ideally with subheadings
- a conclusion which relates to the headline and includes a call to action or invites a response to the points the blogger made
- a timestamp/date indicating when the blog post was published.

Additionally, it could include:
- pictures and illustrations that catch the reader's attention
- tags or hashtags which cross-reference other content that addresses the topic of the post.

Planning stage

Read the task carefully.
- Who is the blog post aimed at? The target group determines the *style and structure of the blog entry.
- What are you going to write about?
- Do you want to post an idea or a topic, start a discussion or contradict somebody else's viewpoint?
- Is it a 'How to ...' guide?

Writing stage

Step 1 Headline
- The headline should not be too long (as with real blog posts, it must fit on the screen).
- It should relate to the main topic of your post.
- It should attract the reader's attention, e.g.:
  - by giving numbers or lists *(Four ways to ..., The ten most important reasons for ...)*
  - by asking a provocative question *(Do you really believe in ...?)*
  - by giving good advice *(How to ...)*

Tip

Some *authors recommend writing the headline last in any kind of text because then they can best assess how to appeal to their readers.

Step 2 Introduction
- Write a captivating introduction.
- Mention the most important, attention-grabbing elements of your post in the first paragraph, e.g.:
  - how you came across the topic of your blog post
  - why it is so important
  - answers to the five *wh*-questions of a story you are going to tell.

Step 3 Main part (body)
- Divide your main part into paragraphs.
- Introduce each paragraph with a topic sentence or highlight the main points of your topic.
- Use subheadings to add structure to your blog post.
- You may add pictures/illustrations, but remember to name your sources.

Step 4 Conclusion

- Do not repeat everything you mentioned in the main part.
- Try to make a connection to the question or thesis you stated in the headline or introduction.
- Bloggers often include a call to action (e.g. *Why don't you ...?, For more information, go to the LINK!*) or invite further comments or responses from their readers.

SF 30 Writing a review

When writing a review, you provide information on a book, film or *play you have read or watched, as well as expressing your opinion about it. Reviews are intended either to recommend the work in question or to discourage people from reading or watching it.

Planning stage

Step 1 Reading, watching or listening to the work

Read the book (*novel, *biography, travel book, etc.) or watch the film/play you want to write about more than once.

Step 2 Making notes of relevant aspects

- Outline the *plot.
- Make notes of interesting, very good or very bad aspects.
- Consider typical elements of the *text type in question.

Step 3 Noting down basic information

Write down important information about the book or film, e.g.:

- title of book/film/play that is being reviewed
- number of pages / running time
- your rating
- year of publication / release date
- author's / director's name.

Writing stage

Step 1 Introduction

- Give your review a catchy title which contains basic facts.
- Start with an introductory paragraph with basic information:
  - type of book/film/play
  - *characters
  - your first reaction.

Step 2 Main part (body)

- First give a short summary of the plot. Be careful not to give away the ending. It could spoil somebody else's pleasure in reading or watching it.
- Comment on the cast/characters.
- Then give your opinion on positive or negative aspects of the book/film/play, e.g. on the plot, characters, *actors, *dialogues, special effects, the 'message'.

Step 3 Conclusion

- Finish your review by summarizing the main aspects.
- Give a recommendation as to whether or not the book/film/play is worth reading/watching.
- Say for which target group you would recommend the book/film/play.

Tips

Writing a review

- Use the present tense.
- Avoid imprecise words like *good, really bad,* etc.

SF 31 Writing a character profile

Characters in *fictional texts are presented through descriptions by the *narrator or other characters (*direct characterization) and through their appearance, language, attitude, behaviour, relationships to other characters, and by their thoughts and actions (*indirect characterization).

Planning stage

Step 1 **Collecting information about the character and their role in the story**

Collect relevant passages in the text and make notes on the following aspects:

- What general information do we get about the character you are dealing with (name, outward appearance, social background, etc.)?
- What role does the character play in the story?
- What does the character say and do?
- What do other characters or the narrator say about the character?
- What does the character say about him/herself?
- Give details about the character, e.g. character traits, ambitions, aims, problems, inner *conflicts, etc.

Step 2 **Analysing the character**

- From your notes, draw conclusions about the character.
- Explain what the character's behaviour, thoughts and actions reveal about him/her. Why does the character act/react in this way?
- Always note down examples from the text (with line references) to give evidence for what you have concluded. ► SF 14: Quoting from texts, p. 213

Writing stage

Step 1 **Introduction**

The introduction should include names, general information, the role the character plays in the story, etc.

Step 2 **Main part (body)**

The main part should include details about the character, e.g. character traits, ambitions, aims, problems, inner conflicts, etc.

Step 3 **Conclusion**

The conclusion should summarize why the character acts/reacts the way he/she does.

Tips

Giving a characterization

- Do not describe what the character does, but explain why he/she says or does.
- Use the present tense.
- Support your findings using quotes from the text. ► SF 14: Quoting from texts, p. 213

Language help

Giving a characterization
- X appears to be ... is portrayed as ...
- This behaviour shows/indicates ...
- Evidence for this can be found in *lines ...
- The way he/she talks implies that ...
- His/Her ... shows ...
- This proves that ... is someone who can be considered courageous/optimistic/trustworthy/unreliable/disloyal/...

SF 32 Writing an (online) article

An article is a text about current events or about a specific topic of general interest published in print (in a newspaper or magazine) or online (e.g. in an online paper or magazine or a blog). There are three types of articles: *news reports ► SF 33: Writing a report, p. 241, feature articles and *leading articles (also called editorials). ► SF 28: Argumentative writing, p. 234

- **News articles/reports** should be objective and unbiased and answer the five *wh*-questions (Who? What? When? Where? Why? And, if possible, How did it happen? What are the consequences?). Sources or people are often quoted.
- **Feature articles** put special emphasis on background information and try to give more (emotional) depth to topical events, people or issues. They are often written in a more narrative style and can also be human-interest stories.
- **Leading articles or editorials** (comparable to comments) express the writer's opinion on a particular topic.

Planning stage

Step 1 Identifying your readership and the kind of article you need to write
- Who is your target audience (e.g. schoolmates in a school magazine, young people in an online blog, people from your area in your regional newspaper)?
- What style/*register is appropriate for your target audience?
- What type of article should you write (e.g. are you reporting on an event, should you write a lively *feature story, or are you asked and allowed to express your opinion in an editorial)?
- Is there a word limit?

Step 2 Researching your topic
- Make sure you can answer all the *wh*-questions.
- Try to find examples, good quotes and anecdotes about the event or people you want to write about that will help you make your point more clearly.
- You could also look for extras such as illustrations, statistics or photos and add them if possible and appropriate.

Writing stage

Step 1 Headline
- A good headline should be short, but not too general. It does not have to be a full sentence.
- Often a question is more provocative because the reader then wants to know the answer.
- You can also add a subheading with additional information.

Step 2 Introduction and main part (body)

- It can be helpful to arrange your ideas in an outline.
- The first sentence or paragraph ('the lead') of a news article gives an overview of the event or story. In the introduction, you need to keep the reader's attention by presenting the most important or most exciting facts so that he/she wants to know and read more.
- After the introductory paragraph, the body of the news article usually gives the most important information first, followed by more minor facts and details. This structure is called the inverted pyramid.
- For each new idea or argument (but not for each sentence) start a new paragraph. Present your ideas/arguments in a coherent order.

Step 3 Conclusion

A good article stays in the reader's mind and makes them think.

- The last paragraph should therefore contain something that the reader will remember.
- If you asked a question at the beginning, you could come back to it.
- If you want to appeal to your readership, you could end your leading article with a call to action, a *rhetorical question or a quote.

Tip

Byline

Don't forget to include a *byline with the author's name at the beginning or end of the article.

SF 33 Writing a report

Reports offer factual information about a recent event. The information is given in chronological order and the language used is objective and *formal.

The following instructions will guide you through the steps of writing a report.

Planning stage

Step 1 Gathering information

- Gather as much information about the event as possible.
- Try to answer the five *wh*-questions:
  - Who [was involved]?
  - What [happened]?
  - When [did it happen]?
  - Where [did it happen]?
  - Why [did it happen]?

  and sometimes also:
  - How [did it happen]?
  - What is the consequence?
- If your report is based on a fictitious event (e.g. from a novel or play), you might need to add missing details such as last names, place names or dates.

Step 2 Ordering the information

Put the information in chronological order. If necessary, add further details.

Writing stage

- Start off with a summarizing sentence.
- Divide your report into paragraphs.
- Use the past tense.
- Use linking words to connect your ideas.
- Make your report sound formal and matter-of-fact by using objective language and the passive voice where possible.
- Do not state personal thoughts, feelings or opinions. Focus on the facts.
- Include quotes or witness statements as evidence. ► SF 14: Quoting from texts, p. 213
- If possible, add a picture/photo with a caption so that the reader can visualize what happened and who was involved.

Language help

Writing a report

- On ..., an incident was reported to the police.
- It is believed/assumed that ...
- ... confirmed/claimed/revealed that ...
- People are concerned about ... / that ...

SF 34 Writing a summary or an outline

When you work with a written or spoken text, you are often asked to write a summary or an outline of the text. While a summary presents (all) the main information from the text in a condensed form, an outline includes only specific information or certain aspects, usually from a complex text. For example, you might be given one of these two tasks on a newspaper article about climate change:

- **Summarize** the article.
  OR
- **Outline** the effects of climate change on biodiversity in Northern Europe as described in the article.

To write a summary or to outline information, you need a good overview of the original text, its content and message. Then you have to decide what to include and what to leave out. The following steps can guide you.

Planning stage

Step 1 **Skimming or scanning**

Read the task carefully so that you know what is expected of you. Then read or listen to the complete text.

- For a **summary:** Take notes or mark the most important words and phrases or sections of the text. Find out which text type you are dealing with, e.g. a *non-fictional text or a fictional text. ► SF 17–20, p. 219
- For an **outline:** Scan the text (or listen out) for the aspect(s) you are asked to include. Mark this information in the text or take notes.

If you have to write a summary, read or listen to the text again and continue with these steps:

Step 2 **Answering the five *wh*-questions**

- Try to answer the five *wh*-questions (Who? What? When? Where? Why? And, if possible, how did it happen? What are the consequences?).

Step 3 **Distinguishing essential and non-essential information**
- Decide which passages of the text contain essential information that needs to be part of your summary and which passages can be left out.
- Do not include examples, numbers, comparisons, quotes, *imagery, *direct speech, etc. in a summary.

Writing stage

Step 1 **Putting the key points in your own words**
- Write an introductory phrase, mentioning the title, author, source of the text as well as the topic and (for a summary) the main message.
- Do not copy from the original text. Remember to use your own words.
- Do not state your own opinion on the matter.
- Use the present tense.
- Use linking words to connect your ideas.

Step 2 **Checking your summary or outline**
- Does your summary contain the most important facts and ideas from the original text?
- Does your outline focus on the aspects in the text as specified in the task?
- Have you left out examples, unnecessary details, etc.?

Tips

Writing a summary or an outline
- Your summary should be (much) shorter than the original text. Sometimes a maximum number of words is given in the task.
- You do not have to follow exactly the same order as in the original text. Rearrange your points so that your summary is logical.
- As an outline only focuses on certain aspects of the text it is usually shorter than a summary.

Language help

Summing up
- The story/article is about ...
- The story takes place in ... (**Not:** The story ~~plays in~~ ...)
- The film deals with ...
- In the podcast the reader gets to know ...
- The topic of the *essay is ...
- The article shows ...
- The author writes/says/states/argues that ...

SF 35 Writing a formal letter or email

When applying for a place at university, asking for information from a company or organization, etc., your *letter or email should follow certain formal rules.

Writing a formal letter

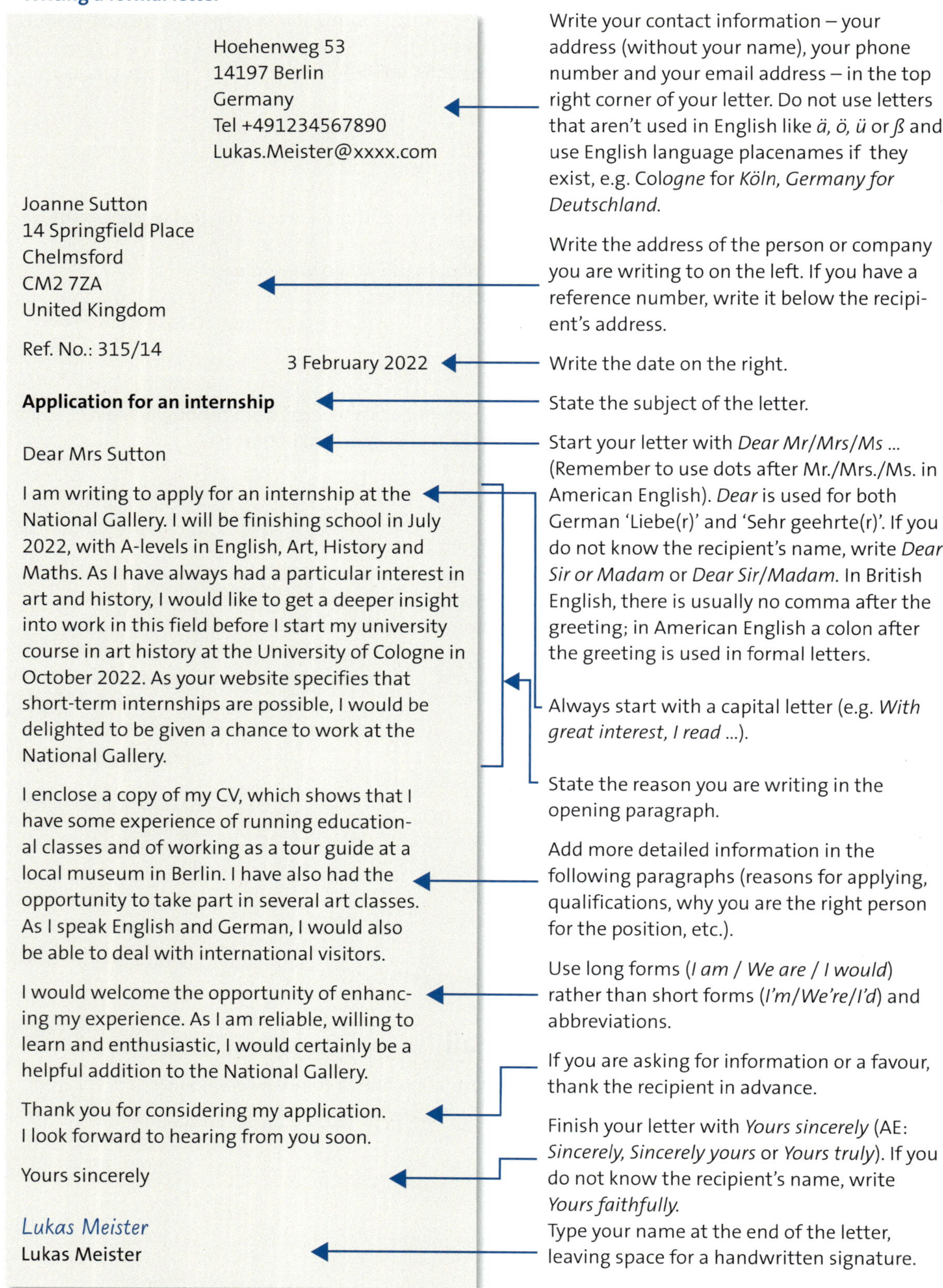

Hoehenweg 53
14197 Berlin
Germany
Tel +491234567890
Lukas.Meister@xxxx.com

Joanne Sutton
14 Springfield Place
Chelmsford
CM2 7ZA
United Kingdom

Ref. No.: 315/14

3 February 2022

Application for an internship

Dear Mrs Sutton

I am writing to apply for an internship at the National Gallery. I will be finishing school in July 2022, with A-levels in English, Art, History and Maths. As I have always had a particular interest in art and history, I would like to get a deeper insight into work in this field before I start my university course in art history at the University of Cologne in October 2022. As your website specifies that short-term internships are possible, I would be delighted to be given a chance to work at the National Gallery.

I enclose a copy of my CV, which shows that I have some experience of running educational classes and of working as a tour guide at a local museum in Berlin. I have also had the opportunity to take part in several art classes. As I speak English and German, I would also be able to deal with international visitors.

I would welcome the opportunity of enhancing my experience. As I am reliable, willing to learn and enthusiastic, I would certainly be a helpful addition to the National Gallery.

Thank you for considering my application.
I look forward to hearing from you soon.

Yours sincerely

Lukas Meister
Lukas Meister

Write your contact information – your address (without your name), your phone number and your email address – in the top right corner of your letter. Do not use letters that aren't used in English like *ä, ö, ü* or *ß* and use English language placenames if they exist, e.g. *Cologne* for *Köln, Germany for Deutschland.*
Write the address of the person or company you are writing to on the left. If you have a reference number, write it below the recipient's address.
Write the date on the right.
State the subject of the letter.
Start your letter with *Dear Mr/Mrs/Ms ...* (Remember to use dots after Mr./Mrs./Ms. in American English). *Dear* is used for both German 'Liebe(r)' and 'Sehr geehrte(r)'. If you do not know the recipient's name, write *Dear Sir or Madam* or *Dear Sir/Madam.* In British English, there is usually no comma after the greeting; in American English a colon after the greeting is used in formal letters.
Always start with a capital letter (e.g. *With great interest, I read ...*).
State the reason you are writing in the opening paragraph.
Add more detailed information in the following paragraphs (reasons for applying, qualifications, why you are the right person for the position, etc.).
Use long forms (*I am / We are / I would*) rather than short forms (*I'm/We're/I'd*) and abbreviations.
If you are asking for information or a favour, thank the recipient in advance.
Finish your letter with *Yours sincerely* (AE: *Sincerely, Sincerely yours* or *Yours truly*). If you do not know the recipient's name, write *Yours faithfully.*
Type your name at the end of the letter, leaving space for a handwritten signature.

Writing a formal email

- You do not need to include the recipient's address or the date in the main part of your email, as they appear automatically in the header.
- Open and close your mail the same way you would when writing a formal letter.
- Do not use emoticons, smileys, etc.
- Type your name and contact details (the email signature) at the bottom.

SF 36 Writing an application: cover letter and CV

If you want to apply for a holiday job or a position in a company (e.g. an internship), you should send a cover letter and a CV (curriculum vitae).

The cover letter

The cover letter for an application follows the rules of a formal letter. ▸ SF 35, p. 243 Since you are presenting yourself, it is important to avoid mistakes and to use formal language. State in what ways you are suited for the position you are applying for. Show that you have collected information about the company you are applying to and that you have a real interest in the position advertised. Mention what documents you are enclosing. At the end of the letter, express hope for a reply or an invitation to an interview.

The CV (American English: **résumé** ['rezəmeɪ])

Your CV gives information about you, about your education, qualifications, etc. to the person you are applying to. A CV should be clear and effective – remember the KISS rule ('Keep it short and simple'). Use a clear and easy-to-read font, highlight particularly relevant information, and do not forget to check your CV for spelling mistakes.

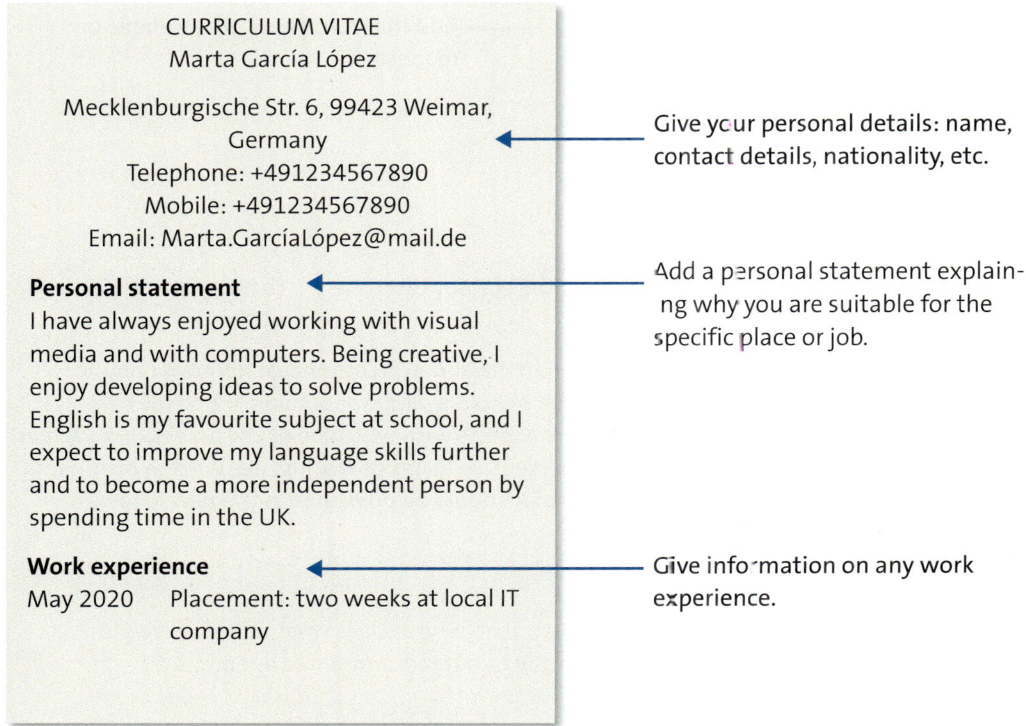

CURRICULUM VITAE
Marta García López

Mecklenburgische Str. 6, 99423 Weimar, Germany
Telephone: +491234567890
Mobile: +491234567890
Email: Marta.GarcíaLópez@mail.de

Personal statement

I have always enjoyed working with visual media and with computers. Being creative, I enjoy developing ideas to solve problems. English is my favourite subject at school, and I expect to improve my language skills further and to become a more independent person by spending time in the UK.

Work experience

May 2020 Placement: two weeks at local IT company

Give your personal details: name, contact details, nationality, etc.
Add a personal statement explaining why you are suitable for the specific place or job.
Give information on any work experience.

Education

2016–date	Secondary/High School: Alfred-Krupp-Schule, Wernigerode
2012–2016	Primary/Elementary School Gartenstrasse, Essen

Show the stages of your education so far (schools, exams, etc.).

Qualifications/skills

IT skills	Excellent knowledge of MS Word, PowerPoint, Excel, web design, Photoshop
Language skills	German native speaker; good written and spoken English, basic French
Technology	Winner of the gold medal 2019 for 'school inventors' in the 'Junior Ingenieur Akademie' (school engineering course)

List your qualifications and present your key skills, especially those the employer is looking for.

Hobbies and interests

Member of school drama club, member of school computer club, member of after-school basketball club. I enjoy listening to and playing music and making films.

Write something about your hobbies or interests.

References

Available on request

Add that references are available on request.

SF 37 Writing a letter to the editor

Newspapers often have a special section for *letters to the editor ('Leserbriefe'). Those on particularly interesting and controversial topics are printed there.

In a letter to the editor, a reader reacts to a *newspaper article and expresses his or her own opinion about it. The reader may agree with the author's opinion or hold a different opinion. He or she can therefore criticize, praise, comment on, add to or correct aspects with which he or she agrees or disagrees. Letters to the editor have a similar structure to other persuasive forms of writing, like written comments. The intention of the writer of a letter to the editor is that it should be published in the newspaper.

Info

Editor
The editor is a person in charge of a newspaper (department) who decides what should be published. Editors also write articles, but usually articles are written by authors and edited by editors.

Writing stage

A letter to the editor follows most of the conventions of a formal letter or email. ► SF 35: Writing a formal letter or email, p. 243

Note the following, however:

- Nowadays, letters to the editor are very often sent by email. Watch out for contact information on the magazine's or newspaper's website.
- Your letter should be brief and to the point.
- Start like this: *Sir or Madam* (leave out *Dear*).
- Refer to the article (give title, date and main topic).
- Omit the closing remarks *(Yours faithfully/sincerely)*.
- End with your name and (postal or email) address.

The main part of a letter to the editor is structured like a comment. ► SF 28: Argumentative writing, p. 234
However, in a letter to the editor, you limit yourself to the arguments that support your point of view.

Language help

Writing a letter to the editor

- I refer to your article '...' about ... published on ... 2022.
- I am writing to you after reading the article '...' about ...
- I am writing to you in response to the article '...' about ..
- I support / agree with / disagree with the author's opinion on ...
- I disagree with this idea / the idea of ...
- I approve of the author's belief in ...
- I do not think that the author understands ...
- In my opinion, it is essential to consider/include the perspective of ...

SF 38 Creative writing

Most creative writing tasks ask you to write ('create') a text based on an existing piece of writing ('material-based writing'). You may have to rewrite part of a story (possibly from a different perspective) or create something new, such as a letter, that is only mentioned in the original text.

Type 1 Continuation of a story

When dealing with fictional texts, a common creative task might be to write an ending to a story.

Planning stage

Step 1 Reread the original text
Look at the *setting, events, dates, characters and their relationships in the original text and watch out for hints as to how the story might continue. Make notes.

Step 2 Check your ideas against the original text
Brainstorm ideas for a continuation and compare them to the original extract to make sure they do not contradict the reality depicted in the story.

Step 3 Analyse the narrative perspective of the original text
Identify the *narrative perspective of the original text (e.g. *first-person narrator) and consider what limitations that specific perspective might have or not have.

Writing stage
Create a new text that corresponds to the original. Try to imitate the style and language used in the original.

Type 2 Change of perspective

A change of perspective means that you take over the view of one of the characters in the story from whose perspective the story is not told. You retell and evaluate ('re-create') the events from this person's point of view, e.g. in a diary entry, a letter or an *interior monologue.

In the case of a non-fictional text (e.g. a *speech or newspaper article), you usually have to evaluate a situation through the eyes of a fictitious character. You might, for example, be asked to read a text on a climate conference and then write an article from the perspective of a reporter who attended the conference.

Example: Writing a diary entry
You may be asked to write a diary entry from the perspective of a literary character.

Planning stage
- Look at the original text and ask yourself what this character thinks, feels, hopes, expects and/or fears in various situations and also what your character knows and does not know.
- Think about a *theme or question that is important to this character. The diary entry should focus on the character's experiences as described in the text.
- Think about what might have led to your character's current situation and/or what you expect to happen next.

Writing stage
- The style of a diary entry is usually informal and it is arranged in chronological order.
- Make it clear at what time, where, in what situation and why you are writing.
- A diary entry usually contains opinions and chit-chat as well as facts. It must not only refer to events but also comment on and evaluate them.
- The diary entry should be written to match the character's personality and language. Age, social status and other features usually determine how someone speaks or writes.

Tips

The difference between a diary entry and an interior monologue
- An evaluation in a diary entry looks back on events and is made in retrospect.
- An interior monologue represents the thoughts and feelings going through a character's mind. It should therefore be conceived as an immediate reaction to the events in the text extract.
- Interior monologues are normally narrated in the present tense.

Type 3 Writing a film script (screenplay)

You may be asked to write the text for a film, including instructions for the actors and directions for filming. A film script has a standard format that is functional rather than attractive to read.

Step 1 Slug line

At the start of each *scene there is a line of text (the so-called slug line) that indicates:

- whether the scene takes place inside or outside (INT. = interior / EXT. = exterior, outside)
- the exact location
- the time of day
- the type of camera shot.

Step 2 Screen directions and dialogue

The slug line is followed by:

- the screen directions (describing the *action, location and objects in the scene as well as the characters)
- the dialogue, i.e. the words the characters speak.

As a rule, the present tense is used for the screen directions, similar to a picture description. The dialogue is usually written in a centre column.

Example:

INT. ARYANE'S FLAT – MIDNIGHT – CLOSE-UP
The two large profiles fill the screen. Aryane kisses the boy firmly, but not passionately. Then her phone rings ...

ARYANE (softly)
Are you feeling better?

GREG (seen from the back, barely audible)
Hmmm ... a little.

You may also be asked to turn a *short story or a key scene from a novel into a film script. In this case, you need to consider which aspects of the original text can be represented in the film and how, and which details can be omitted without changing the message of the text.

Tips

Creative writing

- In a material-based creative writing task, you have to work on and with the original text. Do not move too far away from it, or your own text may become illogical or contradict the events of the original story.
- Think of your task as 'reading between the lines' rather than inventing completely new scenes, etc.
- Pay attention to the text type you are using. If you write a diary entry, you should focus on thoughts and feelings. If you write a letter, you must address the addressee and sign it. ► SF 35: Writing a formal letter or email, p. 243 If you write dialogues, you should use typical elements of spoken language.

Listening and viewing skills

SF 39 Essentials: listening and viewing

The ability to understand spoken English is key to speaking it. Some of the challenges of listening and viewing are listed below.

- In real-life situations, e.g. in conversations, you can usually listen to or look at what you hear or see only once. This is fundamentally different from reading where you can reread the words as many times as you like or feel necessary, e.g. when you get distracted or interrupted.
- When listening or watching, you need to decode both verbal and non-verbal messages, such as *intonation, tone of voice, *pitch, tempo, volume, facial expression and posture. These help you to identify the *speaker's attitude or intentions.
- People speak differently than they write. Many have accents and/or speak too fast, loudly, softly or even very informally. There may also be background noise that makes listening difficult.

There are different listening and viewing skills to be applied depending on the situation or task.

- **Listening/Viewing for gist** enables you to get a general idea of the content or main topic.
- **Listening/Viewing for detail** is necessary if you need to collect information about certain aspects of a spoken text. In exams, you may have to listen/view for specific information.
- **Listening/Viewing and making deductions** is drawing conclusions about the meaning or the speaker's intentions based on the information you hear or see.

A listening or viewing task may be based on a short audio (e.g. an interview, a *speech) or video (e.g. an interview, a documentary, a film clip). Listening tasks often focus on 'Anforderungsbereich I', i.e. text comprehension, and use closed test formats such as multiple choice. Viewing tasks, but also some listening tasks, go beyond simple comprehension and require you to analyse the video or audio more fully. Therefore, make sure you are familiar with the aspects to be tested. ▸ SF 2–3, p. 99

Tips

Listening and viewing strategies

Pre-listening/Pre-viewing

- Read the instructions carefully and make sure you know what to focus on.
- Examine the background information.
- Make predictions about the audio/video and the answers to the questions.

While-listening/While-viewing

- Read all the answers, even if you are sure that you have found the correct one. The differences between the right and the wrong answers are often subtle or tricky.
- If you take notes, only jot down keywords or short phrases.
- If the task is to write a text, note down phrases from the audio/video to use as quotes.
- For viewing tasks, it may be helpful to work with a film diary (viewing log) in which you record the action or individual important scenes as well as your reaction to them.

SF 40 Listening/Viewing for gist and detail

Listening or viewing for gist is when you try to understand what is happening, even if you do not (need to) understand every phrase or sentence. Instead, you try to pick up keywords, intonation and other clues that help you to work out the general meaning.

Listening or viewing for detail is when you listen/watch out for specific aspects or pieces of information to complete a task.

Listening/Viewing for gist

Step 1 Pre-listening/Pre-Viewing

Read the task(s) carefully. If possible, collect information on the following:

- the *text type (e.g. podcast, interview, *feature film) and its addressee(s)
- the situation and *setting
- the number of speakers and their role, e.g. will there be conflicting points of view?
- the topic dealt with and what *points of view or concepts you are likely to encounter.

Try to predict what the listening/viewing will be about and what the speaker(s) might say.

Step 2 While-listening/While-viewing

- Identify the topic / main idea / main point of the text. Ask yourself: What do the speakers talk/think about ...?
- Do not try to understand every detail that is said or shown.
- Listen out for 'signpost expressions' that show somebody's train of thought, e.g. *the biggest issue is ..., the most important argument is ..., on the one hand ...*
- Remember to take notes on key points.

Listening/Viewing for detail

Step 1 Pre-listening/Pre-viewing

- Examine what you know about the audio/video (its speaker(s), addressee(s), situation, setting and/or topic).
- Try to anticipate what might be said/shown in the audio/video.
- Collect keywords that are relevant to your task, e.g. names, dates or numbers.
- Prepare so that you can take notes quickly.

Step 2 While-listening/While-viewing

- Listen/Watch out for the aspects you collected.
- Take notes, using abbreviations and symbols.

Tip

Using the breaks between listening/viewing times

- After the first (or second) listening/viewing, look at your notes and work on the task(s).
- After the second (and/or third) listening/viewing, complete your task(s) and check your answers.

SF 41 Analysing films, series and videos

Watching a film, series or video can make you laugh or cry, feel angry or scared. Such reactions are not only caused by the story itself but also by the way the film or series tells it. Just as written texts can provoke a reaction in their readers through the choice of words and *stylistic devices, films or series can achieve similar responses in their viewers through, for example, the camera work, lighting, sound and editing.

Step 1 **Pre-viewing**

- Find out what film, series or video you are going to watch and get an idea of what to expect by looking at any available information, e.g. film posters, reviews, covers, magazine information.
- Identify the genre: Is it a documentary, a feature film such as a thriller, a science-fiction/sci-fi movie, a *comedy or a drama? Is it a crime series, a non-fiction series, a sitcom or a *soap opera? Is it a news clip, a music video or a *commercial?

Step 2 **While-viewing**

Make notes on the story (setting, location, *plot) and the cast (*actors).

Step 3 **Analysing cinematic devices and their effect**

Watch the film, video or episode once more and have a closer look at the cinematic devices used (e.g. camera work, lighting, sound) and the effect they achieve. You will find details and useful terms below.

Camera range ('Einstellungsgröße')

long shot ('Totale', 'Gesamtaufnahme') a view of a situation from a distance **establishing shot** ('Eröffnungsszene') a long shot at the beginning of a *scene (or a sequence), often an **aerial shot** ('Luftaufnahme') Long shots give an overall impression of the setting.	
medium shot ('Halbnahe', 'Halbnahaufnahme') a shot which shows one or two people from the waist up This allows the viewer to get an idea of the interaction between the *characters.	
close-up ('Nahaufnahme', 'Großaufnahme') a full screen shot of one person's face or one object This allows the viewer to see clearly the emotions a character is experiencing or to consider the role of the object that is shown.	

Camera angle ('Kameraperspektive')

low-angle shot ('Froschperspektive') a shot which looks up at the subject (a person, a building, etc.) from below eye level The character appears to be bigger than others in the scene, thus seeming powerful, dominant or dangerous.	
high-angle shot ('Vogelperspektive') a shot which looks down on the subject (a person, a building, etc.) from above eye level The character appears to be smaller than others in the scene, thus seeming vulnerable, inferior or frightened.	

eye-level shot ('Normalsicht')
a shot which is taken with the camera approximately at human eye level
This has a 'neutral' effect and gives the viewer the feeling of actually being in the scene.

over-the-shoulder shot ('Über-die-Schulter')
a shot of one character over the shoulder of another
In this shot, the viewer sees a character's point of view. It is useful for showing reactions during conversations.

Camera movement ('Kamerabewegung')

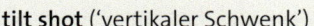

pan shot ('Schwenk')
a shot where the camera moves horizontally (pans) – left to right or right to left – from a static position

tilt shot ('vertikaler Schwenk')
a shot where the camera moves up or down (tilts) from a static position

tracking shot ('Kamerafahrt', 'Mitschwenk')
a shot where the camera moves along tracks beside, behind or in front of a moving person or object

zoom ('Zoom')
a shot from a stationary camera in which the lens achieves the effect of moving towards the subject (zoom-in, 'Ranfahrt') or away from the subject (zoom-out, 'Wegfahrt')

Editing ('Filmschnitt')

Film editing is the technique, practice and art of assembling shots into a coherent sequence.

cut ('Schnitt')
the point at which one shot changes (cuts) directly to another

cross-cutting ('Kreuzschnitt', 'Parallelmontage')
cutting separate actions together to illustrate moments that take place simultaneously

jump cut ('harter Schnitt', 'diskontinuierlicher Schnitt')
an abrupt and unexpected cut from one shot to another where, for example, an element of time or space has been left out

fade-in/fade-out ('Aufblende'/'Abblende', 'Ausblende')
the gradual appearance or disappearance of a shot – usually at the beginning or end of a scene

(cross-)fading ('Überblendung')
fading in (one sound or picture source) as another is being faded out

Lighting ('Beleuchtung[sstil]', 'Lichtgestaltung')

high-key lighting ('High-Key-Beleuchtung[sstil]')
a style of lighting that emphasizes bright and soft lighting with few shadows to create a friendly atmosphere

low-key lighting ('Low-Key-Beleuchtung[sstil]')
a style of lighting where a scene is dominated by shadow, and light is used without producing great contrast

high-contrast lighting ('kontrastreiche Beleuchtung', 'starkes Kontrastlicht')
a style of lighting that results in dark shadows and bright highlights to create eye-catching shots

Sound ('Ton')

soundtrack ('Ton[spur]', 'Filmmusik')
all the sounds, speech and music recorded for a film

on-screen sound ('On-Ton')
sounds, speech or music whose source can be seen in the shot

off-screen sound ('Off-Ton')
sounds, speech or music whose source is not visible in the shot and only the viewers can hear it

voice-over ['vɔɪs 'əʊvə] ('Begleitkommentar', 'Offkommentar')
a spoken commentary while other sounds including voices of the characters continue, often used to convey a character's thoughts or memories

Tip

Viewing log

A viewing log can help you structure your notes. Here is one example. You may choose other categories (e.g. *images, *dialogue, costumes, mood, *characterization, plot) to serve your own purposes.

Scene (What? Where? Who?)	Camera work + its effect	Lighting + its effect	Sound + its effect	Your reaction
...	...	...	...	...

Language help

Film analysis / Describing cinematic devices

Camera work – static shots

- The director uses a long shot of the scene so the viewer can see the group and the setting ...
- There is a medium shot of the two characters so the viewer can see ...
- The viewer sees the character in close-up / There is a close-up of the character ...
- The establishing shot of the film shows ...
- This scene is shot from X's point of view.
- The director uses a high-angle shot of ... in order to ...
- The camera takes a steady position. As a consequence, the action appears slower.

Camera work – moving shots

- The camera pans from left to right / tilts up/down ...
- We first see X as the camera tilts from ... to ...
- There is a tracking shot in this scene as the camera follows . .
- The camera zooms in on ... in order to show ...
- The camera zooms out to reveal ...

Editing

- The director uses a lot of cuts in this scene ...
- There are short shots and a quick succession of cuts to increase the pace of the action and make it more exciting.
- Cross-cutting is used to show X approaching the house, while Y is still asleep.
- *Flashbacks (showing past events) and flash-forwards (showing future events) are used.
- The scene gradually fades in to show ...
- The director uses a fade-in in order to ...
- The use of cross-fading between these two scenes makes the connection stronger / produces a/an ... effect.

Sound and lighting

- The music intensifies/fades as ... / creates/builds tension/suspense/joy/...
- In this scene, the music and lyrics support the plot / underline the feeling of ...
- The soundtrack is eerie and moves towards a *climax.
- The soundtrack helps to ... / underlines/emphasizes ...
- The soundtrack/lighting/editing establishes/reinforces the mood of the scene.

Speaking skills

SF 42 Essentials: speaking

Speaking is a special skill that is determined by the following factors.

- Speaking occurs 'in real time'. This means you have to react quickly in conversations, discussions or even presentations, especially in the case of mistakes or misunderstandings, but also to make your point.
- Speaking takes place in a particular environment, situation or context, i.e. under varying conditions. You react differently to different partners, you deliver a *speech to a certain target audience, you are emotionally involved in a heated argument, etc.
- Speaking tends to be *informal and conversational in *tone and *style, but may also be *formal, e.g. public speeches or academic presentations. ► SF 43–44, p. 257
- Speaking also involves non-verbal forms of communication, and good speakers use them effectively to get their point across.
- Every communicative situation consists of different stages, also called speech acts (e.g. starting it, adding to it, interrupting, contradicting, etc.). Being aware of these stages enables you to keep a conversation going and make it more successful.

Step 1 Preparing for a speaking task

- Analyse the situation:
  - Are you talking to your teacher, classmates, a friend, an interviewer, etc.?
  - Are you taking part in a conversation, discussion, an argument, an interview, etc.?

This will help you to adapt your message to your own needs, those of your communication partner(s) or to your target audience.

- Analyse the task:
  - Is it a *monologue or a *dialogue – with one person or more?
  - Do you have to contribute to a discussion, present an idea, describe a photo or a *cartoon, give an oral presentation, etc.?
- Check you have relevant information/arguments/facts about the topic.
- Collect useful words and phrases for the topic and communicative situation in question.

Step 2 Speaking

Successful speaking involves various expressive and receptive skills, often performed spontaneously or simultaneously. To be effective, it requires paying attention to:

- fluency
- vocabulary (including specialist vocabulary for your topic)
- rules of pronunciation
- rules of grammar
- non-verbal communication, e.g. body language, gestures and facial expression
- in some cases: intercultural communication – to avoid (cultural) misunderstandings. ► SF 12: Communicating across cultures, p. 211

As you speak, react to mistakes or misunderstandings by trying to correct them or by rephrasing what you want to say.

Step 3 **Receiving feedback and acting on it**
Sometimes you will receive feedback from your communication partner(s) or audience on the content of your speech or on your performance. This may be questions, applause, expressions of boredom, etc. Use this feedback to improve your speaking skills.

Tips

Improving your speaking skills
- Study communicative strategies, e.g. how to respond to questions, how to introduce new ideas, how to be persuasive, how to disagree, etc.
- Learn and practise words, phrases and parts of sentences so that you can use them automatically and without thinking when you speak
- Observe other people speaking to learn from their examples.

SF 43 Giving a presentation

Informing an audience about a topic is an important skill to master and one that is useful at school and in later life. To give a successful presentation, these steps can be a helpful guide.

Preparing a presentation

Step 1 **The general framework for your talk**
Find out about:
- the topic of your talk
- the time limit for your presentation
- your audience and their background knowledge of the topic
- the equipment available (smartboard, blackboard, flip chart, digital/video projector, laptop).

Step 2 **Researching your subject** ► SF 13: Doing research, p. 212
- Collect information from different, reliable sources to ensure you cover all the relevant aspects.
- Decide which information is relevant for your presentation.
- Take notes, preferably in English.
- If you are working in a team, decide who is going to work on which aspect.

Step 3 **Structuring your presentation**
- Work out an outline for your presentation.
- Make notes to guide you through your presentation and help you to speak freely.

For team presentations:
- Decide who is going to present which parts.
- Check that the different parts create a coherent presentation.
- Make sure that everybody takes part in the presentation.

Step 4 **Making your presentation interesting, effective and easy to understand**
- Get off to a good start: refer to interesting facts or tell an anecdote to introduce the topic of your presentation.
- Remember the KISS-rule: **K**eep **i**t **s**hort and **s**imple!

- Keep your audience's attention by giving interesting or funny details or examples.
- Explain any difficult or specialist terms so the audience can follow your presentation.
- Avoid extremely long sentences and too many figures or new words. Remember that your audience can only listen to your presentation once.
- If appropriate, prepare charts, visuals, diagrams, etc. to present facts and figures visually.

Step 5 **Using presentation tools**

- Prepare a handout or poster or use presentation software to accompany your presentation.
- Design such material in a way that helps your audience to follow your presentation.
- Proofread your material.

Step 6 **Practising your presentation**

- Check the pronunciation of difficult words in a print or an online dictionary.
  ► SF 8: Working with dictionaries, p. 207
- Practise your presentation in front of friends or record it. If you are doing a team presentation, practise as a team.
- Rehearse with any technology you plan to use. Make sure it is working.
- Do not exceed your time limit.

Doing the presentation

Step 1 **Introducing your presentation**

- Wait until the audience is quiet.
- Then greet them and give an overview of your presentation.
- Say that you will take any questions at the end of the presentation.

Step 2 **Giving your presentation**

- Speak clearly, loudly and not too fast. Make suitable pauses.
- Speak freely and do not read out complete sentences.
- Use 'signposting language' so your listeners can follow what you are saying.
- Refer to your handout, poster or slides without reading from them word for word.
- Maintain eye-contact with your audience.
- Write any new or difficult words on the board and explain them to help your audience.

Step 3 **Rounding off your presentation**

- Summarize the most important aspects.
- Thank your audience for their attention.
- Ask them if they have any questions.

Tips

Making and using effective presentation tools

Handout

- Decide if you should distribute it before the presentation so your audience can follow your talk or afterwards as a reminder of the main points.
- Give it a clear structure. A handout should only contain the most relevant points of your presentation. Usually it should not be more than one page.
- Present the most important information, key quotations, diagrams and/or charts on it.
- Use bullet points, short sentences or keywords and try to avoid any redundancies.
- Indicate the sources you used.

Poster

- Give it a clear structure to guide the reader through the various sections.
- Make it visually attractive and informative.
- Present complex information visually, e.g. with diagrams.
- Keep a good balance between visuals and written information.
- Make sure that the writing can be read from the back of the room.
- Use bullet points, short sentences or key words and avoid redundancies.
- Indicate the sources you used.

Presentation software

- Choose the right font and size.
- Use good-quality images.
- Avoid too many special effects.
- Limit the number of slides.
- Limit each slide to one idea and keep text to a minimum (6–8 lines per slide).
- Do not read from your slides and do not 'speak to them'.

Speaking notes

- Do not learn a full script by heart or read from it.
- Write keywords or notes on index cards.
- Number the cards and use them during your presentation.

Language help

Giving a presentation

Introduction

- Hello everybody. My/Our talk today is going to be on ...
- Today I'm going to talk about ...
- The topic/subject of my presentation is ...
- Today I'll be talking about / discussing ...
- First, I will give you a general idea of ... Then I'll go on to ... After that I'll tell you more about ... And, finally, I'll...
- At the end of my talk, I will explain why ... and give you some examples.
- I'll be happy to take any questions at the end of my presentation.

Starting a new section

- Now, let's turn to ...
- I'd now like to talk about ... / to discuss ...
- The next/second ...
- The next issue/topic/area I'd like to focus on is ...

Conclusion

- So, as I have pointed out, ...
- It's important to keep in mind that ...
- That was my presentation on ...
- Thank you for listening. I hope you enjoyed my/our presentation.
- Do you have any questions? / Are there any questions?

SF 44 Preparing and giving a speech

When you give a speech, you want to get and keep your audience's attention as well as convince them of your point of view on a topic. To do so, plan your speech carefully and deliver it effectively.

Preparing a speech

Step 1 Establishing the general framework for your speech
- Determine the topic of your speech.
- Check the time available.
- Be clear on the purpose of your speech, e.g. to inspire people / lead to a specific action / ...
- Find out about your audience and their background knowledge / attitudes.

Step 2 Brainstorming and/or researching your topic
- Collect any ideas, stories or arguments that fit your topic.
- Form your own opinion on it.
- Make notes.

Step 3 Structuring your speech
- Select the ideas that are the most relevant to the topic and message you wish to get across to your audience.
- Take notes and structure them into introduction / main part / conclusion.
- Put the ideas for the main part of your speech in a coherent order.

Step 4 Preparing the presentation of your speech
- Decide whether you want to prepare a speech script. If so, print out your speech in a format that is easy to read (fonts and margins not too small).
- Write keywords or notes on index cards if you plan to speak freely. Number the cards and use them during your speech.
- Mark passages and words that you want to emphasize.

Step 5 Practising your speech
- Read it out loud to check the pronunciation of difficult words.
- Make your speech sound as if you are speaking freely even if you are using a script.
- Practise it in front of friends or record it.
- Make sure you do not exceed the time limit.

Giving the speech

Remember: Giving a speech is not like reading something out (even if you have written it down).
- Wait until the audience are quiet, then greet them and state your topic.
- Develop your ideas step by step.
- Speak as freely as possible and keep your listeners' attention.
- Speak clearly, loudly and not too fast. Pause in suitable places.
- Try to maintain eye-contact with your listeners. Use facial expressions and gestures to emphasize important points.
- Thank your audience for their attention.

Writing a speech script

If you are not a very experienced speaker, it can be helpful to write down your complete speech. Writing a speech script is also a task you might be asked to do in an exam. A speech script is a type of argumentative text that should have an introduction, a main part and a conclusion. ► SF 28: Argumentative writing, p. 234

Step 1 Writing out your speech
- Choose the correct *register for your specific audience, e.g. scientific, informal.
- Use clear and short sentences. Make logical connections clear by using linking words.
- Be persuasive: use *stylistic devices to convince your audience, e.g. *contrasts, *rhetorical questions, *enumerations, *alliterations, *direct address.

Step 2 Writing the introduction and conclusion
- Write a conclusion: sum up the main points, give a final effective example supporting your message, further food for thought or an appeal for action.
- When you have prepared most of your speech, think of a good introduction, e.g. a true story, a quotation, a rhetorical question, interesting statistics or a joke.

SF 45 Taking part in an interview

At school or when applying for a job, you may be asked to take part in interviews, either asking or answering questions. It is essential to prepare for an interview and to follow some general guidelines.

Preparing for an interview
- On the basis of your role card or the task given, prepare questions to ask (as the interviewer) or think of possible answers to questions you might be asked (as the interviewee).
- For job interviews, you need to be prepared to explain why you are suitable for the position. Research the company you are applying to and prepare some relevant questions. It might be useful to rehearse a job interview with a friend or parent.

Mastering the interview
- Smile when saying hello or thanking your interviewer/interviewee at the end.
- Introduce yourselves and the situation.
- Speak loud enough and clearly.
- Be aware of your non-verbal communication. Maintain eye-contact with the interviewer/interviewee.
- Use a *neutral or formal register.

As an **interviewer:**
- Start off by using your prepared questions but be flexible.
- If an interesting aspect comes up, ask new questions.
- If you feel that your question was not answered fully, ask again in other words.

As an **interviewee:**
- Take time to think about your answers so your reply does not show you in a bad light.
- Do not simply answer questions with *yes* or *no,* but use your answers to show your qualifications or to express your thoughts.
- If you have not understood a question fully, ask the interviewer to clarify it.
- Always be polite.

Language help

Interviewing

Interviewer
- Nice to meet you. / Thank you for coming.
- To start off, would you like to say something about ...? / First, let me ask you ...
- My next question would be ...
- If you think so, then why didn't you ...?

- Let's get back to my original question ...
- You just said ..., how does that relate to ...?
- Thank you very much for taking part in this interview.

Interviewee
- Nice to meet you too. / Thank you for inviting me today. / I am fine, thank you.
- I am not sure I have understood your question correctly. / Sorry, could you rephrase that?
- I'm glad you asked that question because ... / ... is very important to me, as ...
- A good example of the aspect you mentioned is ...
- Let me explain that in some more detail.
- Thank you for the chance to speak to you.

SF 46 Having a discussion

In a (classroom) discussion you exchange ideas and opinions with others. Discussions may be spontaneous or more formal, e.g. in panel discussions or debates. ► SF 47: Having a debate, p. 264 If possible, you should prepare so that you have your arguments and useful words and phrases ready.

Preparing a discussion

Step 1 **Researching the topic and making notes**
- Form an opinion on the topic and note down arguments.
- In a role-play, you may have to take a position which is not really your own, so make sure that your arguments are in line with *your role*.
- Think of counterarguments and of ways to refute them.
- Arrange your notes so that you have the relevant facts ready during the discussion.

Step 2 **Preparing an initial statement**
- A prepared opening statement on the topic will ease your way into the discussion.
- If you are assigned a specific role, be prepared to introduce yourself.

Step 3 **Choosing a chairperson**
It is advisable to choose a chair(person) to lead the discussion. He or she:
- moderates the discussion without taking sides
- steers the flow of the discussion
- is responsible for getting the discussion going and keeping it going.
- must be well informed about the various aspects of the discussion topic.

Holding the discussion

Step 1 **Stating your point of view on the topic**
For example, give your prepared statement.

Step 2 **Listening to what others say and referring back to their statements**
- Say which of the arguments do not convince you and why.
- You might counter an argument by asking a provocative question.
- Remember to bring in the facts you collected to support your view.

Step 3 **Reaching an agreement**
At the end of the discussion, even if you do not fully agree with each other, you need to reach some kind of agreement which you both accept.

Step 4 Summarizing

At the end of the discussion, summarize your point of view or your main arguments. If a chairperson has moderated the discussion, he/she may summarize the main line of the discussion and round it off.

Language help

Taking part in a discussion

Stating/Expressing your opinion

- In my opinion/view, ...
- As far as I'm concerned, ...
- The way I see it, ...
- If you ask me, ...
- It seems to me that ...
- I (personally) think/feel/reckon/believe ...
- First of all, / To start with, I'd like to point out that ...
- There can be no doubt that ...
- I'm (absolutely) convinced that ...

Involving a partner

- What do you think about ...?
- Is there anything you'd like to add?
- Would you agree with that?

Agreeing

- I quite agree.
- I couldn't agree with you more.
- Quite!/Exactly!/Precisely!/Certainly!/Definitely!
- You're quite right.
- I agree entirely/completely.
- That's just/exactly how I see it / how I feel about it.
- You've got a good point there.

Disagreeing politely / Contradicting

- I'm afraid I don't quite/really agree there.
- Well, that's one way of looking at it, but ...
- I'm not convinced that ...
- Well, I have my doubts about that.
- This is true to a certain extent, but ...

Disagreeing strongly

- I doubt that very much.
- That doesn't convince me at all.
- I don't agree with you at all.
- I disagree entirely.
- It's not as simple as that.

Asking for clarification

- Excuse me, I didn't quite catch your point about ...
- I'm sorry, but I don't understand/know what you mean by ...
- Sorry, could you say that again, please?
- Could you give an example / explain that, please?

Interrupting / Signalling that you would like to say something
- May I interrupt? / May I interrupt you for a moment, please?
- Sorry to interrupt you but ...
- Excuse me, I would like to add to that.
- That illustrates perfectly what ...
- Can I just say/explain that ...?
- I would just like to jump in here, to clarify that ...

Adding a point
- Another thing is ...
- We must also consider ...
- I would like to add to that ...
- Have you ever considered / thought about ...?

Buying time / Gaining time to think
- Well, I would say ...
- It's difficult to say exactly, but ...
- If I understood the question correctly, ...
- Well, that's an interesting point.
- I see what you mean.
- Why don't we see what X has to say about that?

Summarizing your point of view
- I have shown that ...
- It has become clear that ...
- Let me just state again that it is vital to ...
- If we don't ..., then ... / In spite of everything we have heard from the other side, ...

Summarizing the course and results of the discussion
- So, to sum up ...
- In brief, ...
- We have seen/heard that ...
- Some are in favour of ..., others against it, but in general you can say that ...
- The general trend seems to be ...
- On the one hand, ... On the other hand, ...
- All in all, this discussion has shown ...

SF 47 Having a debate

A debate is a formal discussion of a 'motion' (proposal) that ends in a vote. Similar to a discussion, the aim of a debate is to present arguments as convincingly as possible. Participants therefore need well-prepared arguments as well as rhetorical skills. There is often a set of rules that the participants have to agree on before the debate.

The starting point for the debate, the 'motion' (i.e. a controversial topic), is normally phrased as a statement starting 'This house ...'.
- 'This house proposes that ... (students should be allowed to use phones during lessons).'
- 'This house believes that ... (minimum wages are a threat to the German economy).'
- 'This house would ... (abolish the death penalty worldwide).'

Step 1 **Preparing the debate**

- Divide the class into two groups: one for the motion (the proposition or 'prop' team) and one against the motion (the opposition or 'opp' team).
- Choose a chair(person), judges (so-called adjudicators [əˈdʒuːdɪkeɪtəz]) and a timekeeper. Then specify a time limit for each speaker (often 3–6 minutes per speaker).
- In your team (either proposition or opposition), research the topic and collect and note down arguments for your side. Your personal opinion on the motion is not relevant here – you must argue for your team. List and rank your team's arguments in order of importance.
- Write your arguments on index cards so that you have them ready during the debate.
- Think of arguments for the opposing view and ways to refute them.
- Choose speakers for your side.
- Remaining group members are the audience, called the 'floor'.

Step 2 **Holding the debate**

A debate follows a clear structure:

- **1st proposal** from the team in favour of the motion
  The first speaker proposes the motion (= argues in favour of the motion) and gives some main arguments.
- **1st opposition** from the team opposing the motion
  The first speaker of this team opposes the motion (= argues against the motion).
- **2nd proposal** from the team in favour of the motion
  The second speaker of the affirmative team presents further arguments in favour of the motion. He/She also responds to the aspects mentioned by the first speaker of the opposing team, outlining where the positions *conflict.
- **2nd opposition** from the team opposing the motion
  The second speaker of the opposing team presents further arguments against the motion and/or restates the position of his/her team. The main task here is to defeat the arguments presented by the team in favour of the motion.

[A short recess may be taken here to prepare for the following 'rebuttals'.]

- **1st rebuttal** from the team opposing the motion
  The team against the motion defends their arguments and tries to rebut the arguments of the affirmative team.
- **2nd rebuttal** from the team in favour of the motion
  The affirmative team supports their point of view and tries to rebut the arguments of the opposing team.
- **3rd rebuttal** from the team opposing the motion
  The opposing team gives their closing statements.
- **4th rebuttal** from the team in favour of the motion
  The affirmative team gives their closing statements.

Info

Rules for the debate

- The chair(person) controls the debate and makes sure that the rules are followed and that time limits are respected. He or she introduces the topic, the judges and speakers and calls on them to deliver their speeches.
- The judges will watch the entire debate and decide at the end which team won.

- Speakers may not interrupt each other at any point. They must wait their turn. However, in competitive debates, a member of the team opposing that of the current speaker may briefly interrupt, offering a POI (point of information) in the form of a short question or a statement (10 seconds or less).
- The time limits as given by the chair must be respected.
- Speakers must remain polite and respectful of the other team.
- Statements must be backed up by examples or proof, by referring to research, experience, etc.

Step 3 Concluding the debate

- The 'floor' (i.e. the audience) may ask questions and/or present their ideas on the topic.
- The 'house' (i.e. everyone present) may take a vote on the motion by a show of hands, not based on what they personally agree or disagree with, but on who made the better case by presenting the better arguments and speaking more convincingly.
- Members of the two debating teams may get some feedback from the audience.
- The judges mark each team on their style, content and strategy, comment on their performance and finally decide who is the winner of the debate.

Language help

Debating

1st proposal

- This house firmly believes that ...
- Not only is ... but also ...

1st opposition

- We strongly advise against following the proposed motion because ...
- The most obvious reason for this is that ...

2nd proposal

- The opposing team has tried to create the impression that ...
- However, we can prove that ...
- It is therefore evident that ...

2nd opposition

- Again, it needs to be stated that by following the arguments, ...
- ... would lead to / cause ...

Mediating skills

SF 48 Essentials: mediating

What is mediating?

Mediating basically means transferring written or spoken information in one language to another language. The main objective is 'to get the message across'. You may also use mediating skills in real-life situations where – as a mediator – you help speakers of English and your own language to understand each other or to understand a text in the other language.

How to do a mediation task

In a mediation task, you should not translate word for word. You should select and pass on only the information that is relevant to another person, the addressee. Usually, the original text is in your native language and the text you need to produce (your mediation text) is in the second language, i.e. English. Pay attention to the following steps when working on a mediation task.

Step 1 Analysing the communicative situation

- Read the task carefully.
- Who is the addressee?
- Will you be writing or speaking? (Speaking allows you to use gestures and other non-verbal means of communication.)
- What *text type are you expected to produce? A (personal or formal) *letter, a (personal or formal) email, a *newspaper article, a school magazine, an internet article, e.g. a blog entry? ► SF 28-38, p. 234

Step 2 Selecting the relevant information

- Select the aspects of the text that are relevant to the given task or situation.
- Answer all of the addressee's questions, but do not give any unnecessary details.
- Decide what ideas, names or technical terms you need to explain.
- Decide which (cultural) aspects or concepts that might not be familiar to the addressee you need to explain. Watch out for possible (cultural) misunderstandings.

Tips

Mediating

- Do not summarize the whole text and do not translate every sentence.
- Use an appropriate *style and *register for the given situation and the text type you are expected to produce.
- Paraphrase words you do not know as well as technical terms. ► SF 50: Paraphrasing, p. 268
- Avoid German-sounding sentence patterns and 'false friends' such as 'spenden'/*spend*.

SF 49 Mediating from German into English

Usually in a mediation task, you are expected to inform your (English-speaking) reader(s) about ideas which you have found in a German text.

Preparing a German-English mediation

- Read the task carefully.
- Check what text type you are expected to produce.
- Make sure you understand the content of the original German text perfectly.
- Bear in mind what specific information the English-speaking addressee needs. Highlight key words and sentences in the German text.
- Take notes on the relevant information you need, then structure it and phrase it in English. Use a dictionary if necessary. ► SF 8: Working with dictionaries, p. 207

Doing a German-English mediation

- Make sure you use the correct text type.
- Sum up the information relevant for the addressee.
- Name the source.
- Include all the necessary explanations.
- Watch out for aspects that are specific to one culture (here: German) and explain them in more detail.
- Paraphrase any words you do not know in English. ► SF 50: Paraphrasing, p. 268
- Structure your text as clearly as possible.
- Remember: the mediated English text will usually be shorter than the original German text because you select only the information that is relevant.

Tips

Mediating information from German into English

- If the original text is German, and the text you need to write is English, you can take notes on the text in either German or English.
- As you are working with a German text, you may find it easier to take notes in German. On the other hand, if your notes are in English, it will be easier for you later to write your own text in English from your notes.
- Find out on your own which method works better for you and use it in all your exams.

SF 50 Paraphrasing

If you paraphrase a text or *speech, you rephrase it in different words, without changing the meaning. Paraphrasing is useful

- for summaries or outlines, i.e. to avoid copying from the original text and to show that you have really understood it
- when you do not know the exact English word or expression, e.g. when mediating into English, when writing a text or in conversation.

There are different paraphrasing techniques.

Using antonyms [ˈæntənɪmz]

*Antonyms denote the opposite of the original word.

Examples:
- 'Reichtum' → *the opposite of poverty*
- 'stumpf' → *the opposite of sharp*

Using comparisons

Comparisons help you illustrate what you mean by creating *images.

Examples:
- 'Handschuh' → *like a shoe for your hand*
- 'Wendeltreppe' → *a set of stairs shaped like a spiral*

Definition or explanation (often using relative clauses)

With definitions or explanations, relative clauses help you add details to general terms such as *person, thing, machine, activity.*

Examples:
- 'Freiwillige/r' → a person who offers to do something but doesn't ask for money in return
- 'Wahl-O-Mat' → an internet website that is designed to help people decide which party to vote for in an election
- 'Apotheke' → a place where you can get something for headaches or other illnesses

Language help

Paraphrasing
- It's the opposite of ...
- It's the same as ...
- It's like ...
- It's similar to ...
- It's somebody / a person who ...
- It's something / a machine / a tool that you use to ...
- It's an animal / a plant / a building / a custom that ...
- It's a place that/where ...

Glossary

An asterisk (*) or an arrow (►) before a term indicates that it can be found as a separate entry in the Glossary.

accumulation [əˌkjuːmjəˈleɪʃn] *Akkumulation, gehäufte Aneinanderreihung*	using a lot of similar words or phrases within a few lines in order to emphasize a description or impression **Example:** *Motorcycles, busses, cars, coaches, bicycles, lorries, vans* were passing by – there was no way to cross the road.
acronym *Akronym, Kurzwort*	a term formed from the first letters of several words **Example:** *NASA* is an acronym for **N**ational **A**eronautics and **S**pace **A**dministration.
act *Akt*	a major division in a *drama Each act is usually subdivided into *scenes.
action *Handlung*	in *fictional texts, everything that happens in the story ► external action, internal action
actor/actress *Schauspieler/-in*	a person who performs in a theatre, in a film, on TV or on the radio, especially as a profession The actors express themselves in the form of *dialogues, *monologues or *soliloquies.
advertisement (infml also: **advert/ad)** [ədˈvɜːtɪsmənt] *Werbung, Anzeige, Annonce*	a text which attempts to persuade people to do something (e.g. buy a particular product or contribute money to a cause) An advertisement normally consists of pictures and text (called *copy)* and is designed to catch the attention of the reader through its *layout.
alliteration [əˌlɪtəˈreɪʃn] *Alliteration, Stabreim*	the repetition of a consonant at the beginning of neighbouring words, or of stressed syllables within such words to produce a rhythmic effect **Example:** A**r**ound the **r**ugged **r**ock the **r**agged **r**ascal **r**an. ► assonance
allusion [əˈluːʒn] *Anspielung, indirekte Bezugnahme*	an indirect reference to something or somebody the reader or listener is supposed to recognize and respond to An allusion may be to a work of literature, a historical event, a well-known person, etc.
alternate rhyme *Kreuzreim, alternierender Reim*	an **a b a b** *rhyme scheme where every other *line rhymes with each other
analogy [əˈnælədʒi] *Analogie, Ähnlichkeit, Vergleich*	the comparison of two things which are similar in several aspects By comparing an object, situation or person to something familiar, the explanation becomes easier to understand. **Example:** What's in a name? That which we call a rose. / By any other word would smell as sweet. / So Romeo would, were he not Romeo called. (William Shakespeare, *Romeo and Juliet)*

anaphora [əˈnæfərə] *Anapher*	the repetition of the same words or group of words in neighbouring sentences, *lines, *stanzas, etc. usually at the beginning of the clause **Example:** **In every** cry of every man, **In every** infant's cry of fear, **In every** voice, **in every** ban (William Blake, 'London', 1794)
antagonist *Antagonist/-in, Gegner/-in, Widersacher/-in*	in *fictional text, the person who opposes the *protagonist
anticipation *Vorwegnahme*	the technique of hinting at later events in a *fictional text so that the reader or audience is prepared for them or can anticipate them
antithesis [ænˈtɪθəsɪs] *Antithese, genaues Gegenteil, Gegensatz*	an idea that is the opposite of an idea (*thesis) already put forward by a writer Often the writer will put forward the antithesis in order to stress his or her own thesis.
antonym *Gegenbegriff, Antonym*	a word meaning the opposite of another word **Example:** *Sweet* is the antonym of *sour* or *savoury*. <> synonym
argumentative text *argumentativer Text*	a text that presents arguments about one or both sides of an issue The main purpose of an argumentative text is to get a certain perspective of an issue across, i.e. the writer tries to convince the reader of his or her opinion on a topic with the help of arguments. Typical examples are *columns, *editorials, *letters to the editor, *speeches, and *essays. ► text type
article *Artikel, Aufsatz*	a story or report in a newspaper or magazine
assonance *Assonanz, vokalischer Gleichklang*	the repetition of the same or similar vowel sounds within stressed syllables of neighbouring words **Example:** the p**o**ppies bl**o**w / Between the cr**o**sses, r**o**w on r**o**w. (John McCrae, 'In Flanders Fields', 1915) ► alliteration
atmosphere [ˈætməsfɪə] *Atmosphäre, Stimmung*	the feeling or mood created by a *narrator in his/her story The *setting, the use of language (i.e. adjectives, adverbs, choice of words, length of sentences, etc.) and *characterization all contribute to the atmosphere.
author *Autor/-in, Verfasser/-in*	a person who writes books, *articles, *essays, etc.
autobiography [ˌɔːtəbaɪˈɒgrəfi] *Autobiografie*	a book written by a person about his/her own life

biography [baɪˈɒgrəfi] *Biografie*	a book written by a person about the life of another person
blog *Blog*	a regularly updated website containing blog posts or blog entries that publish information or discussions on current issues or topics
blurb *Umschlagtext, Klappentext*	the short promotional text on the back cover of a book or a Blu-ray case
byline *Zeile mit dem Namen des Verfassers oder der Verfasserin*	a line at the beginning or end of a piece of writing in a newspaper or magazine that gives the writer's name
caricature [ˈkærɪkətʃʊə] *Karikatur*	a crude representation of a *character which is meant to be laughed at
cartoon *Cartoon, Karikatur*	an amusing drawing in a newspaper or magazine that deals with human nature or a current political or social issue Complex issues are reduced to memorable pictures. Cartoons often include *captions or speech bubbles. Techniques employed by cartoonists include *caricature, *exaggeration, *wordplay and the use of *symbols.
character *Charakter, Figur, handelnde Person*	a person in a *fictional text Characters can be presented through their actions, speech and thoughts as well as through description. Characters can be classified according to their importance as main characters or minor characters and according to their type as *round characters or *flat characters. ► antagonist, characterization, protagonist
characterization [ˌkærəktəraɪˈzeɪʃn] *Charakterisierung, Kennzeichnung*	the way in which the *author of a *fictional text presents his or her *characters to the reader or, in the case of a *drama, to the audience We usually distinguish between two ways of presenting a character: ***direct/*explicit characterization** (*'telling') – somebody tells the reader what sort of person a character is. When the reader has to draw conclusions about a character on the basis of his or her actions and words, we speak of ***indirect/*implicit characterization** (*'showing'). This kind of characterization is predominant in *plays.
chunk *Wortkombination*	words that are commonly placed together, e.g. *collocations or fixed phrases **Examples:** give a presentation, a lame excuse, by the way, a long way off, out of my mind
classified ads / small ads (pl) *Kleinanzeigen*	newspaper or magazine advertisements dealing with job offers, buying, selling or renting something, etc.
cliché [ˈkliːʃeɪ] *Klischee, Gemeinplatz, abgedroschene Phrase*	an expression which has been overused and no longer has any effect
cliffhanger *offenes Ende*	an exciting situation that makes you want to know what will happen next
climax *Höhepunkt, Klimax*	the part of the *plot where the *suspense reaches its highest point ► anti-climax

cluster *Cluster*	spontaneous association of a group of words based around a concept
collocation *Zusammenstellung, Anordnung*	words that are commonly placed together **Example:** strongly suggest, go crazy, economic growth, big decision
colloquial [kəˈləʊkwiəl] *umgangssprachlich*	*informal words and phrases, used in conversation rather than in writing
column *Kolumne; kurzer, regelmäßig erscheinender Zeitungsartikel*	an *article that appears regularly in a newspaper or magazine Columns can be *humorous or serious, and they can deal with any subject, e.g. lifestyle, gossip, personal problems, finances or politics. Any opinion expressed in a column is the opinion of the writer, or 'columnist', and not of the newspaper or magazine it appears in. Thus a column is often an *argumentative text.
comedy *Komödie, Lustspiel*	a type of *drama which deals with a light topic or a serious topic in an amusing way A comedy always has a happy ending.
comic *Comic*	a form of literary text; stories are conveyed with the help of texts and visual elements, often sequential
coming-of-age story / story of initiation *Entwicklungsroman, Initiationsgeschichte*	a *short story or *novel in which the process of growing up is portrayed Usually the *protagonist is a child or an adolescent undergoing an experience which changes his/her outlook on life and marks an important stage in his/her development towards adulthood.
comment *Kommentar, Stellungnahme*	an *argumentative text in which the writer tries to convince the reader of his or her opinion on a topic
commercial (n) [kəˈmɜːʃl] *Werbespot, Werbung*	an *advertisement on television, on the radio or on a website
compound *Kompositum*	Combination of two words to make a new word **Example:** afterlife, daydream, lifestyle, cheesecake
concrete poetry / shape poetry *konkrete Poesie*	*poems in which the printed words form a shape or picture The shape usually reflects the *theme or contents of the poem.
conflict *Konflikt, Kontroverse, Streit*	a struggle or opposition between different forces which produces tension
connotation *Konnotation, Nebenbedeutung, Beiklang*	the additional meaning and association(s) a word has beyond its literal or dictionary meaning
contrast *Kontrast, Gegensatz*	the bringing together of opposing views, words or *characters to emphasize their difference and usually to highlight one of the opposing elements ► juxtaposition
couplet *Reimpaar, Verspaar*	two successive *lines which *rhyme
denotation [ˌdiːnəʊˈteɪʃn] *Denotation, (Haupt-) Bedeutung, Begriffsumfang*	the literal and limited meaning of a word, regardless of the ideas and emotions it might connote

denouement [ˌdeɪˈnuːmɒ̃] *Auflösung, Lösung des Knotens, Ausgang*	the *resolution of the *conflict in a story that is achieved at the end of a play, book, etc.
descriptive text *deskriptiver Text, beschreibender Text*	a text that presents the physical characteristics of living things or objects ► text type
dialogue [ˈdaɪəlɒg] *Dialog, Gespräch*	a conversation in a book, play or film that involves at least two *actors
diction *Diktion, Ausdruck, Wortwahl*	the words a writer chooses for his or her text In many argumentative texts, for example, the writer will use words that have a positive *connotation to support his or her arguments, or words with negative connotations to attack those he or she opposes. The choice of words often reveals the writer's attitudes. A writer can also use *emotive language and so influence the reader to react in a particular way.
direct address *direkte Anrede*	a way of addressing the audience directly in order to establish contact with them
direct/explicit characterization *direkte/explizite Charakterisierung*	a way of presenting a *character directly The *author may provide a description of a character through the words of the *narrator (especially an *omniscient narrator), or another character in the text may comment on the character, or the character may describe him- or herself.
drama / dramatic text *Schauspiel, Drama / dramatischer Text*	a text written to be performed by *actors in a theatre or in a film A drama is usually divided into several *acts. *Tragedies and *comedies are types of drama.
dramatic irony *dramatische Ironie, dramaturgische Ironie*	a situation in a *play when the audience has more knowledge of events or individuals than the other *characters and *actions can take on different meanings for the audience than for the other characters of the play
dramatist/playwright *Bühnendichter/-in, Dramatiker/-in*	the *author of a *play
editorial/leader *Leitartikel*	an *article that expresses the opinion of the newspaper's editor or another member of the editorial staff about an item of news or a political or social issue of topical interest ► argumentative text
ellipsis *Auslassung, Ellipse*	the shortening of sentences by dropping a word or several words which can be understood from the context **Example:** *Coming?* (= *Are you coming?*)
emotive language *gefühlsbetonte Sprache*	words and expressions with particular *connotations that appeal to the reader's or listener's emotions
emphasis [ˈemfəsɪs] *Betonung, Nachdruck, Emphase*	special importance that is given to a word or phrase

enjambement / run-on line [ɪnˈdʒæmbmənt] *Enjambement*	incomplete syntax at the end of the *line where the meaning runs over to the next line without any punctuation at the end
enumeration [ɪˌnjuːməˈreɪʃn] *Aufzählung*	the listing of words, phrases or ideas In *instructive or *argumentative texts, the list of enumerated elements can be given numbers or dashes ('Gedankenstriche') so the reader can see each new element clearly.
epilogue *Epilog, Nachwort*	speech, etc. at the end of a *play, book or film/movie that comments on or acts as a conclusion to what has happened ► prologue
essay *Essay, Aufsatz*	a text form in which a writer expresses his or her personal views on some topic Essays can vary widely in length, subject matter and *tone. Some are serious, others are light-hearted and entertaining.
euphemism [ˈjuːfəmɪzm] *Euphemismus*	a *stylistic device used to hide the true nature of something unpleasant by expressing it in a more pleasant, less direct way **Example:** He passed away. (= He died.)
exaggeration [ɪɡˌzædʒəˈreɪʃn] *Übertreibung*	a strong overstatement Exaggeration may be used to create either a serious or comic effect. **Example:** There were thousands of guests at Tom's party. <> understatement
explicit characterization *explizite/direkte Charakterisierung*	► direct characterization
exposition *Exposition, vorbereitender Teil eines Dramas*	the first part of the *plot, in which the *characters and *setting are introduced The exposition is also the beginning of the *action.
expository text/writing *expositorischer Text*	a *text type in which the writer analyses and explains some relatively complex matter in an objective and precise way
external action *äußere Handlung*	what the *characters do in the 'real', physical world ► internal action
fable *Fabel*	a short *narrative text in which animals represent human types or act like human beings Fables are usually didactic since they intend to teach a moral lesson, make a satirical comment or illustrate some general truth.
falling action *fallende Handlung*	a structural element of a *fictional text, marked by a reduction in the *suspense of the *plot, normally following the *turning point or *climax
feature film *Spielfilm*	a full-length film that has a story and *characters, who are played by *actors A feature film is based on a film script, which the director then turns into a film. Important elements in a film are the *dialogue, the use of camera techniques and the acting.

feature story *Zeitungsreportage*	a piece of *non-fiction news writing that deals with a topic by concentrating on a particular person or on particular people A feature story often takes an individual case as its starting point to discuss the different aspects of the topic on a personal level and leaves the reader to draw more general conclusions from this individual case. The writer of a feature story makes use of direct quotes from the people involved in the story thus relying on first-hand reporting.
fictional text / fiction *fiktionaler Text / Prosaliteratur, Dichtung*	a text or type of literature that does not deal with facts of the real world but creates its own world or reality A piece of fiction can take different forms. The main types are *narrative prose like *short stories or *novels and *drama.
figurative language [ˈfɪɡərətɪv] *bildhafte Sprache, Bildsprache*	► imagery
first-person narrator *Ich-Erzähler/-in*	a *character in the story who refers to him- or herself as 'I' The *first-person narrator tells the *action from his/her perspective so he/she only has a *limited point of view.
flashback *Rückblende*	a part of a film, *play, etc. that goes back into the past to describe or show a *scene that happened earlier in time than the main story but is essential for the *plot
flat character *typisierte Figur („flacher Charakter")*	a *character who only has a limited number of traits and may even just represent a single quality Flat characters are usually minor characters in a *fictional work. ► round character
foot *Versfuß*	a unit of *rhythm in a *line of a *poem consisting of an unstressed syllable followed by a stressed syllable
foreshadowing [fɔːˈʃædəʊɪŋ] *Vorwegnahme*	► anticipation
formal style *formaler (Sprach-)Stil*	a *style that consists of difficult vocabulary, often of Latin origin, and complex sentence structure Formal style is usually only used for serious purposes, e.g. *essays or academic publications, or in official situations, and would not be appropriate in normal everyday conversation.
frame story / frame narrative *Rahmenhandlung*	a *novel or *short story which contains one or more quite independent stories within it (also called 'a story-in-a-story') The main story provides the frame for the other stories. Often the main story consists of a *character in one *setting telling another story in another setting.
free verse *freier Vers, freie Verse*	a literary device that makes little use of *rhyme
genre [ˈʒɒ̃rə, ˈʒɒnrə] *Gattung, Genre*	a type or style of literature, e.g. science fiction

graphic novel *illustrierter Roman*
a piece of *fiction in which a story is told with the help of textual and visual elements; a complex version of the text form *comic

humour (BE), **humour** (AE) [ˈhjuːmə] *Humor*
a quality in something that makes you laugh, e.g. at the strangeness of a *character, an *action or comment, etc. because it is unexpected or unsuitable in a particular situation

hyperbole [haɪˈpɜːbəli] *Übertreibung, Hyperbel*
a deliberate *exaggeration
The purpose of hyperbole is to emphasize something or to produce a humorous effect.
Example: I'm so hungry I could eat a horse.

iambic pentameter [aɪˌæmbɪk penˈtæmɪtə] *fünfhebiger Jambus*
the most common *metre in English, which consists of a *line of five feet (each *foot consists of an unstressed syllable followed by a stressed syllable)
Example: This **ró** / yal **thróne** / of **kíngs** / this **scépt** / red isle.
(William Shakespeare, *Richard II)*

image/imagery *Bild/Bildsprache*
the use of language beyond its normal dictionary definition and meaning
All non-literal (i.e. *figurative) use of language falls into the category of imagery, e.g. *metaphors, *similes and *symbols.

implicit/indirect characterization *implizite/indirekte Charakterisierung*
a way of presenting a *character indirectly
The reader or audience learns of the character through *dialogue and *action, rather than through description.
► explicit characterization

informal style *informeller (Sprach-)Stil, umgangssprachlicher (Sprach-)Stil*
a *style characterized by fairly simple, often incomplete sentences, short forms (e.g. *can't, you'll*), phrasal verbs and *colloquial words
Informal style is used between friends or in a relaxed or informal situation. It may include the use of *slang and/or *taboo words.

instructive text / instruction *instruktiver Text / (Gebrauchs-) Anweisung*
a text that tells the reader what to do in order to achieve a certain goal
Typical examples of instructive texts are travel guides, how-to books or user's manuals. Typical features are the use of imperatives, the use of the passive voice, graphics and illustrations and printing techniques like **bold** or *italic* print, dashes, etc. ► text type

interior monologue [ɪnˌtɪəriə ˈmɒnəlɒg] *innerer Monolog*
a particular kind of *scenic presentation in which the *author depicts the thoughts and feelings passing through a *character's mind
Often an interior monologue does not follow a chronological order because when people think, their thoughts jump from one subject to another. The more common way of portraying thought is through *'reported thought', in which the thoughts are presented as reported speech, introduced by reporting verbs like *think.* ► soliloquy

internal action *innere Handlung*
what takes place in a *character's mind, i.e. his or her thoughts, feelings, memories, associations, etc.
► external action

intonation *Betonung*
(effect created by) the tone of a person's voice as they speak

ironic / irony [aɪˈrɒnɪk / ˈaɪrəni] *ironisch / Ironie*
saying the opposite of what you actually mean
Example: Oh, what a nice present! (when you actually mean 'It is rather ugly').

juxtaposition [ˌdʒʌkstəpəˈzɪʃn] *Gegenüberstellung, Nebeneinanderstellung*	a very strong *contrast of opposing ideas, arguments, views, mostly introduced by words like for example *but, however, nevertheless*
layout *Layout, Aufbau, Anordnung, Gestaltung*	the way elements are arranged on a printed page The layout includes elements such as the type and size of letters, the use of **bold** or *italic* typeface, underlining, headings and sub-headings, bullets (i.e. dots or other symbols used at the beginning of a text passage), the size and number of *columns, the length of paragraphs, the colour and the placement of illustrations. The layout determines whether a text attracts the attention of the reader and is pleasant to read, and it helps writers to structure their texts and to emphasize certain words, phrases or passages. The layout is particularly important when considering *newspaper articles, *advertisements and brochures.
leader / leading article *Leitartikel*	► editorial
letter *Brief*	a handwritten, typed or printed message that is put in an envelope and sent to somebody A letter can be personal or business-oriented, depending on the relationship between the sender and receiver, the occasion and the purpose of the letter. Letters are a very flexible text form and comprise thank-you notes, emails, covering letters (*AE* cover letters), letters of complaint, *letters to the editor, etc. The beginnings and endings of letters follow certain conventions.
letter to the editor *Leserbrief, Leserinnenbrief*	a *letter in which a reader expresses his or her opinion concerning an *article in a newspaper or magazine or a problem which is of public interest A letter to the editor may criticize or support an *article, or state a personal opinion concerning a topic of current interest. ► argumentative text
limited point of view *eingeschränkte Erzählperspektive*	a method of storytelling in which the *narrator sees only what's in front of him/her but does not know everything that occurs, therefore imposing his or her understanding and interpretation on the *action A *third-person narrator can have a limited point of view: the narrator looks at the events and *characters from the perspective of one of the characters or from the outside (as an observer narrator) and so does not have access to the thoughts and feelings of all the characters.
line *Zeile, Vers*	the row of words of a song or poem A *sonnet, for example, always has 14 lines.
literary text *literarischer Text*	a piece of writing that is valued as a work of art, e.g. a *novel, *play or *poem (in contrast to *non-fiction texts) A literary text is often structured and held together by a specific *theme or a so-called *motif, which may be a recurring image or a specific phrase or sentence.

metaphor ['metəfə] *Metapher*	a comparison between two things which are basically quite unlike one another without using the words *as* or *like* The things are meant to create a picture (image) in your mind that sheds more light on a topic. **Example:** There's daggers in men's smiles. (William Shakespeare, *Macbeth)* ► simile
method card	an individual compilation of strategies to help you with skills, language learning or exam preparation
metre (BE), **meter** (AE) ['mi:tə] *Metrum, Versmaß*	the regular *rhythm of words in a *poem The most common metre in English is the *iambic pentameter.
mode of presentation *Erzählweise*	the way a writer narrates events There are two modes of presentation, and usually a combination of both is used in a *narrative text: *scenic presentation and *panoramic presentation.
monologue ['mɒnəlɒg] *Monolog, Selbstgespräch*	a lengthy speech by just one character in the company of others ► dialogue
motif *Motiv, Leitmotiv, Leitgedanke*	a dominant idea in a *fictional text that is often part of the main *theme If the motif is an *image or *metaphor and is repeated often, it may be called a 'leitmotif'.
narrative perspective *Erzählperspektive*	*narrator, *point of view from which a story is told ► narrator
narrative prose *Erzähl-/Prosatext*	a *fictional story told by a *narrator and written in a continuous flow of sentences, not as a *poem or *drama Typical examples of narrative prose are *novels and *short stories.
narrator BE: [nə'reɪtə], AE: ['næreɪtər] *Erzähler/-in*	the person who tells the story in *narrative prose There are two main types of narrator: the *first-person narrator and the *third-person narrator. The third person-narrator can have a *limited point of view or an *unlimited point of view. The third-person narrator with an *unlimited point of view is also known as an *omniscient narrator. A narrator can be *reliable or *unreliable. The narrator is not the same as the *author of a story.
neutral style *neutraler (Sprach)Stil*	the style generally used by educated people Neutral style falls between *formal and *informal style. It is used in *feature stories, *news stories, etc.
news item *Nachricht*	a single report of news about one topic
news(paper) article / news report / news story *Zeitungsartikel, Zeitungsbericht*	a piece of writing about a particular subject that appears in print (in a newspaper or magazine) or digitally (e.g. on a website) News articles can be of any length. In theory, they are meant to be objective and unbiased presentations of the facts, providing answers to the five *wh*-questions, i.e. the questions *who?, what?, when?, where?* and *why?* and often quoting sources or people as support. In practice, however, totally impartial reporting is impossible.

non-fiction / non-fictional text *Sachliteratur, Sachbücher, Sachtexte / nichtfiktionaler Text, Sachtext*	texts that refer to the real world and are classified as *descriptive, *instructive, *argumentative or *expository texts according to their purpose Examples of non-fictional texts are *news stories, *advertisements, *speeches, *letters, *essays.
novel *Roman*	a long and complex type of *fictional *narrative prose often divided into chapters The *plot and structure of a novel are normally more complicated than those of shorter fictional works (like *short stories); consequently there may be a greater variety and a more detailed development of *characters and *setting.
omniscient narrator [ɒmˌnɪsiənt] *allwissende/r Erzähler/-in*	a *third-person narrator with an *unlimited point of view An omniscient narrator can move freely in place and time and can enter the minds of the *characters as he/she wishes.
onomatopoeia [ˌɒnəˌmætəˈpiːə] *Lautmalerei*	the use of a word which imitates the sounds it refers to, e.g. *buzz* or *hum* In a group of words or a phrase, onomatopoeia may evoke a particular feeling, mood, sound or movement. **Example:** Only the s**tutt**e**r**ing **r**ifes' **r**apid **r**a**tt**le. From: Wilfred Owen, 'Anthem for doomed youth' The repetition of 't's and 'r's sounds like the shooting of rifles, which the words describe.
open ending *offenes Ende, offener Schluss*	the ending when a *conflict in a *fictional text is not resolved and the reader is left wondering what might happen next
panoramic presentation *panoramische Darstellung, raffender Bericht*	summarizing in just a few sentences what happens over a longer period of time (e.g. an hour, a week, months) in a story ► scenic presentation
paradox *Paradox(on), Widerspruch in sich*	a statement that seems impossible because it contains two opposing ideas that are both true **Example:** In this rich country, there is a lot of poverty.
parallelism / parallel structures [ˈpærəlelɪzəm] *Parallelismus, Übereinstimmung, Parallelität, Ähnlichkeit / Parallelstrukturen*	the deliberate repetition of similar or identical words, phrases, sentence constructions, etc. in the same or neighbouring sentences Parallelism draws the attention of the reader to certain ideas that the writer may consider important. It may be used to show that the elements are of similar importance, or it may be used in a climactic sequence, with the most important element listed at the end. **Example:** Which alters[1] when it alteration finds, Or bends with the remover[2] to remove. From: William Shakespeare, 'Sonnet 116' [1] **alter** change [2] **remover** person who goes away
parody *Parodie, komisch-satirische Nachahmung*	a *fictional text that copies or imitates someone or something in an amusing way
pars pro toto *Pars pro Toto*	a part or aspect of something representing the whole **Example:** under my roof (= in my house)

personification [pəˌsɒnɪfɪˈkeɪʃn] *Personifizierung*	the technique of representing animals or objects as if they were human beings or possessed human qualities **Example:** the wailing wind
persuasive text [pəˈsweɪsɪv] *appellativer Sachtext*	a text in which the writer attempts to appeal to a reader's or listener's emotions Unlike *argumentative texts, persuasive texts do not use solid arguments. The most obvious example of a persuasive text is an *advertisement, but many *speeches are persuasive rather than argumentative texts. ► text type
pitch *Tonhöhe, Stimmlage, Lautstärke*	how high or low a sound is, especially a musical note
play *Schauspiel*	► drama
playwright *Dramatiker/-in, Bühnendichter/-in*	the *author of a *play ► dramatist
plot *Handlung(sgerüst)*	the structure of events in a *fictional text The plot develops in a number of stages: *exposition, *rising action, the *climax, *turning point, *falling action and the *denouement or an *open ending. A plot will have some element of *suspense and *tension.
poem/poetry *Gedicht/ Lyrik*	a piece of creative writing structured by *lines, *stanzas and *rhythm A poem can express personal thoughts and feelings (lyrical poem) or it can tell a story (narrative poem). Traditional poets make use of *rhyme whereas modern poets often use *free verse. The *speaker is the voice in which a poem is spoken, especially when the personal pronoun 'I' is used. This speaker is not always identical with the voice of the poet.
point of view *Erzählperspektive*	the perspective from which a story is told The concepts of *narrator and point of view are closely related. There can be a *limited point of view, i.e. the *action, etc. are approached from one angle (possibly the point of view of a *character, including a *first-person narrator), or there can be an *unlimited point of view, i.e. the narrator can examine the action, etc. from the point of view of different characters – in this case the narrator is *omniscient.
prologue [ˈprəʊlɒg] *Prolog, Vorwort*	an introductory speech, etc. at the beginning of a *play, book or film
props *(pl)* *Requisiten*	all kinds of objects used by *actors on stage or in a film
prose *Prosa*	a form of written language that is formed by sentences in a continuous flow and is broken up only by paragraphs
protagonist *Protagonist/-in, zentrale Gestalt*	the principal *character in a *fictional text, sometimes also called the hero His/Her opponent is called the *antagonist.
pun *Wortspiel*	► wordplay

quatrain [ˈkwɒtreɪn] *Vierzeiler*	four *lines with a shared *rhyme scheme
quick write	a short written response to an open-ended question or a prompt to reflect your understanding of a topic
refrain [rɪˈfreɪn] *Refrain*	phrases or *lines repeated at intervals throughout a *poem
register *Sprachstil, der für bestimmte Situationen charakteristisch ist; Register*	the level of language used in a text, e.g. *formal, *informal, *neutral, *slang
reliable narrator *glaubwürdige/r Erzähler/-in*	a trustworthy storyteller The reader may take everything the *narrator tells at face value. <> unreliable narrator
repetition *Wiederholung*	the deliberate use of a word or phrase more than once in a sentence or a text to create a sense of pattern or form, or to emphasize certain elements for the reader or listener
reported speech *indirekte Rede*	the reporting of what sb. has said, written or thought **Example:** Direct speech: *Selma asked: 'Is Sam going to the party?'* Indirect speech: *Selma asked if Sam was going to the party.*
reported thought *erlebte Rede*	in fiction: the rendering by the narrator of a character's thoughts using the third-person and the past tense / conditional, but no reporting verb (> *reported speech) **Example:** Direct speech: *Selma asked: 'Is Sam going to the party?'* Reported thought: *Was Sam going to the party?*
resolution *Auflösung*	the moment at the end of a *drama, *novel, etc., where all the *conflicts are solved
rhetorical device *rhetorisches (Stil-)mittel*	► stylistic device
rhetorical question [rɪˈtɒrɪkl] *rhetorische Frage (auf die keine Antwort erwartet wird)*	a question to which the answer seems obvious and is therefore not necessary A rhetorical question pushes the reader or listener to a certain conclusion. For this reason, it is popular in political *speeches, etc. when a person is trying to influence others.
rhyme *Reim*	the similarity of sounds between certain words in *poems, usually at the end of *lines ► rhyme scheme
rhyme scheme *Reimschema*	the way a poet arranges his or her *rhymes in a *poem Small letters are used to show that words share a rhyme. If the words 'day', 'make', 'say' and 'lake' appear at the end of four successive *lines, the rhyme scheme is written as **a b a b.** ► alternate rhyme, rhyming couplet
rhyming couplet *Paarreim, Reimpaar*	a *rhyme scheme that is written a a b b

rhythm *Rhythmus*	the arrangement of stressed and unstressed syllables in a *line of a *poem ► metre
rising action *(an-) steigende Handlung*	the second part of the *plot where the *conflict or the *theme of the story in a *fictional text is developed and *suspense created
round character *runde Figur*	a character in a *fictional text who has several character traits and behaves in a lifelike way Usually a round character develops in the course of the story. The main characters are usually round characters. ► flat character
run-on line *Enjambement*	► enjambement
scene *Szene*	a smaller unit of *action in which there is no change of place or break in time In a *drama a scene is a subdivision of an *act.
scenic presentation *szenische Darstellung*	showing an event or describing a scene in detail as it occurs, using *dialogue, *interior monologue and depicting thoughts and emotions ► panoramic presentation
script *Drehbuch*	the written text of a *play or film
scriptwriter *Drehbuchautor/-in*	a person who creates *scripts for films and television
setting *Schauplatz, Handlungsort*	the time and place (and often the *atmosphere as well) in a *fictional text
shape poetry *konkrete Poesie*	► concrete poetry
short story [ˌʃɔːt ˈstɔːri] *Kurzgeschichte*	a piece of *fictional *narrative prose, but considerably shorter and less complex than a *novel A short story centres around one or two *characters at a decisive moment in their lives. It is limited in its *theme, *setting and *plot by its length.
showing *szenische Darstellung*	► scenic presentation
simile [ˈsɪməli] *Vergleich, Gleichnis, Simile*	a comparison between two things that are not really like each other. Similes use the word *like* or *as*. **Example:** My love is like a red, red rose. (Robert Burns, 1794)
sitcom (= situation comedy) *Sitcom, Situationskomödie (besonders als Fernsehserie)*	a comic *TV/radio series which usually centres around a *character or group of characters The characters are often stereotypes as they do not evolve over the series. A sitcom may be filmed in front of a live audience or have canned laughter added to make the audience aware of or to reinforce the funny lines.
slang *nachlässige, oft fehlerhafte, saloppe Ausdrucksweise; Slang*	very *informal language, mainly used in *dialogue between people of the same age or from a similar background, etc.

soap (opera) *„Seifenoper“, (rührselige) Hörspiel- oder Fernsehspielserie*	a regular TV or radio programme about the everyday lives of a group of people The storyline of a soap (opera), unlike that of a normal *TV/radio series, develops from programme to programme and may often end with a *cliff-hanger to encourage the audience to tune in to the next episode.
soliloquy [səˈlɪləkwi] *Monolog, Selbstgespräch*	a *speech delivered by one of the *characters in a *drama, in which he or she reveals his or her thoughts, feelings or motives to the audience ► monologue
solution *(Auf-)Lösung*	the successful ending of a problem, a *conflict or a difficult situation
sonnet [ˈsɒnɪt] *Sonett*	a special form of a *poem that consists of 14 *lines There are various types of sonnets with different structures and forms. Shakespeare's sonnets comprise three *quatrains (i.e. four lines with a shared *rhyme scheme) and a *couplet (i.e. two successive lines which rhyme).
speaker *lyrisches Ich*	the *fictional person, in theory not identical with the poet, who speaks the text of a *poem
speech *Rede, Ansprache*	a spoken *non-fictional text delivered to an audience The speaker normally wants to convince his/her audience to adopt his/her view on a certain topic. ► argumentative text
spidergram *Wortigel*	a simple diagram for organizing words that belong together because they are of the same type (phrasal verbs, prefixes and suffixes) or they express a key concept
stage directions (pl) *Bühnenanweisungen*	the *dramatist's description of what the stage should look like, and how the *actors should perform the *drama Stage directions may give information about any of the following: the *setting, the objects on stage (the *props), the *characters' appearances, clothes and manner of speaking, as well as their entrances and exits.
stanza *Strophe, Vers*	a group of *lines (*verses) that form a unit in a *poem because they relate to a similar thought or topic
story of initiation [ɪˌnɪʃiˈeɪʃn] *Entwicklungsroman, Initiationsgeschichtes*	► coming-of-age story
style *Stil*	the particular way in which a *fictional or *non-fictional text is written Style includes elements such as *register and *tone.
stylistic device *Stilmittel*	a method and technique used to produce a particular effect in a text and on the reader The most common stylistic devices are: *accumulation, *alliteration, *allusion, *anaphora, *assonance, *contrast, *exaggeration, *irony, *juxtaposition, *metaphor, *personification, *rhetorical question, *simile, *symbol, *understatement, *wordplay.

surprise ending *überraschendes Ende, nicht vorhersehbarer Schluss*	an ending in which the reader's expectations regarding the course of the story are not fulfilled, but an unexpected *resolution to the *conflict is presented
suspense *Spannung*	a feeling of worry or excitement that is created when the reader does not know the outcome of the *conflict or *action
suspension of disbelief *willentliche Aussetzung der Ungläubigkeit*	expecting the reader to accept this world or story as existing or true
symbol / symbolic *Symbol / symbolisch*	a thing, word or phrase signifying something concrete that stands not only for itself but also for a certain abstract idea As in the case of a *metaphor or a *simile the meaning of a symbol goes beyond the literal meaning. **Example:** A red rose is often a symbol of love.
synonym *Synonym*	a word that means the same as another word **Example:** Fast and quick are the synonyms of speedy. <> antonym
taboo word *Tabuwort*	a word that is generally considered obscene, vulgar or shocking and is used only if the writer is trying to make a particular point or shock his or her readers
telling *berichtende Darstellung*	► panoramic presentation
tension *(An-)Spannung*	the feeling evoked in the reader when a story/*drama is full of *suspense, i.e. the reader is curious about what will happen
text type *Textsorte, Textart*	the classification of a text according to the *writer's intentions There are different text types: *argumentative texts, *descriptive texts, *expository texts, *instructive texts, *narrative texts, *persuasive texts.
theme *Thema, Gegenstand, Stoff*	the main idea or *motif (e.g. a recurring image or a specific phrase or sentence) that structures and holds together a *literary text
thesis ['θi:sɪs] *These, Behauptung, Postulat*	an idea or a view that an *author of an *argumentative text presents and discusses in a *formal way ► antithesis
third-person narrator *auktoriale/r Erzähler/-in*	a *narrator who refers to all the *characters as he, she, they or by their names A third-person narrator is not a character in the story. This type of narrator can have a *limited point of view (just like a camera) or an *unlimited point of view. In the latter case, the narrator knows everything and is called *omniscient.
tone *Ton, Stimmung*	the way in which a writer treats his or her topic, thereby reflecting his or her emotional attitude towards that topic and also towards the reader The tone can be *formal, intimate, solemn, playful, serious, *ironic, *humorous, angry, etc.

tragedy / tragic *Tragödie, Trauerspiel / tragisch*
a type of *drama in which the main *character (the *protagonist) goes through a series of misfortunes towards his or her downfall
Usually this downfall is partly brought about by the protagonist's own faults and weaknesses.

turning point *Wendepunkt*
a sudden or surprising change of the *action in the *plot

tv/radio series [ˈsɪəri:z] *Fernseh-/Radioserie*
a regular programme on TV or radio about the lives and problems of a *character or, more usually, a group of characters
Each programme is self-contained, i.e. it deals with a particular issue or storyline which is concluded at the end of the programme. The lives of the characters evolve slowly over the course of a series.

understatement *Untertreibung*
a statement in which the true importance of an idea, event or fact is minimized, so that something is deliberately presented as being much less important, valuable, etc. than it really is
Understatement is often used for *ironic effect. The opposite is *exaggeration/overstatement.

unlimited point of view *uneingeschränkte Erzählperspektive*
a method of storytelling in which the *narrator can move freely in place and time and enter the minds of the *characters at will

unreliable narrator *unglaubwürdige/r Erzähler/-in*
an untrustworthy storyteller
The reader must find out just how much of what the *narrator says can be accepted. *First-person narrators are usually unreliable as they give only one perspective on the *action and the *characters.
<> reliable narrator

verse *Vers*
a single *line of a *poem

volta *Volta, Wendung*
the *turning point in a *sonnet, which can be identified by words like *but*, *yet or* and *yet*
The volta might be a *line of the sonnet.

word family *Wortfamilie*
a group of words with a common base to which other words are added
Example: The words *signal, signature, assign, resign,* etc. belong to the word family of *sign*.

wordplay / play on words / pun *Wortspiel*
the use of a word which may be understood in two different ways or which may be put into a different context to change the meaning
Example: My family bought a boat because it was for sail.

Verbs for tasks

Context Starter uses the same special vocabulary ('Operatoren') for tasks that is used in standard tests, including the 'Abitur'. Be sure you understand what's required of you when you come across one of the verbs below.

'Anforderungsbereich I' COMPREHENSION
refers to text comprehension and definition.

'Anforderungsbereich II' ANALYSIS
focuses on text analysis and comparison, and stylistic devices.

'Anforderungsbereich III' BEYOND THE TEXT
concentrates on discussion, comment, evaluation and text production.

The instructions say	Example	What you are expected to do
analyse *(BE)*, **analyze** *(AE)* ['ænəlaɪz] *analysieren* ANALYSIS	**Analyse** the narrative perspective in the given excerpt.	Describe and explain certain aspects and/or features of the text in detail.
assess [ə'ses] *auswerten, beurteilen, bewerten, einschätzen* BEYOND THE TEXT	**Assess** whether the statement applies to the short story as well.	Give a carefully considered opinion, include all the important aspects of a question.
comment on ['kɒment] *kommentieren, Stellung nehmen, darlegen* BEYOND THE TEXT	**Comment** on the future of multiculturalism in the USA.	Give your opinion, back it up with all the relevant points.
compare *vergleichen, kontrastieren, gegenüberstellen* ANALYSIS	**Compare** X's and Y's views on education.	Tell how things are alike and/or different, use concrete examples.
describe *beschreiben* COMPREHENSION	**Describe** the living conditions of the family.	Give an account in words, present a picture with words.
discuss *diskutieren, erörtern* BEYOND THE TEXT	**Discuss** advantages and disadvantages of introducing full body scanners at airports.	Consider all sides of an issue by providing relevant arguments and concrete examples.
evaluate [ɪ'væljueɪt] *kommentieren, Stellung nehmen, darlegen* BEYOND THE TEXT	**Evaluate** the chances of the protagonist's plan to succeed in life.	Give your opinion, back it up with all the relevant points.

The instructions say	Example	What you are expected to do
examine [ɪgˈzæmɪn] *untersuchen* ANALYSIS	**Examine** the author's use of language.	Name and explain the meaning of specific aspects and/or features of the text and their effects on the reader/audience.
explain *erklären* ANALYSIS	**Explain** the protagonist's obsession with money.	Make clear and plain; give the reason or cause.
interpret [ɪnˈtɜːprɪt] *interpretieren, deuten, auswerten* ANALYSIS BEYOND THE TEXT	**Interpret** the message the author wants to convey.	Explain the meaning or purpose of something.
illustrate *veranschaulichen* ANALYSIS BEYOND THE TEXT	**Illustrate** the narrator's admiration for the main character. **Illustrate** the way in which school life in the USA differs from that in Germany.	Use examples to explain or make sth. clear.
outline *präsentieren, vorstellen, nennen* COMPREHENSION	**Outline** the author's views on lowering the voting age.	Present the main features, structure or general principles of a topic, omitting minor details.
point out *darstellen* ANALYSIS	**Point out** the author's main ideas on ...	Present the main aspects of sth. briefly and clearly.
summarize (*also*: **sum up** / **write a summary**) *zusammenfassen* COMPREHENSION	**Summarize** the main points of the German newspaper article.	Give a concise account of the main points or ideas of a text, issue or topic.
state *darlegen* COMPREHENSION ANALYSIS BEYOND THE TEXT	**State** the author's main arguments ... **State** the writer's opinion on green energy. **State** your reasons for applying for an internship.	Present the main aspects of sth. briefly and clearly.
write/give a characteriza-tion of [ˌkærəktəraɪˈzeɪʃn] ANALYSIS *charakterisieren, detailliert beschreiben und erklären*	**Write** a characterization of the heroine. **Give** a characterization of the hero in the excerpt.	Give a profound analysis of somebody's character and provide suitable examples.

Cover:
Shutterstock.com/C Woods Photography, architects: Hans and Torrey Butzer

Photos
p. 10/11: Shutterstock.com/Sabrina Bracher; **p. 12** top: Shutterstock.com/Livefocus; **p. 12** centre: Shutterstock.com/NDAB Creativity; **p. 12** bottom: Shutterstock.com/Tero Vesalainen; **p. 13** top: Shutterstock.com/dennizn; **p. 13** bottom: CartoonStock/Leo Cullum; **p. 14** top: mauritius images/SuperStock; **p. 14** bottom: Shutterstock.com/Richard van der Spuy; **p. 15** top: mauritius images/Johnér; **p. 15** bottom: Shutterstock.com/TierneyMJ; **p. 16**: Shutterstock.com/Sitophotostock; **p. 17** top: Shutterstock.com/calzone.photography; **p. 17** bottom: Shutterstock.com/Odua Images; **p. 18** top: Shutterstock.com/Overearth; **p. 18** bottom: Shutterstock.com/Rawpixel.com; **p. 19** top: Shutterstock.com/Djomas; **p. 19** bottom: Shutterstock.com/Shine Nucha; **p. 20** top: mauritius images/alamy stock photo/Car Collection; **p. 20** bottom: mauritius images/alamy stock photo/Jess Merrill; **p. 21** top: mauritius images/alamy stock photo/Timothy Swope; **p. 21** bottom: Shutterstock.com/greenaperture; **p. 22**: Shutterstock.com/Ingo70; **p. 23** top: Shutterstock.com/Moor Studio; **p. 23** bottom: Depositphotos/Michael Edwards; **p. 24**: mauritius images/alamy stock photo/Stockimo/emmakearney; **p. 25** top: Shutterstock.com/fizkes; **p. 25** bottom: Shutterstock.com/Fabiophototravel; **p. 26** top: mauritius images/alamy stock photo/khabib alwi; **p. 26** bottom: Shutterstock.com/For your inspiration; **p. 27** top: Shutterstock.com/Overearth; **p. 27** bottom: Shutterstock.com/AnnyStudio; **p. 28**: mauritius images/alamy stock photo/ruelleruelle; **p. 29** top: mauritius images/alamy stock photo/Universal Images Group North America LLC; **p. 29** bottom: mauritius images/alamy stock photo/Steve Skjold; **p. 30** top: mauritius images/alamy stock photo/Audrius Venclova; **p. 30** bottom: Shutterstock.com/Milky Way fa; **p. 31**: mauritius images/alamy stock photo/Christian Bertrand; **p. 32**: Shutterstock.com/Lamai Prasitsuwan; **p. 33**: Shutterstock.com/Urri; **p. 34** top: Shutterstock.com/takasu; **p. 34** bottom: mauritius images/alamy stock photo/Christopher Penler; **p. 35**: Shutterstock.com/PUSCAU DANIEL; **p. 36** top: mauritius images/alamy stock photo/Cigdem Simsek; **p. 36** bottom: Depositphotos/Niyom Tangsiripaisarn; **p. 37**: stock.adobe.com/New Africa; **p. 38** top: Shutterstock.com/marekuliasz; **p. 38** centre: Shutterstock.com/Alexlukin; **p. 38** bottom: stock.adobe.com/Popova Olga; **p. 39** top: Shutterstock.com/New Africa; **p. 39** bottom: mauritius images/TopFoto; **p. 40**: stock.adobe.com/Silvio; **p. 41**: Shutterstock.com/Peter Gueth; **p. 42/43**: stock.adobe.com/alphaspirit; **p. 44** top: Shutterstock.com/NUR AFIYAH; **p. 44** centre right: stock.adobe.com/peopleimages.com; **p. 44** centre left: stock.adobe.com/Pixel-Shot; **p. 44** bottom: mauritius images/alamy stock photo/Jacob Lund; **p. 45** top: stock.adobe.com/commelita; **p. 45** bottom: CartoonStock/Wayno & Piraro; **p. 46**: mauritius images/SuperStock; **p. 47**: mauritius images/Science Source; **p. 48** bottom: mauritius images/alamy stock photo/presidenciamx; **p. 49**: stock.adobe.com/Queenmoonlite Studio; **p. 50**: Shutterstock.com/Nolte Lourens; **p. 51**: mauritius images/alamy stock photo/US Air Force Photo; **p. 53**: Women Deliver; **p. 54** top: stock.adobe.com/deagreez; **p. 54** bottom: Shutterstock.com/Master_shifu; **p. 55**: Shutterstock.com/KatrinKat; **p. 56** top: Shutterstock.com/New Africa; **p. 56** bottom: stock.adobe.com/Martin Debus; **p. 58** top: stock.adobe.com/debramillet; **p. 58** bottom: mauritius images/alamy stock photo/Robert W. Ginn; **p. 59**: stock.adobe.com/WINDCOLORS; **p. 60** top: mauritius images/alamy stock photo/Moviestore Collection Ltd; **p. 60** bottom: stock.adobe.com/khairul; **p. 61**: stock.adobe.com/lithiumphoto; **p. 62**: stock.adobe.com/zzzz17; **p. 63** top: stock.adobe.com/Peter Hermes Furian; **p. 63** bottom: Shutterstock.com/alvarog1970; **p. 64**: stock.adobe.com/Bits and Splits; **p. 65**: Imago Stock & People GmbH/Panthermedia; **p. 67** top: Shutterstock.com/ASCHW; **p. 67** bottom: Shutterstock.com/GoodStudio; **p. 68**: Shutterstock.com/USBFCO; **p. 69**: Shutterstock.com/Volodymyr Nikitenko; **p. 70** top: stock.adobe.com/Andrey Lapshin; **p. 70** centre: Shutterstock.com/Fer Gregory; **p. 70** bottom: Shutterstock.com/delcarmat; **p. 71**: Shutterstock.com/Kite-Kit; **p. 72**: Shutterstock.com/Ground Picture; **p. 73**: Shutterstock.com/Ellagrin; **p. 74**: Shutterstock.com/koya979; **p. 76/77**: Shutterstock.com/FGC; **p. 78** top: Shutterstock.com/Holiday.Photo.Top; **p. 78** centre: Shutterstock.com/Rawpixel.com; **p. 78** bottom: Shutterstock.com/bombermoon; **p. 79**: Shutterstock.com/Maxx-Studio; **p. 80** top left: Shutterstock.com/Drawlab19; **p. 80** top right: Shutterstock.

com/legdrubma; **p. 80** top centre: mauritius images/alamy stock photo/Oleg Nesterov; **p. 80** bottom: stock.adobe.com/Wendelin; **p. 81** top: Shutterstock.com/Mizkit; **p. 81** bottom: stock.adobe.com/IgorZD; **p. 82**: Shutterstock.com/Master1305; **p. 83** top: Shutterstock.com/Rawpixel.com; **p. 83** bottom: Cartoon-Stock/Joe Dator; **p. 84**: Shutterstock.com/Ascannio; **p. 86** top: stock.adobe.com/little_rat; **p. 86** bottom: Shutterstock.com/marhus; **p. 88** top: Depositphotos/Ivan Ushakovskiy; **p. 88** centre: Shutterstock.com; **p. 88** bottom: Shutterstock.com; **p. 90** top: Shutterstock.com/Frame Stock Footage; **p. 90** bottom: Shutter-stock.com/Gorodenkoff; **p. 91** top: mauritius images/Cinema-Legacy-Collection; **p. 91** centre: stock.adobe.com/daviles; **p. 91** bottom: Shutterstock.com; **p. 92** A: Shutterstock.com/i viewfinder; **p. 92** D: Deposit-photos/Monkey Business; **p. 93** B: mauritius images/Fabio and Simona; **p. 93** C: mauritius images/Westend61; **p. 93** E: mauritius images/Westend61; **p. 94** top: stock.adobe.com/DimaBerlin; **p. 94** bottom: stock.adobe.com/forcdan; **p. 95** top: stock.adobe.com/DALU11; **p. 95** bottom: stock.adobe.com/ajr_imag-es; **p. 96**: CartoonStock/Ray Jelliffe; **p. 98**: stock.adobe.com/9nong; **p. 99**: stock.adobe.com/terovesalain-en; **p. 101**: stock.adobe.com/Prostock-studio; **p. 102** top: stock.adobe.com/PR Image Factory; **p. 102** bottom: stock.adobe.com/Dzmitry; **p. 103** top: stock.adobe.com/LP/WESTOCK; **p. 103** bottom: stock.adobe.com/Mariia Korneeva; **p. 104**: stock.adobe.com/Drobot Dean; **p. 105**: Shutterstock.com/TungChe-ung; **p. 106**: stock.adobe.com/2013/Sophie James; **p. 107**: stock.adobe.com/Stephen Finn; **p. 108**: CartoonStock/Crowden Satz; **p. 109**: stock.adobe.com/K Davis/peopleimages.com; **p. 110**: stock.adobe.com/Matthew; **p. 111**: stock.adobe.com/Vittorio Gravino; **p. 112**: stock.adobe.com/Riccardo Niels Mayer; **p. 113** top: stock.adobe.com/Zoran Zeremski; **p. 113** bottom: stock.adobe.com/raywoo; **p. 114** top: mauritius images/alamy stock photo/Keneth Kõgel; **p. 114** bottom: mauritius images/alamy stock photo/Sunshine Seeds; **p. 115** left: stock.adobe.com/Nickolas; **p. 115** right: stock.adobe.com/Mustafa Kurnaz; **p. 117**: stock.adobe.com/Jag_cz; **p. 118** top: stock.adobe.com/waranyu; **p. 118** bottom 1–4 & **p. 119** 5–10: Run Rabbit/Robyn Paterson, New Zealand, 2018/Interfilm Berlin Management GmbH; **p. 120** top: stock.adobe.com/Stephen; **p. 120** bottom: stock.adobe.com/vectorfusionart; **p. 121**: Run Rabbit/Robyn Pater-son, New Zealand, 2018/Interfilm Berlin Management GmbH; **p. 122/123**: stock.adobe.com/C Malambo/peopleimages.com; **p. 123** right: CartoonStock/Megan Herbert; **p. 124** top: stock.adobe.com/Delcio/peopleimages.com; **p. 124** centre: stock.adobe.com/CROCOTHERY; **p. 124** bottom: Shutterstock.com/oneinchpunch; **p. 126**: mauritius images/alamy stock photo/Sunny Celeste; **p. 127**: stock.adobe.com/Yaroslav Astakhov; **p. 129**: stock.adobe.com/insta_photos; **p. 130**: stock.adobe.com/Songsak C; **p. 131**: stock.adobe.com/24K-Production; **p. 132**: stock.adobe.com/JasperSuijten; **p. 133**: Imago Stock & People GmbH/Vedran Vuko; **p. 134**: stock.adobe.com/roibu; **p. 135**: CartoonStock/Chris Wildt; **p. 136**: Imago Stock & People GmbH/Panthermedia; p. 137: stock.adobe.com/SecondSide; **p. 138** top: stock.adobe.com/Александра Замулина; **p. 138** bottom: stock.adobe.com/Torsten Pursche; **p. 139**: stock.adobe.com/Glen; **p. 140**: stock.adobe.com/Ajdin Kamber; **p. 141** top: mauritius images/Superstock; **p. 141** bottom: stock.adobe.com/Malcolm; **p. 143** top: stock.adobe.com/Andrea Izzotti; **p. 143** bottom: Shutterstock.com/Ink Drop; **p. 145**: stock.adobe.com/Henrry; **p. 147**: stock.adobe.com/ballllad; **p. 149**: Imago Stock & People GmbH/Kanelbull; **p. 150/151**: Depositphotos/Pitinan Piyavatin; **p. 152** top: Depositphotos/Anna Tolipova; **p. 152** centre: Shutterstock.com/Andrey_Popov; **p. 152** bottom: stock.adobe.com/aapsky; **p. 153**: Shutterstock.com/Ground Picture; **p. 154** top left: Shutterstock.com/Daisy Daisy; **p. 154** top right: Shutterstock.com/Dmitry Kalinovsky; **p. 154** bottom left: Imago Stock & People GmbH/Addictive Stock; **p. 154** bottom right: stock.adobe.com/thanmano; **p. 155** top: Shutterstock.com/PopTika; **p. 155** bottom: dpa Picture-Alliance/AP Photo/AP; **p. 156**: Shutterstock.com/Roman Samborskyi; **p. 157**: Shutterstock.com/Olga Kashubin; **p. 158**: Shutterstock.com/Gaian child; **p. 159** top: Shutterstock.com/nEwyyy; **p. 159** bottom: Shutterstock.com/Ground Picture; **p. 160**: Shutterstock.com/Ground Picture; **p. 161**: stock.adobe.com/Sophon_Nawit; **p. 162** top: Shutterstock.com/Tatiana Buzmakova; **p. 162** bottom: Shutterstock.com/giedre vaitekune; **p. 163**: Shutterstock.com; **p. 164** top: Shutterstock.com; **p. 164** bottom: Shutterstock.com/tomertu; **p. 165** top: stock.adobe.com/metamorworks; **p. 165** bottom: Imago Stock & People GmbH/Alexander Limbach; **p. 166**: Imago Stock & People GmbH/NurPhoto; **p. 167**: Shutterstock.com/Dim Dimich; **p. 168** top: Shutterstock.com/PX Media; **p. 168** bottom: Shutterstock.com/SNeG17;

p. 169 top: Shutterstock.com/Dima Zel; **p. 169** centre: Shutterstock.com/Piyaset; **p. 169** bottom: Shutterstock.com/Ramcreative; **p. 170**: mauritius images/alamy stock photo/IanDagnall Computing; **p. 171**: Shutterstock.com/TheRightFrameMedia; **p. 172** top: Shutterstock.com/Pandagolik1; **p. 172** bottom: Shutterstock.com; **p. 173**: mauritius images/alamy stock photo/ifeelstock; **p. 174** top: Depositphotos; **p. 174** bottom: Shutterstock.com/FixiPixi_Design_Studio; **p. 175** left: stock.adobe.com/Csaba; **p. 175** right: Imago Stock & People GmbH/Everett Collection; **p. 176** top: stock.adobe.com/Karlo; **p. 176** bottom: Depositphotos/Swee Ming Young; **p. 177**: Imago Stock & People GmbH/Addictive Stock; **p. 178**: mauritius images/alamy stock photo/Jon Davison; **p. 180**: stock.adobe.com/Olga; **p. 181**: Shutterstock.com/Elena Schweitzer; **p. 189**: stock.adobe.com/little_rat; **p. 196**: dpa Picture-Alliance/EPA-EFE/EFE/ALEJANDRO GARCIA; **p. 198** data source: Pew Research Center; **p. 213**: Shutterstock.com/Andrey_Kuzmin; **p. 227** top left: Shutterstock.com/VectorsMarket; **p. 227** top right: Shutterstock.com/Ico Maker; **p. 227** centre left: Shutterstock.com/FallyDesign; **p. 227** centre right: Shutterstock.com/MPFphotography; **p. 227** bottom left: Shutterstock.com/Dychek Marina; **p. 229**: Shutterstock.com/Travel-Fr; **p. 230**: Shutterstock.com/Everett Collection.

Illustrations
p. 254–255: Cornelsen/Roland Beier

Texts
p. 10: Horne, Richard, and Helen Szirtes. *101 Things to Do before You're Old and Boring*. Bloomsbury, 2005 (p.x, xi), (aus didaktischen Gründen verkürzt und verändert); **pp. 14–15**: Fisher, Richard. "Why Teenagers Aren't What They Used to Be." *BBC*, 30 Dec. 2022, www.bbc.com/future/article/20220124-why-teens-arent-what-they-used-to-be.; pp. 20–21: Clement, Jennifer. *Gun Love*. Vintage, 2019, pp. 4–5, pp. 10–12; **pp. 23–25**: Sales, Nancy, Jo. *American Girls: Social Media and the Secret Lives of Teenagers*. Vintage, 2017, pp. 192–197; **pp. 27–28**: Calmbach, Marc, et al. „Wie Ticken Jugendliche? 2020. Lebenswelten von Jugendlichen im Alter von 14 Bis 17 Jahren in Deutschland". *Bundeszentrale für politische Bildung*, 2020, pp. 306–308; **pp. 28–29**: Salinger, J.D. *The Catcher in the Rye*. Penguin Books, 2010, pp. 2–4; **pp. 34–35**: Clement, Jennifer. *Gun Love*. Vintage, 2019, pp. 119–122; **pp. 36–37**: Colaizzo, Paul Downs. *Really Really*. Overlook Duckworth, 2014, pp. 52–53; **p. 38 text 1**: Kaur, Rupi. *Milk and Honey*. Andrews McMeel, 2015, p. 161; **p. 38 text 2**: Addonizio, Kim. "Mermaid Song". *Tell me*. BOA Editions, Ltd E-book, 2000; **p. 38 text 3**: Brooks, Gwendolyn. "We Real Cool". *Poetry*, Vol. 94, Number 6 September 1959, p. 373; **pp. 39–40**: Philip Larkin. "This be the Verse". *Poems*. Selected by Martin Amis, Faber and Faber, 2011, London, p. 96; **pp. 46–47**: King, Martin W., and James Melvin Washington. *A Testament of Hope: The Essential Writings and Speeches of Martin Luther King, Jr.* San Francisco: Harper & Row, 1986; **p. 48** data source: "Human Rights", *Our World in Data*, Bastian Herre, Data comes from the Varieties of Democracy project (v13), sometimes using Lührmann et al's (2018) Regimes of the World classification, and own expansions and refinements, https://v-dem.net/data/the-v-dem-dataset/; **pp. 49–50**: "Interview: In Fighting for Girls' Education, UN Advocate Malala Yousafzai Finds Her Purpose." *UN News*, 31 Mar. 2018, news.un.org/en/story/2017/10/567872-interview-fighting-girls-education-un-advocate-malala-yousafzai-finds-her; **pp. 56–58**: Gibbs, Angelica. "The Test." *The New Yorker*, 8 June 1940, p. 83, www.newyorker.com/magazine/1940/06/15/the-test.; **pp. 60–61**: Platt, Poppie. "From Potato Head to gender neutral dolls: the unstoppable rise of woke toys", *The Telegraph*, 3 March 2021, https://www.telegraph.co.uk/family/life/potato-head-non-binary-dolls-rise-rise-gender-neutral-toys/?utmsource=email (c) Poppie Platt/Telegraph Media Group Limited 2021; **pp. 62–64**: "Ich bin überzeugt, dass Aufklärung nachhaltig wirkt"| *Anyway*. www.anyway-koeln.de/ich-bin-ueberzeugt-dass-aufklaerung-nachhaltig-wirkt; **p. 68**: Collie, Joanne and Gillian Porter Ladousse. "World geography and the rainbow alliance". *Paths into Poetry*, Oxford University Press, 1991, p. 30; **pp. 71–72**: *Noughts & Crosses*, adapted by Dominic Cooke, based on the novels by Malorie Blackman. Nick Hern Books, London, 2008, pp. 88–90; **pp. 73–75**: *Noughts & Crosses*, adapted by Dominic Cooke, based on the novels by Malorie Blackman. Nick Hern Books, London, 2008, pp. 28–30; **p. 76**: Dunthorne, Joe. "I wrote about how one of my favourite children's books, first published 1972, now

reads like a nonfiction account of Jeff Bezos going into space – except with environmentalist dinosaurs." *Twitter*, 10 Dec. 2021, https://twitter.com/joedunthorne/status/1469283072046776325?cxt=HHwWi-oC-_evK-OMoAAAA; **p. 76**: Arceo, Francisco Javier. "Popularity and usefulness are surprisingly uncorrelated on social media." Twitter/X, 12 Jan 2024, https://twitter.com/franciscojarceo/status/1745802623184162925; **p. 77**: King, Stephen. "Hey, kids! It's your old buddy Steve King telling you that if they ban a book in your school, haul your ass to the nearest bookstore or library ASAP and find out what they don't want you to read." *Twitter*, 18 Jan 2023, https://twitter.com/StephenKing/status/1615742233134653442; **p. 80**: Exilus, Mack. "Tech No Language". *One Minute Plays. A Practical Guide to Tiny Theatre*. Edited by Steve Ansell and Rose Burnett Bonczek. London: Routledge, 2017, p. 266; **pp. 82–83**: „Von Werbung verfolgt", Jacqueline Hadasch, *SZ.de* vom 11.08.2020, https://www.sueddeutsche.de/digital/anzeigen-im-netz-von-werbung-verfolgt-1.4988880; **p. 89**: Thompson, Craig. *Blankets*. London: Faber & Faber Limited, 2017, pp. 558–559; **pp. 96–97**: *Lonely Planet The Big Trip 4: Your Essential Guide to Gap Years, Sabbaticals and Overseas Adventures*, 2019; **pp. 98–99**: "Auslandssemester leicht finanziert". *Studieren Weltweit*, 8 Nov. 2022, www.studieren-weltweit.de/auslandssemester-leicht-finanziert; **pp. 103–104**: Sheppard, Emma. "How to Make Sure Your Gap Year Boosts Your Future Career." *The Guardian*, 9 June 2016, www.theguardian.com/careers/2016/jun/09/gap-year-boosts-your-future-career. Copyright Guardian News & Media Ltd 2023; **pp. 105–106**: Friedman, Rachel. *The Good Girl's Guide to Getting Lost – A Memoir of Three Continents, Two Friends, And One Unexpected Adventure*. Bantam Books, 2011, p. 4, p. 9; **pp. 109–110**: Donnelly, Laura. "NHS doctors abandoning UK for better pay and lifestyle overseas", *The Telegraph*, 7 January 2023, https://www.telegraph.co.uk/news/2023/01/07/doctors-nurses-abandon-nhs-better-pay-lifestyle-overseas/ (c) Laura Donnelly/Telegraph Media Group Limited 2023; **pp. 111–113**: Mohamud, Ossob. "Beware the 'voluntourists' doing good." *The Guardian*, 19 Oct. 2022, www.theguardian.com/world/2013/feb/13/beware-voluntourists-doing-good. Copyright Guardian News & Media Ltd 2023; **p. 115**: Rajendra, Cecil. *Bones & Feathers*. Heinemann, Singapore, 1978; **pp. 126–128**: "What Is Globalization Anyway?" *World Economic Forum*, 31 Aug. 2022, www.weforum.org/agenda/2017/01/what-is-globalization-explainer; **p. 132**: *Why Is Biodiversity Important*? 15 Nov. 2018, www.conservation.org/blog/why-is-biodiversity-important; **pp. 138–139**: "Tony Rinaudo – Der Verrückte Weiße Bauer." *World Vision*, www.worldvision.de/aktuell/2015/05/Tony-Rinaudo-FMNR; **p. 142**: Ping, Wang. "Things We Carry on the Sea". *My Name is Immigrant*. Hanging Loose Press, 2020, pp. 7; **pp. 143–144**: Casey, Ruairi. "Young Climate Activists and the Battle to Avert Catastrophe." *Climate Crisis News | Al Jazeera*, 3 Nov. 2021, www.aljazeera.com/features/2021/11/3/youth-climate-activists-speak-of-battle-to-avert-climate-crisis; **pp. 146–148**: Habila, Helon. *Oil on Water*. Cornelsen Verlag, 2010, p. 18, pp. 35–36, pp. 132–133; **p. 156**: Gorvett, Zaria. "Four Teenage Inventors Changing Our World." *BBC Future*, 24 Feb. 2022, www.bbc.com/future/article/20180316-four-teenage-inventors-changing-the-world; **pp. 157–159**: "Interview mit Peter Sänger", *greencity solutions – we grow fresh air*, https://greencitysolutions.de/wp-content/uploads/2022/10/2022-MEDIAKIT-DAS-IST-GREEN-CITY-SOLUTIONS-1.pdf, p. 8; **pp. 159–160**: Malik, Kenan. "Technology Will Never Replace Human Judgment. Look at Football..." *The Guardian*, 17 Nov. 2019, www.theguardian.com/commentisfree/2019/nov/16/technology-will-never-replace-human-judgment-look-at-football. Copyright Guardian News & Media Ltd 2023; **p. 166** data source: Funk, Cary, and Lee Rainie. "5 Key Themes in Americans' Views about AI and Human Enhancement." *Pew Research Center*, 17 Mar. 2022, www.pewresearch.org/short-reads/2022/03/17/5-key-themes-in-americans-views-about-ai-and-human-enhancement/; **p. 173**: Harari, Yuval Noah. *Sapiens: A Brief History of Humankind*. Random House, 2011, pp. 465–466; **pp. 175–180**: Bradbury, Ray. "August 2026: There Will Come Soft Rains". *Collier's Weekly Magazine*, May 6th 1950; **p. 183**: Loomis, Jon. *The Pleasure Principle*. Oberlin College Press, 2001, p. 11; **pp. 192–193**: Blackledge, Sam. "In defence of 'voluntourists.'" *The Guardian*, 19 Oct. 2022, www.theguardian.com/world/2013/feb/25/in-defence-of-voluntourism1. Copyright Guardian News & Media Ltd 2023; **pp. 196–197**: Gorvett, Zaria. "Four Teenage Inventors Changing Our World." *BBC Future*, 24 Feb. 2022, www.bbc.com/future/article/20180316-four-teenage-inventors-changing-the-world; **p. 198** data source: "How Americans View AI and Human Enhancement: 5 Key Themes | Pew Research Center." *Pew*

Research Center, 17 Mar. 2022, www.pewresearch.org/short-reads/2022/03/17/5-key-themes-in-americans-views-about-ai-and-human-enhancement; **p. 233**: Oseman, Alice. *Heartstopper*. Hodder Children's Books, 2018.

Songs
p. 31 *Creep*: Colin Greenwood / Jonathan Greenwood / Albert Louis Hammond / MICHAEL EDWARD HAZLEWOOD / Edward O Brien / Philip Selway / Thomas Yorke; Neue Welt Musikverlag GmbH, Hamburg Concord Music GmbH, Berlin; **pp. 38–39** *Lose yourself*: Jeff Bass / Marshall Mathers / Resto Louis Edgardo; Eight Mile Style Music/Resto World Music/Kobalt Music Publishing Ltd./Printrechte Hal Leonard Europe GmbH.